Governing Growth

Governing Growth

US Industrial Policy from Hamilton to Trump

MARCO R. DI TOMMASO
AND
VINOD K. AGGARWAL

OXFORD
UNIVERSITY PRESS

Oxford University Press is a department of the University of Oxford.
It furthers the University's objective of excellence in research, scholarship,
and education by publishing worldwide. Oxford is a registered trade mark of
Oxford University Press in the UK and in certain other countries.

Published in the United States of America by Oxford University Press
198 Madison Avenue, New York, NY 10016, United States of America.

© Oxford University Press 2026

CIP data is on file at the Library of Congress.

ISBN 9780197850336

ISBN 9780197821787 (hbk.)

DOI: 10.1093/oso/9780197821787.001.0001

Paperback printed by Integrated Books International, United States of America

The manufacturer's authorized representative in the EU for product safety is
Oxford University Press España S.A. of Parque Empresarial San Fernando de Henares,
Avenida de Castilla, 2 – 28830 Madrid (www.oup.es/en or product.safety@oup.com).
OUP España S.A. also acts as importer into Spain of products made by the manufacturer.

"To my lights, my beloved daughters Chiara Alessandra and Francesca Amalia. They know why."

Marco Rodolfo Di Tommaso

"To my grandson Arjun, whose unwavering gaze hints at questions yet unasked and futures yet imagined."

Vinod K. Aggarwal

Contents

Preface

This book was born out of a conversation we initiated about two and a half years ago at Berkeley's Faculty Club restaurant. We reciprocally knew about each other's research activities, but it was the first time we had met in person. Coming from different experiences of work and life, we soon began to discuss international political and economic trends. We were interested in thinking about likely trends in globalization in the wake of the pandemic, and in particular, how global value chains (GVCs) were likely to evolve. Given the changing international order, we were focused on China and discussed whether its state-led model of growth and planning would continue to be successful. We then analyzed the case of the other Asian industrial powers, including Japan, South Korea, and Taiwan. Then we turned our attention to Europe, trying in particular to highlight the situations of the leading manufacturing countries of the old continent, Germany, Italy, and France. Finally, we speculated about the United States and its role in the new evolving global scenario. The first Trump administration was over, and we were in the middle of the Biden presidency. Trump has only recently announced that he would seek the Republican nomination in 2024, but a victory seemed far-fetched at the time. Economic recovery after the pandemic in the United States was going in the right direction. Despite a change in administration, China's rise was still the center of Biden's attention and the shocks associated with the Ukraine war were just coming to our attention.

In that first lengthy discussion, we talked not only about the academic literature but also our personal research experiences in the field in the United States, Europe, and Asia. Our views were in some cases very similar, in others different, but in general, it was clear that we shared knowledge, interests, and intellectual curiosity.

Our conversation on these topics continued in the successive months in other locations, in Italy, in universities in Bologna and Venice, in South Korea, and again in San Francisco and Bologna, where we organized talks, seminars, and conferences, bringing other colleagues and friends into our discussions.

In this setting, we decided to write this new book focusing on industrial policy, broadly defined. Specifically, this book is dedicated to "the American case" with the idea that a long-run analysis of the history of growth of the country should offer elements for the rethinking of our interpretative models and the understanding of our present. A similar approach was adopted in two previous books (Marco R. Di Tommaso and Stuart O. Schweitzer, *Industrial Policy in America: Breaking the Taboo*, Elgar 2013; and Marco R. Di Tommaso and Mattia Tassinari, *Industria governo e mercato. Lezioni Americane*, Il Mulino, 2017), but many of the intuitions of those works were still waiting to be properly developed. This work also draws on Di Tommaso's more recent work, such as Marco R. Di Tommaso, Lauretta Rubini, Elisa Barbieri, and Chiara Pollio, *Industry Organization and Industrial Policy: Production and Innovation, Development and the Public Interest*, Il Mulino, 2024. In addition, the book draws on Aggarwal's joint work, namely Sonia N. Aggarwal and Vinod K. Aggarwal, Rethinking the Political Economy of Industrial Policy, *L'industria*, 2023 and Vinod K. Aggarwal and Tai Ming Cheung, *Oxford Handbook of Geoeconomics and Economic Statecraft*, Oxford University Press, 2025.

In our new book project, we decided to further deepen the analysis of the long-run growth of the United States—a process that began with independence and has unfolded through decades and centuries of transformation, resulting in the America we know today. The topic we chose was very fascinating. We saw a unique and impressive story of structural change, affecting both the economy and society. The process was driven by business and entrepreneurship, but also—and this is our central thesis—by government. Our long-run re-reading suggests that American capitalism has been, and it is, about business and markets but also about government.

In line with this perspective, this book documents the role that government has played in the process of growth, innovation, and structural transformation of the US economy across different eras. In a few words, our research work shows that governing the process of growth has been a common goal for all American administrations, from independence to the present day. We challenge the conventional rhetoric and long-held belief of America as the land of the free market with no government intervention. To support this thesis, we have revisited and debunked key facts from the past and included in the analysis many developments from the fast-evolving present.

We have been impressed, and sometimes surprised, by what we found in the American past: long-run continuity of approaches and attitudes, old new ideas, and similarities with the present. In short, despite a quite consolidated narrative, the American government has always acted to shape the process of growth and structural change of its economy and society.

At the same time, working on the present, we have been challenged by what the daily news has continued to offer to our attention. The Russian invasion of Ukraine and its impact on the world economy and politics; the many crises and conflicts in the Middle East—Syria, Lebanon, Yemen, Iran, and finally Gaza—all of which have opened new fronts of vulnerability in the political and economic order, with specific impacts on GVCs because of the rise of transport and energy costs. Finally, the possible return of Trump that we discussed became a reality, bringing about very radical changes in US policy. While we were writing, we saw the second mandate for President Trump becoming a more likely prospect in the context of the Biden administration's weakness.

The new geopolitics of the new President Trump era has dramatically transformed the institutions and equilibrium of the post-Cold War and WWII era. We have seen unprecedented tensions between the United States and traditional political and economic partners: the European Union, Canada, and Mexico; we have seen a new relationship between the United States and Russia; and we continue to see tensions between China and the United States. In particular, the transformation of American trade policy is particularly striking, with the end of enthusiasm for free trade and free market principles that have been the centerpiece of the US-led global order for over seven decades. In its stead, we see daily US tariff announcements, disregard for global and regional institutions, and a focus on off and on bilateral negotiations with trading partners.

What will the future bring for government intervention in the US economy? What will be the implications of these changes for the global political economy? These questions remain to be answered, but while we can only speculate about the future, we can say with confidence that we are clearly entering a new global order.

Acknowledgments

For their previous contributions to this research line, we are grateful to Prof. Stuart O. Schweitzer, for decades a professor at UCLA, to Prof. Mattia Tassinari of IULM University in Milan, and to Dr. Andrea Ferrannini, researcher at ARCO/University of Florence, and to Dr. Lucia Bazzucchi, former Ph.D. student at the University of Ferrara and now Principal at The Brattle Group.

We are grateful for the many useful comments and ideas in workshops we organized during the writing of this book to (in alphabetical order) Elisa Barbieri, Margaret Kenney, Claudio Petti, Chiara Pollio, Lauretta Rubini, Elena Prodi, and Francesca Spigarelli.

Last but not least, we wish to thank our research assistants, who were critical to the completion of this book. These include Riccardo Rinaldi of the University of Parma, and from UC Berkeley, ably led by graduate students Margaret Kenney and Jiayu Lai, undergrads Denyse Chan, Anjali Dixit, Sophie Duryee, Shantanu Kamat, Anand Mehta, Greta Norris, Ellen Wu, and Carol Xu. For proofreading, we are grateful to Phu Doan, Spencer Lee, Christina Wang, and Amber Yu.

Finally, we would like to thank our families for their support, and to the Oxford University team of James Cook, Lacey Harvey, and Alexcee Bechthold for shepherding the publication of this book.

1

Introduction

1.1 Introduction

At the end of three decades of neoliberal consensus, the 2008 "Big Crisis" that began with the Lehman Brothers collapse opened an unexpected torrent of government intervention in markets throughout the world. Rather than a one-off effort to address that specific crisis, we started to observe the rise of continued interventions with industrial policy coming again into vogue—not only in emerging countries of the "Global South" but also in rich industrialized nations, many of whom had at least in principle eschewed such policies (Aggarwal and Evenett, 2010, 2012; Di Tommaso and Schweitzer, 2013).

Since those years of severe crisis followed by an uncertain recovery, the interventionist trend has been confirmed (see Figure 1.1) by governments' need to respond to long-term transformative megatrends—such as climate change and digitalization/robotization—and to a series of dramatic and unexpected shocks—such as COVID-19, the surge in inflation, the war in Ukraine and the conflicts in the Middle East (Baquie et al., 2025; Evenett et al., 2024; Aggarwal and Aggarwal, 2023; Di Tommaso et al., 2022, 2024; Cherif and Hasanov, 2021; Ferrannini et al., 2021; Saad-Filho, 2021).

In addition, the increasingly tense relationship between the United States and China—and the consequent process of "decoupling"—along with unexpected economic and political contrasts between the United States and a wide range of traditional partners—including the European Union, the United Kingdom, Mexico, Canada, and Japan—have clearly disrupted the existing equilibria within the global value chain, triggering everywhere a further wave of government interventions, targeting a plurality of industries, with a wide range of ambitious goals (see Figures 1.2, 1.3, 1.4).

Examples of government intervention since the 2008 crisis have included policies such as bailouts of national companies, demand-inducement programs, public procurement special programs, measures to protect and support domestic industries, selective policies designed for strategic sectors, actions to guarantee employment, and to support the green transition (Aggarwal and Evenett, 2010, 2012; Aghion et al., 2011; Birdsall and Fukuyama, 2011; Lin, 2012; Stiglitz and Lin, 2013; Di Tommaso and Schweitzer, 2013; Tassinari, 2019; Aggarwal and Aggarwal, 2023).

Governing Growth. Marco R. Di Tommaso and Vinod K. Aggarwal, Oxford University Press.
© Oxford University Press (2026). DOI: 10.1093/oso/9780197821787.003.0001

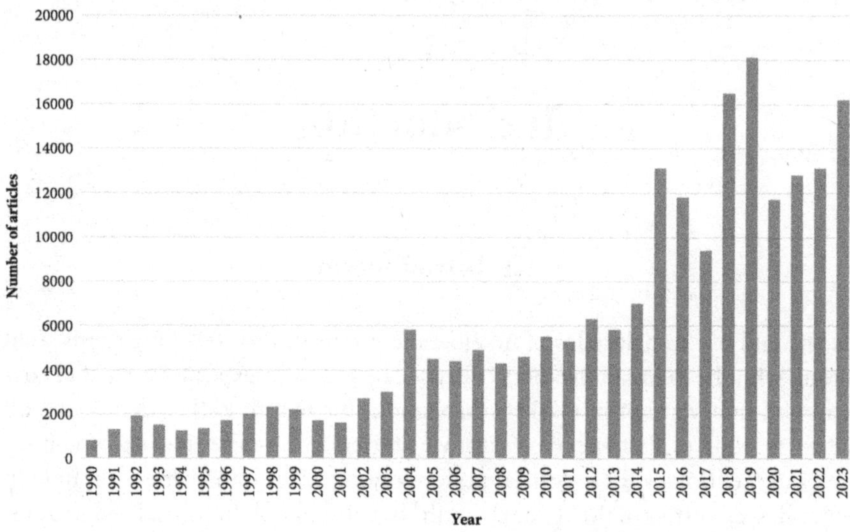

Figure 1.1 Mentions of Industrial Policy in the Major Business Press
Source: Evenett et al., 2024

A more interventionist approach has also characterized the recent history of the United States, a country that, over the past decade, has actively and explicitly promoted industrial policy practices with the support of the Obama, Trump, and Biden administrations—demonstrating a surprisingly bipartisan attitude in this area.

Motivated by the nature of the present relationship between government and industry in the United States as well as President Trump's announcements and actions promoted since the very beginning of his second mandate, we investigate the roots of the existing dynamic equilibria, studying how this relationship has changed over time in American history. Specifically, this book traces the evolution of government intervention in the United States since its independence, identifying elements of continuity and discontinuity.

As we will show, even in the paragon case of supposed nonintervention, which has often been the incorrect ideological perspective on the United States, there has been significant government involvement in the history of growth and structural transformation of the United States. Indeed, some observers have erred by deferring to a political rhetoric and to a history that has often described the United States as a country and society characterized by an unconditional confidence in the market and an innate distrust of government interference (Etzioni, 1983; Schultze, 1983; White, 2010; Ketels, 2007). Yet, as we will illustrate, we have continuously seen efforts by different administrations to engage not only in

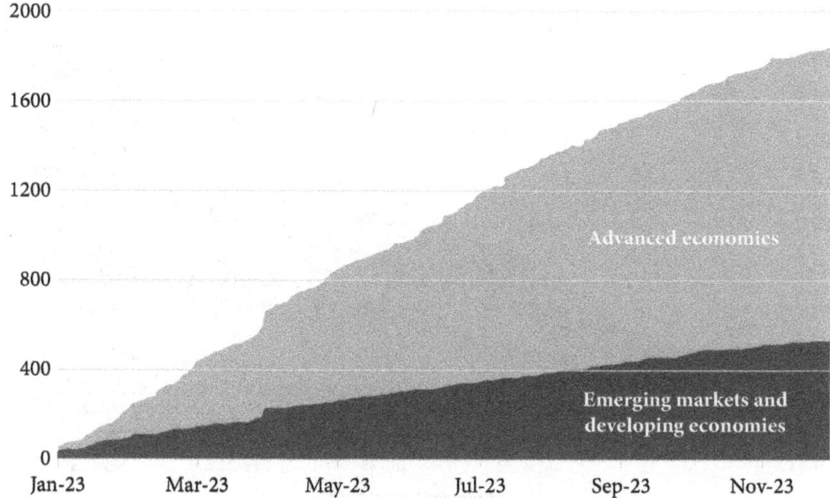

Figure 1.2 Number of Industrial Policy Measures Implemented in 2023
Source: Evenett et al., 2024; IMF staff calculations

broad macroeconomic policies, but also in broad horizontal and sector-specific industrial policies with the goal of governing the process of growth and change. In this book, we propose a new perspective with the goal of offering a different basis on which to analyze our complex present.

Empirically, we start from the ideas of Alexander Hamilton in the years immediately following independence and then retrace all the different phases of American industrialization until the end of Biden's term and the beginning of Trump's second mandate. Beginning with the days immediately after America's independence from Great Britain, policymakers have sought to achieve industrial and economic independence and catch-up with the rest of the world. There is a two-hundred-and-fifty-year-long history of American domestic industry and of government practices that favor it. To understand US policy, we must go beyond the rhetoric found in academic, political, and media circles, which, in many historical periods, have fed off each other. The national government is among the institutions that have supported and governed industrial growth in the United States (Tassinari, 2019; Wade, 2014; Di Tommaso and Tassinari, 2014; Mazzucato, 2013; Di Tommaso and Schweitzer, 2013; Ketels, 2007; Bingham, 1998; Dobbin, 1994; Williams, 1964). In the American history of industrialization, growth, and innovation, the federal government has played a significant role.

This presence should not come as a surprise to most observers and social scientists. The government has played a role in the US economy because, beyond

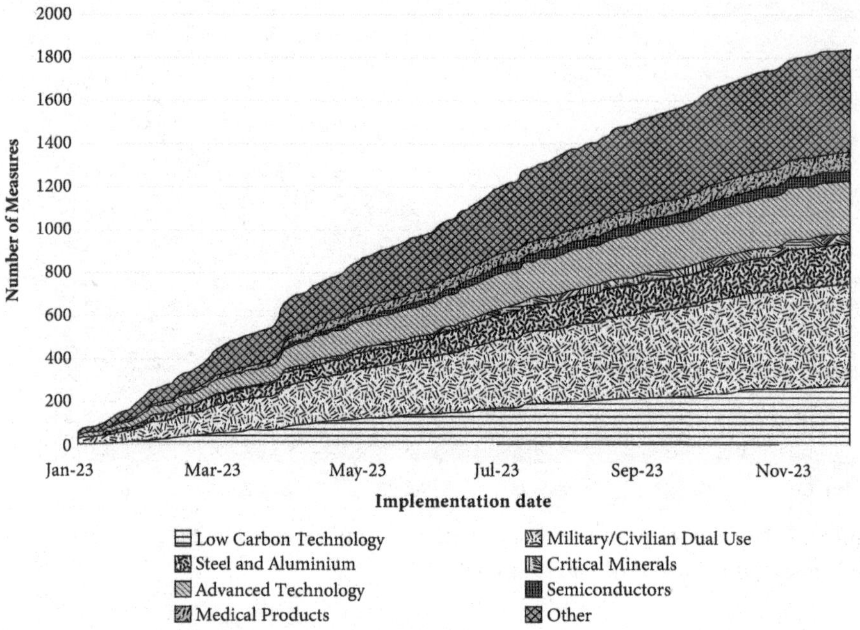

Figure 1.3 Industrial Policy by Sectors (2023)
Source: Evenett et al., 2024

the free-market rhetoric, there has always been demand for such involvement. For example, during George Washington's time, coalitions of politicians and emerging business leaders effectively supported industrial policy interventions from a "catch-up strategy" and "infant industry" perspective (Hamilton, 1791; Rabbeno, 1895; Taussig, 1910; Irwin, 2004; Scheiber, 1987; Chang, 2007; Di Tommaso and Schweitzer, 2013). Later, throughout much of the nineteenth century, some dominant business interests actively supported national trade policy and the maintenance of high tariffs, thus protecting and promoting the growth of the national manufacturing sector (Rabbeno, 1895; Taussig, 1930; Irwin, 2004). Furthermore, since the time of the Sherman Act, the US government has maintained a strong presence—through both action and inaction—in antitrust policy, shaped by the demands of key economic and social stakeholders. Finally, in the example of research, science, and technology policies, the American government has always played a very significant role, driven by the military-industrial complex, which has always demanded and obtained special attention from the US government (Wade, 2012; Di Tommaso and Schweitzer, 2013; Weiss, 2013; Mazzucato, 2013; Tassinari, 2019).

Although specialized scholars have focused on these specific fields, these contributions have been quite fragmented and very often treated as exceptions. In

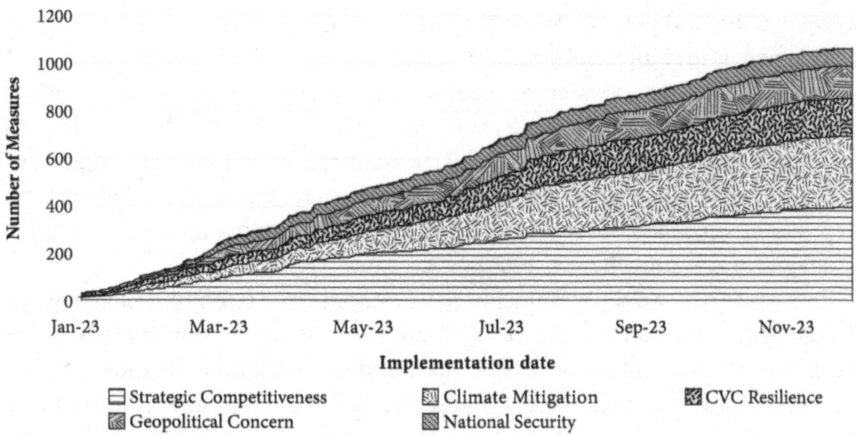

Figure 1.4 Industrial Policy by Goals (2023)
Source: Evenett et al., 2024, Figure 5

contrast, this book offers a comprehensive, long-run analysis of the US government role in managing growth, industrialization, and structural change. Rather than focusing on certain historical periods, specific sectors, or policy goals, we trace the evolution of federal intervention from the founding of the Republic to the present day.

What role did the federal government have, and what role does it continue to have in the dynamics of the country's industrial growth? What have been and what are now the federal government's targets when it intervenes in domestic industry? By what means has the US government intervened and by what means does it now intervene? Is it possible to reconstruct a history of industrial policy practices in the United States that extends to the present day? And is it possible to highlight the elements of continuity or discontinuity that characterize the American case over more than two centuries? As will become evident from our discussion, we take an expansive view of industrial policy in keeping with an analysis of both horizontal and vertical measures. Moreover, we refer to the wide socioeconomic goals that have over time inspired government interventions in industry. From this perspective, social stability, national security, political independence, employment, and environmental arguments are typical examples of why American governments have in different epochs decided to promote actions targeting industry in the name of "meta-economic" rationales.

This chapter begins by theoretically examining how government intervention in industry has been defined, with particular attention to different types of industrial policy. Specifically, section 1.2 of this chapter looks at broad macroeconomic policies and then turns to the analytical rationale for horizontal and vertical industrial policies. We then consider some of the contemporary drivers of this new-found interest in industrial policies.

In section 1.3, we consider the theoretical drivers of industrial policy, focusing on market failure, political goals, and rent seeking by firms. While economists have primarily emphasized market failure, political scientists have identified key political and strategic goals that the government may pursue. An instance of this is rent seeking, where there is now well-developed literature on firm nonmarket strategies and tactics (Baron, 2000).

In section 1.4, we discuss the analytical structure of our empirical chapters. In particular, we identify the key questions that structure our analysis of US government intervention over time. Specifically, we examine the international, domestic, and ideational factors that influenced the different administrations' approach to industrial policy and government intervention. We then assess the main targets of industrial policy in terms of companies, sectors, and regions. Third, we examine the tools that the government used including the legal and administrative mechanisms to implement policies. Fourth, we turn to a political economic analysis of the coalitions in favor or against these policies. Finally, we evaluate the successes and failures of these policies.

Section 1.5 briefly previews our empirical analysis. We begin with the "pre-history" of American industrial policy, tracking how the government has balanced industry and societal needs up until the crisis of the 1970s. We draw parallels between Ronald Reagan and Margaret Thatcher and identify the pivot to neoliberalism in the 1980s. As we shall see, there remained a gap between rhetoric promoting free trade and the actual implementation of protectionist policies. Empirically, the book also compares the recent presidencies of Obama, Trump, Biden, and Trump's second administration, exploring how the vastly different backgrounds and ideologies of these politicians affected US industrial policy. In concluding this chapter, we highlight key themes that recur throughout the empirical work.

1.2 The Logic of Government Intervention: Beyond Macroeconomic Policies?

Arguments about the appropriate role for governments with respect to the market are hardly new, with early advocates calling for a significant state role in helping countries to grow and catch up with their more advanced counterparts (Botero, 1588; de Laffemas, 1597; Serra, 1613; Mun, 1630; Hamilton, 1791; List, 1885).

More recently, some scholars have also highlighted the "hidden hand" of government in the early stages of industrialization of all the "advanced" countries of our time (Chang, 2003; Di Tommaso and Schweitzer, 2013; Reinert et al., 2016; Di Tommaso et al., 2024). Particularly, political economists—including Chalmers Johnson (1982), Frederic Deyo (1987), Bruce Cummings (1984), and Stephan Haggard (1990, 2004)—have focused on the policies of the East Asian "tigers" and examined the role of the state in promoting development through IP (Haggard, 1990; Haggard, 2004).

In recent decades, economists such as Dani Rodrik have also discussed the rationale for state intervention, with a focus on market failures. Other economists such as Justin Lin and Ha-Joon Chang have debated the type of industrial policy strategies that countries might pursue. Nevertheless, most economists from Anglo-Saxon countries have historically been skeptical of arguments supporting industrial policy, as reflected in the work of Howard Pack and Kamal Saggi (2006), who argue that governments are likely to be poor at picking winners and are subject to regulatory capture (Rodrik, 1996, 1998; Lin and Chang, 2009).

The fundamental debate on government intervention can best be understood by distinguishing among macroeconomic policy, horizontal industrial policies, and vertical industrial policies. Macroeconomic policy operates at the economy-wide level, aiming in general to manage aggregate demand and supply to ensure stability and growth. Monetary policy, managed by central banks, uses tools like interest rates and money supply adjustments to control inflation, stabilize exchange rates, and influence economic activity. Fiscal policy, driven by government decisions on spending and taxation, directly affects economic growth, employment, and public investment.

Horizontal industrial policies are generally seen to be nondiscriminatory and aim to improve the general productivity and competitiveness of *all* sectors. They address systemic challenges, such as insufficient infrastructure, gaps in workforce skills, or lack of access to financing. For example, investments in public education enhance human capital, while improvements in logistics infrastructure reduce costs for businesses across the board. These policies are considered (at least in principle) "market-friendly" because they do not distort competition and instead focus on creating enabling conditions that benefit the entire economy. We specify "in principle" because horizontal policies "in the real world" often end up favoring specific sectors, technologies, or firms—intentionally or not—and ultimately acquire vertical characteristics (Di Tommaso et al., 2024).

"Pure" vertical industrial policies target specific sectors or technologies to achieve strategic economic and societal objectives (Di Tommaso et al., 2024). For example, governments may provide subsidies to green energy companies to accelerate decarbonization or impose tariffs to protect nascent industries from foreign competition. As a further example, governments may decide to target the construction industry to mitigate unemployment in post-shock periods. Vertical policies are often motivated by national security concerns as we shall see, or concerns about taking a leadership role in critical emerging technologies—such as artificial intelligence, quantum computing, and synthetic biology.

The fundamental division among analysts has primarily centered around the use of vertical industrial policies. Skeptics of such policies argue that the government is unlikely to have any special insight into selecting policy targets. Moreover, as we shall see, such analysts are concerned that government assistance for specific industries (or companies or technologies) will lead to rent seeking by firms and labor to protect them against competition. In addition, vertical industrial policies are often criticized for their potential to encourage government capture, clientelism, and corruption. We refer here to the typical "government failure" arguments effectively represented by Milton Friedman in few direct words: "...government solution to a problem is usually as bad as the problem" (Friedman, 1975).

Given these concerns, what is driving the current renewed interest in such policies? Several key developments can be identified. First and foremost, the success of the leading Asian industrial powers of our times—Japan, South Korea, Taiwan, and China—in recent decades has attracted the attention of scholars and policymakers. These nations have pursued active industrial policies and achieved impressive rates of industrial growth, competitiveness, and innovation. Their achievements and massive use of selective vertical policies have prompted analysts to reconsider the value of this instrument.

Second, in advanced and established industrialized countries, concerns about deindustrialization and claims about the benefits of promoting "green industries" have driven the IP debate. Widespread concerns about environmental degradation became linked to an interest in promoting the manufacturing of environmentally sustainable goods as a basis for the reindustrialization of developed countries. This theme first gained traction in the United States, Japan, South Korea, Europe, and more recently, China.

Third, with respect in particular to developing countries, the value of creating economic clusters, dynamic learning and spillover, and the importance of inserting themselves in global supply chains has bolstered an interest in IP. In addition to such goals, there has also been a focus on new tools of intervention, including government procurement, general standard setting, and the use of government pressure on companies to secure intellectual property to bolster specific sectors.

Fourth, the evolution of the WTO over the last fifteen years has also led analysts to explore the extent to which international and regional institutions might restrict the ability of countries to pursue IP. The current phase is characterized by a convergence of structural forces—for example, the climate crisis, automation in manufacturing and AI, the COVID-19 pandemic—that require increased coordination through IP in general.

Fifth, COVID-19, the Ukraine war, and increasing geopolitical tensions between the United States and China have prompted a debate on the security of supply chains. Whereas previously, global supply chains followed the logic of pure economic efficiency, the vulnerability of these networks has encouraged countries to increasingly promote onshoring and friend-shoring as a response.

1.3 Drivers of Industrial Policy

We propose three main categories that analysts have identified as drivers of industrial policy: market failures; political, economic, and social goals; and rent seeking by firms. Economic market failures are the classic rationale for why IP might be appropriate. Standard economic theories on imperfect markets and factor market issues are well known.[1] Somewhat newer issues concern the importance of imperfect markets, dynamic scale economies, externalities, public goods, coordination failures, and incomplete information. Our goal is not to be comprehensive on each of these elements, but to point to a few of their central claims.[2] We then turn to understanding how governments might pursue IP for economic, political, and security goals, including inequality concerns, economic growth, and power-based rationales. Finally, we look at how firms may try to capture governments by engaging in a variety of tactics tied to nonmarket strategy: these include classic lobbying, testimony, grassroots efforts, and several others (Baron, 2000).

1.3.1 Economic Market Failures

A key rationale for intervention to correct market failures focuses on imperfect markets. As economists have generally claimed, any deviation from a competitive market is likely to lead to a loss of consumer welfare and generate market inefficiencies (Glykou and Pitelis, 2011). Thus, in the case of monopolies or oligopolies, state intervention to break up firms through legal measures, or regulatory efforts to lower barriers of entry to facilitate efficient functioning of the market or to deter collusion by increasing competition may be called for.

Indeed, the dominant theme in American industrial policy toward the end of the nineteenth century and early twentieth century revolved around "trust busting"—the creation of antitrust laws and anti-collusive statutes to prevent

---

[1] For an updated overview see Di Tommaso et al. (2024).

[2] Pack and Saggi (2006) discuss some key aspects of several of the factors noted in this section. Their treatment is not entirely systematic and thus the discussion here draws heavily on Aggarwal and Aggarwal (2023) and incorporates ideas from Haggard (2004) and Lin and Chang (2009).

excessive industrial concentration. This approach has since enjoyed a revival in the United States with the appointment of neo-Brandeisians under Biden to key political positions. In the case of the European Union, beginning in the 1980s, the emphasis shifted away from nationalization of industry in both the United Kingdom and France toward a focus on privatization and increasing competition through cross-border flows of trade, and investment as a result of the common market (Owen, 2012). More generally, in many developing countries and emerging markets, privatization of former nationalized industries has often led to the replacement of state monopolies with private monopolies or duopolies. Thus, the creation of suitable rules and regulations to encourage competition and encourage efficiency should be viewed as an important form of "industrial policy."

An important motivation for IP is its ability to solve capital market failures in the context of dynamic scale economies. Krugman (1997) and others argue that nascent domestic industries cannot bear the high cost of investment and international competition, so state-led assistance and protection against foreign imports are necessary to encourage development. The basic claim is that through economies of scale that lower per unit costs with expanding production, these industries could be internationally competitive. Although it may appear that an industry lacks competitive advantage at the time, there could be an advantageous endowment structure that would lead to success in the long run. Connected to this argument is the idea that ideally, while financiers should be able to recognize such dynamic arguments, they may be unwilling to do so because of incomplete information (Rodrik, 2013).

Arguments about the need to promote nascent industries are often tied to claims about technological externalities or knowledge spillovers as a result of the formation of human capital. Some industries may be particularly desirable because they lead to widespread diffusion to other sectors of the economy. For example, the US Department of Defense's support to create the Internet demonstrates the "public goods" aspect of investment where private firms may not have a strong incentive to invest in light of possible free riding (Pack and Saggi, 2006, p. 273).

Technological innovation may require government intervention because there otherwise would be a lack of investment. Such innovation can easily diffuse, deterring potential investors who fear that they will not be able to recover the sunk costs of new technology. Consequently, technologically focused products may suffer from a lack of investment owing to this first-mover disadvantage. Moreover, because economic growth comes with significant capital requirements, increased scale of production, and rapid market growth, such improvements must be accompanied by improved educational, legal, and financial institutions, as well as better infrastructure. In addition, production of a new technology requires extensive sunk costs that firms may be unwilling to undertake without government intervention—"once a firm commits to a particular technology, it cannot switch to another technology without big costs—even when changes in the environment are such that a firm would have adopted a new technology" (Chang and Andreoni, 2020, p. 5). Under these conditions, the government can reduce the uncertainty of a technology's success for a firm through guaranteeing demand or making the technology a focal point around which other firms should coordinate (Chang and Andreoni, 2020). The inability or unwillingness of individual firms to single-handedly bring about such changes may thus result in market failure.

Technology may also suffer from coordination failures because of the difficulty for upstream and downstream industries to coordinate their investments. While it may be individually unprofitable to produce computers or software, if private firms in these two sectors invest somewhat simultaneously, both will benefit. But because there is informational uncertainty about the growth of complementary industries, there may be underinvestment, leading to market failure. Tied to these claims, arguments about information inadequacy have been espoused by Dani Rodrik, who argues that industrial policy is more about eliciting information from the private sector about a country's comparative advantage than it is about creating the correct government intervention (Rodrik, 2004, pp. 2–3). The claim here is that it is difficult without complete information to ascertain which industries will have a positive future. In Pack and Saggi's terms, "at the microlevel, entrepreneurs may simply not know what is profitable and what is not" (Pack and Saggi, 2006, p. 277). Hausmann and Rodrik share this view and argue that comparative advantage must be discovered through a form of "experimentation" that depends on "strategic collaboration" between the government and private sector; specifically, the government would help the private sector to "internalize the various externalities associated with the cost-discovery process and to provide many of the public inputs (standards, infrastructure, certification, property rights) that only the government can" (Hausmann and Rodrik, 2003; Hausmann et al., 2008, p. 4).

Arguments about the need to promote industrial policy interventions have also been suggested by cases of public goods (and quasi-public goods)—that is, goods characterized by different combinations of nonrivalry and nonexcludability. Here the problem is well known: because of these two intrinsic characteristics, without intervention, the danger is to accept the underproduction of public goods (and quasi-public goods). This risk supports arguments for industrial policy interventions in strategic fields such research, innovation, technical advancement, and scientific advancement—areas typically supported through public research, patents, subsidies, and tax incentives. More generally, policy interventions in this area could be justified by the fact that these goods often carry great economic and social relevance such as knowledge, culture, health, justice, safety, and security.

1.3.2 Economic, Political, and Security Goals

We next turn to an examination of the variety of economic and political goals that states may wish to pursue, which do not fall easily into the category of "market failure"—although some analysts might see them as such. Some are well known and have long been used as a rationale for government intervention. More recent claims surround the benefits of promoting green industries, both to address environmental degradation and to create a new source of manufacturing jobs, a policy that has been central to the Biden administration's industrial policy efforts.

States can pursue industrial policy as a method of addressing income distribution issues, which can be caused by regional, ethnic, or religious differences. States are often under societal and political pressure to address problems that some see as unequal income distribution. After a period of industrialization, countries often experience a significant increase in income inequality (Kuznets, 1955); though this effect is temporary, governments may face short-term pressure to address these domestic inequalities. Industrial policy strategies have been effective in creating a more equal distribution of wealth in both developed and developing countries. Governments can invest in infrastructure, education, and improved social services in targeted parts of the country that are relatively underdeveloped (e.g., rural versus urban areas).

As an example, both China and India have suffered a wide income gap as a result of rapid industrialization in certain areas. In India, southern states have benefited from India's software boom over the past twenty years, leaving rural areas underdeveloped. China has similarly suffered disparities between its urban and rural residents, as well as regional inequity between inland and coastal cities. More recent legislation by both India and China has worked to address these disparities.

The issue of inequality often extends to ethnic or religious-based economic disparities. States will often promote preferential treatment for certain ethnicities or religions to correct this problem. For instance, Malaysia gives preferential treatment to Malays in education, scholarships, business, loans, and housing to assist its ethnic population and preserve their dominance in various areas. Such policies have come under fire for continuing past the original deadline of 1990 and persisting today (Pang, 2013). Similar preferential policies exist in many other countries.

Neoliberal economists, while generally skeptical of deviations from free markets and the use of protectionism, have almost always agreed that some industries must be protected for reasons of national security. At the same time, industry lobbying groups have often framed their claims for protection in national security terms, knowing that the government may be more amenable to protection in such instances.[3] Some industries such as defense or the oil industry may appear to have stronger claims about their importance. But even these claims warrant scrutiny. For example, in the 1950s the US domestic oil industry argued that imposing quotas on imports of Middle Eastern oil would increase American national security. By 1958, the industry had secured quotas on oil imports based on grounds of national security, claiming that this trade policy would lead to energy independence for the United States. While in the short run this may have been the case, the long-run effect of this policy was disastrous since it led to the depletion of American oil over foreign oil reserves (Keohane, 1984).

Rising tensions between the United States and China have revived the practice of using security to advance industrial policy. For example, in January of 2024 the Department of Defense released its first National Defense Industrial Strategy. The Strategy explicitly mentions the DoD's fear of the "PRC's domination of critical markets" and advocates for supply chain decoupling alongside rebuilding the US industrial base (Department of Defense, 2023). This policy followed the passage of the 2022 CHIPS and Sciences Act which invested $52.7 billion in domestic chip manufacturing. Underlying the decision to invest in domestic production were fears that foreign chip reliance could endanger national security. These developments signal a rise in citing national security concerns as an impetus to craft industrial policy.

In addition to national security claims, governments have often responded to interventions from other countries' IP efforts with either direct negotiations or by working through international institutions such as the WTO. Thus, although industry groups might press for government support, governments may also be independently interested in ensuring that their industries face a level playing field.

1.3.3 Rent Seeking by Governments and Companies

Government bureaucrats, politicians, and business actors may generate rent-seeking dynamics which can sometimes be tied to industrial policy interventions (Krueger, 1974; Buchanan, 1983; Tullock, 1967; Khan et al., 2022). Government officials may be tempted to promote industrial policy interventions for

---

[3] The textile industry, among others, has often made national security arguments.

their own interest. Companies may be desirous to capture government administrators and influence their policy actions. From this perspective, the potential benefits of rent-seeking for both government and business communities should be considered potent drivers of industrial policy interventions.

Public officials may be in a position of opening a market for "rent" that attract the attention of companies, weakening their profit-seeking attitude. It has been suggested that even the mere announcement of a public policy intervention in favor of industries considered in need of support or promotion may trigger rent-seeking among the potential beneficiaries. Private firms can exhibit "rent-seeking" behavior through the pursuit of "nonmarket strategy" (Baron, 2000; Aggarwal, 2001). Thus, in addition to standard market strategies to increase profitability, firms may engage in a variety of tactics to secure personal benefits and avoid competition. With fewer domestic or international competitors, profits are likely to increase.

The most common approach for companies is to lobby governments directly through using connections to legislators (Baron, 2000). Law firms in the United States have large practices devoted to such lobbying, including the so-called K street lawyers. But in addition to lobbying, firms can use a host of other tactics to secure benefits. These include grassroots efforts to generate broad public support to influence office holders, often by appeals to consumers as in the recent case of TikTok in the United States. These grassroots efforts were supplemented by public advocacy efforts by TikTok. Firms also typically build coalitions to secure market intervention on their behalf. The classic example is the textile industry, which built a coalition spanning fiber, textiles, and apparel to increase their political clout in the 1950s and 1960s (Aggarwal, 1985). Firms also actively donate to political campaigns, particularly in the United States, where the use of political action committees is frequent. It is quite common for firms to ensure that their interests are met throughout changing administrations by supporting both Republican and Democratic candidates.

Other tactics include the use of testimony by experts, often with the goal of demonstrating either the economic or security benefits of an industry to secure favorable government policies. Such actions are often supplemented by direct participation on advisory boards. Especially in high technology industries, it is likely that government officials will lack knowledge of key issues in the industry, creating an opening for firms to engage in influence efforts by offering their "expertise." Aside from such direct engagement with government officials, firms often engage in public advocacy for their positions, using social media (directly, as in the case of TikTok, through their own platform). Google and other high technology firms also commonly engage in such tactics. Finally, firms can undertake legal action including antitrust cases, blocking imports under trade laws, and other judicial strategies. Typically, such legal efforts tend to be very expensive, and firms thus attempt to secure favorable outcomes with other tactics that we have reviewed.

1.4 Structuring the Empirical Analysis

Our empirical investigation of historical US government intervention, with a particular focus on industrial policy, is led by a set of guiding questions. We consider each one in turn: First, we discuss international, domestic, and ideational factors that influenced approaches to government intervention and industrial policy. International factors refer to both structural factors (such as shifts in the international political structure with the end of the Cold War) and transactional factors (such as rapidly increasing oil prices). Domestic factors include indicators, such as inflation and/or unemployment. As we shall see, some of these concerns can be tied to international shifts, such as the rise in Japanese automotive imports in the Reagan era or rapidly rising Chinese imports during the 2000s. Finally, we are particularly interested in the role of ideas in influencing policies. Reagan, for example, came to office with a mandate and an ideology of promoting free markets. As he put it concisely, "government is not the solution to our problem, government is the problem" (Reagan, 1981). However, we shall observe that these ideas were often constrained by political realities and pressure from industries such as autos.

Next, we consider the targets of government action, particularly with respect to industrial policy. Over time, administrations have engaged in policies to both target sectors and specific firms, such as the Biden's administration assistance for Intel or subsidies for chip investments in the case of Samsung and TSMC. This kind of direct vertical industrial policy is more common than might be expected from the rhetoric of the free market that we have seen historically in the United States. In many cases, governments have sought to promote regions that have fallen behind, such as the Midwest. These policies are often tied to specific sector policies, as with the bailout of the auto industry owing to fear of severe job losses in this region.

The politics of government intervention can range widely. We have already discussed broad macroeconomic policies such as monetary and fiscal policies, both of which are extremely powerful intervention measures. But administrations have also actively pursued horizontal and vertical policies. The tools span a wide gamut of instruments. For horizontal policies, we have seen technology policies to bolster R&D, tax breaks for investment, educational initiatives, and deregulation policies, among many others. In terms of vertical industrial policies, we have seen a plethora of efforts from tariffs, quotas, and subsidies, to government procurement (as in the defense industry) or the promotion of industrial clusters. To implement such measures, we have seen the passage of laws as well as direct executive action. The latter often entails the use of executive commissions or bodies.

In terms of pursuing government intervention, a key factor in the successful implementation of policies revolves around the political coalitions in favor of or against policies. The United States, as a country with a relatively weak state as compared to, say China or France, has a highly complex policy-making process. Despite various driving factors, be they international, domestic, or ideational, political maneuvering and wrangling is particularly common. Skill in building supporting coalitions is thus critical for the successful implementation of policies.

Finally, we review the successes and failures of different administrations' policies. Assessing such success or failure is not a simple matter, and analysts often have sharply differing views of what constitutes a successful set of policies. And of course, the evaluation of policies often looks very different when evaluated in a broader historical context than in the immediate context of policy implementation. Some analysts have tried to engage in counterfactual reasoning to assess the pros and cons of government intervention and others have tried to develop quantitative measures of net benefits. While we applaud these efforts, on the whole, we do not find them entirely convincing and thus our assessment is more qualitative than quantitative. We believe that our historical approach shows the many forms of intervention that the US government has engaged in over time, and we believe that our analysis points to key contributions of this effort to governing growth.

1.5 Key Themes Across History

Studying the relationship between industry and government in the United States by employing a long-term perspective not only confirms the continued presence of government intervention in industrial dynamics, but also makes it possible to identify some common characteristics that have marked American government intervention throughout time. The process of progressive and radical structural change in the industry, economy, and American society has been accompanied by government intervention that, on some issues, has always been present.

Chapter 2 focuses on the decades following independence until the end of the nineteenth century. During this period, US industrial policy aimed to build a national manufacturing base and manage structural change in a developing nation. The goal of achieving "manufacturing independence" required policies to protect emerging industries and address evolving regional, economic, and social interests. These policies primarily targeted sectors essential for economic growth, such as textiles, iron, steel, and railroads. The government employed high tariffs, subsidies, and land grants to facilitate national infrastructure development. Yet the government also faced new challenges: managing corporate concentration and resolving tensions between capital and labor. While business concentration enabled unprecedented growth, it also posed economic and democratic threats through monopolies and oligopolies. Although early industrial policies successfully fostered economic growth, they created regional disparities, neglected labor conditions, and encouraged exploitative practices. Overall, the period highlighted the complexities of managing industrialization, balancing economic growth with social equity, and governing structural change effectively.

In Chapter 3, we examine the period from 1900 to 1945. US industrial policy became increasingly interventionist, shaped by economic crises, global conflicts, and the desire for international competitiveness. Government policies aimed to stabilize, expand, and consolidate heavy industry through tools like tariffs, subsidies, and defense contracts. World War I, the Great Depression, and World War II demanded unprecedented government coordination, with agencies like the War Production Board implementing centralized planning. While critics argued that government intervention threatened capitalism, most business leaders and labor unions accepted it, benefiting from contracts and public investments. Although US industrial policy successfully positioned the United States as a global economic power, protectionism and favoritism toward large corporations hindered competition and innovation. This period laid the groundwork for the postwar economic order, raising ongoing debates about the proper role of government in fostering economic growth and ensuring national security.

Chapter 4 turns to the post-WWII period until the end of the Carter administration. In this period, US government-led growth led to rising skepticism about state intervention. In the immediate postwar years, government involvement remained central. The Cold War intensified federal support for strategic industries like aerospace, telecommunications, and computing. Economic expansion continued until the 1970s, when oil shocks, inflation, and increased foreign competition disrupted established policies. The economic crisis, coupled with declining manufacturing and social tensions, exposed the limits of government intervention. Keynesian policies lost credibility, and free-market advocates like Milton Friedman gained influence, pushing for deregulation and reduced government involvement. Despite successful infrastructure projects and technological breakthroughs, the late 1970s saw mounting frustration with industrial policy, culminating in the political shift toward market-oriented solutions under Reagan.

Chapter 5 considers the unique approach of Ronald Reagan's administration. While widely considered a free market ideologue, his administration intervened in response to a tumultuous international environment, though vertical industrial policy support was largely avoided. In particular, his industrial policy program bolstered the defense industry, protected domestic automobile companies, and stabilized the agricultural industry. In addition, Reagan worked to deregulate in order to bolster the economy. This approach was supported by the majority of large companies, steel and automobile industries, and defense contractors. However, small farmers and labor unions faced the consequences of his policies and were largely unsupportive.

Reagan's industrial policy was succeeded by the administrations of the 1990s-George H.W. Bush and Bill Clinton, which are discussed in Chapter 6. George H.W. Bush continued the limited intervention, horizontal industrial policy approach of the Reagan administration with a specific focus on the technology sector. R&D support was targeted specifically on computing, electronics, and semiconductor companies. In addition, both the Bush and Clinton administrations invested heavily in creating trade agreements that would enhance economic cooperation and exchange.

Chapter 7 turns to George W. Bush Jr.'s industrial policy program during his administration from 2000–2008. China's accession to the WTO and the subsequent pressure on American industries from the "China shock" put pressure on the Bush administration to intervene. In addition, national security became particularly important in the minds of both the administration and Americans after the 9/11 terrorist attacks. With international and domestic pressure to solve these issues, Bush targeted industrial policy through tax cuts and incentives, in line with his free-market ideology to limit intervention as much as possible. Bush's investment in R&D in the aerospace and defense industries, as well as oil and gas, fostered support among these actors. On the other hand, his policies—in particular the deregulation of gas and oil—were opposed by Democratic lawmakers and environmental groups.

Chapter 8 discusses Obama's approach to industrial policy, which was largely motivated by the 2008 financial crisis. His Keynesian ideological approach manifested in large stimulus packages and sectoral support for manufacturing, renewable energy, technology, and automotives. Republican lawmakers opposed the widespread intervention into the economy. On the other hand, he received support from unions and environmental groups for enhancing their interests through his industrial policy. Obama's industrial policy was instrumental in resolving the concerns of domestic citizens following the 2008 financial crisis and providing a boost to the clean energy sector. However, the short-term nature of these interventions resulted in benefits that were constrained by time.

Chapter 9 documents the first Trump Administration's unique industrial policy program, which heralded an "America First" campaign. In response to rising US-China tensions, the precarity of global supply chains, and domestic manufacturing loss, Trump used tax cuts, deregulation, and tariffs as the main instruments of industrial policy. These policies were particularly supported by manufacturing regions that had experienced unemployment and disinvestment in the last twenty years. However, the strategies were damaging to companies—particularly technology companies—that had extensive supply chains in China.

Chapter 10 illustrates Biden's industrial policy programs. Entering office in the midst of the COVID-19 pandemic, Biden's industrial policy reflects the domestic needs of the American public and the international concern about global supply chains. His industry policy was focused on public infrastructure projects and developing domestic supply chains. The CHIPS Act and Inflation Reduction Act have been broadly successful at improving infrastructure, clean energy, and job growth. These programs have been supported by labor unions, environmental groups, and local governments receiving subsidies. In contrast, Biden has been criticized by international forces—both rivals and allies—for the government's extensive intervention in the economy. The chapter concludes by considering how Kamala Harris would have carried out industrial policy in the United States, had she been elected.

Finally, Chapter 11 documents the second Trump Administration's economic and industrial policy approach, focusing on his second campaign and on the first months of his second mandate. We examine both announcements and President Trump's policies. In particular, we emphasize his focus on tariffs, protectionism, and his policies oriented to the transformation of the international economic and political order.

These empirical chapters illustrate five primary themes that characterize American industrial policy throughout history. First, a key theme has been the enlargement and extension of markets. This is a central question that, in different historical phases, explains much of the role played by the US government. The process of industrialization, as well as structural shifts of the economy and society have required progressive expansion and extension of the markets for domestic industry. Such an expansion was necessary to ensure continued growth, and thus to ensure social and political stability. In this respect, there is no doubt that American governments have always been very careful while playing a particularly active role.

The need to expand westward during the nineteenth century and then integrate into a global market has always guided the government's action in the United States. As highlighted below, this perspective helps to better understand the strategies, conflicts, and military actions undertaken by many American governments. As we shall see, the same outlook explains many of the objectives of trade policy, including bilateral and multilateral international treaties, the other key channels by which US governments favored the growth of national industry.

Second, we have seen policies driven by crises, such as the Great Depression, the end of WWII, or the dramatic rise of China. This has led governments to seek the development and revitalization of domestic industry. Examples include bailouts of private enterprises, procurement rules that impose limits on foreign purchases (for example, Buy American requirements as under the Biden administration), and the continued support and funding of science and technology promoted by numerous departments and agencies.

Third, interventions in favor of science and technology deserve special attention. Leadership in science and technology forms a large part of America's global leadership more broadly. Despite the rhetoric of free markets, American governments have massively invested substantial public resources in the science and technology fields. These are vital areas that are instrumental in maintaining industrial, economic, and military leadership. Regardless of the administration, they are always at the center of the federal government's efforts.

Fourth, the leverage of public procurement is another pillar that has sustained complex government-industry relations. Some interventions followed the Keynesian and Rooseveltian recipes; others, including some of the actions taken by the Bush and Obama administrations, followed different paths but nonetheless embraced intervention. Consider infrastructure investments, which take the form of horizontal actions intended to support the industrial and economic growth of the country. Think of the role that the federal government has had in the development of the railways, the highway system, and more recently, in the growth of data transfer networks. But above all, the Department of Defense has always constituted an extraordinary lever for growth, technological progress, and innovation in large portions of the domestic industry (which in this area has always been able to operate sheltered from foreign competition).

Fifth, and finally, another element of continuity that can be highlighted is the management of tensions between the dynamics of industrial growth and the sustainability of social and territorial divergences. The US government has, from the early stages of industrialization, found itself in the position of having to respond to the needs of companies that drove national growth, while at the same time having to worry about the social sustainability of the changes that stimulated growth. Industrial policy has, in many delicate moments of history, had to mediate between the strong and well-organized interests of industry and the need to mitigate the excesses that industrial capitalism produced. For example, consider the confrontation involving the working class in the early twentieth century and the social and racial tensions of the 1970s. These dynamics clearly led governments to encourage a gradual improvement of living conditions for growing segments of the population, with the result of making inequalities more acceptable and to ensure social and political sustainability during the process of industrial growth.

2

The Beginning

From Independence to the End of the Nineteenth Century

2.1 Introduction

Since the very beginning of US history, government interventions to promote the growth of the young national economy have been at the center of political debate. After achieving political independence, it soon became clear to the new government that economic independence needed to be achieved as quickly as possible. In this context, the first decades of the nineteenth century were marked by discussions on the best way to achieve this desired economic independence.

On one side, some interests—such as agrarian farmers in the South and traders in the Northeast—sought to maintain the existing equilibrium based on the export of raw materials and the import of manufactured goods from the most technologically advanced European countries. On the other side, new emerging interests called for a break from the past and advocated for a different growth model based on the development of a robust domestic manufacturing sector. Analyzing the following decades, it is clear that the latter trajectory was the one America pursued, leading in the nineteenth century to the emergence of a new industrial power progressively capable, in a protected setting, of responding to the fast-growing domestic demand for manufactured goods.

The nineteenth century was an age of accelerated industrialization and change that demanded government attention and action. Promoting manufacturing meant governing growth and the structural transformation of the economy and society, managing tensions and conflicts between interests, and bringing together new coalitions ready to support a manufacturing-driven development trajectory. As manufacturing independence emerged as one of the primary goals of the young nation, the prevailing view on how to achieve this objective involved granting the infant American industry targeted government benefits and protection from foreign competitors. In modern terms, promoting growth, manufacturing, and the resulting structural transformations in the economy and society demanded the implementation of a sophisticated industrial policy plan.

Governing Growth. Marco R. Di Tommaso and Vinod K. Aggarwal, Oxford University Press.
© Oxford University Press (2026). DOI: 10.1093/oso/9780197821787.003.0002

The nineteenth century ended in a changed context wherein new policy challenges emerged: big business concentration and the growing tensions between capital and labor (only partially mitigated by massive flows of immigrants). However, at that point, a new chapter was about to open: American industry was ready to start its trajectory of expansion outside of the continent, enlarging again the extent of its market.

2.2 Political Independence, Economic Independence, and Manufacturing Independence

Following the American Revolution and independence from Great Britain, the new US government soon proved to be very interested in the development of domestic manufacturing (Scheiber, 1987; Chang, 2007; Di Tommaso and Schweitzer, 2013; Di Tommaso and Tassinari, 2017).

One of the first indications of the special attention paid to developing an indigenous manufacturing sector can be seen in the words that President George Washington used in one of his first public speeches as president. In his annual message to Congress on January 8, 1790, he was explicit in defining the strategic role of manufacturing in the new nation:

> ... free people ought not only to be armed but disciplined; to which end a uniform and well-digested plan is requisite; and their safety and interest require that they should promote such manufactories as tend to render them independent of others for essential, particularly military, supplies" (Washington, 1790).

And some years later, close to the end of his last presidential mandate, he was still convinced about the need for a government policy dedicated to the growth of national manufacturing:

> Congress has repeatedly, and not without success, directed their attention to the encouragement of Manufactures. The object is of too much consequence, not to insure a continuance of their efforts, in every way which shall appear eligible (Washington, 1796).

Washington's intuitions and convictions on the matter of domestic manufacturing required his administration to analyze the status quo and discern political support to evaluate possible policy interventions. Soon after Washington's (1790) speech, the House of Representatives requested that Treasury Secretary

Alexander Hamilton submit a report on the infant American manufacturing sector and its potential trajectories of growth:

> ... a proper plan or plans, conformably to the recommendation of the President ... for the encouragement and promotion of such manufactories as will tend to render the United States independent dependent of other nations for essential, particularly for military supplies a plan or plans, conformable to the recommendations of the President for the encouragement and promotion of such manufactories as tend to render the United States independent of other nations for essential, especially military supplies (United States Congress, House of Representatives, 1790).

This request marks the beginning of the "special relationship" between government and industry in the United States. In December 1791, Alexander Hamilton presented to the House the results of a two-year-long study, his "Report on Manufactures." It was a detailed analysis in which one of the government's most influential men produced reflections, perspectives, and information on the present and future of the American economy. In his report, Hamilton proposed an ambitious policy program, aiming to promote the industrial and manufacturing development of the country (Hamilton, 1791). The following words, in which Hamilton began to illustrate the Report, were in line with Washington's ideas. Here we can find the basic motivations that should have led the US government to take care of the development of its manufacturing:

> The Secretary of the Treasury ... has applied his attention ... to the subject of Manufactures; and particularly to the means of promoting such as will tend to render the United States, independent on foreign nations, for military and other essential supplies. (Hamilton, 1791).

The general philosophy of his analysis and the industrial policy plan he was going to propose was quite clear: supporting manufacturing growth to promote the wealth, independence, and security of the nation:

> Not only the wealth, but the independence and security of a country, appear to be materially connected with the prosperity of manufactures. Every nation, with a view to those great objects, ought to endeavor to possess within itself all the essentials of national supply. These comprise the means of subsistence, habitation, clothing, and defense ... (Hamilton, 1791).

The Report first of all openly challenged the general "preference-for-agriculture" assumption rooted in some European thinking (the Physiocrats), which had its followers in the American debate of the time, and suggested that the wealth of nations should primarily be sought in the proper exploitation of the opportunities offered by agricultural endeavors. At the same time, the Report disputed Adam Smith's ideas on the best growth trajectories for the former North American colonies—ideas that were also diffused within the intellectual and political circles of the young nation:

> "It has been the principal cause of the rapid progress of our American colonies towards wealth and greatness, that almost their whole capitals have hitherto been employed in agriculture." (Smith, 1776, p. 365). In North America ... the purchase and improvement of uncultivated land, is ... the most profitable employment of the smallest as well as of the greatest capitals.... (Smith, 1776, pp. 414–415).

Hamilton, who had to be mindful of the interests of a newly independent country, was aware that Smith wrote from a British perspective and that it would have been wrong to, quoting Lionel Robbins, "... suppose that the English Classical economists would have recommended because it was good for the world at large, a measure which they thought would be harmful to their own community" (Robbins, 1953). The Report cut the continuity with the London-centered economic thinking that endorsed the existing equilibrium: on the one side, Britain, which had rapidly consolidated its position as the "workshop of the world," importing raw materials and exporting manufactured goods; on the other side, the colonies, which lacked manufacturing capabilities and were devoted to the export of natural resources. In Washington's and Hamilton's view, newly achieved political independence demanded economic independence that necessarily entailed the rapid growth of "an independent manufacturer" (Hamilton, 1791).

Smith was not quoted in the Report, but there are many clear references in the text showing that Hamilton was familiar with the writings of the Scottish thinker (Bourne, 1894; Rabbeno, 1895). It is also evident that Hamilton, in the Report, had sought to endorse a different approach. His plan implicitly referred to another political tradition that also had migrated to the "new world" and that in Europe had supported a "preference-for-manufacturing" belief. This was a line of thinking that in previous centuries highlighted the crucial role of manufacturing and commerce in achieving growth and prosperity and in catching up to wealthier nations. In this case as well, there are no direct quotations, but in the Report, Hamilton did introduce many of the core ideas of Botero, Mum, Von Hörnigk, and de Laffemas who should be considered the fathers of the "preference-for-manufacturing" European tradition (Reinert et al., 2016; Perrotta, 2014; Roessner, 2016; Di Tommaso et al., 2025).

However, in the Report, there was more than a challenge to the "preference-for-agriculture" assumption: Hamilton deliberately challenged the Smithian laissez-faire principles, such as the idea of the market's metaphorical invisible hand. Not only was the wealth of the nation about manufacturing growth, but, according to Hamilton's approach, this desired growth should be promoted and stimulated by government policies. The Report clearly defined the actions and specific tools needed to promote the infant American industry, in accordance with a strategic vision of the national economy's future: tariffs on imported products, a ban on exports of innovative products and machinery (to prevent appropriation by foreign competitors), direct subsidies to strategic industries, a tax exemption for raw materials, and total support for improving national infrastructure (Hamilton, 1791; Rabbeno, 1895; Taussig, 1931 Irwin, 2004; Chang, 2007; Di Tommaso and Schweitzer, 2013 Di Tommaso and Tassinari, 2017). Industries were treated differently according to their strategic value, and some of them—iron, copper, coal, cotton, glass, gunpowder, and books—received selective preferential government policies (Hamilton, 1791).

In terms of policy tools, Hamilton was particularly determined to describe what he considered to be the advantages of subsidies (bounties), which he believed were superior to tariffs, whose undesirable effects—namely inflation, scarcity, picking winners and losers, and tensions between rival interests—he highlighted:

> ... bounties are one of the most efficacious means of encouraging manufactures, and it is in some views, the best ... though it is less favored by public opinion than other modes (Hamilton, 1791).

However, when the Report entered into the details of the sectors of production that deserved to be protected by tariffs or incentivized by subsidies, the prescription was strikingly narrower and hewed closer to the status quo than Hamilton's strong convictions would lead one to believe: the Report demanded subsidies for comparatively few goods—coal, raw wool, sailcloth, cotton manufactures, glass, bottles, and windows—while maintaining the existing tariff system.

Hamilton was particularly attuned to the need to govern growth and structural change because of the expected tensions between interests representing different economic activities, sectors, and territories. This challenge is mentioned in several parts of the Report, and for this reason, Hamilton suggested the establishment of a government agency in charge of coordinating the promotion of the arts, industry, agriculture, and commerce.

Congress did not warmly welcome the proposal as Hamilton had hoped (Irwin, 2004). The difficulties stemmed from the fact that American policy during those years was influenced by interests pushing in different directions.

Two key groups included those who in some way had maintained a privileged relationship with the British: the merchants and traders of the East Coast, and land and plantation owners from the South (Williams, 1961; Scheiber, 1987; Irwin, 2004; Chang, 2007; Di Tommaso and Tassinari, 2017).

At the center of an industrial policy plan is the pursuit of the national interest. At the end of the eighteenth century, however, the identification of American interests was an open issue. The history of the largest industrial and manufacturing power in the world had yet to be written, and different evolutionary paths were still possible. Industrial policy is not a technical intervention that identifies the optimal means to achieve given objectives. A successful industrial policy plan must manage the balance among the country's various interests (e.g., territories, areas, classes) and help define, from a dynamic perspective, the national interest. As it was clear to Hamilton in his report, industrial policy constitutes a political intervention and not only a technical one, and it requires the government to consider the present and future interests of the country. These interests were not well expressed by a young nation that had just gained independence, and its definition was the subject of tensions between classes and territories, which had different possible paths of development and change in mind (Williams, 1961; Di Tommaso and Schweitzer, 2013).

Reactions to Hamilton's economic plan were divided along party lines (Irwin, 2004). While Federalists supported his proposal for increased government intervention, Democratic-Republicans were impatient with the central government, which emulated the center-periphery relations and typical top-down interventions of the colonial period. Among the ideals that characterized the revolutionary years, there was a picture of a government administered "from the bottom up." Individual states retained vast autonomy, and the decision-making authority was situated at the level of government closest to the citizens. In this scenario, the jurisdiction of the federal government was acceptable only if confined to fields in which local control was not feasible—for example, foreign policy, national defense, and interstate commerce (Irwin, 2004; Dobbin, 1994).

2.3 The Hamiltonian Heritage in the Nineteenth Century: From Quincy to McKinley

Despite this unenthusiastic initial reaction, in the end, the Hamiltonian approach, based on the "preference-for-manufacturing" assumption and on the consequent demand for government special encouragement and protection, characterized the coming decades (Irwin, 2004; Chang, 2007; Di Tommaso and Schweitzer, 2013; Di Tommaso and Tassinari, 2017). The new decade saw years of impressive transformation in which many important industrial sectors developed rapidly, but economic dependency on English imports remained an unsolved issue (see Figure 2.1).

In this context, Hamilton's views on the importance of promoting some strategic industries were put into practice for quite a long time. Moreover, it is also clear that tariffs on foreign manufactured goods were not a temporary characteristic of US government policy: they were kept very high over the nineteenth century and beyond (see Figure 2.2). On average, they remained in a range between 40% and 60% for the whole century. And, as will be elaborated upon later in this book, this protectionist attitude remained after the turn of the twentieth century and the years of the two world wars (Taussig, 1931; Magness, 2023; Klein and Meissner, 2024).

The protectionist aspect of American industrial policy in the nineteenth century generated significant regional tensions, as protection for manufactured goods was supported by the Northern industrialists but not by Southern farmers, who instead were forced to accept low-quality products at high prices. More generally, industrial policy interventions encouraged a structural change in American industry and society that was not welcomed by all. The divergence of interests between North and South continued to widen gradually during the manufacturing industry's growth, soon becoming unsustainable and helping to push the country toward the Civil War. This contrast remained unaltered in the second part of the nineteenth century, when the accelerated growth driven by the manufacturing North made the divergence of interests even larger (Magness, 2023).

These considerations explain why, since the times of Washington and Hamilton and throughout the entire century up to the presidency of William McKinley, tariffs remained a highly disputed issue in American politics, capable of furthering polarization among factions and interests. In a dynamic context of accelerated structural transformations, on one side were the industrial northern states seeking to protect their growing businesses, while on the other stood the southern states advocating for low tariffs. And of course, the scenario was more complex than this, given that in specific historical moments, influenced by domestic and international circumstances, coalitions of multiple interests found different rationales in supporting or opposing protectionist policies. An interesting example is the support for protectionism of some southern sugar producers who sought to defend their market from Caribbean imports and had to politically compete with the powerful, rapidly growing railroad industry that was interested in importing low-price steel from foreign countries (Rabbeno, 1895; Irwin, 2004).

In this setting, the so-called "Tariff of Abominations" of 1828 was a major development and one starting point of this long-lasting political debate: average

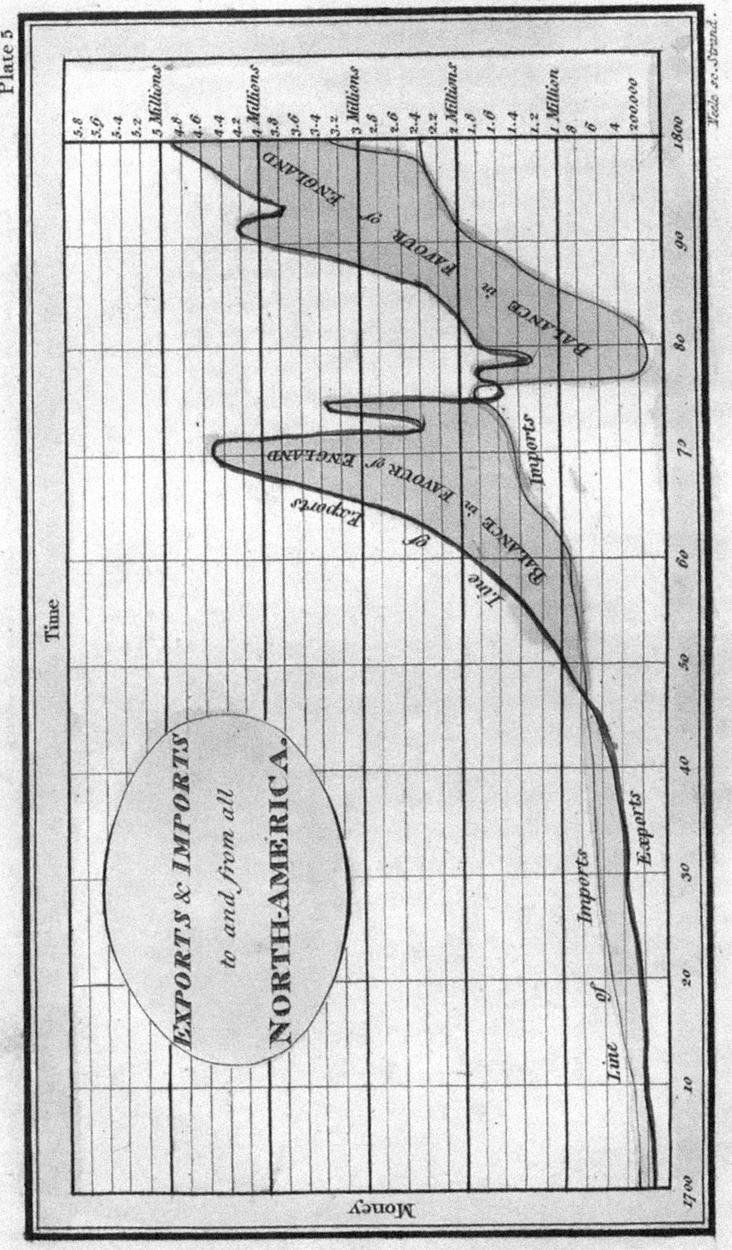

Figure 2.1 US Economic Dependency on the United Kingdom Before and After Political Independence

Source: William Playfair (1805), Statistical Account of the United States of America by D.F. Donnant. London

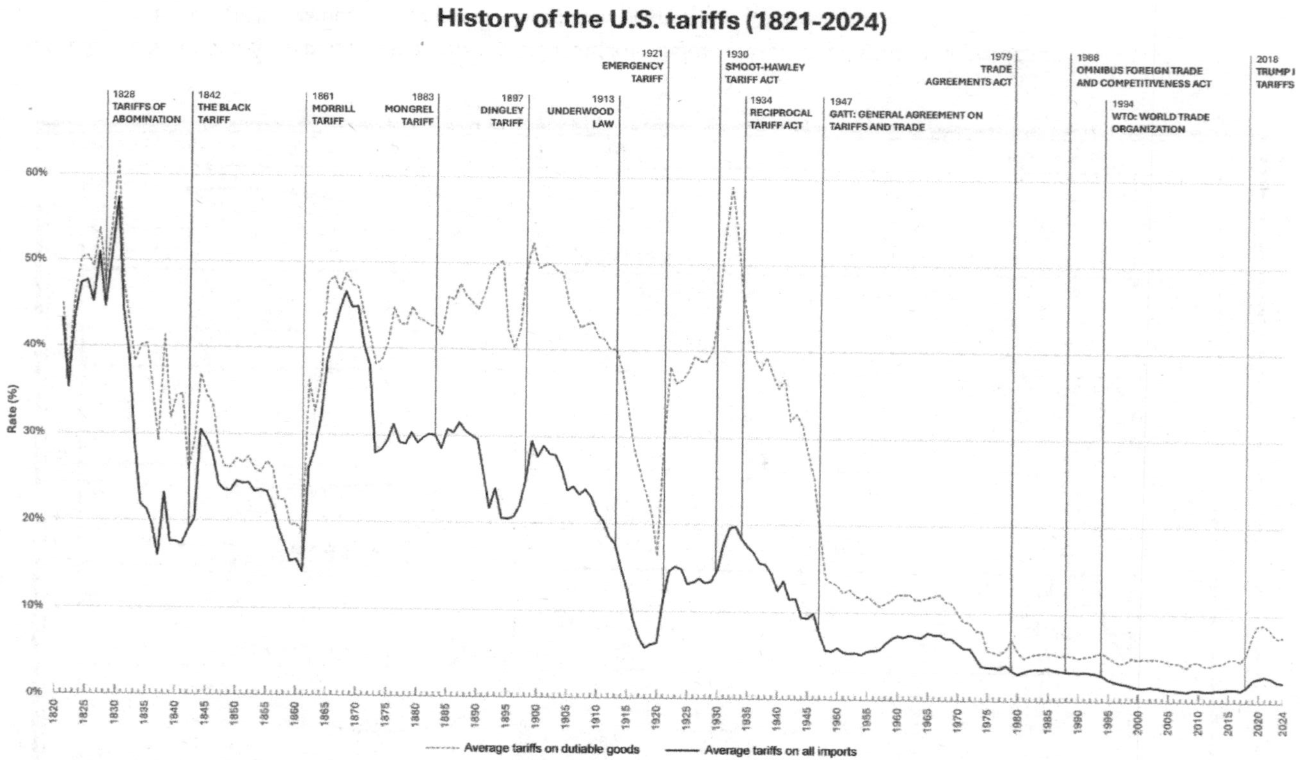

Figure 2.2 The History of US Tariffs

Source: Apple, Charles. A History of U.S. Tariffs. *The Spokesman Review.* www.spokesman.com/stories/2019/may/23/further-review-history-us-tariffs/

tariffs on dutiable imports reached over 60% (Magness, 2023). It was approved by President John Quincy Adams and divided the House of Representatives, which passed it with 104 votes in favor and 94 against. A few years later, after a period of gradual tariff reductions, the protectionist attitude received further support with the so-called "Black Tariff" of 1842, strongly sustained by the Whigs that took control of Congress (Irwin, 2004; Taussig, 1931). In 1861, the discussion of the "Morrill Tariff" was another moment of deep political contrast. However, the protectionist factions prevailed again, also thanks to a wave of southern representatives' resignations from Congress after the election of President Abraham Lincoln. Then, in the following decades, government protection by tariffs continued and became even stronger (Irwin, 2004). We should first mention the 1890 "McKinley Tariff," passed during President Benjamin Harrison's administration: it boosted tariff rates to nearly 50% for many products, mainly on manufactured goods (Magness, 2023).

It is interesting to highlight how intense and polarized the political debate on the issue was during those years, and yet how, in the end, the protectionist perspective continued to prevail for quite a long while. For several decades, the House of Representatives remained a highly divided arena on the issue, with opposing factions deeply entrenched for and against tariffs. The same was true outside the House, given that public opinion representing different territorial and productive interests was very split too. Consider this *New York Times* headline: "Up go the prices now; how the McKinley tariff taxes the necessaries of life. Merchants are marking up almost everything that men wear, eat, or keep house with" (*New York Times, 1890*). And very instructive is the representation offered by the following map published during the 1888 presidential campaign when tariff policy was the principal issue of confrontation: Grover Cleveland demanded a strong reduction in tariffs, arguing that they were unfair to consumers, while Harrison took the side of industrialists and factory workers who wanted to keep tariffs high (see Figure 2.3).

In this context, particular attention should go to William McKinley, quoted by President Trump during his inaugural address on January 20, 2025. McKinley was propelled to the forefront of the debate on tariffs for more than two decades, first as a congressman and then later as president of the United States. His pro-tariff position was his hobby horse since the beginning of his political career when he was only an Ohio congressman. McKinley consciously chose tariffs as his main strategic topic, soon becoming recognizable as a leading congressional expert. Since the late 1870s, in several public speeches he supported the idea that high tariffs forged the United States as that nation: "... without a superior in industrial arts, without an equal in commercial prosperity, with a sound financial system, with an overflowing Treasury, blessed at home and at peace with all mankind" (McKinley, cited in Merry, 2017).

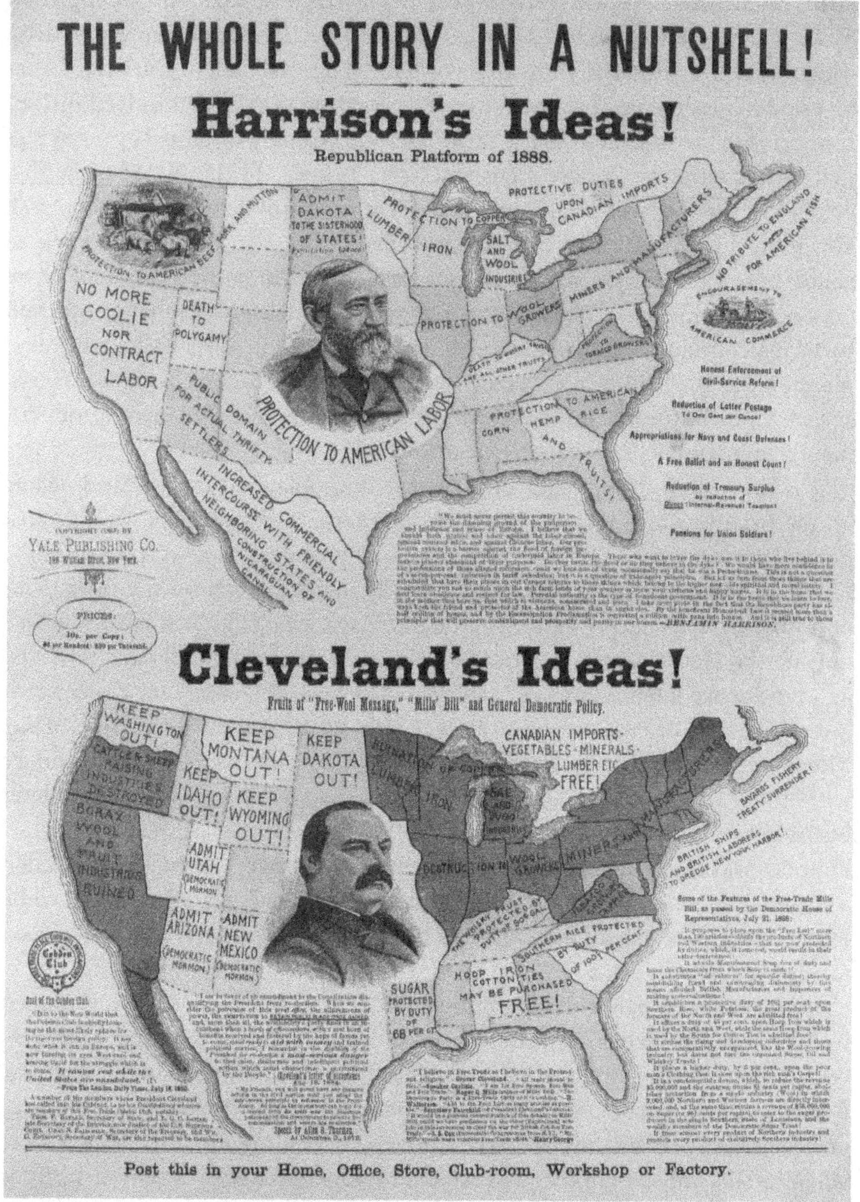

Figure 2.3 The 1888 Presidential Campaign: Tariffs on Imports at the Center of the Debate

Source: Yale Publishing Co., 1888. The Whole Story in a Nutshell! Harrison's Ideas! Cleveland's Ideas! Cornell University Library, Division of Rare & Manuscript Collections: Persuasive Cartography: The PJ Mode Collection. Accession no. 1096.01. https://persuasivemaps.library.cornell.edu/

His faith in tariffs was strong and rooted in his ideas on the positive role of protectionist policies:

"...we are faithfully wedded to the great principle of protection by every tie of party fealty and affection, and it is dearer to us now than ever before. Not only is it dearer to us as Republicans, but it has more devoted supporters among the great masses of the American people, irrespective of party, than at any previous period in our national history. It is everywhere recognized and endorsed as the great, masterful, triumphant American principle—the key to our prosperity in business, the safest prop to the Treasury of the United States, and the bulwark of our national independence and financial honor" (McKinley, cited in Paget, 1896).

McKinley's enthusiasm for tariffs appears quite similar to President Trump's keenness for that policy instrument: "President McKinley made our country very rich through tariffs and through talent" (Trump, 2025c). More than a century earlier, McKinley consistently framed tariff protection as a central pillar of national prosperity, social stability, and political durability, rather than as a temporary or technical policy choice. This conviction soon translated into concrete legislative action. After his election in 1896, one of McKinley's first major initiatives as president was support for the 1897 Dingley Act, which he justified on explicitly protectionist grounds:

In raising revenue, duties should be so levied upon foreign products as to preserve the home market, so far as possible, to our own producers; to revive and increase manufactures; to relieve and encourage agriculture; to increase our domestic and foreign commerce; to aid and develop mining and building; and to render to labor in every field of useful occupation the liberal wages and adequate rewards to which skill and industry are justly entitled. The necessity of the passage of a tariff law which shall provide ample revenue, need not be further urged. The imperative demand of the hour is the prompt enactment of such a measure, and to this object I earnestly recommend that Congress shall make every endeavor (McKinley, 1897).

Focusing on McKinley also allows us to observe the evolution of his positions. The McKinley Tariff of 1890, which he fiercely wanted and obtained, raised tariffs to nearly 50%. Nevertheless, he won his campaign by exploiting his prominent pro-tariff stance, and upon taking office, he lived up to his reputation. However, he revised his position soon thereafter, anticipating a policy attitude that would characterize the following decades of the new century. New times were arriving, and American big business was already consolidated and ready to think globally. Therefore, the new challenge became foreign market penetration. The *McKinley-nomics* principles based on tariffs and protection demanded to be readjusted to the new emerging scenario and the last speech he made before his assassination was exactly in this direction:

> Our capacity to produce has developed so enormously and our products have so multiplied that the problem of more markets requires our urgent and immediate attention. Only a broad and enlightened policy will keep what we have. No other policy will get more. In these times of marvelous business energy and gain, we ought to be looking to the future, strengthening the weak places in our industrial and commercial system, that we may be ready for any storm or strain (McKinley, 1901 cited in Richardson, 1920).

With this new urgent goal in mind, McKinley started to think about bilateral agreements with some selected countries:

> By sensible trade arrangements which will not interrupt our home production, we shall extend the outlets for our increasing surplus. A system that provides a mutual exchange of commodities is manifestly essential to the continued and healthful growth of our export trade. We must not repose in fancied security that we can forever sell everything and buy little or nothing. If such a thing were possible, it would not be best for us or for those with whom we deal. We should take from our customers such of their products as we can use without harm to our industries and labor. Reciprocity is the natural outgrowth of our wonderful industrial development under the domestic policy now firmly established. What we produce beyond our domestic consumption must have a vent abroad. The excess must be relieved through a foreign outlet, and we should sell everywhere we can and buy wherever the buying will enlarge our sales and productions and thereby make a greater demand for home labor (McKinley, 1901 cited in Richardson, 1920).

McKinley's vision on past and future policies was clear:

> The period of exclusiveness is past. The expansion of our trade and commerce is the pressing problem. Commercial wars are unprofitable. A policy of goodwill and friendly trade relations will prevent reprisals. Reciprocity treaties are in harmony with the spirit of the times; measures of retaliation are not. If perchance some of our tariffs are no longer needed for revenue or to encourage and protect our industries at home, why should they not be employed to extend and promote our markets abroad? (McKinley, 1901 cited in Richardson, 1920).

On the role of tariffs in the nineteenth century and beyond, there is an old and interesting debate (Rabbeno, 1895; Taussig, 1910 Irwin, 2017). This debate, following President Trump's first campaign, has been reanimated to support or oppose today's protectionism and economic nationalism (Klein and Meissner, 2024).

President Trump articulated this approach explicitly at the outset of his second term, declaring that he would "immediately begin the overhaul of our trade system to protect American workers and families," replacing domestic taxation with tariffs on foreign countries and establishing an "External Revenue Service" to collect tariff revenues (Trump, 2025c)

In order to examine potential policy implications for our present, we recommend that more studies discuss, with different methodologies, the relationship between tariff protection and economic growth within that specific historical context. A great stock of documents and data clearly shows a temporal coincidence between a long season of tariffs and decades of accelerated industrial growth (Taussig, 1931). However, it has also been argued that tariffs were not supported for industrial policy rationales in the Hamiltonian sense but as a source of funding for a growing public budget (Irwin, 2004, 2017). In other words, even if the existence of very high tariffs during the whole nineteenth century was beyond dispute, it is still possible to argue that this has nothing to do with industrial policy rationales. Moreover, doubts have been raised on the impacts of these tariffs: some scholars suggested that tariffs were ineffective and that successful growth was possible despite tariffs' policy persistence (Taussig, 1931; Klein and Meissner, 2024).

2.4 Growth, Structural Change Sustainability, and Market Expansion

Within the context of continuous and rapid transformations—marked by tensions among competing interest groups—which we have sketched out above, we can trace one of the essential motivations characterizing American industrial policy. This class of interventions, on the one hand, directly supported industrial growth through financial support, protection, and promotion, and on the other, focused on managing the tensions that this very process of structural change created.

This perspective allows us to understand a key means of intervention through which American governments guided this phase of extraordinary industrial, economic, and social change: it consists of supporting the growth and ensuring the sustainability of structural change processes, through actions that first support border expansion and then expanding markets.

The political independence and economic outlook of the United States could no longer be reduced merely to production autonomy from its erstwhile mother country. American industry had already been established, and now it needed to gradually expand. Westward expansion allowed for the acquisition of invaluable new resources and an incredible extension of market opportunities, sustaining industrial growth, and transformation.

President Thomas Jefferson adopted such a view. In his message to Congress on January 18, 1803, requesting money to fund expeditions to the unexplored West, he clearly emphasized the necessity of western territorial expansion to ensure the industrial and agricultural ambitions of the country.[1] By the mid 1850s, American territory had more than tripled in size compared to its size after the Treaty of Paris was signed in 1783 (see Figure 2.4).

Economic development and the nation's industrial growth went hand in hand with the need to claim more territory, thus allowing for gradual market expansion. It was a process that clearly needed military support, transportation infrastructure, and a policy to encourage immigration.

Certain industries had strategic significance with regard to national interests. The railway industry in particular stood at the center of early nineteenth-century economic policy (see Figure 2.5). The government played a crucial role in planning, sponsoring, and coordinating the technical aspects of this sector, recognizing its potential to facilitate economic growth, national integration, and industrial development. It actively regulated prices and competition to prevent monopolistic practices and ensure broad accessibility (Dobbin, 1994).

Initially, local governments and individual states, often in public-private partnerships, took the lead in railway development. These entities played a pivotal role in planning and funding infrastructure, often allocating subsidies and land grants to cities eager to establish railway stations. While private companies were primarily responsible for constructing railway lines, government entities provided critical support through direct financial contributions, regulatory frameworks, and incentives designed to systematically expand the rail network.

Starting in 1860, the scenario changed, and the federal government took an important role in the railway sector, a role which paralleled that of local governments in earlier decades. The federal government decided to intervene to support large national rail projects. In particular, Congress decided to provide land guarantees and loans for the realization of four large transcontinental lines (Dobbin, 1994). The impact of such industrial policies resounded internationally, and other countries emulated the United States. Closely following the completion of the US Transcontinental Railroad, Russia began construction

---

[1] The goal then was also to achieve territorial control of the Mississippi River, which flows into the Gulf of Mexico, and offers an outlet to world markets (Williams, 1964, pp. 216–217).

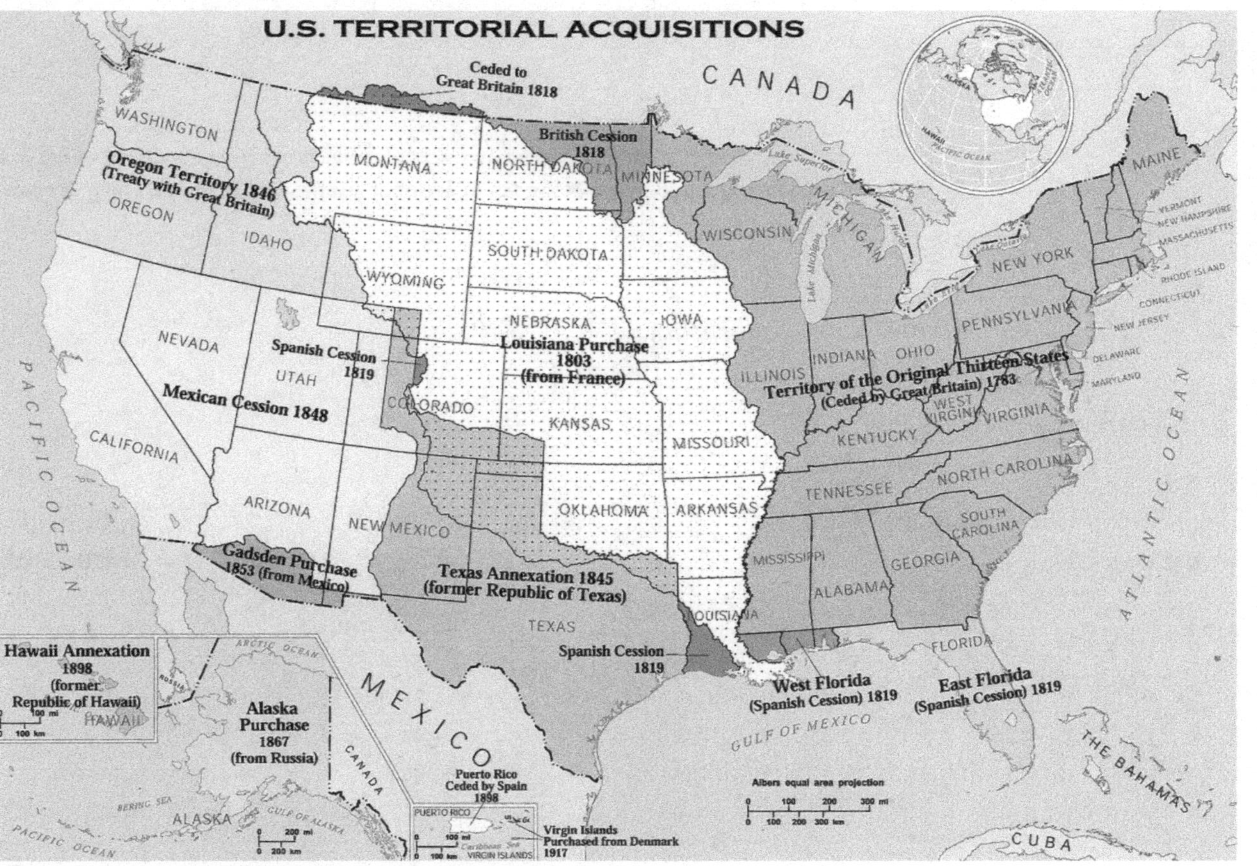

Figure 2.4 "The Border" and the Gradual Market Expansion

Source: Reworking of NationalAtlas.gov

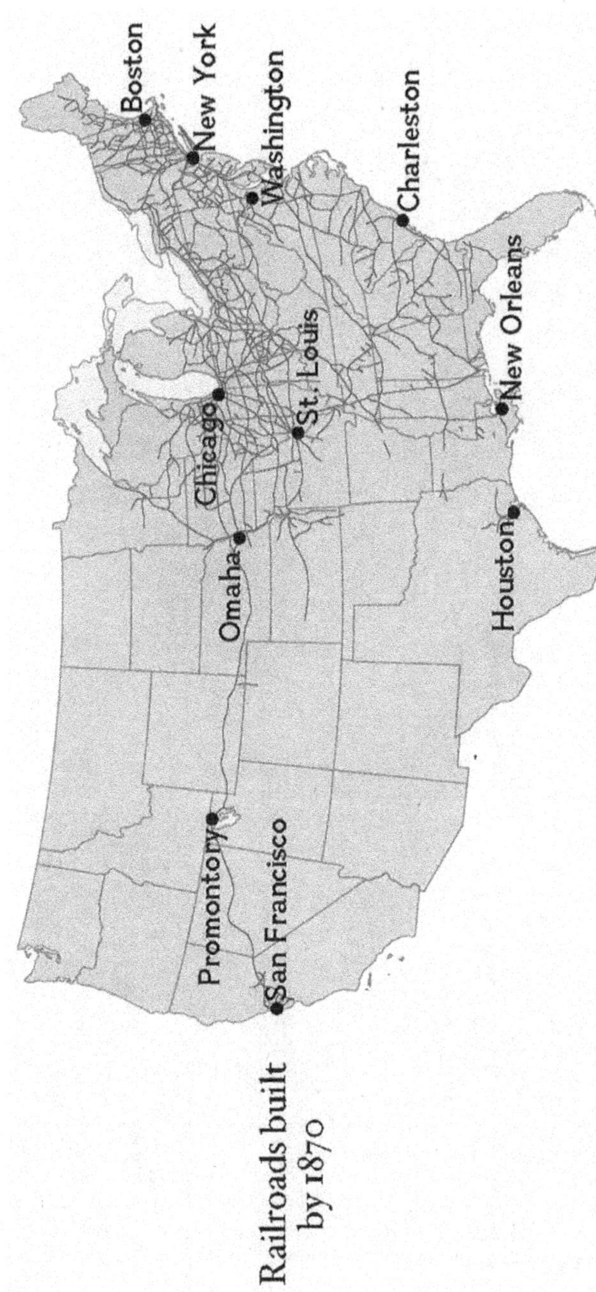

Figure 2.5 The Growth of the Railway Industry in the Second Half of the Nineteenth Century

Source: https://education.nationalgeographic.org/resource/tracking-growth-us/

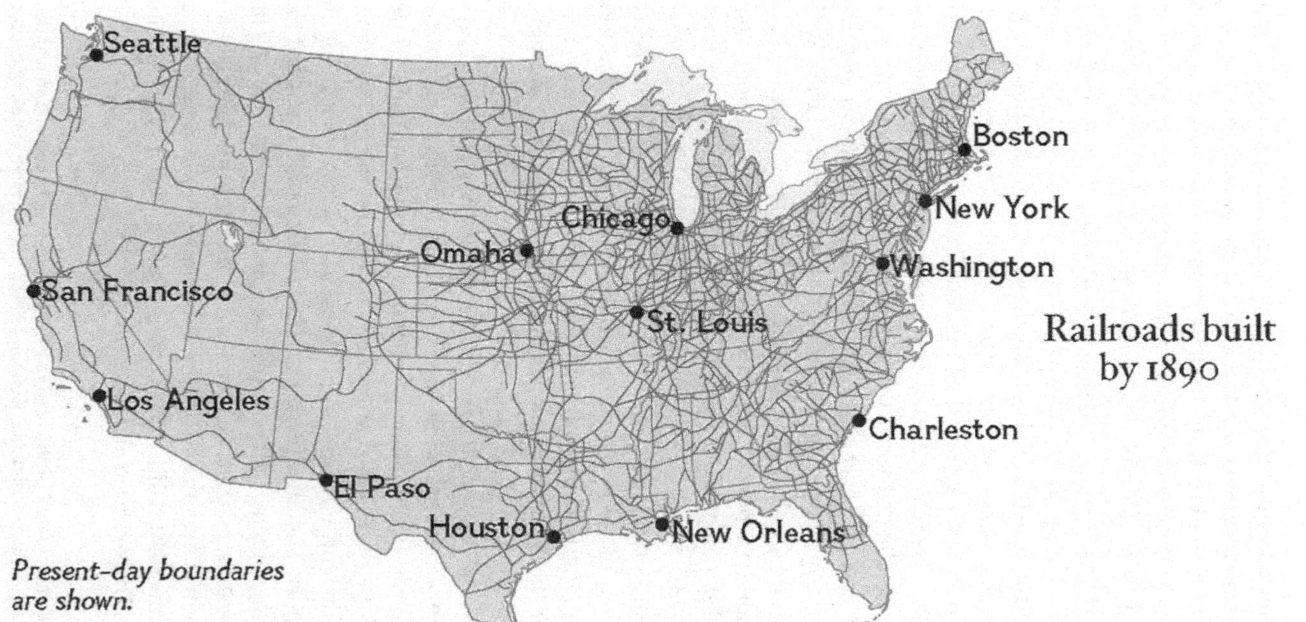

Figure 2.5 Continued

on the Trans-Siberian Railroad, its answer to the US expansion of the railway industry.

In the following decades, the federal government exercised an important role in the growth dynamics of this industry, acquiring a central role in the regulation of the entire national rail system.[2] In those years, it became necessary to exercise control over rail transport prices. In fact, shippers who used the railways began to complain of excessively high and often discriminatory rates. However, the issue went deeper than the shippers' discontentment. The national government did not see railways as an industry like any other, and it was necessary to monitor the dynamics of this highly strategic sector for the national interest.

In 1887, Congress passed the Interstate Commerce Act and the creation of the first federal regulatory agency, the Interstate Commerce Commission (ICC) (Bingham, 1998). The ICC attracted fierce opposition from railway monopolies and other consolidated trusts but received fervent support from ordinary consumers and farmers. This had the effect of strengthening competition in the market, primarily by eliminating abuses and discriminatory tariffs. As pointed out by Dobbin (1994), "Market regulation became the distinguishing feature of American industrial policy. The new American industrial policy paradigm came to symbolize competition among free and equal firms as the mainspring of progress" (p. 28).

The 1920 Transportation Act marked a significant expansion of federal oversight in the railway sector by strengthening the role of the ICC. This legislation not only granted the ICC the authority to set rates in the railway market but also assigned it the broader responsibility of ensuring adequate service levels and industry stability (Bingham, 1998). By formalizing the ICC's role as a regulatory body, the act sought to address inefficiencies in the railway system and protect public interests while ensuring a sustainable transportation network. However, the ICC's influence extended beyond railroads. Throughout the first half of the twentieth century and for decades thereafter, the commission regulated the entire American transportation sector, overseeing multiple modes of transport. The Motor Carrier Act of 1935 further expanded the ICC's jurisdiction by introducing entry control mechanisms for the trucking industry. Through concessions, permits, and the regulation of minimum freight rates, the ICC exerted control over the competitive dynamics of the entire US transport market (Cochran, 1950; Hill, 1951; Carter, 1968; Lloyd, 1982; Dobbin, 1994; Bingham, 1998; Di Tommaso and Schweitzer, 2013.

---

[2] This step was first motivated by the need to respond to extensive corruption and demands to reduce intervention by local governments (Dobbin, 1994). "In the United States, evidenced corruption inherent threat to the political order are posed by expansion. That Americans were certain their Governments had overstepped bounds in offering aid to railroads, and forswore future, government aid to enterprise" (Dobbin, 1994, p. 58).

This regulatory framework reflected the broader New Deal-era philosophy of economic oversight, which sought to balance market competition with state intervention. By stabilizing transportation markets and preventing destructive price wars, the ICC played a crucial role in shaping the evolution of US infrastructure policy well into the late twentieth century.

2.5 The Rise of Large Companies in the Nineteenth Century

The nineteenth century is one in which the American frontier progressively moved southward and westward. This dynamic allowed for a continuous expansion of the internal market. These trends marked decades of continued industrial growth and extraordinary structural change in the American economy and society.

In this context, starting from the years of the Civil War and the presidency of Abraham Lincoln in the 1860s, a limited number of companies and corporations had gradually grown and consolidated significant economic power in many national industries. These were companies that had developed due to the opportunities offered by the expansion of markets and by revolutionizing the organization of production, enhanced by new technologies. It also included companies that had gradually gained strength, also thanks to their dominant positions and preferential relationships with governments. The crises of the 1870s and 1880s had created further pressure toward concentration, increasing the market power of several large companies that had been able to overcome the most difficult moments.

This scenario began to attract public attention and, in some cases, worried governments as well, since these large corporations also sought to influence politics and challenge the government's authority (Stein, 1998; Freyer, 1992; Sandel, 1996; Sullivan, 1991; Prodi and De Giovanni, 1988; Bianchi, 1988). In the words of Senator John Sherman in Congress, the tension was clear:

> If the concentrated powers of this combination are entrusted to a single man, it is a kingly prerogative, inconsistent with our form of government and should be subject to the strong resistance of the State and national authorities. If anything is wrong this is wrong. If we will not endure a king as a political power, we should not endure a king over the production, transportation, and sale of any of the necessaries of life (Sherman, 1890).

The state of affairs demanded federal regulation of competition, which effectively became a tool of negotiation between political and economic power. In this process, we find another fundamental aspect that has characterized the relationship between the federal government and national industry in American history. The emergence of large industrial entities shaped the recurrent pattern of government intervention and nonintervention that would typify US government-firm relations over time. On the one hand, authorities would pursue antitrust actions and competition policies that, at least on paper, aimed to oversee dominant firms' market power and potential abuses. On the other hand, the government tended to seek mediation and mutual accommodation with large industrial groups. These positions, which have continually been in tension, have produced different balances in different circumstances and epochs. Intervention and nonintervention in this field have encompassed the issues of efficiency, innovation, and consumer protection. However, antitrust policy meant much more in American history. The pendulum between antitrust action and inaction has always been a powerful mechanism that allowed American governments to exchange and build political consensus.

From this perspective, we can consider the antitrust debate of the late nineteenth century, during which American industry continued to grow rapidly, and which inspired the 1890 Sherman Antitrust Act and later the 1914 Clayton Antitrust Act (Freyer, 1992; Thorelli, 1955). The first aimed to oversee already consolidated monopolistic power, while the second sought to regulate mergers and acquisitions among companies, preventing further market concentration. However, while the logic behind the two acts was clear, the concrete application of the rules in this field was at times fuzzy, equivocal, or contradictory. Moreover, the specific provisions in which the legislature set out how the laws were to be applied appeared rather imprecise, weakening the government's actual intervention capacity (Stein, 1998; Freyer, 1992; Thorelli, 1955).

This vagueness of the rule allowed for significant judicial discretion, resulting in the effectiveness of the legislative framework being heavily dependent on the actions of judges. For example, attempts at monopolization regulated by the Sherman Antitrust Act from the early twentieth century onward led to few victories for the government against private enterprises, despite the fact that numerous antitrust cases were brought to court.

Early judicial interpretations of antitrust legislation were notably restrictive, as courts required that accusations of monopolization be supported by clear evidence of illegal contracts, collusive alliances, or conspiracies (Prodi and De Giovanni, 1988; Freyer, 1992; Sullivan, 1991; Stein, 1998; Sandel, 1996). This narrow application of the law had significant limitations, as it overlooked the reality that market power could—and often did—develop through normal business strategies, such as economies of scale, vertical integration, and aggressive pricing, none of which were inherently illegal (Stein, 1998; Freyer, 1992; Adams and Brock, 1986). Consequently, this judicial approach effectively legitimized most forms of market concentration, so long as there was no direct evidence of intentional monopolization through unlawful means.

Over time, however, this rigid interpretation of antitrust law gave way to a broader regulatory framework that focused less on the specific methods by which firms acquired dominance and more on the actual existence of excessive market concentration. This shift marked a significant turning point in antitrust enforcement, as regulatory authorities and courts began prioritizing structural economic analysis over the identification of explicit anti-competitive practices. The definition of the relevant market—the geographic and product boundaries within which competition was assessed—became a central point of contention in antitrust cases. However, even under this new approach, which remained dominant until the late 1960s, the federal government struggled to effectively challenge the market power of major corporations. Numerous cases were unsuccessfully litigated against some of the largest American firms, often due to disputes over how the relevant market should be defined to assess monopoly power (Prodi and De Giovanni, 1988; Stein, 1998).

The Clayton Antitrust Act of 1914, which was introduced to address gaps in existing antitrust legislation, sought to prevent market concentration by regulating mergers and acquisitions. The law explicitly prohibited companies from acquiring the shares or assets of another firm if such acquisitions would significantly reduce competition. However, the legislation proved to be largely ineffective in curbing corporate consolidation. Its scope was limited, as it only applied to mergers conducted through the direct acquisition of stock, inadvertently legitimizing other forms of corporate takeovers, such as asset purchases, interlocking directorates, and leveraged buyouts, which became increasingly common (Stein, 1998; Freyer, 1992). Consequently, while the Clayton Act represented an early attempt at strengthening antitrust enforcement, it ultimately failed to prevent the rise of large conglomerates, particularly in the mid twentieth century.

2.6 Big Business after the Turn of the Century

The years of early antitrust legislation and its subsequent weak enforcement formed the ground on which government-industry relationships developed, characterizing the new century. Having legislation on the books allows the government to provide oversight of big businesses, while the discretionary aspect of intervention guarantees the opening of a permanent negotiation table between government and industry. This became a valuable channel for public-private cooperation in its various forms: acceptance of dominant positions and concentrations, public procurement, bailouts, subsidies and incentives, and protection from foreign companies.

The steel sector is emblematic in this regard. The nineteenth-century development of railways greatly contributed to the sector's expansion, which had benefited since the early days of independence from high protective tariffs and from a special relationship with governments. In 1855, the American Iron and Steel Association was founded with the aim of negotiating with the federal government for protection from foreign competition (Nester, 1997; Wilson, 2006). In this framework, even inefficient companies remained in the market for decades despite excessively high prices and low product quality.

The economic crises of the late 1800s quickly exposed deep structural weaknesses in the American steel industry. Many companies, unable to withstand the sharp decline in demand, faced financial ruin and were forced to shut down. This wave of closures not only revealed the sector's vulnerability but also created an environment that favored consolidation as a means of survival. In response, industry leaders pursued mergers as a strategic solution, leading to the emergence of a dominant national oligopoly. This process culminated in 1901 with the formation of the United States Steel Corporation (USSC), the first enterprise to attain a one-billion-dollar market capitalization (Stein, 1998, p. 11). At its inception, the USSC controlled approximately 65% of the national market, a position that was not only tolerated but also justified in the name of national economic stability and industrial growth (Stein, 1998).

Despite the passage of antitrust legislation such as the Sherman Act (1890) and the Clayton Act (1914), these measures had little immediate impact on the steel industry's consolidation. By 1920, USSC's market share had declined to 40%, yet the company faced accusations of predatory behavior. However, the case against it quickly unraveled when the Supreme Court ruled that the Attorney General had failed to prove illegal monopolization practices. No punitive measures were taken, but the proceedings signaled the government's growing regulatory awareness and willingness to engage with corporate power rather than dismantle it outright. This episode marked the beginning of a prolonged phase of negotiation between the steel oligopoly and federal authorities— a relationship that would shape industrial policy and economic governance for decades. As one of the cornerstone industries of the American economy, the steel sector maintained substantial bargaining power with the government, ensuring its influence remained a fixture in US economic and political discourse.

The steel industry was a strategic sector that had to respond to the demands of two world wars—both significant international drivers of American industry policy. Since the early 1900s, this very important sector has become a privileged field of confrontation wherein demands for higher wages and workers' rights, on the one hand, and the interests of big businesses, on the other, were mediated. The industrial policy attitude of American governments in this sector demonstrates how the government intervened in the national industry. It sheds light on the exchange relationship between the political consensus sought by governments and the demands (for action or inaction) of big industrial groups. It explains much of the de facto tolerance toward cartels and oligopolies and why industrial and sectoral policies have often aimed at mediating and managing the potential social conflict between capital and labor (Stein, 1998). It tells us why American governments have had to continue over time to respond to the need to further shift "the frontier" of markets for their industries. The analysis of the major transformations of the early twentieth century that characterized the steel sector and its relationship with the government reveals much about the path that American capitalism was beginning to take. It was a path that needed to open a new phase of the special relationship between government and national industry (Williams, 1964; Stein, 1998).

Following a period in which industrial and political interests were closely aligned, the era of deep suspicion toward big business and corporate dominance gradually subsided. By the early twentieth century, the consolidation of dominant market positions was no longer perceived solely as a threat to fair competition but was increasingly accepted and, in many cases, encouraged. The progressive regulatory battles of the late nineteenth and early twentieth centuries gave way to a more cooperative relationship between business and government, particularly as industrial efficiency and economic stability became national priorities.

This transformation was explicitly acknowledged by political leaders of the time. In 1914, President Woodrow Wilson publicly declared that:

> The antagonism between business and Government is over…the Government and businessmen are ready to meet each other halfway in a common effort to square business methods with both public opinion and public law (Wilson, 1914 cited in Crockett, 2002, p. 114).

Wilson's statement reflected a broader shift in governmental attitudes, where the state no longer saw large corporations primarily as economic threats but rather as strategic partners in modernizing the national economy. This sentiment was echoed by Secretary of Commerce (and future president) Herbert Hoover, who, several years later, observed:

> I believe that we are, almost unnoticed, in the midst of a great revolution—or perhaps a better word, a transformation—in the whole super-organization of our economic life. We are passing from a period of extremely individualistic action into a period of associational activities (Hoover, 1922, cited in Abend, 2014, p. 179).

Hoover's remarks highlighted a fundamental shift in economic governance—from an era defined by unregulated individualism to one that emphasized collaboration between government and industry through associationism, a model that sought to balance economic efficiency with regulatory oversight. This transition became particularly evident during World War I, as the war effort necessitated unprecedented coordination between private enterprise and federal agencies. The War Industries Board (WIB), for example, played a central role in managing production, allocating resources, and stabilizing prices, effectively demonstrating the benefits of industrial coordination for national stability (Hawley, 1974; Weinstein, 2012).

By the end of the war, corporate influence had reached an unprecedented scale, as 31% of all manufacturing activities were controlled by large corporations, employing a staggering 86% of the entire industrial workforce (Williams, 1964, p. 536). This growing corporate dominance reinforced the notion that large-scale industrial organization was not only economically inevitable but also functionally necessary for maintaining national growth and global competitiveness.

2.7 Government, Industry, and Labor in the Early Twentieth Century

Within the framework just outlined, concerns about the sustainability of the entire system were not lacking. While government actions generally responded to the desires of big corporations, enlightened industrial and political circles were aware that the system would face dangerous fractures if it leaned too heavily in this direction (Williams, 1964, p. 506). On the other hand, the message coming from other industrialized countries in the early decades of the twentieth century was clear: ignoring the demands for higher wages and workers' rights could have disruptive effects. The rise of big American industry resulted in the concentration of masses of workers in a limited number of cities and industrial areas. The power that big business had acquired over time allowed the persistence of dreadful living and working conditions: extremely long workdays, dangerous workplaces, precariousness, use of child labor, racial and gender discrimination, the absence of assistance and prevention for accidents and illnesses, and the lack of real pension protection. These conditions were accepted thanks to the enormous and continuous influx of immigrants who, in most cases, were desperate and willing to accept even precarious employment and unhealthy working conditions (see Figure 2.6) (Di Tommaso and Schweitzer, 2013).

The American model of industrial growth and organization produced tremendous success but also harbored a structural conflict that needed to be addressed

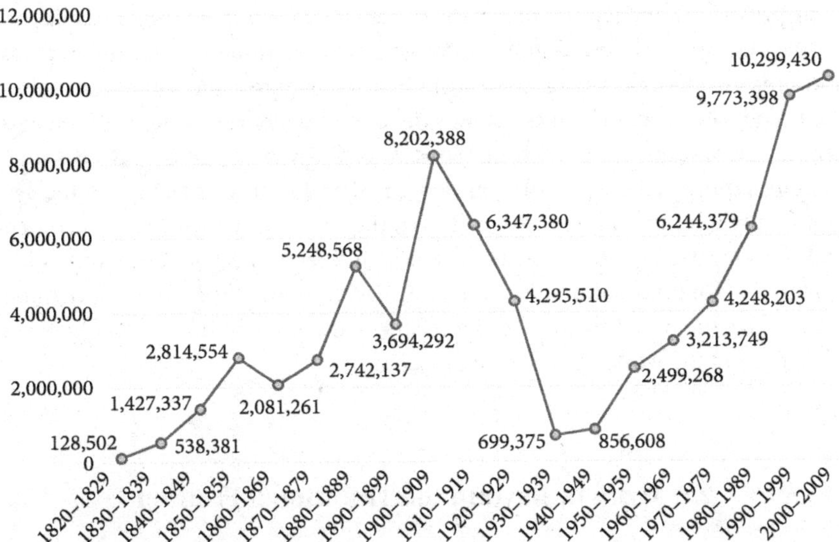

Figure 2.6 Number of Legal Immigrants by Decade
Source: Department of Homeland Security, 2011

sooner or later. The fundamental issue concerned how the government could manage this conflict, and in particular how it could mediate negotiations between interests. The government gained political consensus by responding to the demands of industries that had acquired dominant positions, but simultaneously worked with labor unions to mitigate the excesses of the system. New immigrants—the most desperate, uneducated, and unaware of their rights—helped temper the conflict between capital and labor. At the same time, businesses and unions could exert influence over the government interventions that guaranteed the sustainability of the American economy's growth and structural change.

Since the early 1900s, American governments have intervened in relations between employers and labor in order to encourage a progressive improvement in living conditions for certain classes of workers. Interventions were implemented through negotiation with unions, which had become more institutionalized over time. One prominent example was the rise and progressive co-optation of the American Federation of Labor (AFL), which was founded in 1886 but saw its peak growth in the early decades of the twentieth century. Indeed, it was the AFL that managed the relationship with governments and industry in subsequent years, sharing their fundamental choices, including those related to wartime. The AFL did not question the existing order and represented the demands of all workers whose voices were intended to be heard (Block, 2008; Adams, 1994).

In parallel, other labor organizations declined in importance and did not receive the same privileged status in the negotiations among government, firms, and unions. This was the case with the first labor representation organization, the Knights of Labor, which essentially disappeared by the end of the nineteenth century, as well as the Industrial Workers of the World, whose activists were forcibly suppressed because they posed a real and radical challenge to the system as a whole. In contrast, the AFL was the union in which the government and industry decided to invest, and it was legitimized in negotiations and public debate (Di Tommaso and Schweitzer, 2013; Weinstein, 2012). The government counted on the union to contain big business and prevent the conflict between industry and the working class from escalating.

2.8 Growth Beyond the Traditional Frontier

The governments in the late nineteenth century were primarily concerned with growth and accordingly tended to respond to the demands of large corporations while seeking to avoid excessive social and regional disparities. Governments intervened precisely from this perspective: they worked to promote growth, exchanged support with major corporations, and negotiated with the more forward-thinking segments of capital and labor unions for the progressive improvement of conditions for certain segments of the population. To prevent the system from faltering, it was once again necessary to expand the extent of the market to meet the demands of the growing national industry. To achieve this, it was essential not only to shift the frontier westward but also to support the penetration of American industry, particularly dominant corporations, into foreign markets (Williams, 1964, p. 507).

The need to expand US firms' reach—to further expand the horizons of American product and service markets—pushed government intervention from a national to an international dimension. This was well understood by American politicians in the early 1900s. From the early years of the twentieth century, American presidents pursued the overseas expansion of American markets with remarkable consistency. It was President William Howard Taft who first recognized the need for an active foreign policy capable of securing new markets for American goods and investment, a major turning point in the complex history of American industrial policy. In 1912, Taft stated, "While our foreign policy should not be turned a hair's breadth from the straight path of justice, it may well be made to include active intervention to secure for our merchandise and our capitalists' opportunity for profitable investment" (Taft, 1912, cited in Lens, 2003). Overseas investments, which in those years were primarily directed toward Latin

America and China, increased from $700 million in 1897 to $3.5 billion in 1914 (Williams, 1961, p. 520).

With President Wilson, who took office in the White House in 1913, the American approach to foreign policy continued to be guided by the same insights:

> Prosperity consists in the growth of enterprise and the growth of prosperity in the growth of commerce. America's domestic market is too small: we have reached, in short, a crucial point in the process of our prosperity. It has become a question to us whether it shall continue or shall not continue. If [America] doesn't get bigger foreign markets, she will burst her jacket. There will be congestion in this country which will be more fatal economically than any wider opening of the ports could be (Wilson cited in Williams, 1961, p. 511–512).

With this approach, successive American governments in this new phase intervened and closely coordinated with industry and labor unions. Samuel Gompers, the leader of the AFL, echoed the crux of this approach: "The country that dominates the world markets will certainly control their destinies [...] No obstacle can be put in our path in achieving national glory and human progress" (Stabili, 1984).

2.9 Final Remarks

In the decades after achieving independence, as well as in the decades of accelerated growth during the eighteenth century, industrial policy in the United States had the primary objectives of building a national manufacturing base and governing the process of growth and structural change of the young developing nation. The strategic goal of "manufacturing independence" required policies to support, protect, and manage new and evolving coalitions of various interests. These included regional interests characterized by different industries based on patterns of specialization, as well as rapidly evolving economic and social interests. From this perspective, industrial policy had primarily domestic drivers which generally favored protection from foreign manufacturing. Then, at the end of the period of fast growth and change, once the newly invigorated national industrial capacity finally made American companies stronger and more capable of responding to the rapidly growing internal demand for manufactured goods, industrial policy intervention had to manage two additional complex internal needs: controlling corporate concentration and managing the rising tensions between capital and labor. Again, the main challenge continued to be governing accelerated growth to ensure the sustainability of structural change. Business concentration made possible the rise of unprecedented industrial capacity, but monopolies and oligopolies had costs—in economic terms for sure, but also by posing a challenge to the whole democratic system. Moreover, the great concentration of capital and labor in the nation's most industrialized areas produced social instability that made the model of growth potentially unsustainable.

The key targets of industrial policy were manufacturing sectors considered critical to national economic growth. Early policies focused on textiles, iron, and steel, industries that were both labor-intensive and essential for industrial independence from foreign countries. The transportation sector, and railroads in particular, also became a focal point, as rail networks were crucial for enlarging markets and fostering westward expansion. In regional terms, industrial policies often favored the North, where manufacturing was traditionally concentrated and continued to grow rapidly, while the South remained largely agrarian and relatively isolated from the process of industrialization.

During the eighteenth century, the US government deployed multiple policy tools to foster industrialization and promote structural change in its economy. High protective tariffs shielded domestic industries from foreign competition. Direct subsidies to selected industries and land grants facilitated the development of strategic sectors, while the federal government strongly supported the rapid growth of the national railway network. The legal and administrative mechanisms for implementing these policies included congressional acts, executive directives, and rules promulgated by emerging regulatory agencies.

Since independence, industrial policy has been a very contested domain, shaped by shifting political coalitions. Proponents included northern industrialists, manufacturers, and policymakers. Among the opponents were farmers in the agrarian South and East Coast traders. Republicans, particularly after the Civil War, championed high tariffs and business-friendly policies, while Democrats tended to be free-trade advocates.

The industrial policies of the nineteenth century played a crucial role in the early stages of manufacturing growth and economic development. High tariffs protected and fostered a strong manufacturing base, enabling the United States to emerge as an industrial powerhouse by the late 1800s. The expansion of railroads enlarged the national market, spurred business growth, and contributed to the economic and social progress of the young nation. However, these policies also had their drawbacks. The costs and benefits of tariffs were unevenly distributed, creating tensions between industrial and agrarian regions. Additionally, early industrial policies largely ignored poor labor conditions, leading to widespread worker exploitation and social tensions. Finally, although the consolidation of dominant positions by big businesses led to the establishment of advanced antitrust legislation, its implementation was often inhibited by regulatory capture and interest group pressures.

3

Wars in the Twentieth Century and the Rise of American Power

3.1 Introduction

In the twentieth century, American industry expanded its horizons beyond domestic borders. The United States and its powerful companies became international players in foreign markets and politics. The catching-up period was complete, and American big business—backed by the government—was ready to enter global markets as an emerging industrial power.

American entry into WWI, initially as a provider of goods for the Allies and then as an active participant, is emblematic of a larger system of integration in international business. Protection from foreign competition and big business concentration at home assumed a new strategic rationale in the wartime context, prompting the government to strengthen its relationship with industry. The two world wars justified huge public procurement and investment in technological advancements.

The WWI context inaugurated a new policy attitude with protection from foreign competitors and increased public investment in strategic sectors, boosting American industrial growth and its technological upgrading. Industrialization quickened its pace in the 1910s and 1920s during Fordism, in which innovative experiments of scientific management, modern principles of industrial organization, and product standardization quickly migrated from the automobile sector to other emerging productions—from cars to steel, mechanics, food, textile, construction, electronics, telecommunication, pharmaceutical, chemicals, navy, and aviation.

The same happened in the decade preceding WWII. Military procurement and R&D received special industrial policy attention. The growth of war-related sectors became a national priority, prompting government tariffs, tax incentives, and special programs to enhance efficiency, productivity, and innovation. As it is today, strategic sectors that deserved special treatment were numerous, given that virtually everything was related to national security. For a very long time—from the preparation for WWI to after WWII—American industry was practically managed by a class of government officials, military leaders, and managers of private companies. Their common goal was to

Governing Growth. Marco R. Di Tommaso and Vinod K. Aggarwal, Oxford University Press.
© Oxford University Press (2026). DOI: 10.1093/oso/9780197821787.003.0003

coordinate and manage the entire national production capacity by converting it to meet military needs—a model that did not end in 1918 or 1945. In both cases, inertial dynamics were evident, as returning to "normal times" required time and, in many instances, had to overcome the resistance of the existing interests of bureaucrats and private industry leaders. These interests found new rationales for a special government-industry relationship in the post-war reconstruction and the preparation for potential new military threats.

Finally, the twentieth century was marked by another season of "extraordinariness": the years of the Great Depression. The dramatic period of emergency and consequent policy interventions vested a new relationship between government and industry. The term "industrial policy" had not been coined yet, but the Rooseveltian plan—strongly influenced by Keynesian principles—included interventions that aimed to achieve wider socioeconomic and political goals by targeting specific industries. The government had to ensure the economic and social sustainability of the entire system, and it had to defend the foundations of American democracy from the devastating effects of the unexpected economic crisis.

3.2 Industry, Foreign Policy, and World War I

At the turn of the twentieth century, the government's attention to global issues became a distinctive feature of its interventions in favor of the national industry. Policies focused on economic growth, and those aimed at facilitating the entry of goods and services into foreign markets should be contextualized within the history of military intervention (Bingham, 1998). This refers to the long list of wars and conflicts in which the United States has been a protagonist on the international stage. The American interventionist position has characterized the twentieth century since its very beginning and remains prevalent in the present day (U.S. Army Center of Military History, n.d.).

In the United States—as in other wealthy industrialized countries like France, England, Germany, Italy, and Japan—wars and military threats have always had a significant impact on economic growth and innovation. This led to significant increases in military spending (Figure 3.1). First, the federal government has consistently expressed a substantial public demand for goods, services, and technologies necessary for warfare (Broadberry and Harrison, 2005). Second, this demand has been funded by government resources and met by a national defense industry that required protection from international competition. Third, countries that went through significant

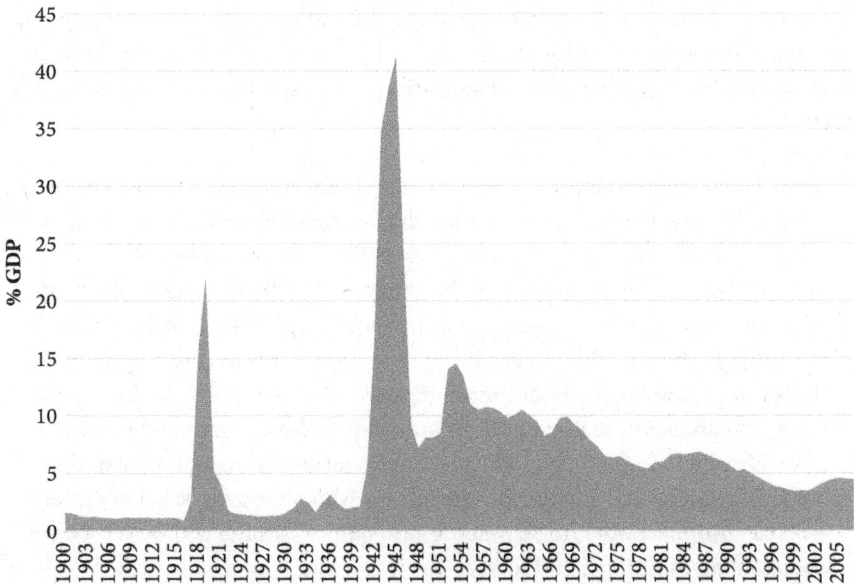

Figure 3.1 Military Expenditures in the United States in Thousands of Dollars, 1914–2007 (base year: 2000)

Source: Chantrill, Christopher. *Defense Spending in Twentieth Century*. US Government Spending. https://www.usgovernmentspending.com/spending_chart_1900_2024USp_XXs2li011tcn_30f_ Defense_Spending_in_20th_Century

reconstruction—such as the European states devastated by the two world wars— have been key markets for American industry (Frank, 1999). In this context, the long-established practice of "special" public support for strategic indus- tries and the involvement of the "public hand" in managing large segments of national production, starting with WWI, became defining features of American capitalism.

The outbreak of WWI inaugurated the system of economic expansion (Frank, 1999). The interests of large companies, acquired rents, and the consolidation of interest groups accustomed to negotiating with the government found new momentum due to the growth opportunities offered in both the domestic and foreign markets: "...entry into the First World War was the expression of a trans- formation that had already begun in American society ... American executives turned to overseas economic expansion as the best strategy to ensure recovery and future prosperity; before the United States became involved in the conflict as non-combatant belligerents or as active military protagonists ... the system began to produce wealth and a sense of community only as a by-product of war" (Williams, 1961, pp. 516–517).

President Woodrow Wilson's speech to the nation—delivered shortly after America's entry into WWI—clearly shows how war became an accelerator of radical structural changes, industrialization, and expansion into foreign markets:

> My Fellow-Countrymen: (...) these are the things we must do, and do well, besides fighting, the things without which mere fighting would be fruitless: we must supply abundant food for ourselves and for our armies and our seamen not only, but also for a large part of the nations with whom we have now made common cause, in whose support and by whose sides we shall be fighting. We must supply ships by the hundreds out of our shipyards to carry to the other side of the sea, submarines or no submarines, what will every day be needed there, and abundant materials out of our fields and our mines and our factories with which not only to clothe and equip our own forces on land and sea but also to clothe and support our people for whom the gallant fellows under arms can no longer work, to help clothe and equip the armies with which we are coordinating in Europe, and to keep the looms and manufactories there with raw material; coal to keep the fires going in ships at sea and in the furnaces of hundreds of factories across the sea; steel out of which to make arms and ammunition both here and there; rails for worn-out railways back of the fighting fronts; locomotives and rolling stock to take the place of those every day going to pieces; mules, horses, cattle for labor and for military service; everything with which the people of England and France and Italy and Russia have usually supplied themselves but cannot now afford the men, the materials, or the machinery to make (Wilson, 1917).

The war required a revolution in production organization and management techniques, which had to be rapidly adapted to meet the enormous and fast-growing demand for manufactured goods, advanced services, sophisticated logistics, and new infrastructure. The nation's energies had to be focused on promoting industrial growth, efficiency, and innovation to support the vast, military-driven demand from both domestic and allied forces:

> It is evident to every thinking man that our industries, on the farms, in the shipyards, in the mines, in the factories, must be made more prolific and more efficient than ever and that they must be more economically managed and better adapted to the particular requirements of our task than they have been; and what I want to say is that the men and the women who devote their thought and their energy to these things will be serving the country and conducting the fight for peace and freedom just as truly and just as effectively as the men on the battlefield or in the trenches (Wilson, 1917).

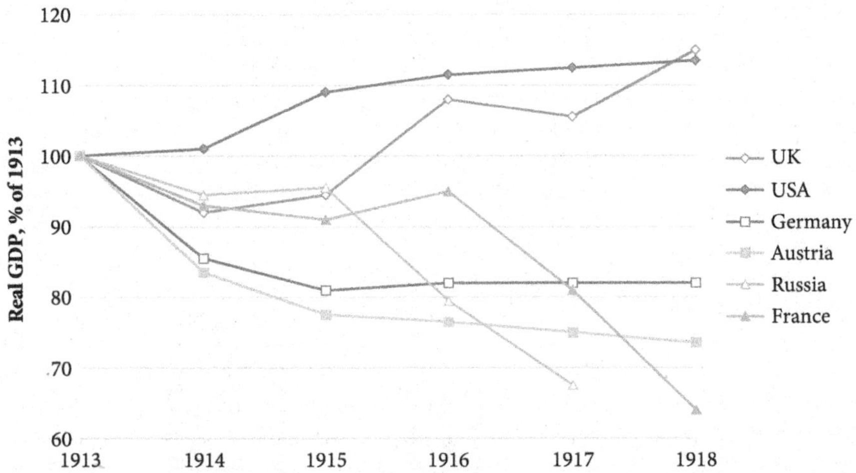

Figure 3.2 The Change in GDP during WWI

Source: Broadberry and Harrison (eds.) 2005, *The Economics of World War I.* Cambridge: Cambridge University Press

President Wilson's expectations were satisfied. The war-driven rise of American industry was fast and effective, with unprecedented effects on economic growth (see Figure 3.2)

During WWI, the United States spent $22 billion in direct costs and authorized a $10 billion loan to the Allies (see Figure 3.3). The total war costs of all nations were about $186 billion. The United States spent about one-eighth of the entire cost of the war, and less than one-fifth of the expenditures of the Allied side (Ayres, 1919).

This huge expenditure of public money, concentrated in very few years, produced a demand for goods and services that rapidly altered the national productive system. In a few decades, the US industry rose to a role of dominance. It moved from a position of technological dependency on the most advanced European producers—the United Kingdom in particular—to a position of autonomy and leadership. This was a process accelerated first by the Allies' demand for military manufactured goods since the beginning of the conflict in Europe, then boosted by the formal entry of the United States into WWI in the spring of 1917 (Ayres, 1919; Woodward, 2014; U.S. Army Center of Military History, n.d.).

The number of men serving in the US armed forces during WWI was 4,800,000, of whom 4,000,000 served in the Army and 116,708 died. During the nineteen months of war, more than two million American soldiers were carried to France. This military-driven growth of those years involved radical

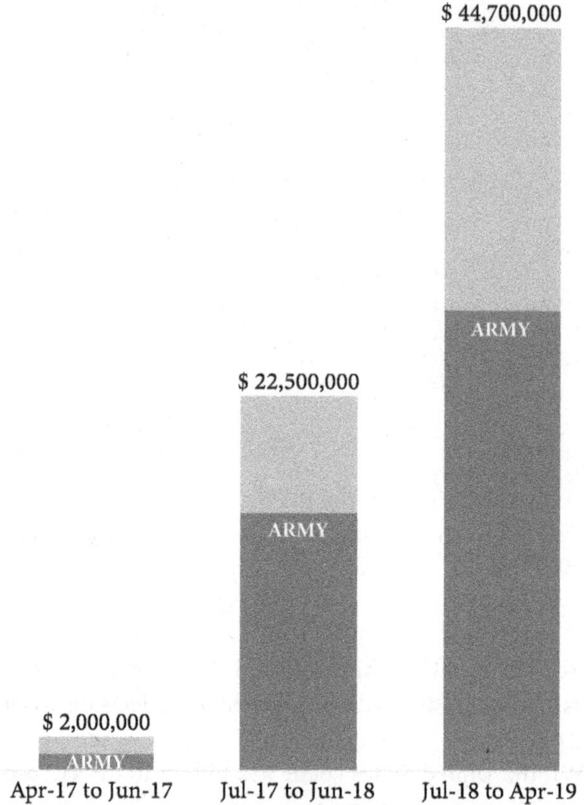

Figure 3.3 Cost Per Day of the Government and the Army

Source: Ayres, L.P., 1919. *The War With Germany. A Statistical Summary*, 2nd edition. Washington: Government Printing Office

transformations in several industries (Ayres, 1919; Woodward, 2014; U.S. Army Center of Military History, n.d.).

In just a few years, the advanced mechanics sector experienced an unprecedented surge in the demand for rifles, machine guns, and ammunition. By the time war was declared, the American company Springfield Rifles had produced nearly six hundred thousand guns for the Army's arsenal (Ayres, 1919). Production continued to ramp up, and the American *Enfield Rifle* was designed and quickly put into production. By the time the armistice was signed, the total production of *Springfield* and *Enfield* rifles had exceeded 2,500,000 units (see Figure 3.4). This boom in armaments production also led to the introduction of a critical new weapon: the machine gun. Prior to the war, machine-gun production was nearly nonexistent, but by 1918, a total of 227,000 units had been produced. Similarly, American small arms ammunition production soared,

Months	Eddystone	Winchester	Ilion	Springfield Armory	Rock Island Arsenal	Total
Before August, 1917	..	..	..	14,986	1,680	16,666
August 1, 1917, to December 31, 1917	174,160	102,363	26,364	89,479	22,330	414,696
1918						
January	81,846	39,200	32,453	23,890	7,680	185,069
February	98,345	32,660	39,852	6,910	2,460	180,227
March	68,404	42,200	49,538	120	420	160,682
April	87,508	43,600	36,377	2,631	..	170,116
May	84,929	41,628	54,477	3,420	550	185,004
June	104,110	34,249	52,995	6,140	619	198,113
July	135,080	35,700	60,413	14,841	2038	248,072
August	106,595	20,030	65,144	27,020	1,597	220,386
September	110,058	31,550	58,027	29,770	3,813	233,218
October	100,214	33,700	53,563	35,920	3,256	226,653
Nov. 1–9, 1918	30,659	9,160	16,338	16,338	808	67,405
Total	**1,181,908**	**465,980**	**545,541**	**265,627**	**47,251**	**2,506,307**

Figure 3.4 Rifle Production Before and After 1917 (base year: 2000)

Source: Ayres, L.P., 1919. *The War With Germany. A Statistical Summary*, 2nd edition, Washington: Government Printing Office

reaching around 3,500,000,000 rounds by the end of the war, with half of these rounds shipped overseas (Ayres, 1919).

Beyond rifles, the surge in military demand had a profound impact on a wide range of other sectors, including textiles, construction, vehicles, aviation, the navy, telecommunications, and the food industry (Ayres, 1919). The garment industry radically transformed its organization and capacity because the government needed an unprecedented quantity of goods: slickers, overcoats, blankets, shirts, breeches, coats, shoes and puttees, drawers and undershirts, socks (see Figure 3.5). The massive demand for garments during the war overwhelmed commercial factories, leading to concerns about supply shortages. By spring 1918, as troop movements intensified, woolen clothing supplies became critically scarce. To ensure sufficient stocks, the Army took control of every stage of production, from sourcing raw materials to inspecting finished goods. For the months before the armistice, the War Department controlled the entire wool industry in the country. If troop movements had continued at the same pace from September 1918 to June 1919, the Army would have needed 246,000,000 pounds of wool, while only 15,000,000 pounds were allocated for civilian use (Ayres, 1919).

A similar situation occurred with the approximately thirty thousand types of other commercial goods the Army purchased to support the troops, including food, forage, hardware, coal, furniture, wagons, motor trucks, lumber, locomotives, railcars, machinery, medical instruments, hand tools, and machine tools

Articles	Total delivered	Articles	Total delivered
Wool stockings, pairs	135,800,000	Blankets	21,700,000
Undershirts	85,000,000	Wool breeches	21,700,000
Underdrawers	83,600,000	Wool coats.	13,900,000
Shoes, pairs	30,700,000	Overcoats.	8,300,000
Flannel shirts	26,500,000		

Figure 3.5 Clothing Delivered to the Army: April 1917 to May 1918

Source: Ayres, L.P., 1919. *The War With Germany. A Statistical Summary*, 2nd edition, Washington: Government Printing Office

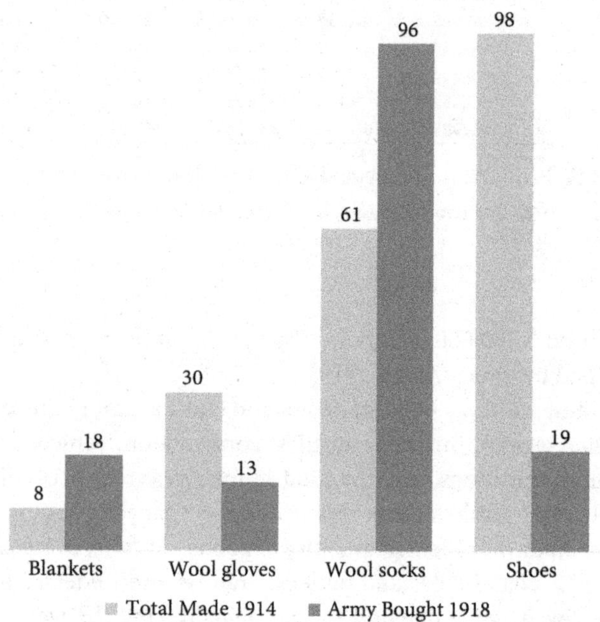

Figure 3.6 Total American Production Compared with Army Purchases

Source: Ayres, L.P., 1919. *The War With Germany. A Statistical Summary*, 2nd edition, August 1, 1919, Washington: Government Printing Office

(see Figure 3.6). The Army relied on nearly all 344 industries recognized by the US Census (Ayres, 1919; Woodward, 2014; U.S. Army Center of Military History, n.d.

In some cases, production required adjustments to existing plants, machinery, and production methods; in others, the challenges of mass production were compounded by the need to create entirely new items. Notable examples include the production of 5,400,000 gas masks—spurred by the use of mustard gas—and 2,728,000 steel helmets by November 1918 (Ayres, 1919).

The direct involvement in European territories also had an impressive scale and important impact on US production capacity. In France, Americans built 17 new ship berths, 1000 miles of standard-gauge track, and 125 miles of narrow-gauge track. In France, the Signal Corps—the Army branch that manages communications and information systems—strung one hundred thousand miles of telephone and telegraph wire. Prior to the armistice, forty thousand trucks were shipped to the Allied forces in France (Ayres, 1919).

The transformation in the production of vehicles for transport—trucks, cars, tanks, planes—before and during WWI is particularly important. From the beginning of the twentieth century, the automotive sector attracted the attention of the federal government. In 1908, Henry Ford introduced the famous Model T automobile to the market, along with new methods of organizing company production processes, later known as Fordism, greatly impacting the trajectory of the industry. Starting in the 1910s in the automotive sector, specialization and mass production radically transformed labor organizations, industries, and society in America and the rest of the world (Di Tommaso et al., 2024, pp. 122–126).

In this context of undeniable entrepreneurial dynamism, the growth and development of the American automotive industry were accompanied by a stable public presence. Firstly, the government protected the sector from foreign competitors: from 1913 until 1934, import tariffs ranged from 25% to 50%, stabilizing at around 10% in the following years (Bingham, 1998). Industrial policy during this period followed what is now known as infant industry protection—a strategy that shields the emerging sector from foreign competition in its early growth phase. This approach is similar to what Japan, South Korea, and more recently, China have done in this sector in recent years (Di Tommaso et al., 2024).

During the same period, the auto sector was strongly encouraged to grow through federal funding of ambitious public works infrastructure programs such as bridges and roads, starting with the two Federal Highway Acts of 1916 and 1921 (Bingham, 1998; Williamson, 2012): "An Act to provide that the United States shall aid the States in the construction of rural post roads, and for other purposes" (United States Congress, 1921). That said, the decades to come were undoubtedly "special" due to preparation for WWI, wartime efforts, preparation for WWII, the war years themselves, and then US global leadership post WWII.

Focusing on the following decades in the next section, it is worth noting the parallels between WWI and WWII. During WWII, the government purchased approximately $30 billion worth of vehicles from the national automotive industry (Bingham, 1998). At the end of the conflict, the Office for War Mobilization and Reconversion was established, which authorized the public purchase of one hundred thousand automobiles in 1945 to initiate conversion to the civilian market (Bingham, 1998). Finally, in the immediate post-WWII period, just as had happened decades earlier, the federal government's attention to the auto industry translated into support for the development of the road network: in 1956, the Interstate Highway Act was signed, initiating a massive federal program for the construction of a futuristic national highway network (Williamson, 2012; Di Tommaso and Schweitzer, 2013).

The national auto industry benefited from protection from abroad, strong and sustained public demand, massive government investments in plants and technology, and preferential access to markets whose industrial structure had been destroyed by the war and which, once acquiring political and economic dependence, would soon experience a strong growth in demand (Di Tommaso and Schweitzer, 2013). Specifically, during the years of WWI, the American Automobile Manufacturers Association was transformed into the Automotive Council for War Production. Under these special conditions, the birth and maturing of the American auto industry coincided with the consolidation of an oligopoly formed by the Big Three producers: Ford, Chrysler, and General Motors. This consolidation was permitted and even encouraged during times of exceptionality by the American government, which nevertheless maintained a "special relationship" with the auto industry (Nester, 1997; Di Tommaso and Schweitzer, 2013; Weiss, 2014).[1]

Similarly, the federal government bolstered the naval industry in this era of world conflicts. During WWI, this sector was the target of government-sponsored industrial support, development, and protection. It was deemed to be in the national interest for the government to possess a merchant fleet capable of supporting foreign trade and addressing wartime needs or national emergencies (NHHC, 2018). The initial problem was that foreign competition could provide maritime transportation services at much lower costs; thus, the government needed to protect the national industry (Bingham, 1998). It was in this context that WWI provided a unique opportunity for the government to finance the construction of an American fleet capable of competing globally in terms of size, strength, and technology.

With the outbreak of the war in Europe in 1914, the United States was not able to offer direct naval assistance to the Allies, and it was necessary to start nearly from scratch, requiring a large initial investment. The American fleet had not yet recovered from the 1898 Spanish-American War, and its standing navy was of modest size and technologically backward compared to those of European

---

[1] This unique relationship spanned the entire twentieth century, and it has remained strong until today, including the Obama administration's bailout interventions (Vlasic, 2011; Ingrassia and White, 1995).

allies and enemies. With the Naval Act of 1916, when it became clear that neutrality was becoming an increasingly difficult choice to maintain, sixty-five new warships were commissioned: ten battleships, five cruisers, and fifty destroyers (NHHC, 2018). However, even in 1917, when the United States directly entered the war, the naval fleet had not changed significantly. Germany's superiority, in particular, manifested primarily through submarine raids between the two Atlantic coasts, which held a large sway in the tide of the war. When diplomatically questioned by the Americans about the necessity to immediately support the Allies, British Prime Minister Lloyd George replied: *"Ships, ships, and more ships!"* (NHHC, 1917).

In this context, President Wilson tasked the United States Shipping Board Commission and the Emergency Fleet Corporation with the execution of an extraordinary program for strengthening the Navy. Priority was given to the construction of 273 destroyers (NHHC, 1917). In parallel, a program of renovation and conversion of existing ships—which also involved private entities—was promoted. The war ended before all the orders placed by the government were completed. However, the unfinished orders were not immediately stopped after the Armistice, and the government continued to support the activities of shipyards well beyond the end of the war (Shonfield, 1965; Bingham, 1998; Mazzucato, 2013).

Again, it is worth noting the continuity of the following decades. Once the WWI hostilities ended, a large portion of the ships that had been produced up to that point were sold to private entities. The privatization was completed quickly and at prices that many commentators of the time considered low and favorable (Bingham, 1998). However, the effects of this contentious operation were particularly negative. The sale of the military fleet collapsed private-sector demand for new ships, causing a severe crisis in the industry even before the onset of the Great Depression. In 1928, the government—seeking to alleviate this crisis—opted to rescue the national industry by providing new subsidies and approving measures to block foreign competition (Bingham, 1998).

With WWII, the long period of exceptionalism and public support for the naval sector continued from its onset during WWI. The United States Shipping Board Commission ceased its activities in 1934 but was replaced by entities with similar objectives, function, and mandate: the US Shipping Board Bureau of the US Department of Commerce (1933–1936) and then, for a notably longer period, by the US Maritime Commission (1936–1950) (Maurer, 1978; Bingham, 1998). In the years of the Great Depression and impending WWII, the government had no reason to change course. If the commitment during WWI was of great proportion, the commission to the naval industry to prepare for WWII was even more imposing in terms of scale and impact on the entire national industry. The close ties between government and the naval industry did not end with the conclusion of WWII (Di Tommaso and Schweitzer, 2013; Bingham, 1998). At the end of the conflict, the American naval industry did not gain efficiency margins, competitiveness in foreign markets, or independence from the public sector. On the contrary, for decades, the sector remained largely tied to public demand and the new military needs that emerged with the onset of the Cold War (Bingham, 1998).

Shifting focus to another key sector, the aviation industry undoubtedly received growing attention since the beginning of WWI. At the time, the American capacity was substantially inferior to the European field, and the military demand constituted a unique chance for catching up. In 1917, the United States had a total of fifty-five serviceable airplanes declared by the National Advisory Committee on Aeronautics as obsolete and inadequate (Maurer, 1978). While European nations—Great Britain, Germany, France, and Italy—had invested considerable sums in recent years to build up their air force, the United States had lagged far behind. Thus, for direct entry in the war, the United States demanded and received specialized support from the Allies in what soon became a very strategic sector (Broadberry and Harrison, 2005; U.S. Army Center of Military History, n.d.). On one hand, the American military authorities had little time to decide to fund the import of finished planes from Europe—3800 units by the end of the war—and on the other hand, they started to promote their own domestic production using the designs and instructions made available by the Allies. Congress approved $640,000,000 to expand airplane production, an act which was signed by President Wilson on July 24, 1917 (Maurer, 1978).

The American government elaborated a detailed industrial plan for the immediate rise of a domestic infant industry:

> There is general agreement ... concerning the governing principle for our American production program: ... First: the United States must provide itself with all airplanes and engines required for training purposes in America. Second: the United States must next provide the airplanes and engines necessary for use strictly in connection with the operation of the American Force in the field. Third: after these first two considerations comes the American program of putting into the field next year air forces in excess of the tactical requirements of its Army in France. It is greatly desired that the United States shall do this. Such air forces should consist of fighting airplanes and bombers (The Boiling Report, 1917, quoted in Maurer, 1978).

The results of the plan were impressive: by the end of WWI, more than 8000 training planes and 16,000 training engines were produced in the United States

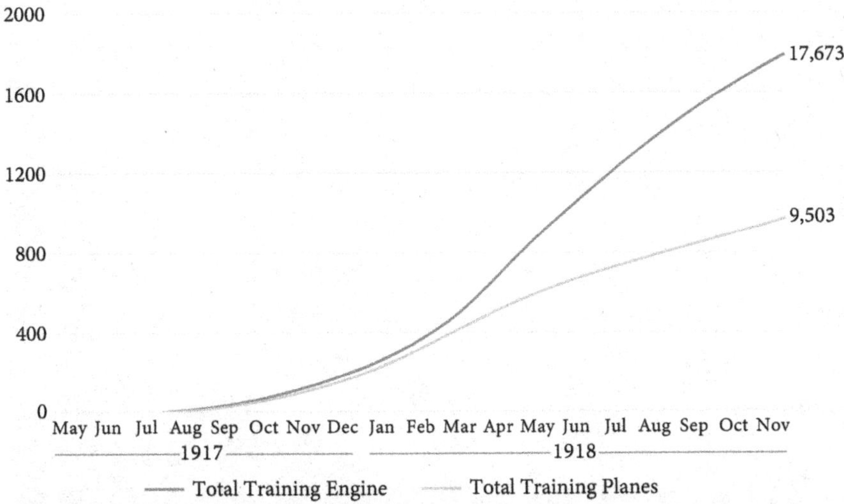

Figure 3.7 Production of Training Planes and Engines at the End of Each Month
Source: Ayres, L.P., 1919. *The war with Germany. A statistical summary*, 2nd edition, August 1, 1919, Washington: Government Printing Office

(see Figure 3.7). Soon thereafter, the British *De Havilland-4*—the surveillance and daylight bombing plane—was also produced in the United States. Before the signing of the armistice, 3227 had been completed at a rate of 100 planes per month, and 1885 were shipped overseas (Ayres, 1919; Maurer, 1978). At the same time, the American aviation industry collaborated with the more advanced French and Italian producers (Ayres, 1919; Maurer, 1978).

The leap forward was evident in the production of airplane engines (see Figure 3.8). As production lines were established by American automobile manufacturers, the manufacturing of the twelve-cylinder Liberty engine became the main American contribution to Allied aviation. Before the end of the war, 13,574 had been completed, 4435 shipped to the expeditionary forces, and 1025 delivered to the Allies (Ayres, 1919; Maurer, 1978).

The rapid growth of plane production greatly increased demand for raw materials, components, sophisticated instruments, and accessories. Production and harvesting of spruce and fir, lubricating oils, linen, protective coatings, and mahogany required great investments and sophisticated organization of supply chains. A force of about thirty thousand men—including both military officers and civilians—was assigned to work in forests and lumber mills to produce enough wood for airplane production. Since castor oil was needed for lubricating airplane engines, 100,000 acres of land were utilized for castor bean cultivation. New lines of production were initiated for other military products: oxygen masks equipped with telephone connections, observation balloons,

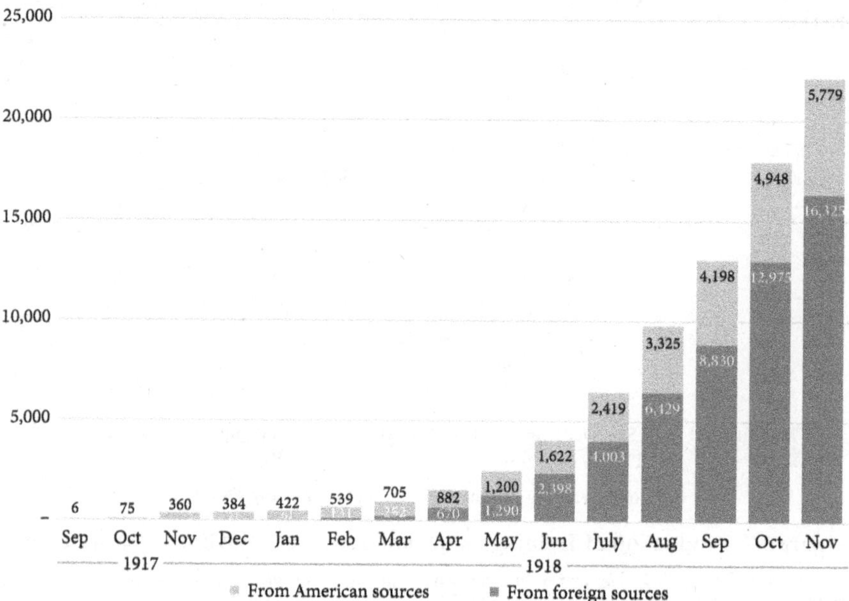

Figure 3.8 Production of Service Engines at the End of Each Month

Source: Ayres, L.P., 1919. *The War With Germany. A Statistical Summary*, 2nd edition, August 1, 1919, Washington: Government Printing Office

electric suits, and electric-heated clothing for aviators, long-focus light-filtration cameras, and wireless telephones (Ayres, 1919; Maurer, 1978).

3.3   The Post-World War I Era and the Great Depression

The focus on the interwar years requires a specific reference to another long "special period" that characterized the relations between industry and the federal government in the United States: The Great Depression and the abrupt halt of the national industrial growth process. The disconnect between real growth and stock market speculation, which led to an increase in stock values unsupported by an actual increase in the sales of goods and services, was among the main causes of the "collapse" of the Wall Street stock market in October 1929 (Dobbin, 1994). The fall in stock values destroyed the stock capital of many savers who, in the climate of uncertainty, withdrew their bank deposits—depriving liquidity to the industrial system—and reduced consumption, leading to an increase in the unemployment rate (see Figure 3.9) (Mazzucato, 2013). The country fell into a crisis spiral that affected all sectors of the economy (Milward, 1979).

During those years, President Roosevelt described a dramatic social condition:

> I see millions of families trying to live on incomes so meager that the pall of family disaster hangs over them day by day. I see millions whose daily lives in the city and on the farm continue under conditions labeled indecent by a so-called polite society half a century ago. I see millions denied education, recreation, and the opportunity to better their lot and the lot of their children. I see millions lacking the means to buy the products of farm and factory and by their poverty denying work and productiveness to many other millions. I see one-third of a nation ill-housed, ill-clad, ill-nourished (Roosevelt, 1937).

One of the government's major concerns, which played a central role in promoting what would be the largest public response to an economic crisis in US history, was related to the social sustainability of this dramatic situation, as then-Secretary of Commerce Harry Hopkins clearly highlighted: "With 12 million unemployed, we are at social bankruptcy and political instability" (Hopkins, 1939, cited in Williams, 1961, p. 514). As with the contemporary financial crisis, the US government decided to intervene deeply in the national industrial system, the economy, and society (Tassinari, 2019). Roosevelt's New Deal sought to reconcile the opposing interests of American society. The Democratic Party rallied behind Roosevelt's Keynesian-inspired interventions, which aimed to connect the interests of the working class—who were severely hit by the recession—with the interests of industry and thus with the broader national interest. However, the Republicans characterized the New Deal as an overexertion of executive authority and as a dangerously broad government intervention into the economy (Shonfield, 1965; Dobbin, 1994).

The economic and political thought that guided the government's intervention sought to balance industry, social stability, prosperity, and democracy (Shonfield, 1965; Stein, 1998). It was in this context that the government, without much hesitation, began to promote public works and contracts and subsidize American industry to stimulate domestic demand. The National Industrial Recovery Act of 1933, which established the Public Works Administration to implement an extensive public works program, proved critical.

> History probably will record the National Industrial Recovery Act as the most important and far-reaching legislation ever enacted by the American Congress. It represents a supreme effort to stabilize for all time the many factors which make for the prosperity of the Nation, and the preservation of American standards. Its goal is the assurance of a reasonable profit to industry and living wages for labor with the elimination of the piratical methods and practices which

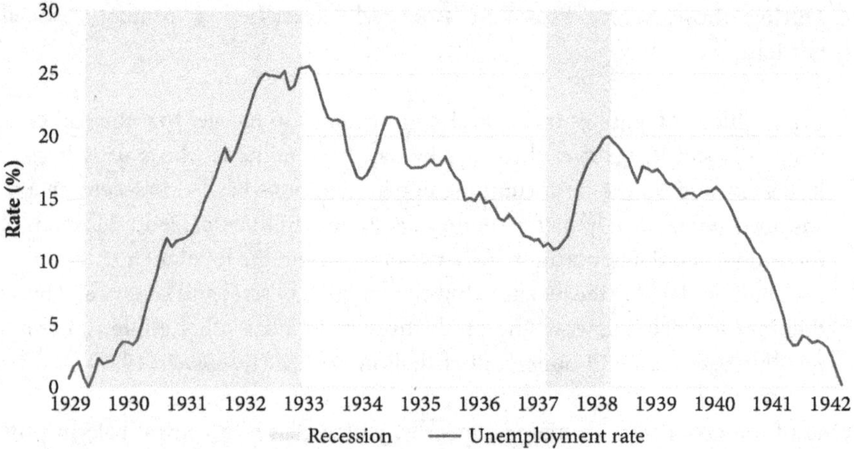

Figure 3.9 Unemployment Rate: The Great Depression

Source: National Bureau of Economic Research, 2021. *Long-Run Trends and the Natural Rate of Unemployment*. https://www.nber.org/reporter/2021number2/long-run-trends-and-natural-rate-unemployment

have not only harassed honest business but also contributed to the ills of labor. While we are engaged in establishing new foundations for business which ultimately should open a return to work for large numbers of men, It is our hope through the so-called Public Works section of the law speedily to initiate a program of public construction that should yearly re-employ additional hundreds of thousands of men. Obviously, if this project is to succeed, it demands the wholehearted cooperation of industry, labor and every citizen of the Nation (Roosevelt, 1933).

On June 16, 1933, Roosevelt announced to the nation that he was ready to launch a massive plan of recovery:

… we should be able to hire many men at once and to step up to about a million new jobs by October 1st, and a much greater number later. We must put at the head of our list those works which are fully ready to start now. Our first purpose is to create employment as fast as we can, but we should not pour money into unproved projects. We have worked out our plans for action. Some of the work will start tomorrow. I am making available $400,000,000 for State roads under regulations which I have just signed, and I am told that the States will get this work under way at once. I have also just released over $200,000,000 for the Navy to start building ships under the London Treaty (Roosevelt, 1933).

Several key initiatives for public works were undertaken in the New Deal. The Civilian Conservation Corps (1933–1942) played a crucial role in environmental conservation, planting 2.3 billion trees, stocking 1 billion fish in waterways, and constructing 2500 cabins in state and national parks. The program also dedicated 6.4 million man-days to fighting forest fires, built 68,000 miles of new firebreaks, and improved the nation's forests and recreational areas (Living New Deal).

Meanwhile, the Public Works Administration (PWA) (1933–1939) focused on large-scale infrastructure projects, constructing 212 dams and canals, nearly 900 sewage disposal plants, 384 airports, and hundreds of college buildings and post offices, strengthening essential public services. The Works Progress Administration (WPA) (1935–1943) improved rural infrastructure by developing over 572,000 miles of roads, building nearly 78,000 bridges, 16,000 miles of new water lines, 23,000 miles of sidewalks, and 325 firehouses (Living New Deal).

The Rural Electrification Administration (REA) (1935–1943) transformed life for farmers by installing 381,000 miles of power lines, bringing electricity to over a million rural households. The National Youth Administration (NYA) (1935–1943) focused on community and educational improvements, producing over 1.3 million pieces of school furniture, establishing 2354 tree and plant nurseries, and constructing or upgrading thousands of recreational facilities, including 407 swimming pools, 9074 tennis courts, and 88 golf courses. Short-lived but impactful, the Civil Works Administration (CWA) (1933–1934) built 255,000 miles of roads, 5000 parks, 2000 miles of levees, and thousands of playgrounds and athletic fields, leaving a lasting mark on public infrastructure (Living New Deal).

Demonstrating a modern attitude at the time, the New Deal programs also aimed to restore and protect natural resources. President Roosevelt and Congress promoted ambitious interventions to revitalize the environment that, in the previous decades, had been severely damaged by mining, timber harvesting, hunting, pollution, and the overexpansion of agriculture, leading to soil depletion (Living New Deal).

The New Deal implemented several major programs to address environmental conservation and infrastructure development. The Civilian Conservation Corps (CCC) planted billions of trees, fought wildfires, and controlled pests, while the WPA improved fisheries, streambeds, and urban greenery. The PWA and Federal Emergency Relief Administration (FERA) tackled sanitation and flood control, building levees, and dredging rivers to reduce disaster risks. The NYA engaged young people in soil conservation, fish stocking, and fire observation efforts (Living New Deal).

The Soil Conservation Service (SCS) promoted erosion control and sustainable farming, while the Parks and Recreation programs expanded national and state parks, adding trails, campgrounds, and visitor centers. Additionally, the Wildlife Refuges initiative established 140 refuges to protect migrating species, funded through the innovative Duck Stamp program. Together, these programs reshaped the American landscape, improving conservation, public health, and recreational access (Living New Deal).

Beyond the public works plan, the Roosevelt Administration launched the Buy American Act in 1933. It was a powerful initiative aimed at stimulating domestic demand by imposing limits on the purchase of foreign products in public contracts, thereby supporting a large part of the national industry (Frank, 1999):

> ... [o]nly unmanufactured articles, materials, and supplies that have been mined or produced in the United States, and only manufactured articles, materials, and supplies that have been manufactured in the United States substantially all from articles, materials, or supplies mined, produced, or manufactured in the United States, shall be acquired for public use unless ... their acquisition [would] be "inconsistent with the public interest or their cost to be unreasonable" (41 U.S.C. § 8302(a)-1).
>
> ...every contract for the construction, alteration, or repair of any public building or public work in the United States shall contain a provision that in the performance of the work the contractor, subcontractors, material men, or suppliers shall use only unmanufactured articles, materials, and supplies that have been mined or produced in the United States ... (41 U.S.C. § 8302(a)-2)

In this context of government intervention, the attitude toward antitrust issues is also relevant. The government was quite ready to ease antitrust pressures on companies, allowing the consolidation of cartels and monopolies for the sake of the national interest (Dobbin, 1994):

> We are relaxing some of the safe-guards of the antitrust laws. The public must be protected against the abuses that led to their enactment, and to this end we are putting in place of old principles of unchecked competition some new government controls. They must above all be impartial and just. Their purpose is to free business, not to shackle it; and no man who stands on the constructive, forward-looking side of his industry has anything to fear from them (Roosevelt, 1933).

In the New Deal, a central role was played by the Reconstruction Finance Corporation (RFC), a national development bank created to direct government loans to companies and industries in need of capital. The RFC was founded by Hoover in 1932 to replace the War Finance Corporation (WFC), an agency created by

President Wilson in 1918 to finance the war industry during WWI. By the end of Hoover's term, the RFC had provided loans of $1.6 billion to numerous financial institutions and the railway sector (Bingham, 1998). During the New Deal years, from 1932 to 1935, the RFC distributed over $2 billion to companies unable to obtain credit from the private sector (Bingham, 1998).

The Roosevelt administration then decided to promote an ambitious reform of the national banking industry, which had shown clear fragilities in the years of the Great Depression. With the Banking Acts of 1933 and 1935, a series of interventions to protect banks were defined. In 1933, the Federal Deposit Insurance Corporation was created, which separated commercial banking functions from investment banking. The Glass-Steagall Act of 1933 introduced Regulation Q, which imposed ceilings on interest rates for savings deposits and required banks to apply a zero interest rate on checking accounts— measures that essentially constituted a permanent subsidy granted by the government to this sector (Bingham, 1998). Also, the banking structures of the Federal Reserve System were reformed. The creation of a new internal body, the Federal Open Market Committee, was entrusted with guiding monetary policy.

During this phase, the steel industry was still the subject of close attention from the government, which responded to the demands of industrialists while trying to avoid aggravating the large masses of workers. For example, the Smoot-Hawley Act of 1930 and the Reciprocal Trade Act of 1934 can be read as key laws to rescue the sector, which was on the verge of collapse (Di Tommaso and Schweitzer, 2013).

The New Deal, in response to the Great Depression, decisively intervened in another important sector of the American economy and society: the agro-industrial sector. A key measure was the Agricultural Adjustment Act of 1933, which sought to ensure higher incomes for agricultural producers. The "fair" prices of agricultural products, set by the Department of Agriculture, were maintained by centrally planning agricultural production (Bingham, 1998). These emergency measures inaugurated a long period in which the relationship between government and this specific sector continued to remain "special." From 1938, Congress required that the Commodity Credit Corporation, the federal agency responsible for regulating agricultural product prices, provide loans to farmers accepting stored agricultural products as collateral. Subsequently, during the Eisenhower Administration (1953–1961), farmers were further subsidized to reduce production and to ensure crop rotations (Bingham, 1998).

Another industry in which the US government intervened during the 1930s was the aviation industry. Once again, this was a special relationship that the government established with one of its most promising infant industries. This sector developed from the postal service. In 1925, Congress authorized the privatization of the air mail service, and private distribution quickly took on the leading role. Initially, the government paid private companies based on the quantity of mail transported, but it changed its policy in 1930 to paying private carriers based on the size of the aircraft and on passenger transport capacity. This payment method provided an incentive for the development of passenger transport services, leading to an increase in demand for new and larger aircraft. These factors promoted innovation in the sector and the development of new commercial services (Bingham, 1998).

In 1938, the Civil Aeronautics Act was passed. It served as a regulatory system that, through the Civil Aeronautics Board (CAB), more structurally promoted air mail, commercial, and military transport. The CAB was responsible for regulating competition among private companies to avoid duplication of services and market dysfunction. The system involved a separation between services operating on main routes and services operating on local routes. From the early 1940s, some main routes no longer required subsidized fares, and the CAB gradually reduced its role, although subsidies remained available for local service (Bingham, 1998). The growth in demand for transportation and technological innovation in this emerging industry then received another formidable public boost in preparation for WWII.

3.4 The Mobilization of Production in WWII

From the mid 1930s, President Roosevelt's attention was directed toward reorganizing the entire American economy to make it ready to respond to the threats of the imminent war. Within a few years, public governance took over many sectors of the national industry to meet military needs. The management architecture of the national industry during WWI was immediately reintroduced and enhanced, leading to the creation of the War Industries Board, the Naval Consulting Board, and the Council of National Defense. Moreover, the National Defense Act of 1920 tasked the War Department with planning the mobilization of the entire economy to prepare it for a potential war. The War Department developed several detailed plans for industrial mobilization in 1930, 1933, 1936, and the last one in 1939 when the war was already on the horizon (Nester, 1997).

The government invested significant resources in the development of the national defense (see Figure 3.10).

The results of this effort were impressive, and manufacturing grew at an unprecedented rate (see Figures 3.11 and 3.12).

	Nominal GDP		Federal Spending			Defense Spending			
	total $	% increase	total $	% increase	% of GDP	total $	% increase	% of GDP	% of federal spending
1940	101.40		9.47		9.34%	1.66		1.64%	17.53%
1941	120.67	19%	13.00	37.28%	10.77%	6.13	269.28%	5.08%	47.15%
1942	139.06	15.24%	30.18	132.15%	21.70%	22.05	259.71%	15.86%	73.06%
1943	136.44	−1.88%	63.57	110.64%	46.59%	43.98	99.46%	32.23%	69.18%
1944	174.84	28.14%	72.62	14.24%	41.54%	62.95	43.13%	36.00%	86.68%
1945	173.52	−0.75%	72.11	−0.7%	41.56%	64.53	2.51%	37.19%	89.49%

Figure 3.10 Federal Spending and Military Spending during World War II (dollar values in billions of constant 1940 dollars)

Sources: Louis J. and Williamson, S.H., 2026. "What Was the U.S. GDP Then?," MeasuringWorth. https://measuringworth.com/datasets/usgdp/. 1941–1945 GDP figures calculated using Bureau of Labor Statistics, "CPI Inflation Calculator," available at http://data.bls.gov/cgj-bin/cpicalc.pl. Federal and defense spending figures from the Government Printing Office, 2004. "Budget of the United States Government: Historical Tables Fiscal Year 2005," Table 6.1- Composition of Outlays: 1940–2009 and Table 3.1- Outlays by Superfunction and Function: 1940–2009

	Aircraft	Munitions	Shipbuilding	Aluminum	Rubber	Steel
1939	100	100	100	100	100	100
1940	245	140	159	126	109	131
1941	630	423	375	189	144	171
1942	1706	2167	1091	318	152	190
1943	2842	3803	1815	561	202	202
1944	2805	2033	1710	474	206	197

Figure 3.11 Manufacturing Growth during WWII

Source: Milward, 1979

	No. of months	Rifles, carbines	Machine pistols	Machine guns	Guns	Mortars	Tanks and SPG	Combat aircraft	Major naval vessels
1939	..	..	..	..	..	..	..	..	..
1940	..	..	..	..	..	..	..	..	..
1941	1	38	42	20	3	0.4	0.9	1.4	544
1942	12	1542	651	662	188	11	27	24.9	1854
1943	12	5683	686	830	221	25.8	38.5	54.1	2654
1944	12	3489	348	799	103	24.8	20.5	74.1	2247
1945	8	1578	207	303	34	40.1	12.6	37.5	1513
Total	45	12330	1933	2614	549[a]	102.1	99.5	192	8812

Figure 3.12 Military Production in the United States: WWII

Source: Harrison, 1998

The rate of acceleration of the production associated with military demand deserves a special mention (Figure 3.11).

The American output of its industrial mobilization for WWII produced incredible results. Allied powers, especially the United States, vastly outproduced the Axis in nearly all categories of weapons and equipment. (see Figure 3.13).

	Rifles, carbines (thou.)	Machine pistols (thou.)	Machine guns (thou.)	Guns (thou.)	Mortars (thou.)	Tanks (thou.)	Combat aircraft (thou.)	Major naval vessels
The Allied powers								
USA	10714	1685	2291	512	61.6	86	153.1	6755
UK	2052	3682	610	317	65.3	20.7	61.6	651
USSR	9935	5501	1254	380	306.5	77.5	84.8	55
Allied total	22701	10868	4154	1208	433.4	184.2	299.5	7461
The Axis powers								
Germany	6501	695	889	262	66	35.2	65	703
Italy	..	..	83	7	11.3	2	8.9	218
Japan	1959	3	341	126	4.3	2.4	40.7	438
Axis total	8460	698	1313	395	81.6	39.6	114.6	1359

Figure 3.13 Military Production in Selected Nations: WWII

Source: Harrison, 1998

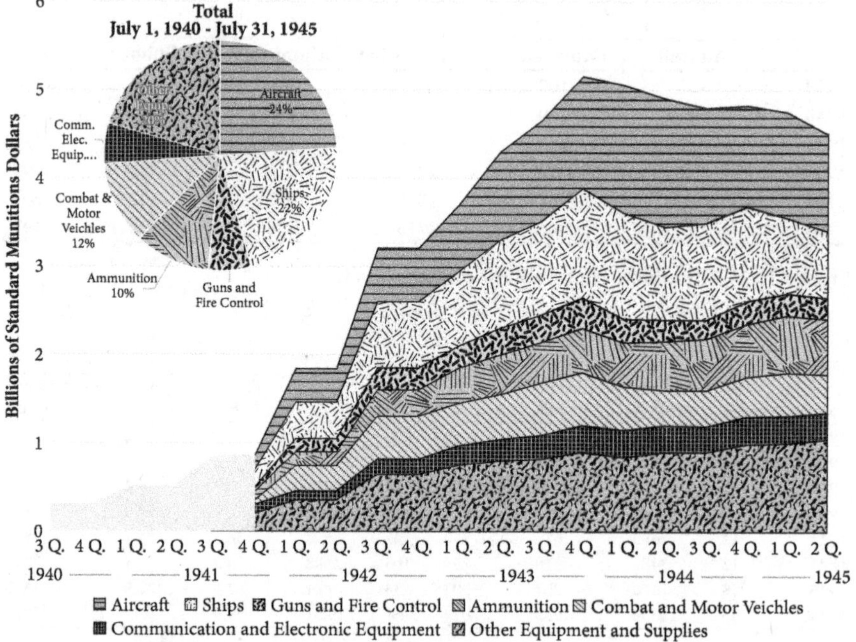

Figure 3.14 The Mobilization of Production: WWII

Source: War Production Board (1945) *Wartime production achievements and the reconversion outlook: report of the chairman.* Washington, D.C.: War Production Board

The mobilization of US wartime production from 1940 to 1945 is massive (Figure 3.14).

In 1940, Roosevelt established the National Defense Advisory Commission Board, which in 1941 was replaced by the Office of Production Mobilization (later renamed the War Production Board). Alongside this agency were the Production Executive Committee and the Office of War Mobilization, which involved government officials, military leaders, and managers of private industries to coordinate and manage the entire national industrial production capacity by converting it to meet military needs. In this context, the Berry Amendment of 1941 excluded foreign competitors from supplying goods and services in the defense sector (Nester, 1997; Weiss and Thurbon, 2006).

Increasing public demand for goods and services from the private sector—along with government funding for research and development conducted for military purposes—translated into strong incentives for economies of scale and learning in a select number of private companies. Only about 100 companies obtained around two-thirds of the contracts (Block, 2008; Weiss, 2014; Dobbin, 1994). For another "special" decade, American industry was not only supported by public demand driven by military needs but was also managed by a select group of public administrators, a select group of military personnel, and a limited number of large private managers (Weiss and Thurbon, 2006; Nester, 1997; Di Tommaso and Schweitzer, 2013). Producing and fighting were the two imperatives that tied the interests of industry and government. In the words of the Director of Production of the War Production Board:

> As a Nation, we have contracted to be the Arsenal of Democracy. It is the biggest and the most responsible contract ever written. If we are to fulfill it on schedule and in good measure, there is no time to lose. There is nothing to do but work, produce, and fight" (War Production Board, 1942).

The relationship between government and industry remained close during World War II, just as it had during the Great Depression and World War I. The period of extraordinary measures had lasted so long that it left its mark on the future of American capitalism (see Figure 3.15). Spanning thirty years from WWI to WWII, the governmental habit of public support and management in certain industries, as well as tolerance toward oligopolies and cartels in sectors strategic for national interest, were characteristics that could not be expected to cease in a few months or years.

Moving in the opposite direction of the response to two military emergencies and the social emergency of the Great Depression was not a simple matter. Assuming that a new administration would choose to do so, the federal government had to contend with the entrenched interests of large companies and powerful special interest groups accustomed to negotiating with the government. That said, after the end of World War II, a "special relationship"

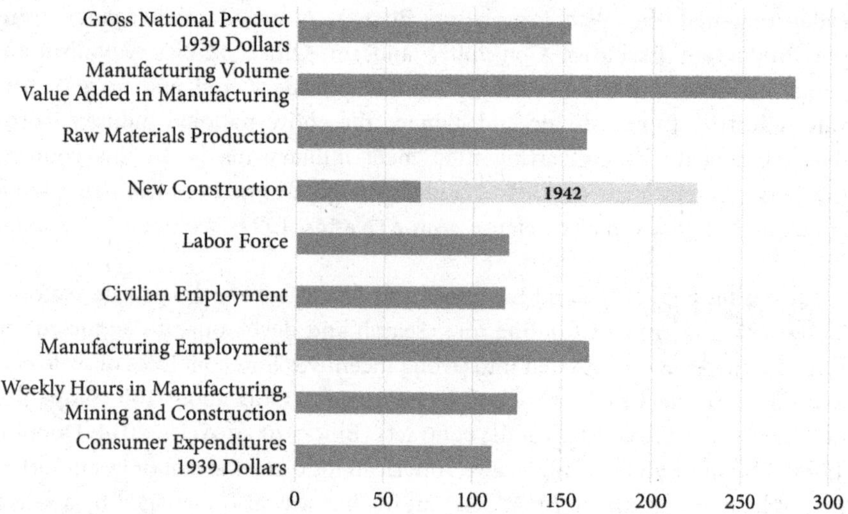

Figure 3.15 Wartime Growth and Transformation: WWII

Source: War Production Board (1945) *Wartime production achievements and the reconversion outlook: report of the chairman*. Washington, D.C.: War Production Board

between the government and certain sectors of the national industry could be justified by a new threat: the Cold War. (Block, 2008; Mazzucato, 2013; Di Tommaso and Schweitzer, 2013; Weiss, 2014).

3.5 Final Remarks Conclusion

From the turn of the twentieth century until the end of World War II, the relationship between government and industry entered a new phase, shaped by both domestic and international factors. At the beginning of the new century, the catch-up period was almost successfully completed, and the American big business was ready to enter the global scenario. The emerging Fordist principles started to demand a larger extension of the market to properly exploit the division of labor and economies of scale (Bingham, 1998; Di Tommaso et al., 2024). In this respect, the fast-growing domestic market was a solid base, but American industry was eager to expand globally in pursuit of wider economies and market opportunities. World War I and later World War II, served as unique opportunities for economic expansion. In general, the United States achieved the status of a new and modern industrial power and thus began on a trajectory of further accelerated growth (Frank, 1999; Broadberry and Harrison, 2005).

American industry penetrated deeper into the richest international markets, starting from Europe. At the same time, the US government was ready to plan an alteration of the existing international political order, which in that period was still European-centered (Milward, 1979).

To achieve this goal, there was growing acceptance of federal involvement in national industry. Government policies helped stabilize, consolidate, and expand domestic demand while simultaneously supporting the entry of American companies into foreign markets (Shonfield, 1965). Government interventions in the national production system were driven by broader goals of social stability and military security (Weiss, 2014). Two world wars and the most significant international economic crisis in history made the government's role in national production both strong and continuous. For a very long period, its influence on both the supply and demand sides of the economy was unparalleled. The outbreak of World War I, the Great Depression, and later World War II required unprecedented government coordination with industry, fueling a shift toward strategic state intervention (Di Tommaso and Schweitzer, 2013).

The two wars required direct government intervention in many strategic sectors, and the New Deal principles and practices promoted during the few years of "peace" confirmed the expansion of government planning and involvement in many industries—starting from construction, infrastructure, and banking. The US government policies accelerated industrialization and—within a highly protected environment that often-barred foreign competition—spurred unprecedented technological advancements in both mature and emerging sectors (Bingham, 1998; Frank, 1999). This enabled the country to catch up with the world's most advanced industrialized nations and facilitated the expansion of big business in both domestic and international markets. In all these years of evident government intervention, the United States witnessed a debate between proponents of free markets and advocates of state-led industrial planning and policy (Shonfield, 1965; Weiss, 2014). Consistent with the latter, Keynesian principles supported concrete military needs and New Deal practices. These policy actions reflected an emerging belief that the government should play a stabilizing role in managing industry, governing growth, and instituting structural changes (Milward, 1979).

Between 1900 and 1945, US industrial policy focused on key sectors that were deemed vital for economic and military strength. Heavy industries, particularly steel, oil, and manufacturing, mechanics, vehicles—starting from cars, trains, planes, and the navy—became the backbone of selective industrial policy, as they were critical for both peacetime growth and wartime production (Bingham, 1998). The construction industry and infrastructure received unprecedented government support because of military needs and government spending during the New Deal years. Regional targeting of industrial policy also took shape, due in part to the public works programs promoted by the Roosevelt Administration (Living New Deal).

The federal government employed a wide range of tools to guide the national production system. Antitrust laws were relaxed during periods of industrial and military mobilization, and protection from foreign competition became particularly important for domestic business (Weiss and Thurbon, 2006). During the Great Depression, public spending programs such as the WPA and the CCC were used to stimulate demand for goods and services and provide employment, aiming to promote social stability. Direct subsidies, investments, and government contracts also became crucial, especially in the many defense-related industries (Living New Deal; Dobbin, 1994). World War II expanded the scope of industrial policy, with the War Production Board overseeing production, price controls curbing inflation, and the military-industrial complex beginning to take shape. The Defense Plant Corporation financed new factories, enabling private firms to scale up wartime production (Weiss, 2014).

To implement these policies, the federal government developed new administrative structures. During the New Deal years, agencies such as the Public Works Administration were created. World War II saw the most extensive use of new administrative mechanisms. The War Production Board, the Office of Price Administration, and the War Manpower Commission managed resource allocation, wage controls, and industrial production (Living New Deal; Bingham, 1998). These agencies demonstrated the effectiveness of centralized planning, although concerns about bureaucratic overreach persisted.

Support for government intervention came from labor unions and of course from big business that, for several decades, strongly benefited from government contracts, public procurement, special public investments, and protection from foreign competition. Great support arrived from a coalition of military, government, and business representatives that together managed the national industry, consolidating a system of economic and political power. Opposition to industrial policy came from the rhetoric of some conservative leaders and free-market economists in academia that described government intervention as a threat to capitalism. However, in the end, these opponents had a very modest impact on the real government-industry relationship (Weiss, 2014; Nester, 1997; Dobbin, 1994; Milward, 1979).

The industrial policies of 1900–1945 had profound successes. The United States emerged from World War II as the dominant global economic power, with a modernized industrial base and a more productive workforce (Block, 2008). The New Deal helped stabilize the economy during the Depression, and wartime industrial policy transformed the United States into the "Arsenal of Democracy," supplying allies and ensuring victory. However, there were also notable negative effects (Broadberry and Harrison, 2005). Protectionist tariffs, weak antitrust application, and the growth of dominant domestic large corporations consolidated a conservative economic and political system that became resistant to the alteration of existing equilibria, economic and social innovation, new entries in markets, and the political arena. Some New Deal programs faced inefficiency and political backlash, while wartime controls sometimes led to shortages and black markets (Di Tomasso and Schweitzer, 2013 Weiss, 2014). Despite public works initiatives, regional economic disparities persisted, and industrial policy often favored existing large corporations over new start-ups and small businesses (Tassinari, 2019).

Between 1900 and 1945, US industrial policy evolved from a largely reactive approach to a more proactive and coordinated strategy. Economic crises and global conflicts forced the federal government to take an increasingly interventionist role, employing a range of tools to regulate, stimulate, and direct industrial development. While debates over government intervention persisted, this period laid the groundwork for the postwar economic order, shaping the modern American industrial economy. The successes and failures of these policies continue to inform contemporary debates on the role of the state in economic growth and national security.

4
American Global Leadership in the Post-WWII Era

4.1 Introduction

Following World War II, the U.S. economy experienced a period of robust growth, driven by government spending and investments in defense, manufacturing, services, infrastructure, and research. In a global context shaped by the Cold War and military demand, the federal government strengthened its relationship with major corporations and played a central role in guiding economic growth, emphasizing technological innovation, productivity, and the expansion of both domestic and international markets. For a considerable time, what we might today call industrial policy focused on key sectors—such as steel, construction, automobiles, the navy, and aviation—while also fostering the development of emerging infant industries like electronics, telecommunications, and aerospace.

In this context, the government continued to play a crucial role in investments, public procurement, technological research, and infrastructure development that resulted in almost three decades of economic prosperity and social cohesion. However, by the 1970s, the situation began to change. Challenges like oil shocks, inflation, unemployment, and rising global competition from Western Europe and East Asia started to disrupt the established model and the existing equilibria. The manufacturing sector faced increasing competition from abroad. Domestically, stagflation and a decline in industrial output raised concerns about the long-term sustainability of the government's economic policy. Despite the success of the previous decades that led America to international leadership in production and technology, the 1970s saw a decline in economic and industrial competitiveness, job losses, and social tensions. Weak government responses to these issues diminished confidence in state-led economic policies. By the late 1970s, neoliberal ideologies advocating for deregulation, tax cuts, and free-market policies began to take hold, paving the way for the rise of Reaganomics in the 1980s and the decline of government-driven industrial policy.

Governing Growth. Marco R. Di Tommaso and Vinod K. Aggarwal, Oxford University Press.
© Oxford University Press (2026). DOI: 10.1093/oso/9780197821787.003.0004

4.2 The End of WWII and the Postwar Years

At the end of WWII, "exceptional times" for the government-industry relationship were supposed to be over. However, the implementation of the New Deal plans was still ongoing, requiring active government intervention. Moreover, for the reconversion from military to civilian production, it became clear that a strong coalition of interests would resist transition. Some plans for future reconversion were being examined even before the end of WWII, and an opposition front consolidated (Janeway, 1951; Bernstein, 1967; Milward, 1979). Senator Harry S. Truman was one of the first to publicly charge that reconversion was being delayed by "... some selfish business groups that want to see their competition kept idle ... [and] by Army and Navy representatives who want to create a surplus of manpower. ..." *Quoted in Bernstein, 1967.* Military leaders, representatives of big business, universities, and federal agencies that had prospered during the pre-war and war years worked together to resist reconversion plans and maintain high defense production, public procurement, and expenditures (Janeway, 1951; Bernstein, 1967; Milward, 1979; Higgs, 1992; Harrison, 1998).

The military expressed concerns about relinquishing control over the economy—a control that had been solidified during the exceptional years of war preparation and execution. This period saw the emergence of the military-industrial complex, where defense contractors and the armed forces established a symbiotic relationship to meet wartime demands. This nexus not only influenced wartime production but also had lasting implications on postwar economic policies.

Concurrently, leaders of dominant large enterprises were reluctant to forfeit the vast, lucrative, and secure markets they had operated in without foreign competition during the war. These corporations sought to maintain their pre-war oligopolistic positions and aimed to prevent the potential market re-entry of small and medium-sized enterprises (SMEs). SMEs were among the first to lose war contracts and were poised to re-enter markets while large manufacturers remained occupied with fulfilling military orders.

The interests of large and small businesses diverged even during the war. Military spending accelerated a concentration process favoring large enterprises. In 1939, small manufacturers accounted for 52% of the labor force employed in manufacturing; by 1944, this figure had decreased to 38%. SMEs received about 30% of war contracts, with approximately one-quarter being subcontracts from large companies. By September 1944, nearly half of the total prime contracts awarded since June 1940 had been allocated to 33 corporations, two-thirds to the top 100, and almost 80% to the top 500 (Bernstein, 1967). This consolidation not only marginalized smaller firms but also entrenched the power of large corporations in the postwar economy.

This tension of interests was represented inside the War Planning Board (WPB) where military and big business interests prevailed. In the WPB, there were members with a past and/or a future in big business that were committed to opposing reconversion: Charles E. Wilson (General Electric), Sidney Weinberg (Goldman Sachs), Lemuel Boulware (Celotex, General Electric), Samuel Anderson (Anderson-Conrow, Lehman Brothers), and Arthur Bunker (Lehman Brothers). This position was supported by military interests: Lieutenant General Brehon Somervell (Chief of Army Service Forces), Major General Lucius Clay, Robert Patterson (Under Secretary of War), James Forrestal (Secretary of the Navy), and Ralph Bard (Navy Under Secretary). On the other side, representatives of SMEs—Maury Maverick, for Smaller War Plants Corporation and labor—Joseph Keenan and Clinton Golden—were too weak to counter the big-business and military coalition. In this context, the defense budget did not decrease in post-WWII times, and this trend was soon justified by the Cold War (see Figure 4.1) (Bernstein, 1967).

Going beyond the domestic market, it is also evident that the post-WWII years paved the way for new and immense opportunities for US production abroad. Victory once again allowed for the shifting of the "frontier," ensuring further expansion of the market to which American industry could cater. The United States had achieved global leadership. The military and political influence over a vast number of nations was a factor that would offer immense economic advantages and extraordinary new opportunities to national industry. Consider, for example, the preferential relationship with some of the countries

	Nominal GDP		Federal Spending			Defense Spending			
	Total	% increase	total	% increase	% of GDP	Total	% increase	% of GDP	% of federal spending
1945	223.1		92.71	1.5%	41.9%	82.97	4.80%	37.5%	89.5%
1946	222.3	−0.36%	55.23	−40.4%	24.8%	42.68	−48.60%	19.2%	77.3%
1947	244.2	8.97%	34.5	−37.5%	14.8%	12.81	−70.00%	5.5%	37.1%
1948	269.2	9.29%	29.76	−13.7%	11.6%	9.11	−28.90%	3.5%	30.6%
1949	267.3	−0.71%	38.84	30.5%	14.3%	13.15	44.40%	4.8%	33.9%
1950	293.8	9.02%	42.56	9.6%	15.6%	13.72	4.40%	5.0%	32.2%

Figure 4.1 Federal Spending and Military Spending after World War II (dollar values in billions of constant 1945 dollars)

Source: Louis J. and Williamson, S.H., 2026. "What Was the U.S. GDP Then?," MeasuringWorth. https://measuringworth.com/datasets/usgdp/; Bureau of Labor Statistics, "CPI Inflation Calculator," available at http://data.bls.gov/cgi-bin/cpicalc.pl; Government Printing Office, "Budget of the United States Government: Historical Tables Fiscal Year 2005."

that had lost the war, such as Germany, Japan, and Italy. These devastated countries, whose industries had literally been razed to the ground, were now under American guidance (and funding), preparing for their reconstruction. And major allies like France and Great Britain needed to reinvent their societies and economies in the wake of the end of the colonial regime.

American aid granted through the Marshall Plan was undoubtedly crucial in fostering rapid economic recovery in Europe, but it was also very important for the American economy itself, fueling demand for goods and services primarily produced in the United States. Secretary of State George C. Marshall described the objectives and motivations of the "Plan":

> The modern system of the division of labor upon which the exchange of products is based is in danger of breaking down. The truth of the matter is that Europe's requirements for the next three or four years of foreign food and other essential products—principally from America—are so much greater than her present ability to pay that she must have substantial additional help or face economic, social, and political deterioration of a very grave character (Marshall, cited in Hogan, 1987).

The aid offered for reconstruction in Europe—and similarly to a long list of other friendly countries—inaugurated another special phase through which the American government supported national growth and its own national industry. European countries had exhausted their foreign currency reserves during the war. The funds made available through the Marshall Plan were the only source with which to finance imports, which were almost entirely met by American companies. Initially, food and fuel were imported, then gradually other types of goods. Of the $13 billion allocated through 1951, $3.4 billion was spent on raw materials and semi-finished products, $3.2 billion on food and fertilizers, $1.9 billion on machinery and vehicles, and $1.6 billion on fuel (Hogan, 1987). The impact of the Marshall Plan should be seen not only in these numbers, but also in the long term. In direct response to the Marshall Plan, the Soviet Union passed the Molotov Plan as the alternative industrial policy plan for much of Eastern Europe. In the aftermath of World War II, the economic interdependence between certain European nations and American industry deepened significantly. This period marked the beginning of intricate dynamics that would tether Western Europe's demand for goods, services, and technologies to the United States and its industrial sector for many years.

Concurrently, the US government spearheaded efforts to restructure international political and economic relations. A pivotal moment in this endeavor was the Bretton Woods Conference in July 1944, when delegates from forty-four Allied nations convened to establish a new international monetary system.

The conference resulted in the creation of the International Monetary Fund (IMF) and the International Bank for Reconstruction and Development (IBRD), commonly known as the World Bank. These institutions were designed to stabilize the global economic system and were significantly influenced by the United States (Hogan, 1987).

The Bretton Woods system also introduced fixed exchange rates, pegging international currencies to the US dollar, which was convertible to gold. This arrangement underscored the dollar's dominance in global finance and facilitated international trade and investment. Shortly thereafter, the General Agreement on Tariffs and Trade (GATT) was established in 1947 to promote international trade by reducing tariffs and other trade barriers. GATT laid the foundation for the World Trade Organization (WTO) and was instrumental in expanding global commerce in the postwar era (Aggarwal and Evenett, 2013).

Collectively, these institutions and agreements, while ostensibly representing the interests of the global community, were profoundly shaped by US economic and political priorities. They played a crucial role in fostering economic cooperation and development, thereby reinforcing the United States' influence in the international arena.

4.3 The Cold War Years

Immediately after the war, it was clear that the extraordinary prospects for American growth and prosperity would be endangered by the ambitions of the Soviet Union. This threat made it necessary and possible to continue the special relationship between industry and government that had characterized the preceding decades. The war had now become cold, but it continued. Military superiority over the Soviet Union was a priority that the government had to ensure. As in WWI and WWII, government investment to address this new conflict was once again an extraordinary tool to support the entire American industrial system.

Government spending in the defense sector continued to fuel a robust and increasing public demand, including for goods, services, and technologies. This channel once again favored American companies sheltered from foreign competition, which could provide the Department of Defense (DoD) with huge production volumes, exploiting economies of scale and learning (Block and Keller, 2011). The massive research and development activities conducted for military purposes, financed by public funds, soon became a source of innovation and dual-use technology that was subsequently applied and commercialized in the public sector (Bonvillian, 2003; Di Tommaso and Schweitzer, 2013). In other words, the DoD—and later many other government agencies such as NASA, National Aeronautics and Space Administration, or the National Science

Foundation—continued to remain at the center of American political and economic balances and once again played a central role in the country's industrial growth and innovation dynamics (Gansler, 2011).

The Cold War was fought on an industrial and technological level as well. In this context, the Vannevar Bush Report of 1945 had clearly indicated that scientific progress, fueled by both basic and applied research, had to be promoted through important public programs. In 1948, with the creation of the National Security Council and the Central Intelligence Agency, the institutional framework for national security was strengthened: it was only the beginning of the forthcoming decades of massive public investments in the many sectors connected to the military industry. In these years, about $16 trillion was spent by the American government, of which $4 trillion was on nuclear weapons. In the years following WWII, the DoD accounted for 80% of the federal government's spending on research and development. By the end of the 1960s, government spending in the defense sector reached nearly 9% of the American GDP (Bonvillian, 2003; Di Tommaso and Schweitzer, 2013; Gansler, 2011).

During the Cold War years, industry support focused on military capacity continued to play a fundamental role in promoting innovation and structural change in the American economy. The intervention of the DoD explains much of the development of industries that were considered nascent at that time. Infant industries, now central to the American economy, developed a "privileged" relationship with the government from those years onward.

A turning point was the reaction, both emotional and political, to the Soviet Sputnik launch in 1957. This Soviet success in launching the first satellite to orbit the Earth highlighted the close relationship between technological superiority and national defense. It stimulated a series of measures in the United States aimed at bridging a technological gap that seemed to have solidified in favor of the Soviets. The immediate reaction was to increase government funds allocated to basic and applied scientific research and a constant effort to increase technological innovation in both military and civilian sectors. In a decade, spending on research and development doubled from 1.5% of the American GDP to over 3% (Di Tommaso and Tassinari, 2014; Gansler, 2011; Block and Keller, 2011).

An industry that could benefit from enormous advantages related to investments in the military field was certainly that of software and computers. The growing demand for computers commissioned during the 1950s and 1960s by the DoD, the Air Force, the Army Signal Corps, the Atomic Energy Commission, NASA, the US Weather Bureau (now the National Center for Atmospheric Research), the National Institute of Health, and the Social Security Administration encouraged private companies in the sector to develop new products and technologies, enjoying precious protection from foreign competition. Public demand and military contracts in this field were not just met by existing large

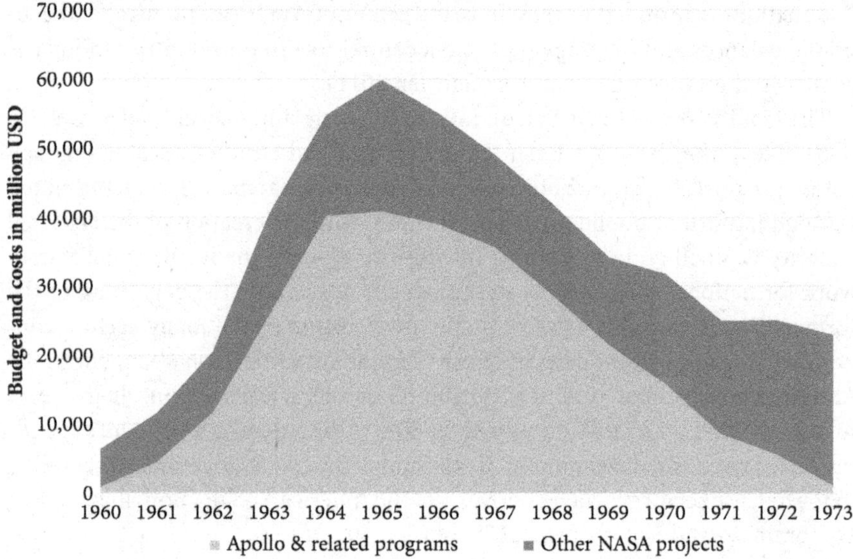

Figure 4.2 NASA's Monetary Obligations Compared to Project Apollo's Total Costs (1960–1973) (in million USD)

Source: Statista, 2023. NASA's monetary obligations compared to Project Apollo's total costs from 1960 to 1973. https://www.statista.com/statistics/1342862/nasa-budget-project-apollo-costs/

companies accustomed to interacting with the government. On the contrary, in this promising sector, a dynamic developed that encouraged the emergence of new, mostly small-sized enterprises. These enterprises found themselves participating in a reasonably competitive context to meet the demand for innovation that, in the Cold War scenario, the DoD and other government agencies expressed (Bonvillian, 2003; Block and Keller, 2011).

The chip industry is a very interesting case. Chips began to be increasingly demanded by the Air Force, which used them in missile construction. And of course, NASA, with the Apollo moon program of the 1960s and 1970s aimed at space exploration, played a very important role in the entire high-tech and computer industry sector (see Figure 4.2).

The Apollo program was planned by the federal government and justified in the name of the national interest. Apollo had a crucial role in the growth of strategic infant industries that because of the Cold War competition with the Soviet Union were heavily protected and funded by the US Government:

First, I believe that this nation should commit itself to achieving the goal, before this decade is out, of landing a man on the moon and returning him safely to the earth. No single space project in this period will be more impressive to mankind, or more important for the long-range exploration of space; and none will be so difficult or expensive to accomplish. We propose to accelerate the development of the appropriate lunar space craft. We propose to develop alternate liquid and solid fuel boosters, much larger than any now being developed, until certain which is superior. We propose additional funds for other engine development and for unmanned explorations (. . .). Secondly, an additional 23 million dollars, together with 7 million dollars already available, will accelerate development of the Rover nuclear rocket. (. . .) Third, an additional 50 million dollars will make the most of our present leadership, by accelerating the use of space satellites for world-wide communications. Fourth, an additional 75 million dollars - of which 53 million dollars is for the Weather Bureau - will help give us at the earliest possible time a satellite system for world-wide weather observation (. . .) I am asking the Congress and the country (. . .): 531 million dollars in fiscal '62, an estimated 7 to 9 billion dollars additional over the next five years. (Kennedy, 1961).

President Kennedy's plan was clear: an unprecedented industrial and technological effort, guided and financed by federal funds, that should have targeted a long list of productive sectors if not the whole national research and production capacity:

(. . .) it will not be one man going to the moon—if we make this judgment affirmatively, it will be an entire nation. For all of us must work to put him there (Kennedy, 1961).

In the 1960s, the US Department of Defense played a pivotal role in fostering technological advancements that have profoundly influenced modern society. One notable endeavor was the development of the ARPANET, the precursor to today's Internet. This initiative was driven by strategic military considerations, particularly the need for a resilient communication system that could withstand potential missile attacks targeting a centralized military installation (Leiner et al., 1997).

During this era, the rapid computerization of military technology led to the concentration of strategic equipment in specific regions, heightening vulnerability to targeted assaults. For instance, the Semi-Automatic Ground Environment (SAGE) system enabled the US Air Force to monitor Soviet bombers and coordinate defensive responses (Gansler, 2011). However, its centralized nature posed significant risks.

To address these vulnerabilities, the Defense Advanced Research Projects Agency (DARPA) initiated funding for the development of a decentralized computer network. This effort culminated in 1969 when computers at the University of California, Los Angeles, and the Stanford Research Institute were interconnected via a telephone line, marking the inception of the ARPANET (Leiner et al., 1997). This milestone represented the genesis of an innovation nurtured within the public sector, initially insulated from external influences, and closely aligned with national military interests amid the Cold War.

The intertwining of technological prowess and national pride was vividly showcased during the 1959 Kitchen Debate, when then-Vice President Richard Nixon highlighted America's technological superiority to Soviet Premier Nikita Khrushchev, emphasizing the ubiquity and quality of American consumer appliances (Bonvillian, 2003; Adams, 1994).

Parallel dynamics influenced the emergence of the biotechnology sector, another nascent industry that garnered substantial public support due to strategic military considerations. This sector's significant growth can be traced back to initiatives under President Richard Nixon's administration. In 1969, the US government decided to repurpose its biological weapons program toward scientific research aimed at advancing the civilian biomedical field (Bonvillian, 2003; Adams, 1994).

This strategic pivot was largely motivated by competitive pressures from Europe, Japan, and the Soviet Union in an industry deemed critical. During this period, agencies such as the National Science Foundation and the National Institutes of Health (NIH) funded pivotal projects, including research on recombinant DNA, which underpinned many successes of the American biotechnology industry.

It is worth noting the risks and costs of this DoD-centric model. It was a model closed to the outside world in which, in the name of national interest, dynamics were accepted that would otherwise be discouraged. It is a scenario in which, in the name of the emergency and the exceptionality of the moment, special relationships are consolidated between a select number of companies and the government. An emergency situation that justifies a confidential relationship and, by its nature, cannot be fully transparent. It is a complex dynamic that characterizes the economic and political balances of the entire nation. It is a scenario that Eisenhower considered unprecedented and on which he expressed himself with concerned lucidity at the end of his term:

> ... we can no longer risk emergency improvisation of national defense; we have been compelled to create a permanent armaments industry of vast proportions. Added to this, three and a half million men and women are directly engaged in the defense establishment. We annually spend on military security more than the net income of all United States corporations. This conjunction of an immense military establishment and a large arms industry is new in the American experience. The total influence—economic, political, even spiritual—is

felt in every city, every state house, every office of the Federal government. We recognize the imperative need for this development. Yet we must not fail to comprehend its grave implications. Our toil, resources, and livelihood are all involved; so is the very structure of our society. In the councils of government, we must guard against the acquisition of unwarranted influence, whether sought or unsought, by the military-industrial complex. The potential for the disastrous rise of misplaced power exists and will persist (Eisenhower, 1961).

4.4 The Post-WWII Boom

The post-WWII era in the United States, spanning from 1945 to 1960, was characterized by significant economic expansion, often referred to as the "Great Economic Boom." This period witnessed a substantial rise in the middle class, leading to increased consumer spending and a thriving domestic market. GDP rose from approximately $200 billion in 1940 to $300 billion in 1950, and to over $500 billion by 1960. This economic prosperity enabled millions of Americans to ascend into the middle class, significantly enhancing their purchasing power. (Higgs, 1992; Di Tommaso and Schweitzer, 2013).

The burgeoning middle class also fueled a surge in consumer spending, creating a vast and eager domestic market. This expansion occurred in a postwar environment where competition from foreign companies was minimal, as many industrialized nations were recovering from the war's devastation. American corporations capitalized on this scenario, meeting the escalating demand for consumer goods and services. The era was marked by relatively low unemployment and inflation rates, contributing to economic stability and consumer confidence. For instance, in 1950, the unemployment rate was 4.3%, and inflation was 5.9%. By 1952, unemployment had decreased to 2.7%, and inflation had fallen to 0.8% (U.S. Bureau of Labor Statistics, 2025; Amadeo, 2024). This favorable economic environment ensured that Americans had more disposable income to spend and consume than ever before.

The 1950s also witnessed significant cultural shifts that further propelled consumerism. The proliferation of television, for instance, played a pivotal role in shaping consumer behavior. By the end of the decade, a substantial majority of American families owned television sets, automobiles, and household appliances, reflecting the era's consumer culture (Di Tommaso and Schweitzer, 2013).

The opportunities for consuming goods and services offered by the new industry had increased extraordinarily in quantity and quality. Low interest rates and government incentives, especially for veterans, allowed millions of Americans to buy their own homes in new suburban areas. The middle class of these years quickly gained extraordinary consumption power that would continue to grow for decades, becoming one of the structural characteristics upon which American society is built (see Figure 4.3).

In this context, the GI Bill (Servicemen's Readjustment Act) was a government-funded initiative of great importance. The plan provided federally funded low-interest mortgages, special loans to start new businesses, unemployment benefits, and scholarships to cover expenses for attending universities, high schools, and vocational training institutes. The primary objective was to manage the economic and social consequences of the return of millions of veterans. However, it was a tool of broader significance for the economy and national industry: the GI Bill transformed millions of war veterans into consumers of the new middle class (Higgs, 1992; Di Tommaso and Schweitzer, 2013).

The actions of the GI Bill had a positive effect on the construction industry, but more generally, they were the first step, financed and inspired by the government, in initiating a radical and progressive structural change in the consumption patterns of millions of Americans. These were the years of the so-called Levittowns, new residential settlements built with federal government funds as part of initiatives for war veterans. They were new urban suburbs that soon became the symbol of the new American middle class: "The dream was mass-produced, single-family, tract housing that, at a cost of $7,000 or $60 a month, ordinary working people could afford . . . Levittown was the American dream come-true for the families that purchased the more than 17,000 two-bedroom homes" (Gans, 1967). They were planned communities consisting entirely of

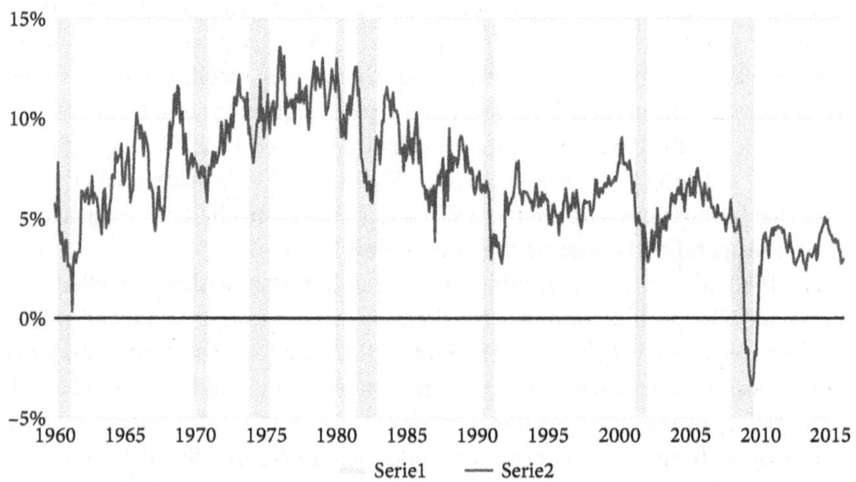

Figure 4.3 Consumption in America (Percentage Change from Previous Year) (1960–2015)

Source: Presentation from *fred.stlouisfed.org*, data from US Bureau of Economic Analysis

homes "... with identical floor plans and constructed using prefabricated units and assembly-line techniques" (Gans, 1967).

Levitt homes were affordable, thanks to low-interest mortgages, and their construction benefited from significant economies of scale, using standard materials and employing unskilled labor that could quickly learn the same assembly patterns and repeat them like on assembly lines. Levittowns and the many subsequent postwar suburbs inspired by them, played a central role in America during those years. By selling thousands of homes with standardized dimensions, structure, and materials, the way was paved for the general standardization of behaviors, needs, and aspirations of family households. This meant the uniformity of demand for a long list of new consumer goods whose production could benefit from extraordinary economies of scale (Gans, 1967). It was only the beginning of an era of mass consumption that seemed to have no limits or boundaries.

4.5 The Great Society Program

In the mid twentieth century, the United States experienced significant economic growth, driven by public demand during the Cold War, expanding foreign markets, and a burgeoning domestic middle class. However, this prosperity was not uniformly shared; notable disparities persisted, particularly among African Americans.

The mechanization of agriculture, which began in the early twentieth century and accelerated during the 1930s and 1940s, brought profound changes to the Southern economy. Technological advancements, such as the introduction of mechanical cotton pickers, reduced the need for manual labor, displacing thousands of unskilled workers, predominantly African Americans. This displacement prompted a mass migration to urban areas in search of employment opportunities. Between 1910 and 1970, an estimated six million African Americans relocated from the rural South to urban centers in the North, Midwest, and West, in what is known as the Great Migration (U.S. Census Bureau, 2012).

While sectors like steel, automotive, and mining experienced automation that facilitated wage growth and improved living standards for many, the mechanization of agriculture had disparate effects. Many African Americans lacked the necessary skills to transition into manufacturing roles, resulting in unemployment and marginalization. As farming was increasingly mechanized, the need for agricultural workers fell sharply, leading to significant demographic shifts (History.com Editors, 2023).

This migration contributed to the urbanization of the African American population, with a noticeable decline in those working in agriculture or domestic labor. Despite these demographic shifts, social imbalances and racial issues remained pronounced, underscoring the complexities of economic and social integration during this transformative period.

National industry was experiencing an unprecedented moment of opportunity: it could rely on the public demand fueled by the Cold War, on the extraordinary opportunities offered by foreign markets, and on the vast and dynamic domestic demand of the new middle class. However, once again, American governments had to address the excesses of the system that could threaten the sustainability of paths of growth and continuous structural change of the economy and society. A large part of American society participated and became middle class, but some segments continued to be excluded (Reischauer, 1986).

The successes of the new postwar America, the improvements in terms of quality of life and opportunities for millions of Americans, clashed with the condition of other millions of Americans who were instead pushed toward paths of unemployment, marginalization, and widespread poverty. It soon became a widespread opinion that the government should intervene to prevent internal differences from persisting, as was happening in many areas of the country. In this context, the words contained in the Economic Report of the President of 1965 are clear:

> The United States has long been a rich country. The abundance of our material output is one of the wonders of the world. [. . .] Yet we know that our society is imperfect. The President has sounded the keynote for a new effort to address ourselves to social problems which have been in our consciousness but which we have failed to attack with the full use of the great technical, social, and economic resources that we possess. World War II, and the long cold war diverted our effort to other matters. [. . .] Today, we have grown accustomed to the ceaseless burdens of being a great power, of preserving nuclear superiority and holding the line around the perimeter of the Western World. [. . .] We are ready to take a large step forward, to put on the agenda tasks long undone, to use our creative powers to build a better America—to move toward the Great Society (ERP, 1965, p. 145–146).

Indeed, it was President Lyndon Johnson, who entered the White House in November 1963 after Kennedy's assassination, who, more than anyone else, attempted to redirect the intervention of the American government, suggesting that it should also act to lay the foundations of a new model of economic and social development. Government action should also be guided by the goal of transforming America into a better society, trying to care for the many who have remained excluded. In his speech at the University of Michigan on May 22, 1964, President Johnson defined what he believed should be the fundamental characteristics of the Great Society he had in mind:

[. . .] we have the opportunity to move not only toward the rich society and the powerful society, but upward to the Great Society. The Great Society rests on abundance and liberty for all. It demands an end to poverty and racial injustice, to which we are totally committed in our time. But that is just the beginning. The Great Society is a place where every child can find knowledge to enrich his mind and to enlarge his talents. It is a place where leisure is a welcome chance to build and reflect, not a feared cause of boredom and restlessness. It is a place where the city of man serves not only the needs of the body and the demands of commerce but the desire for beauty and the hunger for community. It is a place where man can renew contact with nature. It is a place which honors creation for its own sake and for what it adds to the understanding of the race. It is a place where men are more concerned with the quality of their goals than the quantity of their goods (Johnson, 1964).

The Great Society initiative encompassed a comprehensive suite of federal programs targeting advancements in education, healthcare, welfare services, social security, and the eradication of poverty (ERP, 1965, p. 153). While some of these programs had their origins during President Kennedy's tenure, they faced legislative stagnation following his assassination. These interventions aimed to mitigate immediate disparities in Americans' living conditions and, over time, integrate marginalized populations into the broader societal framework. This integration was envisioned to cultivate a new workforce essential for industrial growth, expand the middle class to bolster consumption, and foster citizens who would contribute to political consensus.

Benefiting from a supportive political environment, the Johnson administration swiftly secured Congressional approval for a series of intricate and cohesive legislative measures. The number of federal programs inspired by the Great Society's themes escalated rapidly: from 132 in 1960 to 379 in 1967, with expenditures rising from $8.6 billion in 1963 to $20.3 billion in 1969 (Reischauer, 1986). Notably, several of these programs, such as Medicaid, Medicare, and the Older Americans Act, continued to the present day (Zelizer, 2015).

The Great Society's policies predominantly addressed urban challenges, aiming to enhance the quality of life in metropolitan areas that had experienced significant socioeconomic disparities over time. Initiatives targeted social issues like juvenile delinquency, addressed by the Juvenile Delinquency and Youth Offenses Act of 1963; mental health concerns, through the Community Mental Health Centers Act of 1963; poverty alleviation, via the Economic Opportunity Act of 1964; and urban decay, tackled by the Demonstration Cities and Metropolitan Development Act of 1966 (Piven and Cloward, 2005). These programs primarily focused on inner-city populations, where conditions had often become perilous, unsanitary, and impoverished, in contrast to the middle class that had migrated to suburban locales.

Education was a cornerstone of the Great Society agenda (ERP, 1966). Beyond allocating funds for primary, secondary, and higher education, specific initiatives were introduced to enhance workforce skills and productivity. Efforts were also directed toward optimizing the mechanisms that align labor supply with demand. For instance, programs under the Manpower Development and Training Act offered critical education and training to unemployed individuals with prior work experience. The goal was to update their professional competencies. Between 1962 and the end of 1965, these programs enrolled approximately 370,000 participants (ERP, 1966, p. 99).

Health initiatives under the Great Society had profound implications for workforce productivity and the expansion of health-related industries. The project significantly boosted medical research funding, with total health research expenditures in 1965 reaching around \$1.9 billion, accounting for nearly 9% of the national R&D budget. This figure represented more than a tenfold increase from 1950, reflecting an annual growth rate of almost 18%. Public investments in health research were chiefly funneled through the NIH, whose budget for research, facilities, and training surged from under \$100 million to over \$1 billion within a decade by 1965. In that year, NIH's spending constituted two-fifths of the total medical research expenditure in the United States (ERP, 1966, p. 104).

Despite the initial vigor of the Great Society initiatives, escalating resistance emerged as the Vietnam conflict intensified. The Republican Party adeptly leveraged the Democratic administration's Vietnam decisions to their advantage, leading to a significant erosion of the Democratic majority in Congress during the 1966 midterm elections. This shift in political dynamics had swift repercussions: the Great Society's momentum waned considerably, and the remainder of Johnson's presidency was largely consumed by Congressional pressures advocating for fiscal austerity and reductions in public spending (Helsing, 2000).

4.6 The Crises of the 1970s

In October 1973, the outbreak of the international oil crisis quickly highlighted America's dangerous dependence on oil, which was the main source of power for the national industry. This dependency meant reliance on certain foreign countries, necessitating the United States to closely monitor events in certain areas of the world. American support for Israel in the war against the Arab states had provoked opposition from oil-exporting Middle Eastern countries, which reacted by reducing the global supply of crude oil (ERP, 1974, p. 211). In general,

Western economies were forced to rationalize oil consumption as its price exponentially increased during those years. Particularly, the Arab countries imposed an embargo on shipments to the United States.

The possible repercussions of this situation on the American economy were clear at the onset of the crisis:

1. Limitation of production capacity. Beyond a certain point, inadequacy in energy supply could result in the inability to produce certain goods (or at least the inability to produce them at prices meeting market demand). Obviously, in the case of a significant reduction in national production capacity, the consequence would be a considerable increase in unemployment.
2. Reduction in demand in certain specific sectors. Reduced fuel availability and higher gasoline prices could, for example, limit the demand for large-displacement cars or tourism services. A shortage of heating oil could cut demand for new housing.
3. General loss of welfare due to increased energy costs. All industrial productions using oil as an energy source could experience a significant price increase, resulting in a general reduction in national welfare.
4. Reduction in exports. The reduction in consumption resulting from higher oil prices could severely impact all oil-importing countries, with a general slowdown in markets and global demand, and therefore also affecting American exports (ERP, 1974, p. 24–26).

However, as highlighted in the Economic Report of the President for 1974, the situation in America could have been even more dramatic than it actually turned out to be:

The energy crisis that occurred in late 1973 as a result of the embargo by some of the oil-exporting countries alerted the nation to the risk of depending on imports for a commodity that is vital to our economic well-being, and the supply of which is largely controlled by a few countries. Reductions in oil shipments to the United States and a sharp rise in the price of imported oil have caused substantial economic disruption. Had these events occurred later, when the United States was projected to be even more dependent on imported petroleum, the loss of jobs and the effect on incomes might have been far greater (ERP, 1974, p. 36).

In fact, during the 1960s, the energy policy of the American government had focused on limiting oil imports into the United States to encourage the development of domestic energy resources. Only in the early 1970s, as foreign oil was significantly cheaper than domestic oil, did the government begin to loosen import constraints (ERP, 1974, p. 115). In practice, at the onset of the crisis, forecasts for foreign oil dependence for 1974 revealed that the countries participating in the embargo against America supplied 16% of the oil consumed in the United States, corresponding to 8% of total energy consumption. This was in fact the least oil availability expected from the embargo for 1974 (ERP, 1974, p. 23).

Overall oil consumption and net imports decreased significantly from 1973 to 1975, while domestic production continued to decline. It was only from 1975 onward that domestic oil production began a slight recovery. Although the economic consequences of the oil crisis that began in 1973 were not as dramatic in the United States as in other industrialized economies, the political climate that emerged in this context nonetheless gave the American government new momentum and legitimacy to intervene once again in the industrial system, promoting technological and productive development to reduce dependence on foreign oil:

> Oil imports may become more readily available, and the price may decline. However, the possibility of a subsequent sharp price rise or supply curtailment makes it risky for the United States to remain heavily dependent on imports to supply domestic needs. The nation has the capability to become self-sufficient in energy production. This capability will, however, require substantial capital investment and large expenditure on research and development (ERP, 1974, p. 36).

Initially, it was President Nixon who took steps in this direction. In 1973, he launched "Project Independence," an initiative to address the energy crisis; the FY 1975 budget message proposed federal funding of $10 billion over five years for energy research and development (Nixon, 1973; United States Government, 1974). The main objectives of the program were to improve energy efficiency in consumption and fossil fuel conversion to electricity; increase national production of oil and natural gas; expand coal usage; increase nuclear energy usage; develop renewable energy sources; and reduce environmental effects associated with energy production and usage (ERP, 1974, p. 125).

President Nixon, in addition to imposing price regulations on oil favoring domestic production and limiting imports from abroad, was supportive of creating new nuclear energy facilities. Nixon aimed to boost initiatives in nuclear energy, which had long been an industry that American governments had invested in (Clarke, 1985; Duffy, 1997).

In the aftermath of World War II, the US federal government initiated support for research centers dedicated to the development of nuclear energy for civilian applications. The Atomic Energy Commission (AEC), established under the Atomic Energy Act of 1946, was tasked with overseeing and coordinating these research endeavors. A key institution in this initiative was the Argonne National Laboratory, managed by the University of Chicago, which played a pivotal role in advancing nuclear technology (US Department of Energy).

In 1954, under President Dwight D. Eisenhower, the Atomic Energy Act was amended to promote the commercial development of nuclear power. This legislative change encouraged technological advancements in nuclear energy production and facilitated private sector participation. Subsequently, the AEC launched the Power Demonstration Reactor Program, fostering collaboration between the federal government and private companies to develop the first generation of nuclear reactors (US Department of Energy; Davis, 2014).

Between the late 1950s and early 1960s, federal funding further propelled the nuclear sector, leading to the construction of the first nuclear power plants. A notable milestone was achieved on December 20, 1951. Argonne National Laboratory's Experimental Breeder Reactor I produced the world's first usable amount of electricity from nuclear energy, illuminating a string of four light bulbs, a step toward the emergence of a new industry focused on civilian energy production (Argonne National Laboratory; Clarke, 1985).

The 1970s witnessed significant growth in the nuclear energy sector, driven by the international oil crisis and escalating global tensions. The federal

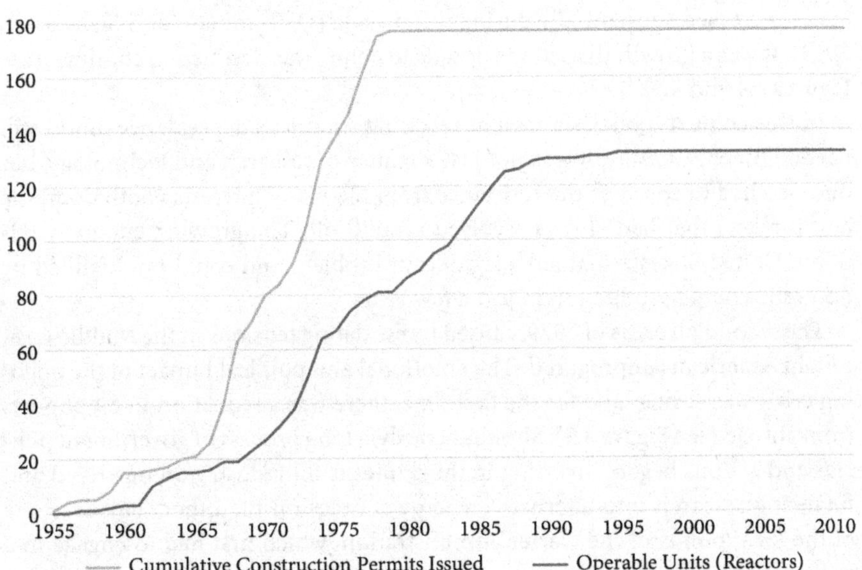

Figure 4.4 Nuclear Power in the United States: Construction Permits and Operating Reactors (1955–2011)

Source: Elaboration from EIA—US Energy and Information Administration, 2012

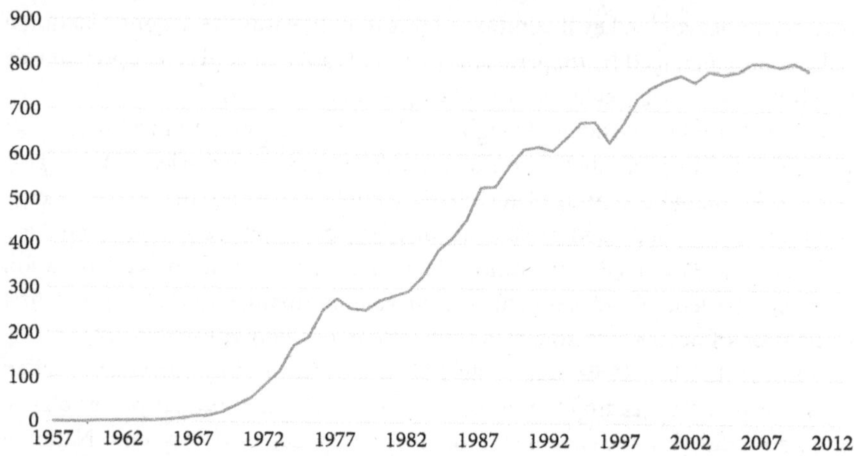

Figure 4.5 Nuclear Electricity Production in the USA in Millions of Kilowatt-Hours (1957–2014)

Source: Elaboration from US *Energy Information Administration (table 8.1)*

government, recognizing the strategic importance of energy independence, invested heavily in nuclear energy. Despite safety concerns raised by various stakeholders, the number of operational nuclear power plants in the United States increased substantially during this decade (Di Tommaso and Schweitzer, 2013). It was a growth that, in the decade to come, was destined to continue (see Figures 4.4 and 4.5).

In this context, policies aimed at reducing America's dependence on oil still needed time. Naturally, it was not just a matter of research and technology, but one also had to consider the resistance from the many interests (both domestic and foreign) that had always revolved around oil. The growing energy needs of the United States remained a significant problem and could not be filled by domestic energy production in just a few years.

The second oil crisis of 1979, caused by escalating tensions in the Middle East, caught Americans unprepared. The emotional and political impact of the ongoing crisis was strong, and for the first time, there was a reduction in oil imports from abroad (see Figure 4.5). Simultaneously, a long process of government policies and actions began, investing in the domestic oil industry on one hand and financing research into alternative energy sources on the other. This was one of the focal points of the Carter administration, which first had to engage in a policy of price regulation.

On the industrial front, one of the major initiatives promoted by the Carter administration to reduce dependence on oil was the launch of the Synthetic Fuels program. By the end of Carter's term in 1980, the Synthetic Fuels Corporation

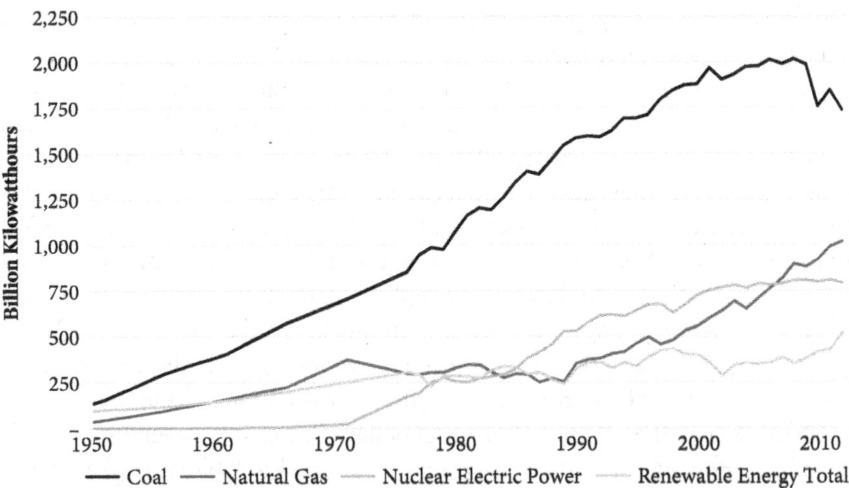

Figure 4.6 Electricity Generation in the USA by Sector in Billions of Kilowatt-Hours (1949–2011)

Source: US *Energy Information Administration (table 8.2a)*

was created with the Synthetic Fuels Corporation Act, aimed at financing the development and implementation of commercial synthetic fuel plants as alternatives to imported fossil fuels (Di Tommaso and Schweitzer, 2013).

However, the arrival of the 1980s did not bring stable solutions in this field. As Figure 4.6 clearly demonstrates, the process of diversifying energy supply sources required numerous decades and can hardly be said to be concluded today. The issue of how to meet domestic energy demand remains one of the major unresolved issues that continues to affect the American economy, society, and politics. The complex relationships with oil lobbies and America's military engagement in many areas of the world are clear evidence of how much still needs to be done.

4.7 Final Remarks

In the four postwar decades, the US industry-government relationship continued to be influenced by international challenges and military threats, coalitions of domestic interests, and rapid social and economic transformations. The years immediately following the end of WWII were marked by a relatively slow process of converting military production into civilian production, with government spending and defense activities remaining central to economic growth and innovation. Resistance to reconversion and the arrival of the Cold War made possible the preservation of existing established interests supported by big business, military, and government circuits.

In this context, the expected decline in demand at the end of the war did not happen. On the contrary, rising domestic demand accelerated business growth for about three "golden" decades. Years of accelerated transformations of domestic and international markets, where the role of the federal government remained central in research, production, and infrastructure. The postwar government was committed to promoting economic growth, granting military security, and providing and fostering people's welfare. By the 1970s, however, the situation began to change dramatically. Oil shocks, economic stagnation, inflation, and rising international competition disrupted the established economic, social, and political equilibria, sparking debates about the need to revise policy and reduce state intervention. Industrial policy oscillated between the continuity of government-led initiatives—mainly connected to Cold War demand for advanced military goods and services—and a push for market-driven solutions.

The Cold War fundamentally shaped US industrial policy, as national security considerations led to sustained government support for key industries, particularly aerospace, defense, sciences, research, and technology. Moreover, the Marshall Plan designed to rebuild European economies, ensured a vast and stable market for American producers of goods and services. By the 1960s, international competition intensified. Japan and West Germany, having recovered from wartime devastation, emerged as formidable industrial competitors, particularly in manufacturing and consumer electronics. The 1970s oil shocks and the rise of the Organization of Petroleum Exporting Countries further underscored the vulnerability of the US industry, economy, and society to international dynamics.

Domestically, the first postwar decades were marked by high growth, rising productivity, rapid technological upgrading, and a strong labor market, supported by federal policies. However, by the 1970s domestic issues connected to stagflation, unemployment, and manufacturing decline challenged the economic model that had underpinned industrial policy since the New Deal. In particular, the evident crisis of the American industrial system, boosted by oil shocks and foreign aggressive competition, led to a reconsideration of business strategies and government policies. The American postwar model was under attack: economic slump and uncertainty were accompanied by severe social tensions. A radical change of attitude became urgent. Government policies, including industrial policies, started to be considered "the problem," not the solution. The issue quickly and easily polarized the national political debate, becoming a central topic in the 1980 presidential campaign.

During this period, economically dominant thinking shifted from a general acceptance of government intervention in the economy to a growing emphasis on free-market principles and solutions. The Keynesian consensus of the 1950s and 1960s, which endorsed active government management of the economy, came under strain as inflation and unemployment rose in the 1970s. By the end of the Carter administration, a new neoliberal ideology was gaining traction, advocating for deregulation, tax cuts, and reduced government intervention. The Keynesian positions drastically lost their consensus, both in academic and political circuits. The rhetoric of Reaganomics, supported by the Chicago School, was destined to prevail very soon. In this new emerging scenario, there was no longer room for industrial policy arguments.

Industrial policy after the end of WWII focused on several key sectors, often driven by Cold War imperatives. The defense industry remained a primary recipient of government contracts, leading to the growth of what President Eisenhower termed the "military-industrial complex." Aerospace (Boeing, Lockheed), telecommunications (AT&T), and computing (IBM) all benefited from federal support, particularly through military procurement and research funding. The automobile industry was a dominant force in the postwar economy but began struggling by the 1970s as Japanese manufacturers introduced more fuel-efficient and reliable cars. The energy sector, particularly domestic oil and nuclear power became a key focus of industrial policy after the oil shocks of 1973 and 1979. Regionally, federal investment targeted infrastructure development, with projects like the Interstate Highway System (begun in the 1950s) facilitating economic expansion. However, by the 1970s, the Rust Belt suffered significant job losses as factories closed, prompting discussions on industrial revitalization.

The federal government played a central role in financing technological innovation. Agencies such as NASA, DOD, and NSF supported R&D that contributed to advances in computing, aerospace, and materials science. However, industrial policy also relied on regulatory frameworks to manage economic activity. The 1960s and 1970s saw increased environmental and workplace safety regulations, such as the Clean Air Act (1970) and the Occupational Safety and Health Administration. These policies aimed to mitigate industrial externalities but were criticized for increasing business costs. Trade policy fluctuated between protectionism and liberalization. While tariffs and quotas were used to shield domestic manufacturers from foreign competition, the United States also promoted free trade agreements, particularly under the GATT. Keynesian fiscal policy was a major tool through the 1960s, but rising inflation in the 1970s led to a shift toward monetarist policies, particularly under the Federal Reserve's leadership. President Carter, facing economic stagnation, struggled to balance stimulus measures with inflation control.

After the end of WWII, coalitions in favor of active industrial policy included established big business, labor unions, military representatives, government officials, and progressive politicians who supported federal investment. The defense sector, high-tech firms, and infrastructure-heavy industries supported government intervention in funding and procurement. Opposition came from some emerging new business leaders demanding to lower entry barriers to the markets, free-market economists, conservative politicians who favored deregulation, public budget cuts, and lower taxes. By the 1970s, frustration with economic stagnation fueled calls for reducing government involvement in industrial planning. The rise of supply-side economics, championed by figures like Friedrich Hayek and Milton Friedman, set the stage for a major ideological shift in the Reagan era.

Since the end of WWII, the US economy has experienced decades of unprecedented economic growth and expansion associated with rising technological advancements and living standards. Federal investments made possible American technological leadership and dominance in strategic sectors like telecommunications, computing, aerospace, and pharmaceuticals. Heavy public investments and procurement made possible impressive infrastructure development: the construction of highways, airports, and energy plants was one of the key factors able to support economic expansion and the rise of Americans' living standards.

After three decades of unprecedented economic growth and quality of life improvements, however, the 1970s saw dramatic changes. Industrial decline and companies' crisis led to job losses and social tensions especially in urban and manufacturing areas. Government answers to rising unemployment and business failures were inadequate. The same was true for policies that needed to rethink the American energy industry and its dependency from abroad: government responses to oil shocks were weak and inconsistent, with price controls and alternative energy programs yielding uncertain results. Moreover, the combination of high inflation and stagnant growth made the traditional Keynesian approach obsolete, lowering confidence in government-led industrial policy. Industrial policies' answers to urgent economic and social problems became less credible, paving the way to the rise of radical free-market alternatives.

The period from 1945 to 1981 saw the rise, peak, and gradual decline of government-led industrial policy in the United States. In the early postwar decades, industrial policy played a pivotal role in driving economic growth, expanding both domestic and international markets, advancing infrastructure, fostering technological innovation, and strengthening military capacity. However, by the 1970s, economic stagnation, inflation, and growing global competition began to challenge the prevailing models of state intervention. While government involvement, particularly in defense and technology, remained central to the American growth model, the deepening economic crisis and mounting social tensions prompted a shift in both rhetoric and attitudes toward the role of government and industrial policy. This era set the stage for ongoing debates about the state's role in shaping the economy and society, a highly polarized discussion that continues to shape American political discourse today.

5

The Paradoxes of Reagan's Time

Rhetoric and Practice

5.1 Introduction

Public intervention in industrial dynamics has always been one of the most controversial issues in the American debate. However, starting from the early 1980s, the theme assumed an obvious political centrality. These were years of crisis, international instability, and big changes. It was a complex period for the world economy. This stage coincided with the rise of the Washington Consensus (Williamson, 1989) and thus with the support for a series of neoliberal prescriptions shared by the US Department of the Treasury, the World Bank, and the International Monetary Fund.

During this period, the public gained a greater theoretical awareness of the unresolved problems associated with government intervention and the acceleration of the process of globalization. As a result, the academic and political paradigm shifted toward a market-oriented approach and a drastic reduction of public intervention in the economy (Stiglitz and Lin, 2013).

5.2 The Debate During the Washington Consensus Era

The words "industrial policy" entered the American lexicon only at the end of the 1970s, during the Carter administration (Reich, 1982; Dumke, 1984; Norton, 1986; Eisinger, 1990; Bingham, 1998; White, 2010; Di Tommaso and Schweitzer, 2013). The strong pressure of foreign competition, in particular from Japan, was an issue to be addressed. The problems were real, but to get adequate political support they could also exploit emotional levers, i.e., national pride, which could not easily accept that the enemies defeated in the last war were coming back to challenge the leadership of the United States of America (Engelhardt, 1995). Nevertheless, industrial policy interventions need political consensus, and these kinds of considerations were very useful to build it.

Governing Growth. Marco R. Di Tommaso and Vinod K. Aggarwal, Oxford University Press.
© Oxford University Press (2026). DOI: 10.1093/oso/9780197821787.003.0005

President Carter made use of a committee of experts—the Economic Policy Group (EPG)[1]—that, as soon as he took office in 1977 was tasked with studying and proposing solutions to the problems of the complex present situation: inflation, unemployment, slowdown of growth, decline in productivity, and fall in the competitiveness of American industry. In this scenario, the EPC was tasked to draw up a national industrial policy plan (Biven, 2002). In reality, the working group did not produce any public documents for a long time, in part because the internal positions within the EPC were not always homogeneous on many issues (Graham Jr., 1992). It was only in 1980 that Carter, in a speech during his second election campaign, announced the launch of the Economic Revitalization Program (ERP, 1981; Bingham, 1998).

The ERP proposal for industrial policy planned to set up one institution to be entrusted with directing intervention: a federal agency that had the specific task of formulating and then managing national industrial policy strategies. This agency was also supported by a council with representatives of government, enterprises, and workers, who had the task of collecting information on the domestic industry, thus offering a basis for informed consent to the industrial policy interventions that would be promoted. Finally, a federal development bank was planned to deal with financial and credit issues.

Government intervention followed two major approaches. The first focused on providing assistance and instituting temporary trade protections—primarily against Japanese imports—for weakening or declining industries. The second approach aimed to support sectors that struggled to attract sufficient capital from the private banking system, particularly in emerging industries where private investors were perceived as overly risk averse. These measures were seen as critical for addressing the extraordinary economic challenges of the time and for accelerating the adaptation of the US production system to evolving competitive pressures (ERP, 1981).

The government pursued its overarching goals of stimulating economic growth and facilitating the structural transformation of American industry with determination. However, the ERP ultimately remained unrealized. With President Carter's electoral defeat, the initiative never came to fruition, as the incoming Reagan administration embraced a fundamentally different economic philosophy.

As it is well known, President Reagan in the United States and Prime Minister Thatcher in the United Kingdom were the main promoters (and effective media disseminators) of this change of perspective. Milton Friedman and the

---

[1] The EPC was led by the Secretary of the Treasury, the Director of the Office of Management and Budget, the Chairman of the Council of Economic Advisors, along with the Federal Reserve Chairman. In addition, the Secretaries of State, Commerce, Labor, Housing and Urban Development and the National Security Advisor also participated (Graham, 1992).

Chicago School represented the academic reference for a vast international network of scholars, who globally spread the precepts of the neoliberal paradigm (Friedman, 1951; Cárcamo-Huechante, 2006; Jones, 2014).

Reagan began his term at a time of economic crisis when a radical policy change was required. There were serious concerns about oil and the Middle East. The world had recently been shocked by two major oil crises, one in 1973 and another in 1979. The 1973–1974 shock occurred as OPEC decreased oil output in response to the United States' continued sympathies toward Israel during conflicts between Arab governments and Israel (Hammes and Wills, 2005). The decrease in oil supply increased prices worldwide, "shocking" many nations that had previously been relying on Middle Eastern oil imports. The second oil crisis was caused by a decrease in oil imports from Iran just before the 1980 election, once again from a Middle Eastern conflict. The resulting crisis didn't last more than one year, but it raised gas prices at the pump by around 20 cents a gallon. The Department of Energy attempted to ease gas prices by making larger refineries sell crude oil to smaller ones, as well as instilling price controls and increased inventory requirements. These actions may have, in the end, increased incentives to withhold oil from the market, worsening the crisis (Verleger et al., 1979). These two crises showed how the political volatility of other nations could affect American national security and economies, while the American people realized the unreliability of government intervention.

In addition, the Cold War was not over yet. The 1979 invasion of Afghanistan by the Soviet Union after years of support for pro-Soviet leaders prompted a response from the United States and its allies. President Carter announced the US doctrine of protecting oil-producing countries in the Middle East from Soviet influence, leading to embargoes on Soviet goods as well as a boycott of the 1980 Olympic Games (Office of the Historian, 1978–1980, n.d.). This only increased tensions between Washington and Moscow running up to the 1980 election which had previously been easing by the early 1970s. The first Strategic Arms Limitation Talks (SALT) led to the Antiballistic Missile Treaty, which reduced the number of arms both nations could develop. Furthermore, the Helsinki Final Acts provided a channel for trade and cultural exchange as well as the stability of established political borders (Office of the Historian, 2019). The Soviet invasion of Afghanistan threw the United States back into rising tensions with the Soviet Union and placed foreign affairs at the top of election issues and a topic of key concern for Reagan as soon as he entered the Oval Office in 1981 (Reagan, 1985).

Inflation and unemployment were problems at the center of the political agenda. The 1970s was a decade of "stagflation": a confluence of high unemployment and low output, on the one hand, and high inflation, on the other. Stagflation, which was previously dismissed as an unlikely phenomenon for a

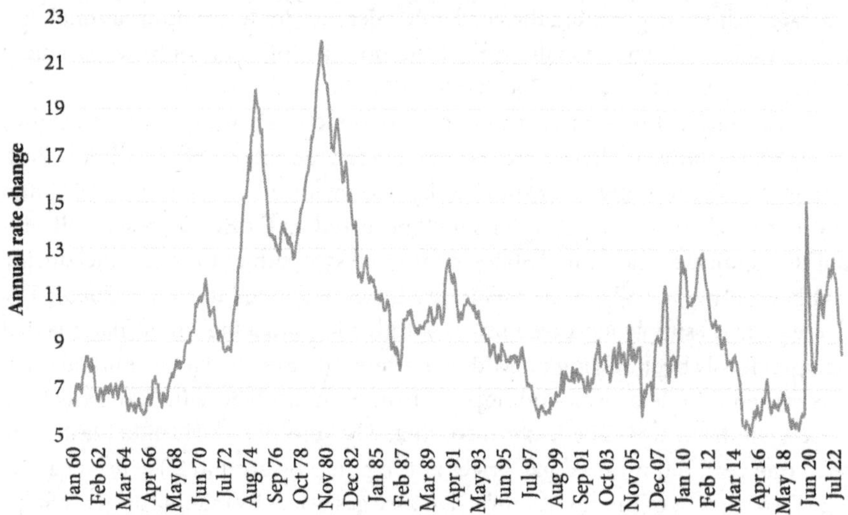

Figure 5.1 Annual Rate of Change of Misery Index

Source: Statista, 2023. Annual rate of change of the misery index (unemployment rate plus
consumer price index) in the United States from January 1960 to September 2022. Available at:
https://www.statista.com/statistics/1324607/us-misery-index/

protracted period of time, took a toll on the American people. The starkness of
the 1970s is captured by the rocketing "misery index"—a crude, but telling, measure of economic health equivalent to the sum of the unemployment rate and the
annual rate of inflation (Statista, 2023).

Consumers were left reeling from higher prices in grocery stores and at the
pump and faced shortages of fuel and key goods. This fueled widespread discontent with the economic state of affairs in the United States. In the November
1979 Gallup survey, only 19% of respondents reported that they were satisfied with the way things were going (Satisfaction With the United States, 1979).
This simmering dissatisfaction is one reason, and perhaps the most powerful
one, that explains the election of Ronald Reagan, the conservative governor
of California, as president twelve months later. Reagan indeed referenced the
"misery index"—over 20% during election season—in political debates, wield-
ing it to illustrate the increasingly tough economic situation Americans were
finding themselves in during the Carter administration and his predecessors
(see Figure 5.1) (Baker, 2024). The stagflation of the 1970s had several causes,
not the least of which was the oil price shock. But Reagan and other policymakers, economists, and thinkers also implicated poor domestic macroeconomic policy, excessive government spending, and overregulation. These sorts
of ideas formed a key basis of one side of a bubbling grand economic policy

debate in the years to follow. Social tensions and conflicts also grew. Competition from Germany and Japan threatened the national industry in many sectors.

In this context, a polarized debate started in the United States. On the one hand, making special reference to the experience of Japanese industrial growth, some argued for an urgent intervention in industrial policy (Etzioni, 1983; Bingham, 1998). On the other hand, those declaring themselves to be defenders of the values of the free market criticized any intervention by the government, whose excessive activism was to be considered the real American problem. As it is known, this last position prevailed: the administrations of Reagan and Bush (between 1981 and 1993) were always hostile to any national industrial policy plan.

> The Administration remains strongly opposed to any sort of industrial policy, which would involve second-guessing private investment decisions by selecting particular firms, industries, or commercial technologies for favorable tax treatment or direct subsidies. History provides strong support for the view that private market participants, who have profits and jobs at stake, have sharper incentives and better information than government decision-makers and, as a consequence, make sounder investment decisions (ERP, 1990, p. 25).[2]

This rhetoric was very important for acquiring buy-in to the policy agenda since the first Reagan election campaign of 1980. Such rhetoric was also shared by Bush and, partially, also by the subsequent Clinton administration (1993–2001). However, as we will see in the next pages, those words did not prevent the successive administrations from continuing to support the national production system through various channels (Di Tommaso and Schweitzer, 2013; Di Tommaso and Tassinari, 2014; Tassinari, 2014).

However, it must be said that the program had a lasting impact on the debate of those years. The public discussion on the themes of the program did not characterize only the election campaign in 1980 but also the Reagan administration. Use of the term "industrial policy" continued for a long time to characterize the political debate, having been employed by supporters and opponents alike. Many of the problems that the revitalization program wanted to address remained open and unresolved. However, the persistence of disputes in the Reagan era is also explained by another factor: "industrial policy" proved to be one of the great themes capable of polarizing positions in the national public debate, offering easy political capital to the contenders who used it (Bingham, 1998; Norton, 1986).

[2] See also Becker (1985).

Public opinion was fragmented, and so were the media, academia, and Congress. Starting from the proposal of industrial policy elaborated by the Carter administration, two antagonistic positions gradually consolidated. The first, in line with supply-side economics, was in favor of substantial freedom for market mechanisms to function and was by definition contrary to industrial policy. The second supported an active role for the government and continued to suggest the need to promote a comprehensive national industrial policy plan that would revive the American economy (Reich, 1982). In the academic field, these positions were respectively supported by the Chicago School (which had great trust in the ability of the market to contribute to efficiency) and the Harvard School, which was more inclined to recognize the need for public intervention in some circumstances (Grillo and Silva, 1989). At certain times, it was a bitter, strongly ideological debate, often further amplified by the media. It was a debate in which politicians, scholars, and opinion leaders confronted each other, adopting arguments that were too often prejudiced. This opportunity was exploited by Reagan, who used powerful rhetoric to build a great deal of political consensus on this debate since his first election campaign (Richman, 1988).

The discussion was monopolized by big issues of a general nature. The United States found itself rediscussing the role of the state and the virtues of the market. Politicians and academics were confronted in the media about the underlying principles that should have guided the political action of governments and on the role that the state should have had in the economy (Reich, 1982; DiLorenzo, 1984; Dorn, 1984; Johnson, 1984).

The supporters of industrial policy during the Reagan era were inclined to promote broader government action, including industrial policy interventions whose objectives went beyond efficiency to goals such as employment or the rebalancing of socioeconomic disparities. According to this perspective, policies could contribute to achieving objectives in the general interest, which went beyond those of individual companies and individual sectors addressed by the intervention (Ketels, 2007; White, 2010).

In the industrial policy debate, proponents of government intervention emphasized five key arguments (Reich, 1982, 1984). First, the government was already deeply involved in supporting national industries through military procurement and R&D financing programs. Given the substantial allocation of public resources, a more deliberate assessment was necessary to understand how these initiatives influenced the competitive strength of the industrial sector.

Second, rather than allowing lobbying pressures to dictate the distribution of commercial protections and costly benefits to select industries, businesses, or regions, policymakers needed to adopt a more systematic and coherent national strategy for economic support.

Third, industries losing their international competitiveness require structured, long-term interventions instead of ad hoc bailouts. If left unaddressed, the decline of labor-intensive industries would lead to job losses, significant social costs, and the formation of protectionist interest groups resistant to necessary economic transitions. Because workforce retraining and relocation were slow and costly processes, industrial policy was seen as essential—especially given the reluctance of banks and private investors to fund ventures with limited short-term profitability.

Fourth, the government needed to increase investment in public goods—such as infrastructure, education, and healthcare—that would serve as foundational pillars for sustaining American industry's future competitiveness.

Finally, an industrial policy was needed to address strategic economic initiatives undertaken by other advanced countries. This meant fostering emerging industries with strong potential for global competitiveness by promoting economies of scale and technological innovation through targeted incentives.

Opponents of intervention—who supported the rise and consolidation of President Reagan—espoused completely different ideas. For the supporters of supply-side economics in those years, industrial policy intervention was always to be avoided. During public speeches, Reagan and supporters of his positions highlighted how selective industrial policies—those in which governments choose to intervene in some sectors, some territories, or some specific businesses—were undesirable. Directing policies to particular targets in a preferential way was wrong, had high costs, uncertain expected benefits, and negative effects on efficiency. A precise set of interventions was challenged, as the single tools used by the government were the problem: direct subsidies to companies, tax breaks, and commercial protectionism. Critics who were inspired by Reagan's position claimed that selective interventions would have altered the competitive mechanisms and that they would not have been able to promote the efficiency of the industrial system and of businesses.

Similarly, interventions in the field of antitrust and competition were not encouraged by Reagan and his political and academic supporters. This approach suggested that the market should be entirely self-regulating, thanks to the freedom of entry and exit. In the majority of cases, it was not necessary for governments to intervene: competitive markets offered their own solution to the problems of abuse of dominant position (Baumol et al., 1983).

The government would not have had to replace the market in determining the structural adjustment of the economy, in deciding the allocation of capital to the various production activities (e.g., by granting public loans to emerging industries) and in the "choice of winners" protecting old declining industries (ERP, 1984). The reasons underlying this perspective were mainly linked to a literature that in those years was becoming very influential, i.e., the one on government failure[3] (ERP, 1982, pp. 37–42).

First, it was emphasized how the government had a high probability of failing in its intervention due to structural difficulties in finding and processing information about the policy targets on which it intended to intervene. This literature contested the idea that the government had sufficient knowledge (about the industry or enterprises) to select the best actors to turn its attention toward. On the other hand, it was argued that competition and well-functioning markets were the best tools to select the most efficient productive activities, which therefore deserved the competitive positions they had been able to achieve (Etzioni, 1983; Schultze, 1983; DiLorenzo, 1984).

In addition to the problems concerning information, the literature highlighted that the government tended to fail in pursuing political objectives that represented the public interest. This was due to two undesirable dynamics, considered in any case hard to improve. On the one hand, the organizational complexity that characterized the government and the many subjects (ministries, departments, divisions, agencies, etc.) that in fact implemented its action. On the other hand, the inevitable pressures that the government suffered came from society. In this regard, public intervention tended to favor the activity of some well-organized groups triggering mechanisms of non-virtuous search and hoarding of rents (i.e., rent seeking), which could easily degenerate into corruption, clientelism, and non-transparent exchange with the political power (Dorn, 1984; Krueger, 1990; Chang, 1994; Di Tommaso and Schweitzer, 2013).

These writings on government failures highlighted the weaknesses of public action and served to feed the idea that industrial policy, although in some cases necessary, was always undesirable because it was hopelessly destined to fail. The costs associated with the intervention were argued to be greater than the expected benefits.

Supporters of supply-side economics, along with policymakers influenced by this school of thought, sought to emphasize in the political arena that the government's role should be strictly confined to setting the "rules of the game"— namely, safeguarding property rights, ensuring adherence to private contracts, and maintaining the integrity of the price system (DiLorenzo, 1984).

Proponents of this framework considered substantial tax cuts for businesses and savers as essential, given that they were expected to stimulate investment and drive employment growth. Additionally, reducing public regulation was seen as a way to mitigate government-induced distortions in the market. Given these principles, the government should not be responsible for explicit industrial policy interventions. Reagan was clear in his opposition to such measures, making it a cornerstone of his political agenda (Reagan, 1985).

---

[3] For a synthesis of the debate on government failures see, among others, Krueger (1990); Le Grand (1991); Chang (1994); Buigues and Sekkat (2009); Di Tommaso and Schweitzer (2013).

This stance was reinforced in the 1984 Economic Report of the President, which dedicated an entire chapter to rejecting proposals that advocated for a more structured and interventionist approach to industrial policy (ERP, 1984, Ch. 3). Reagan's perspective was not about debating the existence of an industrial policy per se; rather, he argued that the government should not expand its role in shaping the structural evolution of American industry beyond its existing functions. The 1984 Economic Report of the President clearly articulated this position:

> It is true that many Federal policies affect industrial output. But the argument about whether they constitute industrial policy, like all arguments about definitions, is pointless. What is relevant is whether the proposals of industrial policy advocates are a good idea. Should the U.S. Government have a larger role than it now has in deciding the composition of U.S. industry? The answer is no. An industrial policy would not solve the problems faced by U.S. industry and would instead create new problems (ERP, 1984, p. 88).

The Reagan administration rejected the notion that the United States was undergoing a widespread and inevitable process of de-industrialization that threatened the overall competitiveness of its industrial sector. Instead, it attributed rising unemployment during that period primarily to gains in labor productivity. Following this logic, addressing job losses through industrial policy measures targeting struggling sectors was deemed unnecessary.

Rather than intervening in declining industries, the administration argued that the appropriate response was to provide direct assistance to displaced workers and facilitate their transition into new career fields. Industrial policy interventions, it was contended, could hinder the adoption of more efficient production methods, prolong the survival of uncompetitive businesses through continued financial support and protection, and ultimately lead to higher prices and welfare losses for consumers (ERP, 1984).

5.3 Trade Relations with Europe and Japan

In terms of commercial policy, in perfect harmony with the general policy perspective that the administration had publicly adopted, President Reagan's rhetoric promoted the idea of liberalizing markets at the international level:

> Our policy toward other nations' barriers to trade and to investment or export subsidies is one of strong opposition. Our trading partners must recognize that it is in their own interest, as well as ours, to assure that international trade and investment remain a two-way street (ERP, 1984).

This perspective carried significant consequences for the American economy. Because foreign competitors held an advantage over US industries, American businesses were expected to enhance their competitiveness independently—without government intervention—or redirect resources toward more productive sectors (Baldwin and Richardson, 1987).

However, this approach ultimately proved unsustainable. By 1985, the US trade deficit ballooned to $114 billion annually, fueling widespread support for protectionist policies aimed at mitigating the crisis, preserving jobs, and shielding struggling industries from competition (ERP, 1986). This sentiment aligned with past measures, such as the Trade Act of 1974. Under Section 201 of this Act, "safeguards" could be implemented—through tariffs or quotas—to protect industries threatened by foreign competition until they regained competitiveness. Domestic industries could petition under this provision, prompting a federal investigation to determine whether such protections were warranted (CRS, 2021).

A stark contrast emerged between Reagan's public rhetoric and the actual trade policies his administration pursued. Many scholars of the time highlighted this inconsistency. For instance, Richman (1988) titled his analysis of Reagan's trade policy *The Reagan Record on Trade: Rhetoric vs. Reality*. In a similar fashion, in an article, William Niskanen—a key member of the Council of Economic Advisers during Reagan's first term—underscored the widening gap between theory and practice.

> U.S. trade policy turned sharply protectionist during the Reagan years. Moreover, all of the new trade restraints imposed were initiated or approved by the administration, despite a general endorsement of free trade in its public rhetoric (Niskanen, 1988).

Similarly, other authors argued:

> On the basis of its "Statement on U.S. Trade Policy," one would have expected the administration to follow a very tough stance against import protection. However, on the surface at least, the administration's actual performance in granting import relief does not seem to differ significantly from the varied record of other recent administrations (Baldwin and Richardson, 1987, p. 136).

In reality, a radical change in the postwar balance of power was taking place. The strategy adopted by the United States in the postwar period to respond to the international tensions of the Cold War had been based on a strong political, military, and economic alliance with Europe and Japan. European countries (primarily West Germany) and Japan could count on economic support and preferential relations with the United States, which for many decades also represented their most important foreign market (Buigues and Sekkat, 2009).

In the years following World War II, this strategy worked well. The foreign economies had been destroyed by the war, and the superiority of the American industrial system muted concerns raised about the economic costs associated with a foreign policy aimed at favoring foreign imports. However, when in the early seventies some European and Japanese industries began to reach, if not exceed, the competitive capacities of their American counterparts, the United States found itself at a crossroads. On the one hand, several sectors of the national industry needed commercial protection and incentives to relaunch investments and modernize production. On the other hand, this kind of intervention would have angered important allies and thus incurred political costs. President Carter at the time hesitated until the end of his term to implement an industrial recovery plan, paying high social costs caused by rising unemployment. As noted, his industrial policy plan eventually remained in the drawer. Reagan faced the same problems: negative trade balances and potential social conflicts that arose precisely in sectors and areas of evident industrial decline (Stein, 1998).

Moreover, large manufacturing enterprises and the territories where they were located demanded remedies. Trade unions, which represented millions of workers employed in declining industries, had similar objectives. In this context, the Reagan administration chose the path of intervention without renouncing the neoliberal rhetoric. The government promoted a series of protectionist actions targeted toward those sectors that were most affected by international competitive pressures. Reagan justified the government's actions as a response to dumping and other unfair practices undertaken by competitor countries (Richman, 1988). It should be noted that the scope of these policies seems hardly justifiable on these grounds alone.

The previous administrations had been attempting to increase labor-friendly policies and union membership rates since the New Deal of the Great Depression. However, this all took a turn during the Reagan administration. Reagan's labor board attempted to distance the government from involvement in labor relations by deregulating employer conduct and allowing for more latitude in involvement in union campaigns. The Reagan administration also oversaw a key watershed moment during the 1981 air traffic controllers' strike, which resulted in the strikers being fired and non-union members being hired (Farber and Western, 2002). Reagan's policies were a part of the neoliberal shift to a more laissez-faire approach, in this instance giving employers more leeway in controlling employees and in the collective bargaining process. It was not just to remove government involvement, but also to improve relations with industry and increase production by limiting strikes and other interferences from labor unions.

By the late 1970s, the automotive industry was among the sectors facing the most severe challenges, prompting decisive intervention from the Reagan administration. Imported vehicles had captured 30% of the US market, and Chrysler—despite being one of the nation's three major automakers—had laid off 40% of its workforce and teetered on the brink of collapse. Given its size and economic significance, Chrysler was deemed "too big to fail," leading the government to intercede with a bailout (Richman, 1988; Di Tommaso and Schweitzer, 2013).

The intervention began in 1979, during the final months of the Carter administration. Congress passed the Chrysler Corporation Loan Guarantee Act, allowing the company to secure $1.5 billion in federally backed loan guarantees, along with an additional $3.5 billion in capital and concessions from labor unions (Di Tommaso and Schweitzer, 2013).

Carter's plan involved direct government oversight of Chrysler's operations to ensure that financial assistance was tied to structural reforms aimed at enhancing the automaker's competitiveness. The goal was to prevent the company from merely receiving aid without implementing the necessary changes to strengthen the automotive industry as a whole (Graham Jr., 1992).

After Reagan's election, the incoming administration did not strictly follow the path of reducing government intervention, as the rhetoric of the recently concluded electoral campaign would have indicated. On the contrary, it altered the government's policy stance from federal support to a single company, Chrysler, to a more sweeping action that intervened on behalf of the entire automotive sector. Of course, Reagan immediately wanted to ease public interference in the management of Chrysler, but that meant something else. The company's management and shareholders certainly appreciated the initiative. This gave way to more calls for another kind of support. The company and the entire automotive sector—which has always been dominated by a few large companies—demanded protection from what they labeled as tantamount to a Japanese commercial invasion. In this context, the administration acted with determination and immediately assumed an active role at the international level by exploiting its political and military leadership (Richman, 1988; Di Tommaso and Schweitzer, 2013).

Another traditionally struggling industry that Reagan intervened in was agriculture. Farmers were facing declining land values as well as a decrease in exports. Thus, the Reagan Administration passed the Food Security Act of 1985 in order to provide security and stability for American farmers. They utilized policies from the Agricultural Support Act of the 1930s, such as price support for the dairy industry. Another important aspect was the income support for grain producers as well as price-supported loans based on the world market price.

The target was to make agricultural prices at a level that would increase American agricultural exports and competitiveness (Glaser, 1986).

Another program meant to increase exports was the 1990 Agricultural Export Program. This program primarily targeted the wheat market, encouraging exports through subsidies. Particularly, the Export Enhancement Program (EEP) was targeting the European Community, which had risen as a strong US competitor in the international agriculture market due to its own export subsidy program. US exporting firms would compete for sales in the foreign markets and subsidies would be awarded based on successful bids that fit the Foreign Agricultural Service's price targets. After the introduction of the EEP, US wheat exports started to increase and government stocks began to drop, causing the EEP to be considered a success by policymakers (Goldberg and Knetter, 1997). These actions illustrate the Reagan Administration's willingness to interfere in order to rigorously support US exports against competitors.

In the first half of the 1980s, the Reagan administration exerted pressure on the Japanese government to obtain a "voluntary export restraint" that would reduce the export of cars to the United States (Aggarwal et al., 1987). In March 1982, the agreement limited car exports to 1.68 million. In the following years, the limit progressively moved upwards but remained in force until 1985 when the limit was set at 2.3 million cars (Niskanen, 1988; Richman, 1988; Bingham, 1998). This represented an invasive intervention that clashed with the precepts of the free market and free trade. Despite the alleged "voluntariness" of the "voluntary export restraint," the action should be read as a showdown of the American government toward its ally and former enemy.

One cannot find a justification for the export restraint in the theoretical roots on which Reaganomics relies, but it confirms long-term dynamics that we have already referred to in previous pages by analyzing other historical periods. The industrial policy intervention, inspired by the same simple principles that have always justified protectionism, welds the interests of the government with those of the manufacturing industry and trade unions. The Reagan administration responded to the big manufacturing industry's demands, gathered the support of trade unions, and consolidated political support for the effort.

In the same period, the Reagan administration also agreed on other similar actions, whose underlying logic resembled that in the Japanese automobile export restraint case. First, it agreed on a second important "voluntary export restraint" with Europe about steel. The restraint was justified as an anti-dumping measure in response to the subsidies that many European governments granted to their steel companies, with (economic and political) motivations quite similar to those that led the American government to offer protection to the same sector in the United States. However, the agreement set a 5.5% blanket limit on European steel exports to the American market, regardless of the amount of subsidy received by European firms. A similar limit was also applied to pipe imports. In 1984, more complex and ambitious negotiations began with the goal of impacting the global steel industry. The government's purpose was to agree on export restrictions with all major steel-producing countries (Niskanen, 1988).

The textile industry, too, saw the Reagan administration intervene in important ways that displayed continuity with previous administrations. Reagan did not hesitate to renew the Multi-Fiber Arrangement (MFA), i.e., a quota system adopted by industrialized countries to limit imports from developing countries, and at the same time tried to modify the rules that restricted the export possibilities of the most industrialized countries toward the developing countries themselves (Aggarwal, 1985). The MFA was supposed to be a temporary arrangement. It came into force in 1974 as an extension of the 1962 Long Term Agreement Regarding International Trade in Cotton Textiles promoted during the Kennedy Presidency under the auspices of the GATT. The MFA was negotiated by Ford and adopted by Carter, but then survived throughout the Reagan era and beyond, being completely dismantled only in 2005. The MFA represents a history of protection and support of the national textile industry by seemingly different administrations (Aggarwal, 1985). These administrations have passed the baton for decades, using foreign policy as an instrument of industrial and commercial policy, and the Reagan years exemplify the extent to which such policy can be implemented and its impact on American industry.

Support for the increasingly vital semiconductor industry also became a key focus. Beginning with the 1986 U.S.-Japan Semiconductor Agreement, the Reagan administration exerted significant pressure on Japan to establish a Commerce Department that determined "fair" market prices for memory chips used in computer manufacturing. As part of the agreement, Japan was required not only to reduce the volume of its semiconductor exports but also to ensure that American chips accounted for approximately 20% of its domestic market. Additionally, Japan had to apply the agreed-upon price to exports to third-country markets (Irwin, 1996).

While Japan complied with the pricing mandate, it was accused by the US government of failing to enforce the same pricing structure in third-country markets and of not increasing the share of American semiconductors in its domestic market. The Japanese government, lacking direct control over individual firms, struggled to meet these obligations. In response to these perceived violations, the United States took decisive unilateral action, imposing a 100% tariff on $300 million worth of unrelated Japanese imports (Niskanen, 1988; Richman, 1988; Irwin, 1996).

The Reagan administration also demonstrated a strong commitment to export promotion policies. A key legal foundation for this effort was "Section

301" of the Trade Act of 1974, which required the Office of the United States Trade Representative (USTR) to take all necessary measures to eliminate foreign policies, laws, or practices that violated international agreements or unjustifiably restricted US exports (CRS, 1974). The 1988 Omnibus Trade and Competitiveness Act, signed by President Reagan, reinforced this approach by introducing two new provisions—"Special 301" and "Super 301"—that further expanded the USTR's authority in protecting American exports (CRS, 1988).

The Reagan administration also promoted the strengthening of intellectual property rights, both internationally through the GATT and nationally with the Omnibus Trade and Competitiveness Act of 1988. The latter established greater power for US patent holders to block imports or claim compensation for damages from foreign companies that sell products made with processes patented in the United States. Furthermore, the Drug Price Competition and Patent Term Restoration Act of 1984 extended the duration of patents in the pharmaceutical field (ERP, 1989).

Another measure taken in an attempt to even out the American trade deficit was the signing of the 1985 Plaza Accords by the five largest industrialized countries (G-5). The nations agreed to bring down the value of the dollar by selling dollars in exchange for other currencies. The dollar had been increasing in value continuously, and the decrease in competitiveness by the United States was harming the trade balance. After this accord, the dollar was devalued by 40%, leading to a decrease in the trade deficit and decreasing the barriers for US exports. This helped prevent Congress from having to take more extensive protectionist measures and also established a closer financial relationship between the top industrialized nations that exists in the form of the G-7 today (Frankel, 2015).

As a whole, Reagan's commercial policy, which has firmly supported the American industry in the international context, adopted an approach that has been defined as aggressive unilateralism (Bingham, 1998). This definition describes a scenario in which the United States managed to reduce barriers to US exports and investments with countries that threatened competition with US goods on domestic and foreign markets. The United States forged aggressive unilateralism through negotiations with allied and politically weaker countries, leading to an aggressive policy that managed to shape agreements to the advantage of its own national industry through threats of retaliation and usually without any mutual concession (Niskanen, 1988; Bingham, 1998):

The administration stepped up pressure on other governments to open their markets to U.S. goods. The general tactic was to threaten limits on their exports to the United States in order to induce them to reduce their limits on U.S.

sales in their markets. The Reagan administration initiated ten such cases during its first term and 22 such cases after September 1985, when trade policy became markedly more aggressive. These measures had some success. Japan reduced or eliminated tariffs on aluminum products, cigarettes, and leather products, and substituted high tariffs for very restrictive quotas on beef and citrus. Korea reduced its barriers on U.S. movies and television programming. Taiwan opened its market to beer, wine, and cigarettes. Europe reduced restraints on imports of corn and citrus, and so on (Niskanen, 1988, p. 5).

5.4 Public Procurement and Incentives for Research and Development (R&D)

Operating in parallel with the direct management of commercial relations with the main competing countries, other measures continued to play an even more direct role in terms of protection and support to the suffering American industry during the years of the Reagan presidency. Among these, the development of science and technology was an important priority of the Reagan administration.

In this field, a variety of direct intervention tools were used. They include public funds for research in particular areas considered strategic for the national interest, funding for universities or public laboratories, policies for technological transfer, tax incentives for the private sector (i.e., tax credits), policies for the protection of intellectual property, and policies aimed at encouraging research cooperation between companies. Special attention was paid to basic research, which was largely commissioned to public and private universities and research centers (Economic Report of the President, 1988).

Public procurement practices—i.e., the government's purchase of goods and services from the private sector—continued to play a key role during the years of the Reagan administration. It was also a channel that could be "armored" thanks to the old Buy American Act,[4] to which US government agencies and companies could continue to appeal. The large volume of public demand encouraged the growth of companies that, in an environment protected by foreign competition, could benefit from economies of scale and learning (Weiss and Thurbon, 2006). In some cases, public orders were able to stimulate the emergence of new entrepreneurial endeavors that would then exploit, over time and even outside national borders, the advantages associated with their special relationship with the government.

---

[4] The Buy American Act, issued in 1933, was subject to subsequent adjustments that did not alter its underlying philosophy. See Luckey (2009) for more information.

In this context, the Department of Defense (DoD) continued to play a central role through the financing and purchase of private goods and services, an activity that continued to produce important spillovers by transferring new technology from the military to the civilian sector (Reich, 1982; Weiss, 2014). Over half of the Reagan administration's R&D funds were allocated to the DoD. In 1987, the defense sector absorbed 69% of total government spending on R&D, which amounted to 60 billion dollars, corresponding to almost half of the national budget (Economic Report of the President, 1988).

The DoD actively supported the machine tools and semiconductor industries, both of which were threatened by foreign competition, particularly from Europe and Japan. In 1986, supported by federal funding, a research consortium known as the National Center for Manufacturing Sciences sought to develop new production technologies in the field of machine tools (ERP, 1989). The activities of the center began with $10 million of financing from the Michigan Strategic Fund and then with an important $5 million order from the US Air Force.[5] In 1987, Semiconductor Manufacturing Technology Initiative (SEMATECH), a consortium of American semiconductor manufacturers and users, was born. SEMATECH started its activities in Austin, Texas collaborating with the University of Texas and counting on the presence of the Microelectronics & Computer Technology Corp, a consortium of 19 companies founded in 1983. SEMATECH received an initial $500 million five-year loan from DoD. In the following years, the consortium continued to be financed with public funds until 1996, when its mission was considered complete (ERP, 1989; Block, 2008; Wade, 2012; Di Tommaso and Schweitzer, 2013).[6]

Another DoD initiative was the Very High Speed Integrated Circuits (VHSIC) technology program during the 1980s. Launched in 1980 and beginning its first phase of technology development in 1981, the VHSIC program aimed to develop silicon integrated circuits for data and signal processing and to integrate those chips into military systems (U.S. Department of Defense, 1986; U.S. General Accounting Office, 1985). The goal was to remedy DoD's advanced tech procurement problems that hamstrung its ability to access cutting-edge commercial technologies leveraged by commercial sectors (U.S. Department of Defense, 1986). Within its first few years, the program expanded by providing direct subsidies to contractors to further accelerate tech development and ensure that it

---

[5] NCSM is still active today. In almost thirty years of activity, it has promoted collaboration agreements worth a total of $840 million of which: $455 million has been allocated by the DoD, $115 million by the DoC (Department of Commerce), $90 million to the DoE (Department of Energy) (see https://www.ncms.org).

[6] The activities continued even after the mid 1990s, when SEMATECH started a restructuring process that partly transformed its mission and organization, in particular: the International SEMATECH project started in 1996, which involved a selected number of foreign companies; the agreement with the State of New York and the Albany's College of Nanoscale Science and Engineering signed in 2003.

remained on schedule (U.S. General Accounting Office, 1985). Among the main contractors associated with the VHSIC program were Honeywell, Hughes Aircraft Company, IBM, Texas Instruments, TRW Automotive, and Westinghouse (U.S. General Accounting Office, 1985). While the project was beset by delays and inefficiencies, it did eventually boost yields and promote the integration of integrated circuits in military systems (U.S. Department of Defense, 1986; U.S. General Accounting Office, 1985). The subsidies and total expenditures ran well into the hundreds of millions of dollars, and perhaps more than $1 billion (U.S. General Accounting Office, 1985).

The words contained in the 1989 ERP show the impact of the DoD intervention on the national industry:

> The existence of NCMS and SEMATECH raises fundamental questions about the DoD's role in supporting civilian commercial technologies. The Department clearly needs semiconductors and advanced machine tools and, in special circumstances, may not want to rely on foreign suppliers. But DoD's demand for these products is only a small portion of the total market, and DoD alone does not need and cannot support a large domestic production base. Requiring DoD to provide R&D support for an industrial base larger than it needs, however, diverts its resources from military technologies that the private sector would never fund on its own (ERP, 1989, p. 248).

These words show a certain tension in the relationship between the supply and demand of policies. An administration that declares itself opposed to intervening in market dynamics faces a dilemma when it feels compelled to respond to commercial challenges with tangible actions. On the one hand, a national industry in crisis (mechanics and semiconductors in this case), which was clearly vulnerable to foreign competition, and a reality made of companies that asked for extraordinary interventions, support, and public funds. On the other hand, the military lobbies were prone to do their part as in the past, but not willing to be dragged too far toward objectives that threatened to weaken the national defense system.

With regard to R&D of military systems, the Reagan administration proposed the Strategic Defense Initiative (SDI). First announced in 1983, Reagan intended to leverage the nation's best and brightest scientists, engineers, and experts to build groundbreaking technologies that would collectively allow the United States to detect and destroy incoming Soviet intercontinental ballistic missiles as they fly toward their targets (Strategic Defense Initiative,1983). Reagan hoped that the SDI would help "render ballistic missiles impotent and obsolete," as he put it in a government report issued in January 1985 (Reagan, 1985). His critics, on the other hand, argued that the SDI's success could only be achieved with futuristic technology (earning it the derisive moniker "Star Wars"), that it would be needlessly expensive, that it would imprudently abandon Cold War deterrence, and that it would complicate negotiations with the Soviet Union. The SDI would have represented a dramatic break with the doctrine of mutually assured destruction and would upend or reorient US deterrence to a nonnuclear foundation in the context of Soviet arms buildup (Strategic Defense Initiative). Reagan described the SDI as follows:

The Strategic Defense Initiative (SDI) is a program of vigorous research focused on advanced defense technologies with the aim of finding ways to provide a better basis for deterring aggression, strengthening stability, and increasing the security of the United States and our allies. The SDI research program will provide to a future President and a future Congress the technical knowledge required to support a decision on whether to develop and later deploy advanced defense systems (Reagan, 1985).

He continued,

Through the SDI research program, I have called upon the great scientific talents of our country to turn to the cause of strengthening world peace by rendering ballistic missiles impotent and obsolete. In short, I propose to channel our technological prowess toward building a more secure and stable world. ... the quality of our future is at stake ... I would also ask you to consider the SDI research program in light of both the Soviet Union's extensive, ongoing efforts in this area and our own government's constitutional responsibility to provide for the common defense. I hope that you will conclude by lending your own strong and continuing support to this research effort—an effort which could prove to be critical to our nation's future (Reagan, 1985).

In other words, the SDI's goal was to funnel federal funds for the purposes of national defense and global security. This is a theme that recurs in the Reagan years and beyond: justifying government investments in industry on the grounds of military necessity.

Beyond the national defense sector, several other federal departments and agencies—including the Department of Energy, NASA, the National Science Foundation, and the National Institutes of Health—played a crucial role in advancing research and industrial development in the United States. Their approach to intervention followed a consistent pattern: these agencies commissioned universities and laboratories to conduct research in specialized fields, effectively extending government-led initiatives into the broader industrial landscape.

A crucial focus of policy efforts was facilitating technology transfer from government entities to the commercial sector. Prior to 1980, federal agencies commonly patented the results of research they funded, offering nonexclusive licenses to private companies for their use. However, demand for these nonexclusive licenses remained low. The passage of the 1980 Bayh-Dole Act (University and Small Business Patent Procedures Act) marked a turning point by allowing private universities, small businesses, and nonprofit institutions to claim exclusive ownership of patents derived from federally funded research, thereby establishing them as key players in commercializing innovation (Audretsch, 2003).

In 1983, the Reagan administration expanded these provisions to include public universities and nonprofit institutions, further strengthening the link between publicly funded research and private-sector development. As a result, the number of university-held patents surged from 230 in 1976 to approximately 900 by 1987 (ERP, 1989).

Several pivotal legislative measures further promoted technology transfer. The Technology Innovation Act of 1980 and the Federal Technology Transfer Act of 1986 enabled federal laboratories to establish research partnerships with private companies. Additionally, these laws allowed federal institutions to retain a portion of the royalties generated from private-sector use of government-funded research (ERP, 1989).

Science and technology policy was also advanced through incentives designed to stimulate private-sector investment in R&D. The Economic Recovery Tax Act of 1981 introduced a 25% tax credit for research expenditures that exceeded a company's average spending over the previous three years. Unlike a direct subsidy, this tax credit applied only to the increase in research investment rather than total R&D expenditures. However, its overall impact remained relatively modest. Originally set to expire in 1986, the tax credit was extended until 1989 under the Tax Reform Act of 1986, though at a reduced rate of 20% (ERP, 1989).

Private-sector research efforts were further incentivized through a more lenient antitrust policy, which allowed firms to benefit from economies of scale by engaging in collaborative research initiatives. The National Cooperative Research Act of 1984 fostered cooperation among researchers in the early stages of product development prior to commercialization in the market. To qualify for these antitrust exemptions, industrial research consortia were required to register with the Justice Department and the Federal Trade Commission. By the end of Reagan's presidency, more than 100 consortia had been established under this framework (ERP, 1989).

During the 1980s, several key programs were introduced to foster local economic development and support small businesses. Among them, the Small Business Innovation Research Program (SBIR), established in 1982, played a particularly significant role. This initiative created a consortium involving the Small Business Administration and multiple federal agencies, including the Department of Defense, the Department of Energy, and the Environmental Protection Agency. Under the program, these agencies were required to allocate a portion of their research budgets to fund projects led by small private companies. SBIR not only facilitated the growth of numerous innovative start-ups (Lerner, 1999; Audretsch, 2003; Mazzucato, 2013) but also played a crucial role in strengthening a broader innovation ecosystem. By fostering collaboration between local, state, and federal institutions, the program helped create a network capable of providing capital and strategic support for entrepreneurial ventures (Block, 2008; Weiss, 2008, 2014; Buigues and Sekkat, 2009; Schrank and Whitford, 2009; Block and Keller, 2011; Wade, 2012; Di Tommaso and Schweitzer, 2013; Mazzucato, 2013).

Another major initiative launched during this period was the Manufacturing Extension Partnership (MEP), introduced in 1988. Designed to enhance the productivity, competitiveness, and technological capabilities of small American businesses, the program established a network of state and local centers that provided companies with technical support, managerial guidance, and business development services (Shapira, 2001; Stone & Associates and Center for Regional and Economic Competitiveness, 2010).

Alongside these programs, the 1983 Orphan Drug Act was important for the innovation and growth of the biotechnology sector. The objective of the law was to provide incentives—i.e., subsidies—for the development of medicines for the treatment of "rare" diseases. The protection and support that the law provided to the companies of the sector proved to be decisive for increasing the innovative capacities of the entire pharmaceutical market, with the consequent emergence and consolidation of large companies, such as Genzyme, Biogen, Amgen, and Genentech (Lazonick and Tulum, 2011; Di Tommaso and Schweitzer, 2013; Mazzucato, 2013).

5.5 Final Remarks

Ronald Reagan's approach to industrial policy was driven by international factors including the Cold War, rising global competition from Japan and West Germany, and Middle East instability that drove up oil prices. These factors shaped both domestic concerns and the administration's response in light of Reagan's free-market ideas.

The Cold War was in full swing when President Reagan was elected, marked by the Soviet invasion of Afghanistan in December 1979. Although Reagan emphasized free-market principles, his decision to compete with the Soviet Union to ensure its collapse entailed a significant defense buildup, which included the promotion of advanced technology. Key industries that were essential to this task included aerospace, electronics, and computing, and the government provided defense contracts to these industries. In addition, greater competition from Japan, particularly in the auto sector and semiconductors led to efforts to restrict Japanese imports. The instability in the Middle East, in particular the Iran-Iraq war of 1979–1980, significantly pushed up oil prices, leading to efforts to promote alternative energy sources including nuclear power as well as deregulation to boost oil production.

These international factors deeply influenced the US economy negatively, with high inflation driven in part by oil prices. Indeed, Reagan's focus on "the misery index" that combined inflation and unemployment boosted his election prospects. From his perspective, a key domestic factor in this increasing index was excessive government spending and overregulation. Domestic constraints also included the strength of labor unions.

In terms of ideas, Reagan believed that the United States needed to defeat the "evil empire" of the Soviet Union and not continue to pursue a policy of détente. This meant that US allies needed to refrain from providing technology to the Soviet Union. Combined with a free-market philosophy that included supply-side economics, the type of industrial policy that Reagan sought was significantly different from his predecessors. But still, with international drivers, free-market principles gave way to support for significant defense spending, technology development, and trade restrictions.

Reagan's industrial policy sought to steer between his belief in allowing markets to freely operate on the one hand with the international and domestic constraints that his administration faced on the other. In particular, with an emphasis on competing with the Soviet Union, he emphasized defense-related industries and technologies. Major defense contractors such as Boeing, Lockheed Martin, and Raytheon were important beneficiaries of this largesse. Support for defense bolstered the South, which had fewer regulations and non-unionized labor. A key example of the need for increased government expenditure was his promotion of the SDI that was to be a space-based defense system—deviating sharply from the longstanding American (and Soviet) approach of deterrence. Other industries also proved to be beneficiaries of government largesse. These included companies in computing, telecommunications, and aerospace, such as IBM, Texas Instruments, and Lockheed Martin. The semiconductor industry in particular came closest to direct vertical industrial policy, with both a research consortium (SEMATECH) and pressure on the Japanese to promote US semiconductor exports.

The dramatic increase in competition from the Japanese autos in the wake of the 1973–1974 oil crisis, with their market share going over 20% of the US market also led to pressure to help this industry, leading Reagan to seek Voluntary Export Restraints from Japan. A similar logic applied to the steel industry, which had become uncompetitive over time despite trade restraints going back to 1968.

In agriculture, a perennially subsidized and protected industry, the 1980 grain embargo imposed on the Soviet Union by President Carter in 1980 (in response to the invasion of Afghanistan) reduced a major export market for US farmers. Demand for agricultural products also fell with a strong dollar driven by high interest rates to tackle inflation in the early 1980s.

With respect to tools and implementation, Reagan's administration eschewed direct vertical industrial policy support for the most part, but many of the specific trade and defense support measures clearly benefited specific industries. From a horizontal industrial policy perspective, consistent with his free-market philosophy, he emphasized deregulation as a means to improve US competitiveness.

The most important liberalization measure was no doubt the Economic Recovery Tax Act of 1981, that lowered personal income tax rates significantly and provided accelerated depreciation for capital investments, particularly benefiting industries like manufacturing and technology. Specifically, it gave companies a tax credit of 25% on the amount of research spending that exceeded the average level of spending over the previous three years. The 1986 Tax Reform Act also lowered the corporate tax rate from 46% to 34%. Accompanying lower taxes was the administration's effort to deregulate a host of sectors, including telecommunications and transportation.

In terms of more macro policy, it is worth noting that the 1985 Plaza Accord, which Reagan's administration supported, successfully led to the devaluation of the dollar, particularly against the Japanese yen, thereby making US exports cheaper.

With respect to trade policies, drawing on the president's foreign policy authorities and eschewing the need for Congressional approval, Reagan negotiated VERs with the Japanese on autos in 1981 to avoid facing pressures from the GATT that called for compensation if a country-imposed quotas. He was also able to negotiate VERs with the Japanese, Koreans, and the EEC among others, in light of steel companies filing cases under Section 201 of the Trade Act of 1974 and antidumping laws. Section 201 allowed industries to petition the government for relief if they could prove that imports were causing or threatening serious injury to a domestic industry. But as with autos, VERs avoided any oversight from the GATT that would have come with the use of quotas.

Reagan also strongly targeted the semiconductor industry, both through trade policy and a private-public partnership. The 1986 U.S.-Japan Semiconductor

Agreement called for greater access to the Japanese market for US semiconductor exports as well as preventing dumping of Japanese semiconductors. As with autos and steel, behind this agreement was the threat of US trade law, in this case Section 301 of the Trade Act of 1974, which allowed the United States to unilaterally launch investigations against countries engaging in a variety of "unfair" trading practices.

In addition to trade measures, the public-private SEMATECH Consortium (1987) was funded by both private companies and the government. It promoted R&D in semiconductor manufacturing, with the goal of enhancing the competitiveness of US chipmakers. The industry also benefited from DoD investments, including the Very High-Speed Integrated Circuit (VHSIC) initiative.

Finally, in agriculture, a traditionally heavily protected sector, the Reagan administration secured passage of the Food Security Act of 1985 aimed to stabilize farm income with price support mechanisms and loans. It also provided direct payments to farmers to offset losses caused by low market prices. To promote exports, the administration created the EEP (1985) to provide subsidies and credit guarantees to US exporters to help compete with heavily subsidized European agricultural products in foreign markets. In addition, the government pursued Section 301 measures to pressure countries such as Japan and groupings such as the EEC.

As expected, Reagan's industrial policies and deregulation efforts were enthusiastically supported by manufacturers and large corporations. More specifically, favored industries included defense contractors, agriculture, autos, steel, and technology industries. On a regional basis, states in the Sunbelt region, such as Texas, Florida, and California were supportive given the focus on technology, defense, and aerospace industries. In particular, R&D incentives benefited high-tech companies and start-ups in Silicon Valley.

Older industries such as automobiles and steel also were supportive, albeit not to the extent one might expect given the protectionist measures that Reagan pursued. The VER with Japan provided the auto sector with breathing room to restructure, but auto manufacturers were slow to adapt, and the VER encouraged Japanese automakers to upscale and threaten higher value-added luxury cars. Similarly, while the steel industry was pleased with the VERs they secured, they criticized the inability of the United States to prevent imports that circumvented the VERs by shifts in production to other countries or exporting semi-finished steel products. In addition to trade measures, their wish list included direct subsidies and support for comprehensive modernization programs.

Unions also proved less supportive than might have been anticipated. With layoffs continuing, they called for longer-term protection. Unions were also critical of the lack of efforts to promote modernization and workforce development. From their perspective, the United States needed to modernize steel mills with government assistance, expand training for workers, and invest in infrastructure to promote steel demand.

In the agricultural sector, small farmers were supportive of subsidies, but the high interest rates in the early 1980s as a result of tight monetary policy increased their debt burden. By contrast, agribusinesses were strongly supportive, as they were the primary beneficiaries of subsidies and price controls. They were also more likely to benefit from support for exports.

More generally, broad-based labor unions saw Reagan's policies as unfriendly to labor, with his focus on deregulation and tax cuts for the wealthy. His firing of striking union members in the 1981 Professional Air Traffic Controllers Organization strike created sharp tension with labor groups. Other groups, such as environmentalists and farmers also had grievances. Groups such as the Sierra Club and the Natural Resources Defense Council opposed Reagan's rollback of pollution standards and favoritism toward resource extraction industries.

Political support for opposition to Reagan and Republican priorities came from Democrats, who criticized his tax cuts and deregulatory measures, viewing them as "trickle-down" economics. They argued that these policies would increase income inequality and called for better support for the working class, education, and social welfare programs.

Reagan's industrial policy approach combined a pro-market, defense-focused, and deregulatory strategy with targeted sectoral policies.

6

The 1990s, George H. W. Bush and Bill Clinton

The United States in Command

6.1 Introduction

The 1990s, encompassing the administrations of George Bush and Bill Clinton, were critical in shaping the structure of the American economy. The collapse of the Soviet Union, ending the Cold War, gave the United States global political leadership that was undisputed and considered by many to be definitive (Fukuyama, 1992). In a euphoric atmosphere in which the majority of Americans felt proud to have won this war, the US government was well-positioned to benefit from the new global context.

For American industry, there was once again the possibility of moving the "frontier" and expanding markets. The American government, as it had done many times in the past, intervened by offering policy support to encourage entry into new markets. First of all, there were the satellite countries of the Soviet Union, suddenly left as political and economic orphans after 1990, changing the dynamic for these European countries. Moreover, a long list of developing countries that had gravitated around the Soviet bloc in their post-colonial period also found themselves in a new world. The United States could now look at developing new economic and political relations with these countries. These were also the years when a new accommodating relationship with China began to be tested, as China was beginning a slow but progressive process of openness and industrialization. The "frontier" of new markets could then move to Latin America and Africa, continents that had actually served as arenas for confrontation during the Cold War but now posed no major obstacles to American economic expansion. These regions served as easy outlets for the export of goods and services, as well as access to unique natural resources.

In this novel context, the Bush Senior (1989–1993) and Clinton (1993–2001) administrations demonstrated continuity in behavior and a common strategic line. The central instrument for the promotion of American industry in this decade was the signing of multilateral and bilateral agreements. This was the

Governing Growth. Marco R. Di Tommaso and Vinod K. Aggarwal, Oxford University Press.
© Oxford University Press (2026). DOI: 10.1093/oso/9780197821787.003.0006

channel that widened the expansion of markets and with which the government responded to the internal demand of companies, supporting a new phase of growth. These negotiations and important agreements, in the absence of overarching political leadership at the international level, allowed the United States to simultaneously penetrate new markets while protecting the domestic market from foreign imports.

During this period, the United States effectively defined the rules of international competition. Under American leadership, the conclusion of North American Free Trade Agreement (NAFTA) in 1995, Asia-Pacific Economic Cooperation (APEC) in 1989, and efforts to conclude a Free Trade Area of the Americas (FTAA) beginning in 1994 put pressure on countries to conclude the GATT Uruguay Round negotiations (Aggarwal, 2009a, p. 9). The newly created WTO in 1995 saw a movement away from trade only in goods to a focus on services, where the United States was highly competitive (Aggarwal, 1992), and the emergence of Trade-related Investment Measures (TRIMs) and Agreement on Trade-related Aspects of Intellectual Property Rights (TRIPs). These efforts were a continuation of the Reagan administration's emphasis on strengthening intellectual property rights with GATT and the Omnibus Trade and Competitiveness Act of 1988. The United States held the power to influence the behavior of a long list of foreign governments through anti-dumping measures and voluntary export restraints. Through its influence on the World Bank and the International Monetary Fund, the United States also oversaw the transition process of the former Soviet bloc and influenced the policies of developing countries.

Contrary to expectations, the end of the Cold War did not fundamentally alter the relationship of the government to the military-industrial complex. The reasons for the continuation of a special relationship were, in part, the same as in the past. First, the inertia of a relationship that had lasted for decades: the massive defense apparatus that had been built during the decades of "cold" confrontation with the Soviet bloc could not be dismantled in a few months, given the Soviet Union's rapid collapse. Projects, orders, and financing that linked the government to the defense industries extended over a medium- to long-term horizon. The relationship between the military-industrial complex and government had been at the center of the American economy for so long that it was difficult for it to be withdrawn. Just as at the end of WWI and WWII, there could have been a problem of industrial reconversion requiring significant time. However, this scenario did not arise. New dangers and emergencies were on the horizon and soon began to justify governments' continued investment in defense and security. Indeed, American military interventions in the 1990s were not lacking: the First Gulf War (1990–1991), Somalia (1992–1995), Haiti (1994–1995), Bosnia (1994–1995), and Kosovo (1998–1999). Subsequently, another decade of conflict unfolded: the war in Afghanistan (2001–2014), the Second Gulf War

(2003–2011), and the enduring war on terrorism which started soon after the attacks on the Twin Towers.

Finally, the 1990s were a decade in which the American government offered strong support to the national scientific research system. This intervention, partially driven by military demand, also followed independent dynamics. Such attention to research was justified as a response to market failures (Stiglitz, 1989; Chang, 1994; ERP, 1994) and a choice that was also framed as the desire to support specific strategic visions of what the government believed to be the future of the national industry (Eisinger, 1990; Chang, 1994; Di Tommaso and Giovannelli, 2006; Di Tommaso and Schweitzer, 2013).

6.2 The WTO and International Agreements

The objectives and instruments of the new phase were clear. As stated in the 1990 ERP:

> As global integration advances and competition intensifies, the United States must increase its efforts to lead the world toward a system of free trade and open markets. The Administration remains strongly committed to those efforts and staunchly opposed to managed trade. That commitment means actively removing trade barriers and resisting inevitable calls for protection – thereby opening markets, not closing them. The President's highest priority in trade policy is to further the role of the General Agreement on Tariffs and Trade (GATT) as a rules-based system for liberalizing trade and settling trade disputes (ERP, 1990, p. 30).

Showing an evident continuity, the path established by Bush (1989–1993) was later reaffirmed by the Clinton administration (1994–2001):

> This Administration, like its predecessors, has responded to these changes by pursuing liberalization and the promotion of exports at a variety of negotiating levels. The American approach has been of nondiscrimination: negotiated reductions in trade barriers should apply to all trading nations; individual nations should not cut deals that benefit themselves at the expense of others (ERP, 1995, p. 203).

One of the most important multilateral initiatives was the creation of the WTO in 1995. This accord was negotiated in the Uruguay Round which began in 1986 and involved 123 countries across three administrations (Reagan, Bush, and Clinton). The Uruguay Round negotiations pursued three main objectives: the reduction of barriers to trade, the extension and adaptation of GATT rules to new sectors, and the enhancement of the dispute settlement mechanism. Two extensions to the scope of the GATT stood out: the regulation of foreign investment (TRIMS) and the protection of intellectual property (TRIPS). Among the other notable points in the WTO were quality standards for homogeneous products, the regulation of special safeguard measures (such as voluntary export restraints and antidumping measures), as well as the creation of the Dispute Settlement Body (ERP, 1991; ERP, 1995; Greenaway, 1992; Shenkin, 1994).

Within this multilateral context, special "safeguard measures" under GATT were often invoked, enabling countries to temporarily restrict imports and adapt their national industries to the new competitive environment. However, difficulties in challenging improper foreign use of these measures discouraged these practices, instead encouraging the emergence of bilateral agreements on the limitations of imports that were more easily controlled. In many circumstances, the United States used these agreements to its own advantage (e.g., Voluntary Export Agreements) (Aggarwal et al., 1987).

The birth of the WTO, along with other trade agreements signed in those years, gradually imposed restrictions on member countries regarding government intervention in the economy, establishing a uniform framework of rules at the international level. This strongly discouraged any industrial policy interventions aimed at supporting and defending national industries (Pack and Saggi, 2006). The United States demanded that all countries in multilateral and bilateral negotiations comply with these rules, regardless of a country's historical context or industrial capacity.

The creation of the WTO aroused worrying resistance. Some argued that US sovereignty would be impaired by the WTO (ERP, 1995, p. 212). The issue was how to protect the United States from international rules that in some specific circumstances could go against the American national interest. This was the case, for example, with the acceptance of deregulation processes that envisaged the adoption of less stringent health and safety standards than those in the United States.

In reality, the procedures for implementing international rules would in no way have harmed American sovereignty (ERP, 1995). The trade agreements established within the WTO had no legal force in the United States without implementing legislation. Moreover, the US government, if it deemed it necessary, could always refrain from applying certain international rules by offering compensation for liberalization in other areas, or accepting trade barriers to US exports in areas of interest to other countries (ERP, 1995).

6.3 International Disputes on Public Procurements

With hegemonic power in defining international rules, a key issue was the creation of rules on government or public procurement. It was a powerful tool that, as in the past, continued to allow the US government to promote national industrial development and to protect certain sectors of its economy. Moreover, in the new international context, it seemed more than possible for American companies to capture significant portions of foreign public demand. This was particularly evident in the liberalization and privatization programs that in recent years involved a long list of countries in transition and developing countries under the guidance of the World Bank and the International Monetary Fund. It was a process that revolutionized the prospects and expectations of many American companies. Governments in Eastern Europe and many developing countries were induced to sell their public companies and outsource production and services, a process of substantial scale from which American companies, supported by government agencies and diplomatic channels, drew huge profits.[1]

The process aiming to liberalize the international public procurement market actually started at the end of the 1960s as part of the GATT rounds. The agreement was initially signed by the United States, Canada, fifteen Member States of the European Union, Japan, Israel, Korea, Norway, and Switzerland (Hoekman and Mavroidis, 1997; Trionfetti, 2000). The first two Government Procurement Agreements (GPAs) entered into force in 1981 and 1988, respectively. However, the most significant regulations emerged from the negotiations between 1986 to 1994 within the Uruguay Round which led to the signature of the WTO GPA 1994 which came into force in 1996. Resolving the issue of discrimination against foreign companies in accessing public procurement markets—which has still not been fully resolved—was particularly tortuous during the 1990s, leaving significant room for bilateral disputes and agreements.[2]

Simply put, although the establishment of the WTO occurred in a formally multilateral climate, as the main political, military, and economic power of the time, the United States held a significant position of power. Negotiations

---

[1] The United States Agency for International Development (USAID) has played an important role in this process. There was a bond that created between the American industry and privatizations, for example in Eastern Europe: "In Hungary and Czechoslovakia, USAID provided support for privatization with interested foreign acquirers. USAID funded teams of International Executive Service Corps volunteers and investment bankers to work with state property agencies to prepare large enterprises for sale and negotiate those with individual foreign buyers. Preparation included identifying companies the government had decided to sell, valuation, negotiation of starting price, and managing the information disclosure process" (USAID 2013).Page: 6

[2] As we will discuss later, the Buy American Act was also repeated in the stimulus package implemented by Obama in 2009 in response to the crisis, raising significant criticism (Hufbauer and Schott, 2009).Page: 7

consistently managed to safeguard and support the interests of the American economy and industry. The agreements that the United States pursued were often driven by heavy lobbying by industries, with a key example being the role of pharmaceutical companies and service sector industries (Aggarwal, 1992). As the 1995 ERP noted:

> Although the principle of one country, one vote has always characterized the GATT, in fact GATT votes were almost never taken; decisions were reached on the basis of consensus among members. In practice, the United States has always had a major influence over the course of GATT policy, not because it has had a larger formal vote but, in baldest terms, because it brought the largest market to the table. (ERP, 1995, pp. 212–213).

The "commercial war" between the United States and the European Union that began in the early 1990s serves as a notable example of trade tensions. In 1993, the EU Public Procurement Directive required Member States to apply a 3% price preference for European suppliers, disadvantaging third-country competitors. The United States immediately viewed this measure as discriminatory. In response, the US government invoked Title VII of the 1988 Omnibus Trade and Competitiveness Act, unilaterally imposing sanctions on eleven European Community states that had implemented the directive. These sanctions targeted procurement contracts for goods, services, and construction projects below specific value thresholds, as well as all service contracts awarded by the Tennessee Valley Authority and the Power Marketing Administrations of the Department of Energy. Additionally, the sanctions applied to fourteen service categories procured by federal agencies, including broadcasting, R&D, legal services, healthcare, and telecommunications. The European Community, in turn, retaliated with equivalent countermeasures against the United States.[3]

In reality, the regulation on public procurement envisaged in the WTO-GPA framework left individual states a wide margin of autonomy in implementing national public procurement programs that could continue to discriminate against foreign suppliers. Countries could therefore exploit the margins of this discretion depending on their international political weight. In this context, the United States evidently had unique advantages. International regulation offered the opportunity for the United States to use more influence than others in order to obtain the opening of foreign procurement markets without ever being forced to truly open its own market. In essence, it was a matter of either applying the

---

[3] See the Regulation (EEC) No 1461/93 of the Council (OJ L 146, June 17, 1993). Sanctions on public procurement remained in force for both parties until 2006. See also the Proposal for Regulation (EC) by the Council repealing the Regulation (EEC) No 1461/93 concerning the access to public procurement by candidates and tenderers from the United States.

provisions of the WTO-GPA rules or undertaking bilateral negotiation routes to obtain, thanks to their political weight, agreements that were advantageous for American industry. These same instruments and the same discretion in their application allowed the US government to restrict foreign access to its domestic procurement market in many circumstances (Weiss and Thurbon, 2006).

The US approach to the GPA proved to be a very powerful industrial policy instrument that served two functions: support for national industry to penetrate foreign markets and protection of the domestic market from foreign competition. American international political leadership translated into economic advantages for the national industry. Liberalizing international procurement meant that the United States could win the public demand for a long list of friendly countries without significant fear of foreign companies entering its domestic market (Weiss and Thurbon, 2006).

6.4 NAFTA and Other Important Regional Agreements

Among the regional commercial policy initiatives undertaken by the United States, the most important was NAFTA involving the United States, Canada, and Mexico. The signing of NAFTA, framed in the long run, is nothing but an additional step in the ongoing process of expanding the "frontier" which has been repeatedly referred to. From this perspective, extending the market toward Canada and Mexico was a natural progression and a strategic goal for American industry.

The US government had engaged in the process of extension and enlargement for some time. Several years passed from the first proposals to the entry into force of the treaty. At the beginning of his first term, President Reagan publicly proposed the idea of a "North American Agreement." After years of negotiations, the United States-Canada Free Trade Agreement was signed in 1988. Following this agreement, Mexico's involvement was discussed during long trilateral negotiations. Eventually, NAFTA was signed by President Bush in 1992, a few days before the end of his term (Aggarwal, 1994). In 1993, the Clinton administration ratified the agreement and integrated some subsidiary agreements, particularly concerning work and environmental standards. NAFTA, along with its subsidiary agreements, officially came into force on January 1, 1994.

President Clinton, like his predecessor, saw NAFTA as beneficial for the American economy:

> I believe that NAFTA will create 200,000 American jobs in the first 2 years of its effect. I believe if you look at the trends—and President Bush and I were talking about it this morning—starting about the time he was elected President, over

one-third of our economic growth and in some years over one-half of our net new jobs came directly from exports. [. . .] I believe that NAFTA will create a million jobs in the first 5 years of its impact. [. . .] NAFTA will generate these jobs by fostering an export boom to Mexico, by tearing down tariff walls which have been lowered quite a bit by the present administration of President Salinas but are still higher than Americas'. Already Mexican consumers buy more per capita from the United States than other consumers in other nations. Most Americans don't know this, but the average Mexican citizen, even though wages are much lower in Mexico, the average Mexican citizen is now spending $450 per year per person to buy American goods (Remarks by President Clinton, President Bush, President Carter, President Ford, and Vice President Gore in Signing of NAFTA Side Agreements, 1993).

Labor unions, on the other hand, became the fiercest opposing coalition against NAFTA, fearing that the trade agreement would lead companies seeking lower production costs to move factory operations to Mexico, resulting in manufacturing job losses in the United States and heavy wage stagnation. In response to NAFTA, union members staged massive demonstrations around the country, protesting in front of the Capitol in Washington and in other major industrial states (Gonyea, 2013).

One key issue that was addressed in the negotiations leading up to the establishment of NAFTA was the phased elimination of most trade barriers (both tariff and non-tariff) over ten years for industrial goods and fifteen years for agricultural goods. NAFTA also introduced common investment rules, liberalization of the financial sector, improved land transport and telecommunication services, and reinforced labor and environmental laws. Furthermore, in 1993, the Clinton Administration incorporated subsidiary agreements that established a dispute resolution mechanism and a system for protecting intellectual property rights into the final treaty.

However, there were concerns over possible economic instability caused by the increased imports from Mexico and Canada, prompting measures to facilitate structural adjustments to the US economy. Thus, safeguards were put in place to temporarily restrict imports that posed a significant threat. The Transitional Adjustment Assistance (TAA) program was introduced to support affected workers, offering employment and training services, unemployment benefits, and relocation allowances. In 1994, the NAFTA-TAA program provided aid to approximately 12,000 workers (ERP, 1995).

While Canada and Mexico were immediate targets in America's expansion strategies, administrations in the 1990s aimed to extend the "frontier" further. In addition to NAFTA, the United States undertook several other regional liberalization initiatives, focusing on Asia, the Pacific, and Latin America.

In the East, APEC was established with the Pacific Economic Cooperation Council playing a key driving role, aimed at promoting Asia-Pacific economic cooperation (Aggarwal, 1993, 1994; Ravenhill, 2000). Initially created in 1989 with only twelve countries involved, APEC's activities began with a series of interlocutor meetings. While the Bush administration saw little progress, Clinton viewed Asia as a strategic priority for the economic interests of the United States and had significant interest in the project. By the time of the Clinton administration, APEC had expanded to eighteen members, including China, Singapore, South Korea, Malaysia, and Thailand.

APEC was viewed as a key forum to address trade and economic challenges in the region, which at the time represented about 30% of world trade, as well as a spur to the European Union to conclude the Uruguay Round. The APEC agenda was driven in large part by American corporate interests. With its rapid growth, Asia represented a key frontier. The first APEC summit was held in 1993 in the state of Washington and was enthusiastically promoted by the Clinton administration. In his inaugural speech, we find the motivations that led President Clinton to invest politically in the APEC project, alongside the American industry:

> [C]reating jobs and opportunities for our people at home requires us to be engaged abroad, so that we can open foreign markets to our exports and our businesses. [...] [T]he growth of Asia can and should benefit our Nation. Over the past 5 years, our exports to every one of these nations has increased by at least 50 percent. Much of what Asia needs to continue on its growth pattern are goods and services in which we are strong: aircraft, financial services, telecommunications, infrastructure, and others. [...] (Clinton, 1993).

President Clinton was determined to build a new community of government representatives (which excluded Europe, with which negotiations were held at other venues) that would serve a transnational community of corporations centered around American economic and commercial interests. One of the first American proposals was "the formation of an Asia-Pacific business roundtable to promote greater discussion within the region's private sectors" (Clinton, 1993), which came to be known as APEC Business Advisory Council (ABAC).

The APEC community continued its efforts toward economic integration with a second summit in 1994 in Bogor, Indonesia, where leaders adopted the Bogor Goals, committing to free and open trade and investment by 2010 for developed economies and by 2020 for developing economies. This marked a significant milestone in APEC's evolution, setting a long-term vision for trade liberalization in the Asia-Pacific region (Aggarwal, 2000).

Building on this momentum, APEC held its third summit in 1996 in Osaka, Japan, where members formulated the Osaka Action Agenda to outline concrete steps toward achieving the Bogor Goals. The agenda aimed to facilitate market access by addressing quotas and tariffs, services, investment regulations, competition policies, and deregulation. It emphasized voluntary, non-binding commitments based on "concerted unilateralism," allowing economies to liberalize at their own pace while maintaining collective progress (ERP, 1996).

APEC's approach to trade liberalization was unique compared to formal trade agreements such as NAFTA or the WTO, as it relied on consensus-based decision-making rather than legally binding commitments (Aggarwal, 1994). This flexibility helped accommodate the diverse economic conditions of its members, ranging from highly developed economiès like the United States and Japan to developing nations in Southeast Asia.

The work plan laid out in the Osaka Action Agenda was explicit and direct:

The principles embodied in the Action Agenda ensure that liberalization in each country will be comprehensive, covering all products, services, and investment, and require each country to achieve results that are balanced and comparable to those of other APEC members (ERP, 1996, p. 242).

Beyond Asia, Clinton's strategy also envisaged concentrating on another area of the world: Latin America. The Free Trade Area of the Americas (FTAA), launched by Clinton in December 1994 in Miami, was an ambitious initiative that aimed at establishing a free-trade area between the countries of the Western Hemisphere, with thirty-three countries participating in this first Summit of the Americas (Aggarwal, 2009b).

As stated in the joint declaration by the governments participating in the Summit, the central idea behind the FTAA was that the promotion of prosperity (of all participating countries) could be achieved through economic integration and free trade:

A key to prosperity is trade without barriers, without subsidies, without unfair practices, and with an increasing stream of productive investments. Eliminating impediments to market access for goods and services among our countries will foster our economic growth (First Summit of the Americas: Declaration of Principles, 1994).

Free trade and economic integration between the countries of the American continent were also expected to foster improvements in living standards, working conditions, and environmental protection (First Summit of the Americas: Declaration of Principles, 1994). The US government sought to focus on a growth path driven by the ability of American companies to expand into foreign markets. Thus, the Clinton government was prepared to play its part in Latin America as well:

> We must in the United States not only create jobs but raise incomes. And we can only do that if we train people for higher wage jobs and if we create those jobs. One of the only ways we can create those jobs is to expand trade, especially in this hemisphere. So that's why every American worker in every part of the United States should be glad we are all here today at the Summit of the Americas (Clinton, 1994).

Even more explicitly, Clinton outlined the numbers that highlighted the importance of this initiative for American industry and trade unions:

> Latin America is already the fastest growing region in the world for American exports. Of every dollar Latin Americans spend on exports, 44 cents buy goods made in the USA. Despite trade barriers that are, on average, 4 times higher than ours, Florida alone sold almost $9 billion worth of goods in the Americas in last year alone. And by the year 2005, if current trends continue, our country will sell more to Latin America than to Western Europe or Japan. That's why we're here. That's an investment worth making. Creating a free trade area would be good news throughout the Americas. Here in the United States, our exports to Latin America could literally double by the year 2005. That would create over one million new jobs (Clinton, 1994).

President Clinton was determined to move forward in this direction and the benefits the United States could draw from the FTAA are clearly included in the 1996 Economic Report of the President:

> The United States should reap significant benefits from the establishment of the FTAA. It will create a market of over 850 million consumers with a combined income of roughly $13 trillion. [. . .] The FTAA will also level the playing field for U.S. exporters, reducing Latin American trade barriers that are currently three times higher on average than U.S. barriers (ERP, 1996, p. 241).

Following President Clinton's endorsement, efforts to establish the FTAA gained momentum, with the goal of creating a transregional accord by 2005. A series of high-profile summits and ministerial meetings were convened to negotiate the terms and framework of the proposed agreement. The initiative formally began at the 1994 Summit of the Americas in Miami, where leaders from thirty-four countries agreed to work toward a hemispheric free-trade zone.

Key summits included Santiago (1998), Quebec City (2001), Monterrey (2004), and Mar del Plata (2005), each aimed at refining the FTAA's structure and scope. Parallel to these summits, trade ministers engaged in negotiations through ministerial meetings in Denver (1995), Cartagena (1996), Belo Horizonte (1997), San Jose (1998), Toronto (1999), Buenos Aires (2001), Quito (2002), and Miami (2003). These meetings sought to resolve contentious trade issues and deepen economic cooperation across North and South America.

To facilitate negotiations, permanent working groups were established to focus on key trade policy areas, including agriculture, government procurement, investment, competition policy, intellectual property rights, services, dispute resolution, subsidies, anti-dumping, and countervailing duties. Discussions centered on eliminating tariff and non-tariff barriers, reforming and harmonizing customs procedures, promoting investment, and standardizing technical and health regulations. A crucial aspect of the negotiations involved reconciling existing sub-regional trade agreements—such as NAFTA, MERCOSUR (Southern Common Market (Mercosur; Spanish: *Mercado Común del Sur*), the Andean Community, and the Caribbean Community (CARICOM)—to create a cohesive and comprehensive Pan-American free-trade area (ERP, 1996).[4]

Despite significant progress, the FTAA faced growing opposition from several Latin American countries, particularly Brazil, Argentina, and Venezuela, which argued that the agreement disproportionately favored US interests while limiting their ability to protect domestic industries. Disputes over agricultural subsidies, labor and environmental standards, and dispute resolution mechanisms further stalled negotiations. By the 2005 Mar del Plata Summit, the initiative had largely collapsed, with left-leaning governments in Latin America pushing for alternative trade frameworks such as the Bolivarian Alliance for the Peoples of Our America (ALBA) and reinforcing regional blocs like MERCOSUR (Schott, 2004).

While the FTAA never came to fruition, its negotiations influenced subsequent trade agreements, including bilateral free-trade deals between the United States and Latin American countries (e.g., CAFTA-DR, US-Chile FTA, and US-Peru FTA), as well as broader economic cooperation initiatives within the Organization of American States (OAS) and the Inter-American Development Bank (IDB).

6.5 Support to Economies in Transition

The Bush administration's primary objective in the transition of former Soviet bloc countries' markets was to ensure support for economic growth and international market openness. "A renewed commitment to open markets and

---

[4] See Aggarwal (1998) on nesting smaller regional arrangements in larger ones. Page: 17

policies that encourage competitive and undistorted markets and greater productivity are keys to growth—for both industrial countries and economies in transition" (ERP, 1992, p. 233).

Support for countries in transition was driven by ideals linked to freedom, opposition to tyranny, and the promotion of democracy. The longest war of the century was over, and the United States had once again won by defeating totalitarianism. This led to a period of "reconstruction," with the fall of the Berlin Wall symbolizing a shift in the "frontier" of the reference markets for American industry. In President Bush's rhetoric, assistance and business merged into one path:

> The advance of democratic ideals reflects a hard-nosed sense of our own, of American self-interest. [. . .] the global spread of free markets, by encouraging trade, investment, and growth, will sustain the expansion of American prosperity. In short, by helping others, we help ourselves (Bush, 1992).

The Bush administration pursued important bilateral initiatives with the so-called transitional economies to complement the multilateral negotiations undertaken within the Uruguay Round, aimed at opening up and liberalizing markets. These include the Trade Enhancement Initiative for Central and Eastern Europe, the Andean Trade Preference Initiative—which involved Bolivia, Colombia, Ecuador, and Peru—and the Enterprise for the Americas Initiative (ERP, 1992; Trade Enhancement Initiative for Central and Eastern Europe, 1991).

In the following years, the Clinton administration continued this approach, and the United States assumed a central role in guiding the transition of former Soviet bloc economies toward market economies. Consistent with the preceding Reagan and Bush administrations, the Clinton administration recognized the US international leadership in those years and pledged to spread the American economic model globally. This strategy aligned perfectly with the goals of supporting American industrial growth. The 1997 ERP states:

> We are looked to for leadership in part because our economy remains the largest in the world, and in part because we are the sole remaining superpower. How do we intend to exercise that leadership? Among the most important objectives of U.S. economic policy are to ensure that the United States itself benefits fully from the integration of these emerging markets into a globalized economy (ERP, 1997, p. 257).

Already by 1990, the United States developed a plan to support the economic and political transition of Eastern Europe after the collapse of communist regimes.

The Support for Eastern European Democracy Act of 1989 allocated $944 million in grants and over $1 billion in additional assistance to programs in order to facilitate market reforms, economic stabilization, and democratic institution-building in former Soviet countries (United States Congress, 1989).

Along with direct financial assistance, the United States also committed $200 million to help individuals privatize, such as through technical assistance programs, management training, market economics education, privatization efforts, legal and financial sector reforms, and the strengthening of democratic institutions. Emergency aid, such as food aid, was also another critical component of American intervention. $260 million was allocated for emergency food supplies, including $112 million directly for Romania as one of the hardest-hit nations during the transition to a market economy (Haggard and Kaufman, 1995).

In terms of broader multilateral assistance for Eastern European economies, the United States leveraged its influence over international financial institutions. In 1991, the IMF allocated $5 billion in structural adjustment loans, while the World Bank committed $9 billion in development financing between 1991 and 1994. Between 1991 and 1996, the European Bank for Reconstruction and Development (EBRD) provided $7 billion in loans focusing on infrastructure development, financial sector reform, and support for small and medium-sized enterprises (White House, 1991; EBRD, 1996).

The end goal of this financial technical assistance by the United States and other Western nations was to integrate Eastern Europe into global markets and democratic frameworks. These efforts were complemented by the European initiatives, like the PHARE (Poland and Hungary: Assistance for Restructuring their Economies) program, which provided funding for institutional and economic forms in post-communist states (Grabbe, 2006). Some nations such as Poland and Hungary rapidly adapted to market economies, while others such as Romania and Bulgaria faced prolonged economic struggles due to slower institutional reforms and political stability. This made measuring the success of these interventions harder (Bideleux and Jeffries, 1998). The US intervention in Eastern Europe during the early 1990s set the foundation for the area's integration into Western political and economic structures as well as laid the groundwork for the NATO and EU enlargement that would follow in the late 1990s and early 2000s.

In this context, the Russian case warrants a brief investigation. Concessions of financial aid,[5] privatization, and liberalization were dangerous dynamics in a country that had lost the Cold War and had been hit by a sudden wave of dramatic political, social, and economic changes. Russia had to transition to a

---

[5] In 1992, USAID granted approximately $2 billion to Russia with the Freedom Support Act (ERP, 1997).

market economy in the context of being on the brink of civil war. However, these challenges presented unique profit opportunities for industry, banks, and foreign consultancies. The United States, under these circumstances, was especially concerned about the management of nuclear arsenals, the weakness of the government, and supporting American industry to fully exploit the collapse of the Soviet system (Rice, 2000; Sakwa, 2008).

During this period, Russia remained in a precarious balance for a sustained period of time. Substantial opportunities for profit, institutional vacuums, and political turmoil facilitated the rise of a class of powerful new oligarchs who began doing business with American and European entrepreneurs, consultants, and investors. Unlike what happened at the end of World War II with Germany, Japan, and Italy, the United States opted against investing in the growth of a new national ruling class or launching a new Marshall Plan. The United States, first with Bush and then with Clinton, decided to settle for Yeltsin, which guaranteed reasonable control of nuclear arsenals and acceptable prospects for political stability (Rice, 2000; Sakwa, 2008). At the same time, American companies, banks, and consultants were left free to pursue business with an emerging economic class composed largely of former state managers, members of the KGB, and party officials (Dunlop, 1993).

6.6 The Debt Crisis and Aid to Developing Countries

The United States played a central role in managing the Third World debt crisis of the 1980s and 1990s, something that would completely reshape economic policies in many developing countries. The debt crisis had its roots in the mid 1980s, when developing countries, particularly in Latin America, Africa, and Asia, borrowed extensively from major international banks. Many of these banks were American institutions, like Citibank, Chase Manhattan, and Bank of America as the OPEX price increases created large surpluses that ended up in international banks. These loans were then used to finance infrastructure, industrialization, and social programs instead of generating revenue that could service the debts (Aggarwal, 1987, 1996). At the beginning of the 1980s, the situation changed dramatically when, during the Reagan administration, interest rates skyrocketed due to the US Federal Reserve's aggressive tightening of monetary policy using the so-called "Volcker shock" to combat stagflation. Many debtor nations found themselves unable to meet their repayment obligations as the cost of borrowing soared on variable interest rate loans. The crisis truly erupted in 1982 when Mexico declared that it could no longer service its debt, which then triggered panic across international financial markets. More nations followed suit afterwards as Brazil, Argentina, and other highly indebted countries sought urgent financial relief (Aggarwal, 1987).

In response, the American and other Western commercial banks holding a substantial portion of developed countries' debt started taking measures to avoid a financial collapse. They began strengthening their capital reserves, increasing provisions for bad loans, and reducing new lending to developed nations. This created a credit crunch for debtor nations and exacerbated economic conditions, leading to stagnation, hyperinflation, and unemployment (Sachs, 1989).

The United States and other international institutions took a more interventionist approach to prevent a full-scale disaster. They promoted debt rescheduling and restructuring as a strategy for crisis management. According to Aggarwal (1996), the debt rescheduling negotiations become complex strategic interactions between creditor and debtor nations. Each side was attempting to minimize its losses while ensuring continued access to global capital markets. The United States, along with the IMF and the World Bank, imposed structural adjustment programs that required debtor nations to implement austerity measures such as cuts to social spending as well as trade liberalization, currency devaluation, and privatization of conditions for new loans or rescheduled debt payments (Williamson, 1994).

Several initiatives were launched to address this crisis. The first was the Baker Plan (1985), which was spearheaded by the US Treasury Secretary James Baker. This plan sought to promote economic growth by encouraging new lending to highly indebted middle-income countries. This plan largely failed, however, due to continued instability and a lack of investor confidence (Aggarwal, 1996). Another was the 1989 Brady Plan which was introduced by then-Treasury Secretary Nicholas Brady. The Brady Plan shifted the strategy by advocating debt reduction rather than just debt rescheduling. This allowed for the conversion of blank loans into tradable bonds with guarantees, which provided debtor nations with a more sustainable long-term solution. The IMF and the World Bank supported this initiative, and it proved more successful than previous attempts at mitigating the debt crisis, providing the foundation for debt restructuring in Latin America and beyond (New York Times, 1989; Aggarwal, 1996).

Aggarwal (1996) notes that these debt negotiations did not just include economic decisions, but also political and strategic calculations. With the United States playing a dominant role in shaping the terms of debt relief, the United States' influence over global financial institutions and emerging markets was maintained while also ensuring that financial stability was restored. On one hand, by the late 1990s, many debtor countries had managed to reschedule or reduce their debts which led to renewed economic growth for some nations. But the legacy of austerity measures and IMF-imposed reforms remained controversial as they often resulted in rising inequality, social unrest, and long-term dependency on foreign capital (Stiglitz, 2002).

The Latin American debt crisis transformed the landscape of international finance while reinforcing the dominance of the US-led financial institutions and changing the ways developing countries approached sovereign debt management and economic policy.

Regarding developing countries in general, the Clinton administration authorized $6.7 billion in aid in 1996. A 10% increase was then requested in the 1998 budget. The main aid strategy of the 1990s was to direct aid toward specific states (i.e., Egypt, Israel, Ethiopia, Haiti, India) and priority regions (i.e., sub-Saharan Africa and Latin America) (ERP, 1997). However, aid to developing countries often did not produce the anticipated outcomes and as Stiglitz (2002) notes, such policies often had not just neutral or slightly positive effects, but had negative effects given the lack of developing countries' competitiveness in the global market economy (Saad-Filho, 2005).

That said, here we are interested in highlighting the impact of these policies on the United States. Regardless of whether these interventions provided any benefits to the recipient countries, there is no doubt that these policies yielded returns for the American economy and industry—a goal pursued consistently by the Reagan, Bush, and Clinton administrations. In line with Bush, Clinton also believed that the United States ought to provide aid to the development of the poorest countries as it served the interests of American companies:

> When our aid helps countries grow, we benefit from increased exports. For example, 20 countries have achieved a sufficient level of development to graduate from lending programs of the International Development Association (the World Bank affiliate that lends to the poorest countries on a concessional basis). These countries bought $61 billion in U.S. exports in 1995, or 6.3% of our total exports. And by deepening our economic relationship with developing countries through aid, we also make it more likely that they will turn to U.S. firms for products in the future (ERP, 1997, pp. 260–261).

6.7 China and Japan

In 1978, under Deng Xiaoping, China began the long process of change and opening: a process of continuous, slow, and relentless structural change in the Chinese economy and society which, over three decades, reshaped the global industrial geography and more generally, the current geopolitical balance (Di Tommaso et al., 2013).

In fact, China's transformation owes much to its special relationship with the United States over time—a relationship that has been politically tense at times. Until the Trump administration, the relationship between the United States and China was solid, adapting to new economic and political conditions. It was a relationship that grew in light of substantial complementarity, where each country's structural changes supported those of the other. In other words, while the two countries continued to challenge each other on different political fronts, they actually shared an interest at the time of China's gradual but radical economic opening.

The centrality of this relationship was already evident in the early 1970s, when President Nixon personally decided to reopen diplomatic ties between the two countries:

> This was the week that changed the world, as what we have said in that Communique is not nearly as important as what we will do in the years ahead to build a bridge across 16,000 miles and 22 years of hostilities which have divided us in the past. And what we have said today is that we shall build that bridge (Nixon Goes to China, 1972).

However, it took another ten years for a second visit by an American president to China. In 1984, Reagan took a significant step toward reopening relations between the two countries. By then, China's process of change and industrialization had successfully taken its first steps, and the United States had become its primary political and economic partner. The complexities of the Cold War, particularly issues related to Taiwan, limited further political progress. Nevertheless, American businesses and capital had already identified extraordinary opportunities to grow in China. The entry into China marked one of the most important "frontier movements" to which the American industry would have dedicated itself in the decades to come.

During the 1990s, China's industrialization began accelerating at an unprecedented rate amid political and economic transformations, pushing the United States to finally engage in substantive trade negotiations with China. This was despite the temporary stall in the US-China relations caused by the 1989 Tiananmen Square crackdown. It was during this diplomatic strain that the George H. W. Bush administration initiated the first significant bilateral agreement. Despite domestic criticism, the administration based its approach on the belief that engagement with China was a strategic imperative for global economic stability and long-term US interests (Foot, 1995).

A major milestone in establishing economic relations with China came in October 1992 Market Access Agreement, which the US government presented as a means to expand American export opportunities (ERP, 1993). This agreement facilitated the entry of US goods into Chinese markets by removing the export restrictions on hundreds of products, simultaneously setting the stage for a deeper economic relationship. While on one hand Americans framed the deal as a win for US businesses, it also reflected China's desire, under Deng Xiaoping's "reform and opening-up" policies (改革开放), to integrate into global trade networks (Fewsmith, 2001).

By the late 1990s, the economic relationship between the two countries had intensified; however, this expanding relationship was accompanied by a growing trade imbalance. China had become the United States' fourth-largest trading partner, but US exports to China were increasing at an annual rate of 8%, while Chinese imports to the United States by 21%. By 1996, the US trade deficit with China was approximately $40 billion. This raised concerns among American policymakers, industries, and labor unions who were worried about the effect the trade deficit would have on American companies. Government officials claimed this trade imbalance was caused by Chinese trade barriers such as high tariffs, quotas, discriminatory regulations, and limited access for US companies to operate in Chinese markets (Lardy, 1998).

The Clinton administration responded to the mounting pressure from American businesses and labor groups by increasing their efforts to negotiate China's accession into the WTO. The administration argued that China's inclusion in the WTO would ensure that China complied with international trade norms which would create a more stable and transparent framework for US businesses operating in China and open up the country for further negotiations regarding trade. The United States also sought to integrate China into the global economic order to prevent it from forming an alternative trade bloc similar to the Soviet trade bloc (Shirk, 2007).

This push for WTO accession led to the US-China Bilateral Trade Agreement of 1999, which set the conditions for China's formal entry into the WTO in 2001. This agreement required China to open up its market further by reducing tariffs, eliminating quotas, and allowing greater foreign investment. It also addressed concerns over intellectual property rights and state subsidies inhibiting competition (Naughton, 2007). While some Chinese industries resisted entrance into the WTO, Beijing believed that WTO membership was essential for sustaining its current economic momentum and further securing foreign investment (Huang, 2008).

The 1990s was the beginning of the deep economic interdependence between China and the United States that would come to the forefront of industrial policy in the twenty-first century. While it is true that US businesses expanded their reach by accessing Chinese markets, the flood of cheap Chinese imports raised doubts about the benefits of freer trade due to job losses, trade deficits, and economic insecurity. These concerns would shape US policy in the twenty-first century, leading to more protectionist trade measures and disputes (Breslin, 2013).

American public opinion was not always convinced of the benefits of China's entry into the WTO. Many were concerned about the impact of this entry on the American industry, showing skepticism and resistance. It was clear that the entry of China would have had both positive and negative effects, benefiting some sectors while posing challenges to others. In other words, China's entry into the WTO required the United States to accept a structural change in the American economy and society that would create both winners and losers.

In the end, everything was solved by extolling the substantial benefits that China's entry would bring:

> The WTO agreement will move China in the right direction. It will advance the goals America has worked for in China for the past three decades. And of course, it will advance our own economic interests. Economically, this agreement is the equivalent of a one-way street. It requires China to open its markets—with a fifth of the world's population, potentially the biggest markets in the world—to both our products and services in unprecedented new ways. All we do is to agree to maintain the present access which China enjoys. Chinese tariffs, from telecommunications products to automobiles to agriculture, will fall by half or more over just five years. For the first time, our companies will be able to sell and distribute products in China made by workers here in America without being forced to relocate manufacturing to China, sell through the Chinese government, or transfer valuable technology—for the first time. We'll be able to export products without exporting jobs. Meanwhile, we'll get valuable new safeguards against any surges of imports from China. We're already preparing for the largest enforcement effort ever given for a trade agreement (Clinton, 2000).

Even within Congress, members were divided by party lines on China's bid to join the WTO. Ultimately, however, the House of Representatives saw 73 Democrats vote alongside 164 Republicans in favor of the agreement, which, once passed, was another trade legislative victory for Clinton. It was clearly the largest of the trade agreements that promised significant opportunities in the coming decades—an immense new opportunity for American industry to once again expand its "frontier." It was a unique economic scenario that did not prevent the Clintonian rhetoric to emphasize, to those who wanted to believe it, that it was not just an opportunity to sell more goods and services: "By joining the WTO, China is not simply agreeing to import more of our products; it is agreeing to import one of democracy's most cherished values: economic freedom" (Clinton, 2000).

During those years, if China represented the "new frontier" to look at in the future, Japan stood out as the other great Asian country with which the United States had long been engaged. As noted earlier, even before the Clinton administration, various agreements had been negotiated between the two countries. These accords sought to reduce trade barriers that limited market access to American products: both those of a structural nature (such as the distribution systems used, excessive regulation, and lack of transparency in procurement practices), and those related to specific sectors (such as that of semiconductors, wood products, mobile phones, and buildings).

At the beginning of the 1990s, dissatisfaction with the results led to continued negotiations. This issue also served as fodder for political rhetoric seeking consensus, particularly concerning the influx of Japanese products into the United States. Many American companies also complained about the longstanding asymmetry in the relationship, accusing Japan of not sufficiently opening its domestic market.

In the 1980s and 1990s, as Japanese firms expanded their dominance in key sectors of the American market, such as in automobiles, consumer electronics, and semiconductors, the economic rivalry between Japan and the United States intensified. US exporters struggled to penetrate the Japanese market, which was comparatively more protected and structurally resistant to foreign competition due to its complex distribution networks, keiretsu business groups, and government policies favoring domestic industries (Johnson, 1982; Lincoln, 1990). This gave the air of an unequal trade relationship and as a result, US officials accused Japan of engaging in unfair trade practices, including non-tariff barriers, restrictive business regulations, and implicit collusion between government agencies and domestic corporations (Prestowitz, 1988).

The United States looked to counter these alleged unfair trade practices through both multilateral and unilateral measures. Some measures were pursued under the GATT, where the United States filed complaints and pushed for greater market liberalization in Japan. However, Washington would later take a more aggressive stance through domestic trade legislation. This can particularly be seen in the invocation of "Super 301"—a key provision of the Omnibus Trade and Competitiveness Act of 1998. This provision empowered the US Trade Representative to identify and retaliate against countries with unfair trade barriers.

Japan quickly became a primary target of this legislation (ERP, 1998; Destler, 1995).

Using Super 301, the US government launched several high-profile trade disputes with Japan, mostly in sectors where American firms faced significant obstacles like in the aforementioned industries of auto, consumer electronics, and semiconductors. One of the key cases was in semiconductor manufacturing, which led to an agreement in 1986 (Tyson, 1992), with a subsequent renewal in 1991 (that expired in 1996). Regarding automobiles and auto parts, the Clinton administration accused Japan of restricting imports from US suppliers and favoring domestic businesses, leading to retaliatory tariffs which were prevented by an 11th-hour deal (Schoppa, 1997). Furthermore, in computers and satellites, the United States pressed Japan to open public procurement contracts from 1994 to 1996, which resulted in agreements that expanded access for American tech firms (ERP, 1998).

Against this backdrop, under the joint efforts of first the Bush and then Clinton administrations, the US-Japan Framework for a New Economic Partnership Agreement was signed in 1993. The Americans' primary objective was to break down the barriers to entry in the Japanese market while looking for tools that would allow them to protect themselves more effectively from Japanese imports. Moreover, during this period, a wider range of issues concerning the structure of the national economic institutions of the two countries was dealt with through bilateral negotiations (i.e., the "Structural Impediments Initiatives"), which focused mainly on savings and investments, territorial planning policy, price mechanism, distribution system, antitrust policy, and Keiretsu (companies owning each other's capital assets) (ERP, 1990).

6.8 Innovation

In the early 1990s, during the Bush administration, the US government's rhetoric about technology advances and innovation policies had not changed since the 1980s as set forth by Ronald Reagan. According to the Bush administration, the role the government had to play was minimal. In this context, the government had to influence economic structural adjustment as little as possible, leaving the markets with the greatest possible flexibility: "Flexibility enhances the ability of a market economy to respond to change and rewards innovation" (ERP, 1991, pp. 111–112).

From this perspective, the focus was on changes in market demand, consumer tastes and preferences, and the capacity of private enterprises to stimulate and respond to such changes (ERP, 1991). The promotion of innovation and tech-nological advancement of the American industry should rely on governments, and the administration rejected advocating for industrial policy interventions to foster innovation:

> Some have argued for a broad new Federal role: choosing specific civilian tech-nologies and financing their development or commercialization by special tax treatment or direct subsidy—a so-called industrial policy. Such an expansion of the current Federal role is strongly opposed by this Administration (ERP, 1990, p. 116).

Instead, the focus was on deciding whether it was necessary to encourage sav-ings and private investment in physical, intellectual, and human capital. The only policy instrument that was explicitly proposed was the reduction of the tax rate on capital gains (corporate capital gains) that would have allowed the domestic industry to invest more in innovation (ERP, 1990, p. 25, 109). Despite recog-nizing that the natural structural adjustment of the economy could impose high social costs in the short-term, the administration emphasized that:

> [s]uch shocks may increase unemployment temporarily, but a flexible economy adjusts to new circumstances effectively and can return rapidly to full employ-ment. [. . .] This reallocation of resources occurs without government planning. [. . .] the government is not nearly as good as the market at organizing the real-location of resources that must accompany innovation. [. . .] Such qualitative changes are very difficult to predict, and government interference in market forces can suppress them without anyone even being aware of the loss (ERP, 1991, pp. 111–112).

However, the approach promoted by the Bush administration was not intended to prevent these negative consequences, but rather to intervene afterwards, mit-igating social costs and facilitating retraining and re-employment of the labor force (ERP, 1991). In this regard, both the federal and state-financed unemploy-ment insurance system and other measures sought to increase workforce skills were justified (ERP, 1992). It was precisely in this area of intervention that the Bush administration proved to be particularly active.

6.9 Education and Training

Technological shifts reshaped the American economy, creating an increasing demand for specialized labor, thus causing the Bush Administration to quickly recognize the importance of workforce development and prioritize business training. The administration built upon existing federal initiatives such as the Economic Dislocation and Worker Assistance program that was introduced by Reagan in 1998. In 1992, the Job Training 2000 program launched. It was designed to serve as a coordinating force for the more than 600 private industry-led committees that were responsible for implementing federal vocational training programs, creating greater efficiency and cooperation between these various programs. Job Training 2000's goal was to modernize vocational training by shifting its focus from a welfare-based initiative to a system that was driven by market needs and business demand (ERP, 1992).

The Bush administration also pursued education reforms alongside its workforce training initiatives. It hoped to shape the national education system to align better with broader economic and social objectives. George H. W. Bush famously declared his intention to be "the education President," striving to generate a revival in the excellence of American schools, seen following the passage of the Defense Education Act. Historically, primary and secondary education in the United States had remained under the jurisdiction of local and state governments, with limited federal involvement. However, due to the changing economic climate and new technological demands in the job market, the Bush administration recognized the need for national coordination. Thus, he embarked on a series of significant educational initiatives from the beginning of his term (ERP, 1990).

In September 1989, a major step toward this goal occurred when President Bush convened an Education Summit in Charlottesville, Virginia. This summit brought together key members of his administration and state governors, resulting in the formulation of national objectives for primary and secondary education which were then later outlined in the National Education Goals: A Report to the Nation's Governors (1990). Some of the key goals were increasing the high school graduation rate, improving science education, raising literacy, enhancing adult learning programs, and addressing social issues like school violence and drug use (ERP, 1991). This marked an important shift in federal education policy as these goals emphasized measurable outcomes and national standards within a historically decentralized US education system.

Building on the momentum set by the National Education Goals, the first Bush administration launched America 2000, a long-term strategy intended to achieve substantial education improvement by the turn of the century. One of the main components of this strategy was the Educational Excellence Act of 1991. This act sought to allocate federal funding for the construction of new schools, rewards for high-performing institutions and educators, as well as supporting states in implementing alternative teacher certification programs. This bill also proposed broader reforms to enhance overall school quality and accountability. However, since education had been deemed as being under the jurisdiction of the states, there was significant resistance to this initiative in Congress. Some lawmakers were concerned that this initiative was an overreach of federal authority into the rights of local and state governments. As a result of this, the Educational Excellence Act never passed (McAndrews, 2006).

While this was a blow to the legislation for the Bush administration's educational agenda, the initiatives laid the ground for future federal efforts in education reform, influencing later policies under the Clinton and George W. Bush administrations such as Goals 2000 and No Child Left Behind. The shift to a push for higher standards, accountability, and federal-state collaboration in education policy reflected an evolving recognition of education's role in economic competitiveness and workforce development at the national level due to the increase in service and technical jobs.

6.10 Research, Science, and Technology

The Bush administration strongly believed in bolstering the development of science and technology. Financial support for basic research, protection of intellectual property rights, tax incentives for research and development conducted by private companies, among others, were part of these interventions. For example, in 1989, a 20% tax credit was granted for research and experimentation costs.[6] However, significant support for science and technology also came through another important channel: the demand generated by government agencies and departments. As in the past, and as already noted, the role of the Department of Defense remained central, alongside the Department of Energy, NASA, the National Science Foundation, the National Institutes of Health, universities, and government laboratories.

The federal government, in general, played an important role in funding universities and research laboratories to conduct basic research, most importantly in areas that were not directly aligned with the objectives of specific federal agencies, thus framing this funding as for the public and economic good. This investment in scientific inquiry fostered technological advancements that often found subsequent commercial applications in the private sector, especially in research-heavy industries like pharmaceuticals, leading to the development of new products, processes, and industries (ERP, 1994). In financing fundamental

---

[6] In this regard, as mentioned, the government intervened on the international protection of intellectual property, the adoption of internationally uniform basic standards to which traded goods should be subject, and continued support for the elimination of "unjustified" regulations, in particular through the Uruguay Round negotiations (ERP, 1990).

research, the government made sure that universities and research institutions had the resources to research and develop cutting-edge scientific fields, creating the foundation for long-term innovation and economic growth.

Historically, federal support for scientific research has been instrumental in major technological breakthroughs. In the postwar period, investments in fields such as computing, materials science, and biomedical research led to life-changing developments. The Internet was one of these major developments, which was originally funded through the ARPANET project by the Department of Defense. Other notable advancements were made in semiconductor technologies and in pharmaceuticals (Mowery and Sampat, 2005). This model of government-funded R&D would continue in the 1990s, with increased funding going specifically to newer fields such as biotechnology, nanotechnology, and artificial intelligence (AI), which ensured the United States and its research institutions remained at the forefront of scientific discovery (ERP, 1994).

A significant impact of this federal investment was the propagation of university-affiliated start-ups and spin-offs, particularly in high-tech industries. Both public and private universities were increasingly active in commercializing research through technology transfer offices and partnerships with the private sector. Foundational policies such as the Bayh-Dole Act of 1980 enabled universities to retain the intellectual property rights to federally funded research, which encouraged faculty and researchers to patent their discoveries and then license them to industry for profit (Mowery et al., 2001). This dynamic continued to develop, and by the early 1990s, there was a surge in start-ups, particularly in sectors of strategic interest such as biotechnology (e.g., Genentech), software development, and advanced materials (Shane, 2004).

Likewise, federal research funding supported multi-disciplinary research collaborations. These collaborations fostered innovation ecosystems that helped integrate university researchers, private companies, and government agencies. Independent institutions such as the National Science Foundation (NSF) and the National Institutes of Health (NIH) played key roles in financing long-term, high-risk research, while partners with federal laboratories and industry leaders helped accelerate commercialization pathways (Rosenberg and Nelson, 1994).

Through its investment in innovative research, the federal government not only advanced scientific knowledge, but also furthered US industrial competitiveness, ensuring that cutting-edge discoveries led to real-world economic and technological leadership (ERP, 1994). These policies laid the foundation for the rapid development of biotechnology clusters such as Silicon Valley and Boston's biotech corridor, both arising around key research universities and emerging as global hubs of innovation and entrepreneurship.

By the 1990s, the DoD remained the central force behind government-supported R&D, continuing its legacy as both the primary funder of scientific research and the largest public purchaser of American technology and industrial products (Weiss, 2008). This dual role—sponsoring cutting-edge technological advancements while serving as a major market for innovations—has historically driven breakthroughs in fields such as computing, aerospace, and advanced materials.

As noted in the 1994 ERP:

In this manner, the Federal Government supported the development and diffusion of jet aircraft and engines, semiconductor microelectronics, computers and computer-controlled machine tools, pharmaceuticals and biotechnology, advanced energy and environmental technologies, advanced materials, and a whole host of other commercially successful technologies (ERP, 1994, p. 193).

Certainly, for a brief euphoric moment, defense costs had seemed less necessary, at least to public opinion. Undoubtedly, this perception could suggest a future contraction of spending for military purposes. However, if this hypothesis were confirmed, there would have been a downsizing of research spending in a number of defense-related sectors—a downsizing that would have imposed a consequent rethinking of the whole system of national research:

The circumstances that allowed the United States to rely primarily on a defense-led model have changed. With the end of the cold war, demand for new defense systems is now less than it was. Commercial product spinoffs from military research have also diminished from their heyday of the 1950s and 1960s, and American companies face intense international competition from increasingly capable foreign firms (ERP, 1994, pp. 193–194).

As noted previously, hopes for drastic reductions in US military interventions did not materialize. Similarly, those who expected a massive reduction in spending for national security purposes were wrong:

One possible additional concern with cuts in defense spending is their potential effect on the defense industrial base and U.S. technological superiority. In managing the proposed spending cuts, the ability of the United States to continue to produce the equipment needed to fight future conflicts should be maintained. Furthermore, the advantage the United States has in defense technology should be protected through continued investment in research, although some of the priorities may be shifted. The defense technology base can also be protected by relaxing procurement regulations, particularly those that restrict the transfer of defense technology to civilian uses (ERP, 1991, p. 151).

These final remarks appear decidedly clear and accurately capture the attitude of those years and foreshadow what would have happened. In this scenario, the Clinton administration embarked on a reassessment of the national research system, which had appeared excessively dependent on military demand:

> The development and deployment of new technology have long been of interest to the government. But technology policy is especially critical in a period of large-scale defense cutbacks, because more than half of total Federal support for R&D has traditionally been related to national defense. With less need for research on weaponry, the Federal Government must now make a choice. Will we reduce total research support, or will we shift the research dollars into civilian technologies? The president believes that the latter is the wiser course, which is why the Administration is reorienting the research capabilities of the Defense Department and the national laboratories toward R&D partnerships with industry (ERP, 1994, p. 45).

As a result of this debate, the years of the Clinton administration were particularly important for American science and technology research. Recognizing biotechnology as a key growth industry, Clinton promoted policies to support biotech research and development. His administration encouraged public-private partnerships to stimulate innovations in life sciences, making significant investments in the Human Genome Project and other biotech research initiatives. While the focus on military demand persisted contrary to some expectations, Clinton inaugurated an industrial policy phase dedicated to innovation and scientific and technological research:

> The administration's technology initiatives are shifting the composition of Federal R&D from military to civilian concerns, and the composition of military R&D toward the development of so-called dual-use technologies—those with applications to both military and commercial products (ERP, 1994, p. 194).

These interventions sought academic legitimacy in schools that dealt with market failures and the ability of governments to intervene legitimately to solve the markets' inability to lead to efficiency and innovation. They emphasized the production of public goods, management of externalities, and tackled issues related to information asymmetries and non-competitive markets. These factors underscored the rationale for industrial policy interventions aimed at promoting innovation and scientific-technological progress (Stiglitz, 1989; Chang, 1994; ERP, 1994):

> While the bulk of research and development (R&D) must and should be done by private industry, support for basic and generic research has long been recognized as a legitimate function of government because of informational externalities. New technology is expensive to discover but cheap to disseminate. So what one company learns passes quickly to others, making it impossible for the innovator to capture all the returns from its discovery. In fact, estimates find that innovating businesses capture less than half of the social returns to their R&D (ERP, 1994, p. 44).

This approach represented a continuity with the past but also departed from the free-market theses of Reaganite rhetoric by accepting the possibility that, in some specific circumstances, government intervention might be necessary to correct the malfunctioning of market mechanisms.

However, the most significant departure from previous administrations was an economic policy approach that argued that it might be necessary to intervene in national industry by defining its underlying strategies. The motivations behind the industrial policy interventions promoted by the Clinton administration, which during those years heavily invested in the national scientific research system, came from the belief that government intervention could be guided by a long-term public strategy, especially in areas such as scientific research (ERP, 1997, p. 19).

Another notable shift from Reaganite rhetoric was the idea that government intervention was not structurally destined to fail, and that the effectiveness and efficiency of public administration action could be improved: "The Administration recognizes the need for change not only in what the government does, but also in how it does it" (ERP, 1996, p. 33).

This shift was exemplified by initiatives like the National Performance Review (NPR), later renamed The National Partnership for Reinventing Government, launched in March 1993. Led by Vice President Al Gore, it was tasked with reforming and streamlining the way in which the federal government operated (Kamensky, 2001). The 1994 ERP states:

> The NPR identified 384 ways that the Federal Government could save money without reducing the level of service and, indeed, often while improving governmental performance. Its report concluded that, by shifting to a market-like focus on customer service, by introducing competition where possible, and by streamlining internal government processes to facilitate better management, we could have a government that «works better and costs less» (ERP, 1994, p. 171).

. NPR, initiated by Vice President Al Gore in 1993, emphasized improving the public procurement process, enhancing budget controls, optimizing services to customers, streamlining the management of financial and human resources, and integrating information technology systems into government affairs (ERP, 1994). The NPR was a part of the broader "reinventing government" initiative which sought to make federal agencies more efficient, responsive, and cost-effective, following along the lines of increasing liberalization within the government. The NPR shifted the focus toward performance-based budgeting and deregulation with the aim to modernize the public sector to better match the global economic shifts that were reshaping the economic-political landscape in the 1990s.

The Clinton administration also targeted key industries that had a high potential for economic development. One of the most critical sectors was the Information and Communication Technology (ICT), which was regarded as pivotal in driving productivity gains and sustaining economic competitiveness. The emphasis on ICT was partially due to the need to compensate for the declining role of the defense sector in technology after the shift to consumer-consumption oriented development following the end of the Cold War (ERP, 2001).

Due to the increase in ICT investment, between 1990 and 2000 the ICT sector grew from 5.8% to 8.3% of GDP, with private investment in the sector increasing at a rate of 28% annually since 1995 (ERP, 2001). This rapid growth of ICT heralded a new wave in technological innovation that reshaped economic organization. This shift marked the rise of the "New Economy"—or a nation with a knowledge-based, digitally connected economic landscape.

To further support these developments, the Clinton administration introduced several new initiatives to support the ICT sector and a broader digital presence within the economy. One of these initiatives was the Information Technology for the Twenty-First Century (IT21) program, aimed at advancing software development, supercomputing, and network infrastructures. Federal funding for IT21 increased from $309 million in 2000 to $704 million in 2001 (ERP, 2001). This demonstrated the administration's dedication to technological advancement. Furthermore, additional policies such as the Internet Tax Freedom Act temporarily suspended internet access taxes, seeking to foster the expansion of the internet economy, thus encouraging greater online commerce. The administration extended its commitment to digital economic transformation on the international level by playing a key role in negotiating and signing the WTO's Information Technology Agreement and Basic Telecommunications Agreement, which facilitate the liberalization of markets for high-tech goods and services (Aggarwal and Ravenhill, 2001).

To enhance market competition and innovation in the ICT sector, Clinton introduced the landmark Telecommunications Act of 1996. This bill deregulated the telecommunications industry which opened local and long-distance markets to new entrants, thus encouraging healthy competition among service providers (ERP, 2000). By opening up competition, this act expanded consumer choice, reduced prices, and accelerated broadband deployment across the United States.

The Clinton administration extended support for scientific and technological progress beyond the ICT into other strategically important sectors, most notably in healthcare and biotechnology. The federal government significantly increased funding for scientific research, showing its recognition of the potential for biomedical research to drive economic growth and improve public health outcomes. The funding for the NSF grew by more than 60%, while the budget for the NIH, the primary sponsor for biomedical research, increased by over 80% over eight years (ERP, 1999; ERP, 2001). These investments fostered key advancements in medical sciences and supported the US biotechnology industry, leading to innovation in pharmaceuticals, genetics, and bioengineering.

Besides the sector-specific interference, the Clinton administration pursued "horizontal" policies that strengthened collaboration between the government and private industry in research and development. One of the key developments of this approach was the Advanced Technology Program (ATP), administered by the National Institute of Standards and Technology (NIST). The ATP encouraged public-private partnerships to accelerate technological innovation by providing funding for high-risk, high-reward research projects with good long-term commercial potential. Such programs played a vital role in aligning federal priorities with industry needs, ensuring that government-supported advancements translated into real economic and societal benefits for the public good. As noted in the 2001 ERP report, "Over 460 ATP awards—many of which have gone to cooperative ventures between firms and universities—have been made in fields as diverse as photonics, manufacturing, materials science, information technology, and biotechnology" (p. 116).

By encouraging a policy environment that fostered innovation and global competitiveness, the Clinton administration positioned the United States at the forefront of digital and knowledge economies. These strategic initiatives laid the foundations for the sustained economic growth seen in the twenty-first century.

The Clinton years had other noteworthy examples of collaboration between the government and the private sector. One of these being the Partnership for a New Generation of Vehicles (PNGV), established in 1993. The PNGV directed the development of fuel-efficient, environmentally friendly vehicle technology by bringing together the three major American automakers—General Motors (GM), Ford, and Chrysler. These were alongside more than 300 automotive suppliers, universities, and even seven federal agencies, including the Department of Energy and the Environmental Protection Agency (ERP, 2001). The PNGV initiative represented the overall trend of public-private partnership that was the forefront of the Clinton administration's approach to industrial policy, chiefly in sectors where technological advancements were seen as critical to economic and environmental sustainability (Yergin and Stanislaw, 2002).

Despite the administration's efforts to push for collaboration and innovation, America's antitrust legislation posed challenges to expanding cooperative efforts. However, the Reagan administration had already taken early steps to address this in the 1980s with the National Cooperative Research Act of 1984. This act reduced legal uncertainties by specifying the conditions under which cooperative research was exempted from antitrust regulation, thus encouraging firms to engage in joint ventures without the fear of persecution or penalties (Kwoka, and White, 1999). The Clinton administration built on the foundation of the National Cooperative Research Act with the National Cooperative Research and Production Act of 1993, which expanded legal protections to also cover joint production ventures, not just research. This extended protection proved instrumental in cultivating greater industry collaboration. Already by 1998, there were approximately 740 registered joint ventures, with a high concentration in high-tech sectors such as communications, electronics, and transportation (ERP, 2001; Jorde and Teece, 1992).

Along with the aforementioned acts, the Antitrust Guidelines for the Licensing of Intellectual Property was issued in 1995. These guidelines aimed to provide a balance between promoting innovation and protecting competitive markets by clarifying how intellectual property rights could be shared or licensed among companies, facilitating the diffusion of cutting-edge technologies while minimizing antitrust pushbacks (U.S. Department of Justice and Federal Trade Commission, 1995). The Clinton administration aimed to provide clearer regulatory frameworks that created an environment where technological advancements could thrive. They hoped that this would ultimately contribute to the broader goals of economic modernization and international competitiveness (Porter, 1998).

This legislation and policy reforms were emblematic of the evolving role of the federal government in an increasingly globalized American economy. The administration encouraged strategic alliances and reduced regulatory barriers, aiming to enhance the American industry's capacity to innovate and adapt to rapidly changing technological landscapes. It was not simply about maintaining economic growth; these efforts were also about ensuring that the United States remained a global leader in key industries critical to national security and economic prosperity.

6.11 Final Remarks

Starting with driving forces, there is little doubt that the most dramatic change that influenced the policies of the 1990s was the end of the Cold War. With a reduced emphasis on competing with the former Soviet Union, the administration's priorities shifted to the strong competition that the United States faced from Japan. Within this context, the Bush administration continued with the noninterventionist stance that we have seen in the Reagan administration, although as noted in the case of Reagan, there were many cases of direct intervention to bolster specific industries. Surprisingly, given the difference in political parties, President Clinton's policies were remarkably similar to the Bush administration as we have seen.

The dramatic end of the Cold War led George H. W. Bush's administration to focus on the growing competitive threat from Japan. This pressure on American industries, particularly in the high-technology and auto industries, continued from the Reagan administration period. But aside from some defensive measures, Bush sought to look to new markets, with a focus on both NAFTA and the Uruguay Round of GATT negotiations. He also pursued a Latin American strategy with the FTAA. Clinton continued these policies, with the Uruguay Round and NAFTA being concluded—and passed—with significant Republican support. He also promoted a similar Asian strategy as Bush, with his enthusiasm for APEC. Both Bush and Clinton believed that a more open trading system would help domestic industries become more competitive.

The dramatic domestic shift with respect to the military-industrial complex, the onset of new wars, including the First Gulf War and conflict in Somalia, meant that the expected peace dividend did not fully materialize. More urgently, under Bush, the United States faced a recession, pushing his administration to balance fiscal conservatism with the need for economic revitalization. But with significant deficits, Bush was limited in the extent to which he could support industrial policy through federal spending. Clinton was more open to pursuing industrial policies, particularly in high-technology industries. But with continued budgetary challenges, Clinton avoided heavy-handed industrial planning efforts. Rather, he focused on targeted support for key sectors.

In terms of beliefs, Bush pursued a free-market approach inherited from the Reagan administration. Rather than vertical industrial policy, the focus was on horizontal measures such as stimulating private sector-led growth with tax incentives for R&D rather than direct subsidies. And consistent with the horizontal approach, he also sought to support innovation, science, and technology development. Clinton also was highly focused on technology support, and while he rejected Reagan's free-market ideology (more in theory, than in practice), he was much more open to promoting markets and improving the skills of workers to compete in the global economy.

Within a primarily horizontally focused approach, the Bush administration viewed several sectors as critical for economic growth and his administration thus followed a more vertical approach than Reagan. In particular, a key focus in the face of Japanese and European competition was high-tech industries, especially those related to computing, electronics, and semiconductors. R&D support was also targeted on these high-tech industries and included infrastructure for emerging industries like telecommunications and computing. And despite the end of the Cold War, the aerospace and defense sectors continued to benefit from government support, with companies such as Boeing, Lockheed Martin, and Northrop Grumman receiving ongoing contracts and government backing. Defense contractors, given their expertise in high-tech and advanced manufacturing, were also encouraged to pivot toward commercial uses, leading to a "dual-use" approach of using military technologies for civilian applications.

The US auto industry, particularly companies like Ford, General Motors, and Chrysler, faced strong competition from Japan. Yet the VERs that Reagan had negotiated were phased out by 1991, and Bush's focus was on encouraging the creation of a broader North American market through NAFTA, which came into being under Clinton. The Bush administration also supported green industries, including encouraging the auto sector to become more fuel-efficient. In addition, it targeted sectors linked to clean energy and environmental technology such as wind and solar. And it promoted "clean coal" technology to reduce emissions from the traditional energy sector, while eschewing direct intervention.

The Clinton administration built on Bush's efforts, with Al Gore promoting the "Information Superhighway." This effort to build out a national telecommunications infrastructure was a critical component in developing a digital economy. It also sought to promote biotechnology through public-private partnerships and make investments in the Human Genome Project. Here again, it was the Bush administration that had initiated this project on October 1, 1990, but under Clinton, it gained significant visibility and support. Continuing with Bush's "green" efforts, the Clinton administration promoted renewable energy sources, energy-efficient technologies, and green jobs, providing companies with incentives to invest in cleaner production methods and technologies.

In terms of regions, the Bush administration focused on the "Rust Belt" in the Midwest and Northeast regions, which had faced industrial decline and job losses, particularly in manufacturing and steel. Again, the support was indirect, with workforce retraining programs and incentives for businesses to reinvest in these areas. It also provided tax incentives and support to help small businesses grow and compete. Here again, the focus was on broad horizontal measures such as removing regulatory burdens, offering loans, and promoting entrepreneurship.

Clinton continued Bush's efforts to help the Midwest and Northeast by encouraging investments in emerging sectors within these regions, such as advanced manufacturing and tech. Key initiatives included Empowerment Zones and Enterprise Communities, which provided tax incentives and grants to distressed urban and rural areas to attract private investment. At the same time, Clinton helped to boost established and emerging tech hubs like Silicon Valley, Austin, and Boston. Policies included grants for R&D and educational initiatives to produce skilled workers for the new tech-driven economy. In particular, while eschewing help to specific companies, Clinton's horizontal policies included tax credits for R&D, grants for tech innovation, and support for large defense firms to focus on commercial applications.

With a free-market emphasis, the primary approach of the Bush administration was on horizontal policies. These included R&D tax credits, with a focus on companies investing in modernizing equipment and facilities, particularly in manufacturing and capital-intensive industries. Another broad policy approach was a reduction in capital gains taxes to encourage investment in technology start-ups and manufacturing firms.

The administration also supported public-private partnerships between federal research institutions like the National Institutes of Health and the Department of Energy and private companies. They also included the ATP program, initially passed by Reagan in 1988, as part of the Omnibus Trade and Competitiveness Act. This program was implemented by the Bush administration to fund high-risk, high-reward R&D efforts that would benefit multiple industries. Bush also continued to support the SEMATECH consortium, a public-private partnership created under Reagan in the late 1980s to help US semiconductor manufacturers compete against Japanese firms.

As detailed at length, the key focus of the Bush administration was on pursuing regional, transregional, and global trade arrangements: APEC was negotiated in 1989, followed by the NAFTA accord signed by the Bush administration in 1992 (ratified under Clinton in 1993). The GATT negotiations of the Uruguay

Round also continued, with the inclusion in particular of intellectual property provisions, trade-related investment measures, and a stronger dispute settlement mechanism—all provisions supported by most US businesses.

With respect to the auto sector, VERs under Reagan expired by 1985 and were not renewed. Instead, when Bush came into office, he pushed for the SII with Japan (1989–1990) to increase US exports, including those for autos. Still, under pressure from the steel industry, the administration pursued a two-fold policy: supporting claims of dumping and imposing countervailing duties; and continuing export restrictions that had been negotiated under Reagan.

On the environmental front, the administration signed the Clean Air Act Amendments of 1990, setting stricter environmental standards and encouraging a shift to cleaner technologies. Indeed, Bush had run as the "environmental president" and thus continued to push for green technologies. The Amendments to the earlier 1970 Clean Air Act gave the law greater teeth. It also had generally positive effects on acid rain, smog, toxic air pollution, and the ozone layer as CFCs were phased out.

With respect to technology, passage of the Telecommunications Act of 1991 promoted more competition in telecommunications, helping industries dependent on advanced communications infrastructure. The administration also enhanced the 1982 Job Training Partnership Act (JTPA) to help workers transition into higher-skilled industries, helped disadvantaged youth, and sought to align workforce skills with the demands of a modernizing economy.

The George H. W. Bush administration implemented its industrial policies through a range of legal and administrative mechanisms that reflected a preference for indirect market-oriented strategies. In addition to formal laws, Bush used executive orders to streamline and focus government priorities. An example was directing federal agencies to support dual-use technologies that benefited both defense and civilian applications. Along these lines, the National Technology Initiative encouraged private sector R&D through collaborative programs with federal research institutions.

During the Clinton administration, the US government implemented a range of policy tools to shape industrial policy, foster innovation, enhance global competitiveness, and revitalize distressed regions. The administration pursued a market-oriented approach that relied on targeted tax incentives, investments in research and development (R&D), public-private partnerships, trade agreements, and workforce development programs.

One of the primary tools used to encourage innovation was the R&D tax credit, which incentivized private companies to invest in research, particularly in high-tech sectors such as biotechnology, information technology, and clean energy. By lowering the effective tax rate on R&D expenditures, this policy sought to increase technological advancements and global competitiveness (ERP, 2001). Additionally, the administration expanded investment tax incentives, including accelerated depreciation for capital-intensive firms and tax deductions for small businesses to stimulate entrepreneurship and economic diversification (Jorgenson, 2005).

Federal investment in R&D played a central role in Clinton's industrial policy. Funding was channeled through key agencies such as NSF, NIH, and DOE, with emphasis on emerging technologies. The Human Genome Project, one of the most ambitious federally funded R&D programs, positioned the United States at the forefront of biotechnology research (Collins et al., 2003). The Advanced Technology Program (ATP), administered by the National Institute of Standards and Technology (NIST), provided cost-sharing grants for high-risk, high-reward technological advancements in partnership with the private sector (National Research Council, 2001).

The Clinton administration also followed up on Bush's trade efforts. NAFTA, signed into law in 1993, created a free-trade zone between the United States, Canada, and Mexico, aiming to increase exports and enhance the competitiveness of US manufacturers (Hufbauer and Schott, 2005). Additionally, Clinton's support for the WTO facilitated American participation in global trade negotiations, reducing tariffs and ensuring intellectual property protections for high-tech industries (ERP, 1999).

Public-private partnerships played a significant role in Clinton's industrial strategy. The Partnership for a New Generation of Vehicles (PNGV), launched in 1993, brought together the three major American automakers, over 300 suppliers, universities, and federal agencies to develop fuel-efficient and environmentally friendly vehicles (ERP, 2001). Other collaborations included the Manufacturing Extension Partnership (MEP), which helped small and medium-sized manufacturers integrate new technologies into their production processes (Shapira, 2001).

Recognizing the importance of workforce readiness in a global economy, the Clinton administration introduced several job training and educational programs. The School-to-Work Opportunities Act (1994) facilitated vocational education and apprenticeships to better align the labor force with emerging industries (Bailey and Merritt, 1997). Additionally, the Workforce Investment Act (1998) consolidated federal workforce programs, improving training and job placement services, particularly for displaced manufacturing workers (Holzer, 2001). Federal support for community colleges was also expanded, strengthening ties between education and industry.

To address economic disparities, the administration implemented regional economic development programs such as Empowerment Zones and Enterprise

Communities. These initiatives provided tax incentives and grants to attract private investment to economically distressed urban and rural areas (Turner et al., 2002).

Regulatory and intellectual property (IP) protections were strengthened to promote industrial competitiveness. The Antitrust Guidelines for Licensing of Intellectual Property (1995) clarified how firms could collaborate on technology while maintaining market competition (U.S. Department of Justice and Federal Trade Commission, 1995). The Telecommunications Act of 1996, the first major overhaul of US telecommunications law in six decades, deregulated the industry to encourage competition and innovation, laying the foundation for the expansion of broadband and wireless communications (Crandall, 2005).

The Clinton administration utilized multiple legal and administrative mechanisms to implement these policies. Key legislative measures included the NAFTA Implementation Act (1993), Telecommunications Act (1996), and Workforce Investment Act (1998), each passed through Congress to establish legal frameworks for trade, industrial development, and labor market reforms (ERP, 2000). Additionally, executive orders and presidential directives were used to direct federal agencies in implementing economic development programs, such as the designation of Empowerment Zones (Clinton, 1993). Federal agencies like the NIST, NSF, and DOE played a central role in administering grants and research initiatives, ensuring that industrial policies aligned with national economic priorities.

Political coalitions under Bush reflected both his pro-business stance and focus on trade accords to help American companies find new markets. But his interest in promoting green industries ran into opposition from traditional energy industries. Key supporters of Bush's initiative included high-tech, defense, and aerospace companies, which greatly benefited from tax incentives, defense contracts, and dual-use technology initiatives.

GM, Ford, and Chrysler were all supportive of Bush's effort to open up the Japanese market, but continued to press for more aggressive protectionist measures. They were unsuccessful in this effort. However, auto suppliers were pleased with the increasing opportunities arising from Bush's support of great Japanese investment in the auto sector (which was driven in large part by Reagan's VERs).

For the most part, small businesses were enthusiastic about the efforts to help them, and organizations like the National Federation of Independent Business (NFIB) and the US Chamber of Commerce supported Bush's tax incentives and regulatory adjustments. In addition to these groups, large multinationals stood to benefit from trade opening and endorsed his multi-prong trade opening strategy. Agricultural groups also generally supported NAFTA, with the promise of expanded markets for US agricultural exports.

The effort to expand the scope of the GATT to include TRIPS and TRIMS also garnered significant support. US business groups, particularly the International Intellectual Property Alliance and Business Roundtable, were active in lobbying the administration, and pharmaceutical companies, the music industry, and the movie industry all were strongly supportive of TRIPS. TRIMS, which sought to regulate national policies that discriminated against foreign investors, had strong supporters in firms such as Coca-Cola, General Motors, and ExxonMobil, as the accord would reduce the need to source a certain percentage of inputs locally and export a certain proportion of their output.

With his environmental push, many groups such as the Environmental Defense Fund and the Natural Resources Defense Council supported his legislative efforts. But they were not always uniformly supportive. For example, the Sierra Club and Greenpeace argued that Bush's approach to energy policy did not do enough to address climate change or reduce reliance on fossil fuels. Meanwhile, he faced significant opposition from old energy producers, including coal-burning utilities and oil companies, automakers who resisted the stricter tailpipe emissions standards, and industrial manufacturers who were concerned about the costs of complying with rules on toxic air pollutants.

With respect to trade policies, Bush faced significant opposition. Groups concerned about market opening included labor unions, economic nationalists supported by populist politicians, and less competitive industries such as steel and autos. In this effort, they were supported by some progressive economists and social policy advocates, who argued that trade opening would lead to great inequality. Congressional Democrats, particularly those representing industrial states, opposed Bush's free-trade agenda. They called for direct support to the struggling manufacturing sector and argued that open market policies would lead to further deindustrialization and job losses.

The Clinton administration reflected a continued strategic commitment to globalization, technological advancement, and trade liberalization pursued by Bush. These priorities created both strong alliances and significant opposition coalitions, as various political, business, labor, and social groups responded differently to Clinton's economic agenda. While his policies garnered support from pro-business factions, technology leaders, and centrist Democrats, they also faced considerable resistance from labor unions, progressive Democrats, protectionist Republicans, and anti-globalization activists.

High-tech and telecommunications companies were among the strongest supporters of Clinton's policies, benefiting from initiatives such as the Telecommunications Act of 1996, which deregulated the industry and facilitated internet expansion (Crandall, 2005). Similarly, biotechnology firms and dual-use technology contractors welcomed increased federal funding for R&D, particularly through programs like the Advanced Technology Program (ERP, 2001). Clinton's "Third Way" economic approach sought to balance market-oriented reforms with social investment (Hacker and Pierson, 2005). Centrist and moderate Democrats supported trade liberalization and pro-business policies, aligning with Clinton's push for NAFTA and the WTO agreements. Additionally, pro-trade Republicans and export-oriented corporations favored these policies, viewing expanded market access as crucial to US economic leadership (Hufbauer and Schott, 2005).

While some environmentalists opposed trade liberalization, many supported Clinton's green technology initiatives, which promoted R&D in renewable energy and energy efficiency (Vogel, 2012). Community colleges and workforce training providers also backed the administration's workforce development programs, such as the School-to-Work Opportunities Act, which provided funding for vocational education (Bailey and Merritt, 1997).

Labor unions, particularly manufacturing and industrial workers' organizations such as the AFL-CIO, opposed NAFTA and WTO agreements, arguing that they facilitated job losses and wage stagnation due to increased foreign competition (Levinson, 2019). Progressive Democrats also criticized Clinton's trade policies, contending that they undermined labor protections and environmental standards, benefiting corporations at the expense of workers. In this opposition, they had allies in a faction of protectionist Republicans and small manufacturing firms who resisted Clinton's free-trade agenda, fearing that increased foreign imports would hurt domestic industries (Bivens, 2007). Similarly, economic nationalists opposed globalization, arguing that it eroded US industrial capacity and prioritized multinational corporations over American workers. Finally, anti-globalization activists and grassroots environmental groups expressed concerns that trade agreements weakened environmental protections and enabled corporate exploitation of developing nations (Stiglitz, 2002). They argued that policies like NAFTA led to "pollution havens," where industries relocated to countries with weaker regulations, undermining global environmental efforts.

Bush's industrial policies, primarily horizontal in nature and heavily focused on market opening, were helpful in supporting technological innovation. Ironically, his efforts to promote NAFTA, soon thereafter passed under the Clinton administration, proved to be a key issue in his electoral loss.

His support of environmental regulation also achieved significant reductions in pollutants. But in terms of the concerns about deindustrialization, his efforts to promote trade adjustment and labor retraining proved insufficient. Traditional industries such as steel, textiles, and automotive continued to face significant import competition; market opening did not help these industries as their exports were simply not competitive with more efficient foreign suppliers, particularly those based in Asia. With respect to retraining, while some of his programs worked, they were not sufficiently funded and did not directly affect manufacturing losses. Although globalizing policies were carried forward by the Clinton administration, the rise of populist politicians continued to grow over time, eventually leading to Trump's victory in both 2016 and 2024.

Government intervention under the Clinton administration produced a mixed legacy. While it contributed to economic expansion, technological leadership, and fiscal discipline, it also exacerbated job losses in manufacturing, income inequality, and backlash against trade liberalization.

Clinton's policies coincided with one of the longest periods of peacetime economic expansion in US history. Between 1993 and 2001, GDP grew steadily, unemployment declined to 3.9% by 2000, and inflation remained low (ERP, 2001). The administration's emphasis on technology, trade, and deficit reduction helped increase investor confidence and drive economic activity (Jorgenson, 2005). Additionally, rapid expansion in the information technology sector created millions of jobs, positioning the United States as a leader in the digital economy (Crandall, 2005). His deficit reduction strategy, enacted through the 1993 budget plan, combined spending cuts and tax increases on high-income households. This policy led to budget surpluses by the late 1990s, reducing national debt and strengthening investor confidence (Hacker and Pierson, 2005). Foreign investment in US markets increased as a result, further stimulating economic growth.

The administration played a crucial role in fostering technological advancements. The Telecommunications Act of 1996 deregulated the telecom industry, accelerating internet expansion (Crandall, 2005). Federal investments in biotechnology, including the Human Genome Project, strengthened US leadership in life sciences, contributing to long-term economic and medical advancements (Collins et al., 2003). Clinton's support for NAFTA and the WTO also expanded global market access for US businesses, benefiting export-oriented industries such as agriculture, manufacturing, and technology (Hufbauer and Schott, 2005).

Despite overall economic growth, the United States lost hundreds of thousands of manufacturing jobs between 1993 and 2000, partly due to trade liberalization and outsourcing (Bivens, 2007). NAFTA, in particular, made it easier for companies to relocate production abroad, disproportionately affecting Rust Belt communities reliant on industrial employment (Levinson, 2019). While the high-tech sector experienced wage growth, incomes for low- and middle-income workers remained stagnant, exacerbating income inequality (Stiglitz, 2002). Clinton's workforce retraining programs, though well-intended, failed to provide displaced manufacturing workers with sufficient skills to transition into high-wage industries (Holzer, 2001). While some Empowerment Zones saw improvements, many distressed areas experienced limited economic growth. The scope of these programs was insufficient to counteract structural economic shifts, leading to persistent economic disparities between prosperous tech hubs and struggling industrial regions (Isserman and Rephann, 1995).

7

George W. Bush

Between September 11 and the Crisis's Outbreak

7.1 Introduction

The eight years of the George W. Bush administration from 2001 to 2009 were marked by two important historical events: the attack on the Twin Towers and the onset of the Great Recession. These events profoundly reshaped the relationship between government and industry, pushing the administration to follow a path that justified unprecedented choices.

George Bush, Jr. faced a difficult election, leading him to center his campaign around traditional Republican positions. The electoral outcome proved to be very uncertain, and thus during the electoral campaign it was necessary to propose themes capable of polarizing the consensus. Among these, opposition to "Big Government" was still a major issue that allowed the future president to attract the attention of some important segments of the electorate: "My guiding principle is government if necessary—but not necessarily government" (Bush, 1999).

After a narrow victory, Bush began his administration under the banner of national bipartisan unity which by necessity sought a certain continuity with the actions of the Clinton administration. During his victory speech, he stated: "Americans share hopes and goals and values far more important than any political disagreements. Republicans want the best for our nation. And so do Democrats. Our votes may differ, but not our hopes." (Bush, 2000).

Over these months, Bush sought to create political continuity with the previous presidential administration. This included the development of international treaties and investments in research for civil uses without neglecting the special relationship with the "military-industrial complex." However, this period was short-lived: On September 11, the national and international political scene radically changed. The global war on terrorism became the priority, and the whole system was redirected toward creating an economy that prioritized national defense and security (Weiss, 2014). At the same time, the world economic order was changing (Moran et al., 2005). America's dominant role in international relations had allowed it to orchestrate favorable terms of trade. While these

Governing Growth. Marco R. Di Tommaso and Vinod K. Aggarwal, Oxford University Press.
© Oxford University Press (2026). DOI: 10.1093/oso/9780197821787.003.0007

policies had previously benefited the United States, American industrial dominance faltered following the development of new industrial powers, primarily China.

7.2 Military Expenditure, National Security, and Technological Innovation

The Bush government reacted to the attack on the Twin Towers on September 11, 2001, on several fronts, all aimed at ensuring internal and global security. Among the actions with the greatest impact and greater visibility, in a climate characterized by strong emotion, President Bush decided to invade Afghanistan in 2001 and then in Iraq in 2003. The Bush administration claimed that there were weapons of mass destruction in Iraq, and that military intervention was critical for defending national security. The fear of terrorism gripped the country, and as a result, military demand immediately regained a central role in the American economy (Weiss, 2014; Buigues and Sekkat, 2009). In these years, the budget allocated to the Department of Defense grew from 15.6% of the total budget of the federal government in 2001, to 19.9% in 2008. This increase is reflected

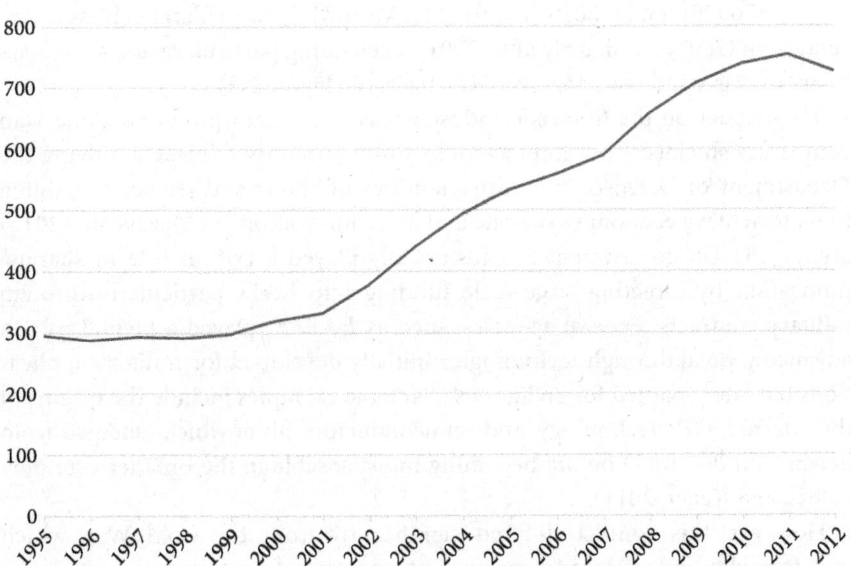

Figure 7.1 National Defense Spending and Investments in the United States: 1995–2012 (in billions of dollars)

Source: Elaboration from Economic Report of the President (ERP, 2013)

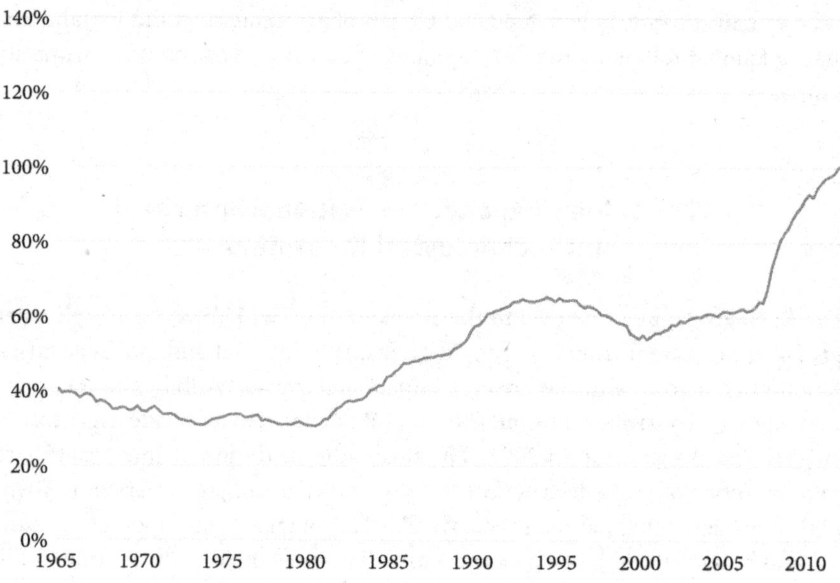

Figure 7.2 US Federal Debt as a Percentage of GDP

in the steady rise in national defense spending from under $300 billion in 2000 to over $700 billion by 2010 (Figure 7.1). Meanwhile, US federal debt as a percentage of GDP rose sharply after 2001, accelerating particularly after the 2008 financial crisis and reaching over 90% by 2010 (Figure 7.2).

The impact on the domestic industry was once again profound. American companies shielded from foreign competition found themselves supplying the Department of Defense with vast quantities of goods and services, enabling them to achieve economies of scale and drive innovation. As Mazzucato (2013) argues, the US government has historically played a critical role in shaping innovation by directing large-scale funding into R&D, particularly through military contracts. Federal agencies, such as DARPA, played a pivotal role in advancing breakthrough technologies initially developed for military applications but later adapted for civilian use. Notable examples include the origins of the internet, GPS technology, and semiconductors, all of which emerged from defense-funded R&D before becoming indispensable in the broader economy (Block and Keller, 2011).

However, this conflict differed significantly from the Cold War, which had formally ended decades prior. The concept of "national security" had evolved to encompass a far broader range of threats beyond conventional military engagements. While traditional defense expenditures remained crucial to addressing the direct demands of warfare, the security agenda expanded to include pandemics, bioterrorism, international terrorism, environmental crises, and cyberattacks (Weiss, 2014). This redefined security landscape meant that the war effort was no longer limited to foreign encounters but had significant implications for domestic governance as well.

As a result, an extensive array of public agencies—ranging from the Department of Homeland Security to the National Institutes of Health—became deeply engaged in a security framework that demanded vast investments in specialized and highly sophisticated research initiatives. The scale of these investments underscored the growing interdependence between military and civilian technological advancements, reinforcing the notion of dual-use innovations that blurred the traditional boundaries between defense and economic development (Moretti, 2012).

Bush's investments led to the further development of Unmanned Aerial Vehicles. Before 9/11, the United States had under 170 UAVs, but by the end of the administration, it had over 6,000. The development of UAVs has important civilian applications such as land surveying and delivery capabilities (World Bank, 2017). The development of GPS under the Bush administration has not only been critical for defense but has also enabled significant advancements in nonmilitary technology. GPS advancements have revolutionized industries, creating new strides in agriculture, tracking goods for business logistics and transportation, mining, utilities, navigation, automated driving, surveying statistics, smartphone applications, and more (GIS Geography, 2023).

In response to the evolving security landscape following the 9/11 attacks, the US government undertook a sweeping reorganization of its security infrastructure. In 2003, the Department of Homeland Security (DHS) was established, consolidating twenty-two federal agencies under a unified command to anticipate, prevent, and respond to national emergencies, particularly terrorist threats (MacMartin et al., 2025). Within DHS, the Homeland Security Advanced Research Projects Agency was created to drive innovation in security-related technologies, mirroring the defense-oriented model of the Defense Advanced Research Projects Agency (DARPA), which had long been instrumental in military R&D (Weiss, 2014).

This period witnessed a dramatic surge in R&D funding across multiple security-related sectors. The US Army significantly expanded its R&D budget to maintain technological superiority in military operations, with a strong emphasis on network-centric warfare, autonomous systems, and counterinsurgency technologies (Gansler, 2011). Concurrently, the Department of Energy (DOE) launched the Advanced Research Projects Agency-Energy (ARPA-E) in 2007, following the precedent set by DARPA in fostering high-risk, high-reward innovations (ARPA-E, 2023). Unlike other defense-related agencies, ARPA-E focused on the energy sector, which was relatively insulated from the disruptions caused by the ongoing War on Terror and geopolitical instability in the Middle East and Central Asia. Its mission reflected growing concerns over energy security and the need to develop alternative energy sources to reduce dependence on foreign oil (Grubler and Wilson, 2014).

The overall budget for national security-related R&D expanded rapidly. HSARPA alone controlled a budget of $6.6 billion in its first five years of operation following the Twin Towers attack (Weiss, 2014, pp. 48–49). In parallel, the National Institutes of Health (NIH), the Department of Defense (DoD), and the National Science Foundation (NSF) collaborated to establish a biodefense consortium. This consortium coordinated a $5 billion initiative under Project BioShield, aimed at developing, procuring, and stockpiling vaccines and medical countermeasures to combat biological threats (Franz and Zajtchuk, 2002). The initiative underscored the increasing intersection of national security and public health in the wake of bioterrorism threats, such as the anthrax attacks of 2001.

During the two terms of the Bush administration, a multitude of special projects emerged under the umbrella of national security, many of which extended into cutting-edge technological fields. Research in nanotechnology, robotics, and renewable energy experienced rapid growth, reflecting the broader securitization of scientific innovation (Weiss, 2014, p. 123). The convergence of these efforts illustrated a recurring pattern in US industrial policy: military and security-driven investments frequently served as catalysts for broader technological advancements that later found applications in civilian industries (Mazzucato, 2013).

The attention to the demands of defense and national security had, in fact, interrupted one of the lines of intervention of the Clinton administration, which, from a strategic point of view, had promoted huge public investments in research and new technologies for civil use. Clinton's industrial policy was met with domestic resistance. The Bush administration initially opposed this policy, but after some time, they found interest in diversifying government investments (Ruttan, 2006).

In an effort to bolster American innovation and maintain global economic leadership, the American Competitiveness Initiative (ACI) was launched in 2006 under the Bush administration. This plan, developed by the Office of Science and Technology Policy (OSTP), aimed to double federal investments in civilian R&D over the next decade (OSTP, 2006). The initiative sought to increase funding for federal agencies engaged in scientific research, including the National Science Foundation (NSF), the Department of Energy's Office of Science, and the National Institute of Standards and Technology (NIST). The ACI responded to warnings from economists and industry leaders that the United States was at risk of losing its competitive technological edge to rising powers like China and India (Atkinson and Mayo, 2007).

However, despite its ambitious vision, the ACI struggled to gain traction. Congress failed to provide sustained financial support, and the initiative was effectively abandoned within a few years (Buigues and Sekkat, 2009). The lack of congressional backing for mainstream science and technology programs had cascading effects on earlier industrial policy efforts, particularly those launched in the 1980s and 1990s aimed at enhancing US technological competitiveness. Among the casualties was the Advanced Technology Program (ATP), an initiative administered by NIST that played a key role in fostering public-private partnerships to develop cutting-edge commercial technologies. Initially established in 1988, the ATP had supported high-risk, high-reward innovations that private firms were reluctant to fund (Bonvillian, 2003). Yet, under mounting political pressure from free-market advocates criticizing government involvement in industrial policy, the ATP's budget was gradually slashed throughout the early 2000s, culminating in the program's official termination in 2007 (Wade, 2014, p. 392).

The failures of the ATP and ACI highlighted the Bush administration's reluctance to embrace long-term, strategic industrial policy for the civilian economy. Despite occasional resistance from certain policymakers and industry groups, the administration largely subscribed to a minimalist vision of government intervention in industrial development. Rather than investing in broad-based innovation programs, Bush's approach prioritized short-term economic growth driven by public demand from the defense sector (Block, 2008).

Indeed, during the Bush years, defense-related R&D thrived, driving significant advancements in unmanned aerial vehicles (UAVs), GPS technology, and precision-guided munitions—areas where military funding delivered a clear and immediate return on investment (Gansler, 2011). While these innovations benefitted defense contractors and generated some spillover effects in civilian industries, they failed to lay a foundation for long-term, diversified industrial growth (Weiss, 2014). The absence of a comprehensive strategy for industrial renewal left key sectors such as advanced manufacturing, clean energy, and information technology without the sustained public investment needed to maintain long-term competitiveness (Mazzucato, 2013).

In short, by prioritizing military-driven technological development while allowing civilian industrial policy initiatives to languish, the Bush administration reverted to a narrow and reactive industrial strategy. This approach not only failed to address structural challenges in the US economy but also weakened the nation's ability to compete in emerging high-tech industries in the decades that followed.

7.3 Commercial Policy and International Treaties

At the outset of its first term, the Bush administration remained committed to upholding international trade agreement strategies that had defined US policy since the 1980s. The post-Cold War era continued to grant the United States significant global political influence, enabling it to shape international trade rules through multilateral frameworks such as the World Trade Organization (WTO). However, the early 2000s marked the beginning of a shift in global economic power. The era of US-led multilateralism was increasingly challenged by the rise of emerging economies, most notably China (see Figure 7.2).

A pivotal development in this transformation was China's accession to the WTO. After years of negotiations, China reached an agreement in 1999 to join the WTO, which became official at the start of George W. Bush's first term in 2001. This agreement was contingent on a five-year transitional period for China which required reducing its average tariff rate from 24.6% to 9.4%, eliminating restrictions on foreign direct investment, enhancing intellectual property protections, and allowing foreign firms greater access to supply state-owned enterprises (Kiely, 2015, p. 47).

Although these extended negotiations were designed to slow China's formal integration into global trade governance, China had already begun a decade-long transformation into the world's leading manufacturer and exporter. Throughout the late 1990s and early 2000s, China leveraged its low labor costs, aggressive industrial policies, and strategic state support to become the world's dominant manufacturing hub (Di Tommaso et al., 2013; Barbieri et al., 2015). By the time China's WTO membership was fully implemented, its economic ascent had already begun reshaping global trade.

China's rise was just one of many challenges facing the US-led multilateral trade framework. The WTO's launch of the Doha Development Round in 2001 aimed to liberalize global trade further by reducing tariffs, removing non-tariff barriers, and addressing agricultural subsidies (WTO, 2016). However, despite extensive negotiations, the Doha talks repeatedly failed to produce a final agreement. The most contentious issues involved US and European agricultural subsidies, trade protections in developing economies, and disagreements over services trade liberalization (Hopewell, 2016).

The failure of the Doha Round highlighted the growing shift away from US-driven trade multilateralism. The Bush administration, recognizing this limitation, increasingly pursued bilateral and regional trade agreements instead. The objective remained clear: expand market access for US exports while mitigating the competitive pressures of foreign imports.

According to data from the ERP (2009), by 2007, 41% of US exports were directed to countries with which the United States had a trade agreement, while only 31% of imports came from these same countries (ERP, 2009). These figures reinforced the belief that trade agreements remained an essential tool for supporting US industry and led to the rapid growth of both imports and exports (see Figure 7.3).

Despite efforts to open foreign markets to US exports (see Figure 7.4), the United States increasingly faced a growing trade deficit, particularly with China (see Figure 7.5). From 1990 to 2005, US imports from China and Hong Kong surged from 5.7% to 15% of total US imports, making China the single largest contributor to the US trade imbalance (Schwartz 2009b, cited in Kiely 2015, p. 106).

This widening trade deficit revealed a declining competitiveness in certain US industries, particularly in manufacturing sectors that struggled to compete with China's low-cost production. The pattern was stark: while the United States was importing more than it was exporting, China's trade surplus mirrored the US deficit, indicating a structural shift in global economic power.

Not all industries experienced the same degree of trade pressure. As illustrated in Figures 7.4 and 7.5, some sectors managed to maintain a balanced trade position or even improve over time. Among the industries expected to maintain or improve their trade balance in the 2000s were pharmaceuticals, beverages, tobacco, and iron and steel.

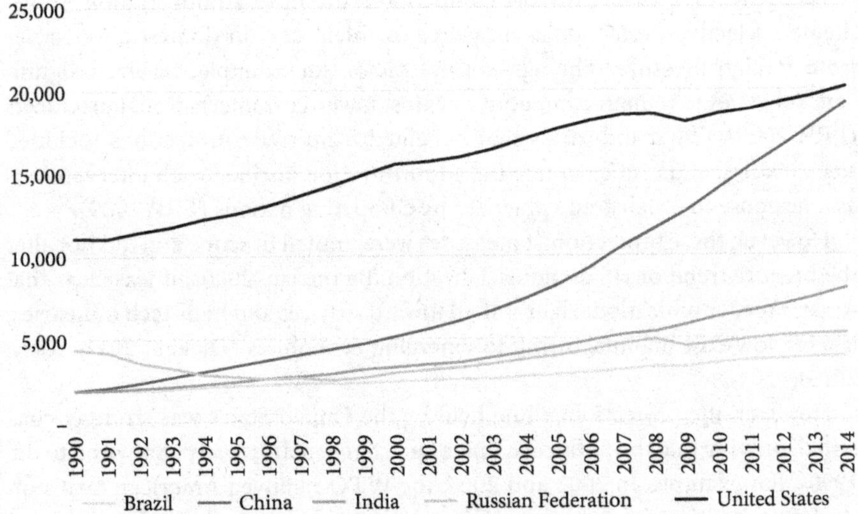

Figure 7.3 US and BRIC GDP: 1990–2014 (in billions of dollars)
Source: Elaborations on IMF and UN data

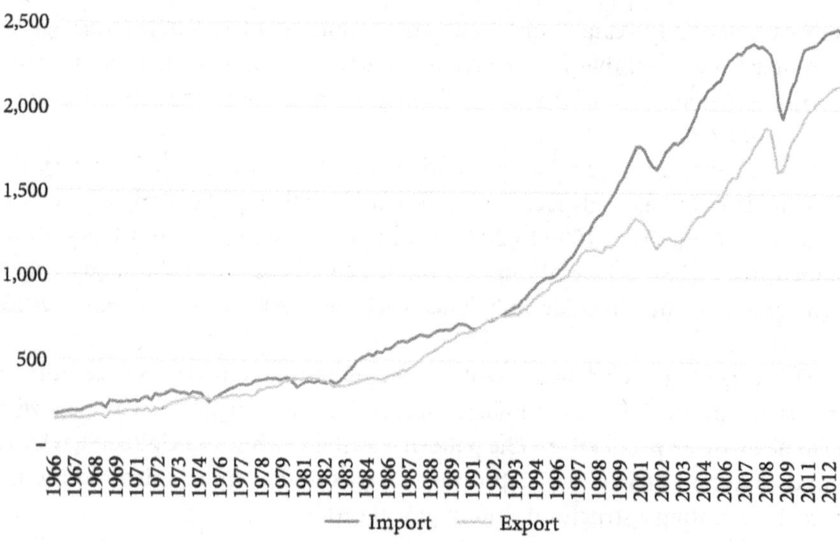

Figure 7.4 US Real Imports and Exports: 1996–2012 (in billions of dollars)
Source: Elaboration from Economic Report of the President (ERP, 2013)

However, other key industries experienced a significant and persistent trade deficit with China, including automobiles, machinery and electrical equipment, mechanical machinery, optical and precision instruments, plastics, and footwear.

Faced with increasing import competition, the Bush administration implemented selective protectionist measures to shield certain domestic industries from foreign pressure. The agricultural sector, for example, received significant subsidies to remain competitive against lower-cost international producers (ERP, 2009). Other industries that benefited from trade protections included steel, textiles, and timber, where the administration justified such interventions as a response to unfair trade practices by competing nations (ERP, 2009).

However, these protectionist measures were limited in scope and did not alter the broader trend of US deindustrialization. By the late 2000s, it was clear that America's economic model had shifted toward services and high-tech industries, leaving low-cost manufacturing to emerging economies (Dicken, 2011; Kiely, 2015).

However, the protectionist line held by the United States was strongly contested, proving that the political climate had changed drastically compared to the 1990s. For example, in 2003 and 2004, the WTO removed American tariffs on steel. Bush's industrial policy regarding steel was shaped by both domestic and international factors. The surge in cheap steel imports, particularly from China, resulted in significant challenges for the US steel industry. This contributed to

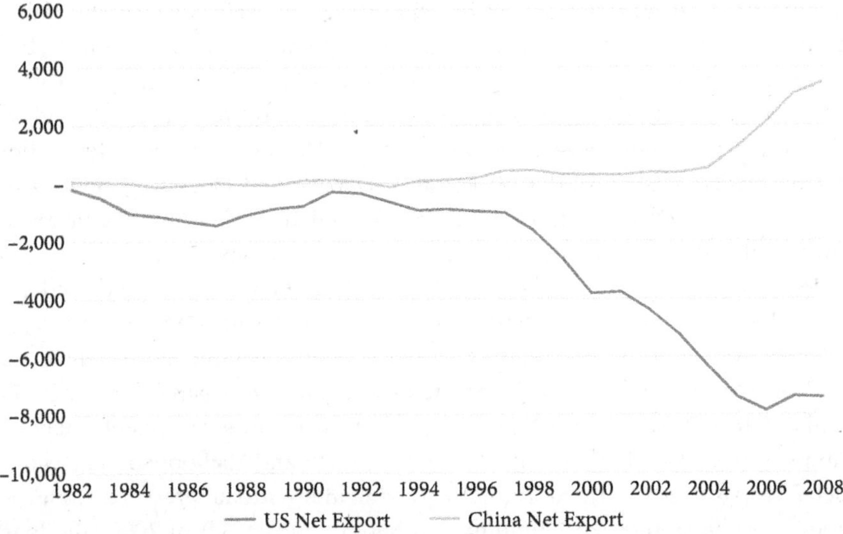

Figure 7.5 US and Chinese Net Exports: 1982–2008 (in billions of dollars)
Source: Elaborations on IMF and UN data

growing concerns about the loss of American manufacturing jobs and the trade deficit, prompting the administration to take action. The punishing tariffs varied between 8% to 30% on several types of steel imports, most heavily impacting tin mill steel—the main product of Weirton Steel, one of the largest employers in West Virginia, a state Bush won in the 2000 election, partially because of his campaign promise to safeguard the steel industry (IATP, 2002).

Notably, Canada and Mexico were exempt from the tariffs as the United States would incur penalties under prior free-trade agreements; developing or impoverished countries such as Argentina, Thailand, and Turkey were also exempt (IATP, 2002). The move drew swift criticism from American allies, some of whom the tariffs hit the hardest, with the European Union warning of potential retaliation in a similar fashion. Under threat of a global trade war, Bush lifted the steel tariffs on December 4, 2003, asserting confidence in the steel industry's recovery regardless of industry player protests (Knowlton, 2003).

Aside from steel tariffs, Bush also implemented additional sectoral policies that sought to bolster the green energy industry by targeting fossil fuel companies based in Alaska and the Gulf of Mexico. The Energy Policy Act of 2005 (EP Act) served as the primary instrument for conducting such industrial policy, hailed by Republican supporters as "the first major energy law enacted in more than a decade" (Federal Energy Regulatory Commission, 2020). Notably, Obama had voted in favor of the Act as senator, a harbinger of his administration's future direction in supporting the renewable energy industry (U.S. Congress, 2005). The Act supported grant programs, demonstration projects, and tax incentives to promote alternative fuels and advanced vehicles, offering loan guarantees for companies that innovate or use technologies that negate the production of greenhouse gases (U.S. Environmental Protection Agency, 2024). Crucially, the EP Act also strengthened federal regulations on fuel economy testing and against market manipulation to safeguard consumers from exploitation (Federal Energy Regulatory Commission, 2020).

In addition to the EP Act, Congress passed the Economic Growth and Tax Relief Reconciliation Act of 2001 and the Jobs and Growth Tax Relief Reconciliation Act of 2003, enacting tax cuts that disproportionately benefited the top 1% of households and widened the income inequality gap (Horton, 2017). Dubbed the "Bush tax cuts," the wide-scale rollback of government intervention led to weaker-than-average economic growth and "ballooned deficits and debt" (Horton, 2017). In 2007, under growing international pressure, Congress abolished the Continued Dumping and Subsidy Offset Act of 2000 (the Byrd Amendment), which established that funds obtained from duties on imported products were distributed to firms facing difficulty (an amount of about 840 million dollars for the years from 2001 to 2003).

The World Trade Organization (WTO) ruled against the United States' Foreign Sales Corporation provisions, determining that the associated tax exemptions constituted prohibited export subsidies. This decision led to significant changes in US tax law to comply with international trade rules (Pierce and Schott, 2012). Although US manufacturing employment remained relatively stable from 1965 to 2000, it experienced a sharp decline of 18% between March 2001 and March 2007. This downturn was further exacerbated by China's rapid economic growth and its integration into the WTO, which intensified competition for US manufacturers. The decline in US manufacturing was exacerbated by China's growth, and subsequent integration into the WTO. While US manufacturing declined, this trend was not represented in the bullish housing market, which continued to overestimate the wealth of American homeowners.

Despite the displacement of workers, a decline in industrial production, and an increase in surplus going to Chinese imports, the stock market continued to rise. The Industrial Select Sector SPDR Fund (XLI), a key index for the industrial sector, grew by just under 31.5% in nominal value and 13.8% in real value from the end of 2000 to late September of 2007. It took six more years for the SPDR to reach the nominal level it was at in late September of 2007 (Microsoft Network Watchlist). In contrast, the S&P 500 only grew by about 11.6% nominally in this same time period. There was actually a 6.1% decrease in the real value of the S&P 500 (Macro Trends, 2024). While Chinese imports quickly reduced American manufacturing, its full effect on the US economy was substantially delayed.

7.4 The Outbreak of the Crisis: 2008

In 2008, we saw the outbreak of the financial crisis. This sudden explosion forced Bush to intervene when he was at the end of his second term. Nothing had been foreseen until a few weeks before. The crisis resulted in one of the most aggressive interventions of a government in American history, undoubtedly clashing with the Republican rhetoric, which had been opposed to government interference since the first Bush election campaign. However, there was no time to hesitate: it was necessary to intervene with the utmost urgency.

On September 15, 2008, Lehman Brothers formally initiated a bankruptcy procedure, a decision taken after the bank had to acknowledge that no buyer was willing to save it and that the US government would not intervene to prevent bankruptcy. With a debt of about $613 billion, failure would potentially create systemic risk. The Lehman crash had no comparable precedent, and, in a few hours, panic broke out in America and around the world.

The United States, at the time, was in the midst of a full presidential election cycle. Republican candidate John McCain concurred with the decision not to use taxpayers' money to save Lehman. Nonetheless, Bush shifted positions, declaring himself seriously worried about the economy. Prompted by suggestions of government intervention, Bush declared: "We are working to reduce disruptions and minimize the impact of these financial market developments on the broader economy" (CNN, 2008).

In any case, it had to be clear that it was an intervention legitimized only by the exceptional nature of the moment. The premise was that the basic ideas that inspired Republican thinking remained solid.

> History has shown that the greater threat to economic prosperity is not too little government involvement in the market, it is too much government involvement in the market [...]. While reforms in the financial sector are essential, the long-term solution to today's problems is sustained economic growth. And the surest path to that growth is free markets and free people. [...] Free market capitalism is far more than economic theory. It is the engine of social mobility – the highway to the American Dream. [...] If you seek economic growth, if you seek opportunity, if you seek social justice and human dignity, the free market system is the way to go (Bush, 2008b).

In addition, no protectionist temptation could make its way abroad without repercussions. It was important not to be questioned by friendly countries about what had been done in previous decades through bilateral, multilateral negotiations, and the promotion of free-trade areas.

Just as important as maintaining free markets within countries is maintaining the free movement of goods and services between countries. When nations open their markets to trade and invest, their businesses, farmers and workers find new buyers for their products. Neo-classical economics assumes consumers benefit from more choices and better prices. Entrepreneurs can get their ideas off the ground with funding from anywhere in the world. Thanks in large part to open markets, the volume of global trade today is nearly 30 times greater than it was six decades ago – and some of the most dramatic gains have come in the developing world (Bush, 2008b).

However, despite this ideological commitment, it was clear to the Bush administration that the exceptional nature of the moment required extraordinary government intervention. The intervention was indeed requested by the banks and the national industry. And so it was:

These are not normal circumstances. The market is not functioning properly. There's been a widespread loss of confidence. And major sectors of America's financial system are at risk of shutting down. The government's top economic experts warn that without immediate action by Congress, America could slip into a financial panic (Bush, 2008a).

In October 2008, amid the worst financial crisis since the Great Depression, the Troubled Asset Relief Program (TARP) was launched. President George W. Bush urged Congress to approve a $700 billion bailout plan to stabilize the collapsing financial system. The legislation authorized the federal government to purchase toxic assets—primarily high-risk, mortgage-backed securities whose values had plummeted with the real estate market collapse (Paulson, 2010; Blinder, 2013). Bush had justified the intervention, stating: "The government is the only institution patient enough to buy these assets at their current low prices and hold them until their prices return to normal" (Bush, 2008a).

Despite the urgency of the crisis, the roots of the Great Recession had been developing for years. Among the many contributing factors of the meltdown, one of the most significant was America's economic relationship with China and its broader impact on US financial markets (Krugman, 2009; Stiglitz, 2010). Throughout the 2000s, American households became increasingly indebted due to cheap credit, financial deregulation, and an overvalued real estate market (Saad-Filho, 2011). A critical aspect of this growing debt was that it was largely financed by capital inflows from China. At the same time, the US federal deficit ballooned, largely due to the War on Terror and increased defense spending after 9/11 (Stiglitz and Bilmes, 2008; Blanchard et al., 2012).

China, benefiting from a trade surplus with the United States, reinvested much of its earnings in US Treasury bonds, effectively lending money to the US government and consumers (Bernanke, 2005; Kiely, 2015). This influx of liquidity kept interest rates artificially low, making it easier for banks to expand lending, particularly in real estate (Bianchi and Mendoza, 2010). At the same time, American consumers relied on debt-fueled consumption, enabled by: 1) Cheap Chinese imports, which lowered inflation and increased purchasing power despite stagnant wages; 2) Easy access to subprime mortgages, allowing households—including low-income buyers—to purchase homes with minimal down payments and weak credit histories (Moessner and Allen, 2011); and 3) Rising real estate values, which encouraged speculative investments and further borrowing.

This system was self-reinforcing: as home values surged, Americans borrowed more against their rising home equity, increasing speculation in the housing market (Blinder, 2013; Stiglitz, 2010). However, once home prices peaked and demand began to slow, the debt-driven model became unsustainable. By mid 2007, the first signs of distress appeared in the real estate market. As inflation rose, the Federal Reserve raised interest rates, making mortgages more expensive. Many subprime mortgage holders—those with weak credit—could no longer afford their payments. As a result, foreclosures skyrocketed, driving property values down and triggering a domino effect throughout the financial system (Edey, 2009; Attali, 2010; Bianchi and Mendoza, 2010).

The crisis was further exacerbated by a host of things: financial institutions that had issued loans without adequate collateral, assuming ever-rising housing prices would offset risks (Krugman, 2009); packaged and sold mortgage-backed securities as safe investments, even though they were based on risky subprime loans (Blanchard et al., 2012); and engaged in complex financial engineering, including derivatives like collateralized debt obligations (CDOs) and credit default swaps, which spread risk throughout the global economy (Barnett-Hart, 2009). As property values collapsed, America's debt-fueled economy crumbled. Banks that had overleveraged themselves on risky mortgage-backed securities began failing or required massive government bailouts to survive. Financial giants like Lehman Brothers collapsed, while others, such as Bear Stearns, AIG, and Citigroup, required unprecedented government intervention (Akyüz, 2014).

The crisis sent shockwaves through the global economy. US consumption contracted as households cut spending and increased savings out of fear for the future. It also led to a drop in imports, particularly from Europe and China, which depended on US consumer demand. And it led to a financial crisis in Europe, where banks had heavily invested in US mortgage-backed securities (Allen and Moessner, 2012).

The financial collapse in 2008 marked the beginning of a global recession, the effects of which would last for years. It spurred major financial reforms under the Obama administration, including the Dodd-Frank Act and new rules governing Wall Street (Blinder, 2013). While the TARP bailout temporarily stabilized the financial system, it did not address the fundamental economic issues of the crisis. As the global economy adjusted, debates over free trade, financial regulation, and America's economic relationship with China intensified, setting the stage for future policy shifts (Stiglitz, 2010; Kiely, 2015).

7.5 The Rescue

As the Great Recession unfolded, the Bush administration initially focused its intervention where the crisis had begun—the real estate market. Recognizing the potential for systemic collapse, policymakers moved quickly. Without much warning, Congress passed the Housing and Economic Recovery Act (HERA) in July 2008, seeking to stabilize a financial sector that was beginning to unravel (Bernanke, 2015). One of the primary concerns was the fate of Fannie Mae (Federal National Mortgage Association) and Freddie Mac (Federal Home Loan Mortgage Corporation), two government-sponsored enterprises that together managed approximately $5 trillion in mortgage-backed securities (Frame et al., 2015).[1]

In the 1990s, under the Clinton administration, both agencies adopted more aggressive lending strategies, facilitating the issuance of subprime mortgages to borrowers with higher credit risks (Acharya et al., 2011). However, as housing prices plummeted in 2007–2008, these institutions found themselves financially vulnerable and faced massive losses. In response, the Bush administration placed them under federal conservatorship in September 2008. The Federal Housing Finance Agency assumed control, while the Treasury Department provided an emergency bailout totaling $187.5 billion to keep the two entities solvent (Frame et al., 2015). Henry Paulson, the Treasury Secretary who accompanied the announcement of the government's intervention, explained the decision to prevent their bankruptcy:

> Fannie Mae and Freddie Mac are so large and so interwoven in our financial system that a failure of either of them would cause great turmoil in our financial markets here at home and around the globe. This turmoil would directly and

[1] Originally established under President Franklin D. Roosevelt (U.S. Congress, 1938) and President Lyndon B. Johnson (U.S. Congress, 1970), these institutions played a significant role in expanding homeownership.

negatively impact household wealth: from family budgets, to home values, to savings for college and retirement. A failure would affect the ability of Americans to get home loans, auto loans and other consumer credit and business finance. And a failure would be harmful to economic growth and job creation. That is why we have taken these actions today" (Bush, 2008b).

Recognizing the systemic risks of the 2008 financial crisis, President George W. Bush's administration took decisive measures to stabilize banks and prevent the collapse of key financial institutions. One of the most significant actions was the implementation of TARP in October 2008, authorized under the Emergency Economic Stabilization Act of 2008 (U.S. Congress, 2008). Initially, TARP was conceived as a $700 billion fund aiming to restore liquidity and confidence in the financial system by purchasing toxic assets from distressed financial firms (Congressional Budget Office, 2024). However, the program evolved into a direct capital injection mechanism, with the federal government acquiring equity stakes in major banks and other financial institutions, shifting its focus to recapitalization (U.S. Government Accountability Office, 2023).

During this critical period, financial stability dominated the 2008 presidential campaign. Both major candidates, Barack Obama and John McCain, actively engaged in discussions over the financial rescue. Ultimately, both endorsed the TARP initiative, recognizing that failure to act could trigger a catastrophic collapse. In a joint statement, Obama and McCain said:

> The American people are facing a moment of economic crisis. No matter how this began, we all have a responsibility to work through it and restore confidence in our economy. The jobs, savings, and prosperity of the American people are at stake. Now is a time to come together—Democrats and Republicans—in a spirit of cooperation for the sake of the American people" (Zeleny, 2008).

Approximately half of the allocated funds were managed under the Bush administration, while the remaining balance, often referred to as "TARP II," was implemented under President Obama (Mishkin, 2011). By the end of his term, Bush had disbursed roughly $350 billion in TARP funds to prevent the collapse of major financial institutions. The Treasury Department released a detailed list of approximately 300 banks that received TARP funds before Bush left office, with the largest 25 recipients receiving a total of $177 billion by January 20, 2009 (see Figure 7.6).

However, TARP was not limited to financial institutions. Recognizing the dire situation in the American auto industry, the Bush administration extended financial assistance to struggling automakers through the Automotive Industry Financing Program (Webel and Canis, 2015). General Motors (GM) and

N.	Date	Institute name	City	State	Investment ($)
1	28/10/2008	Bank of America Corporation	Charlotte	NC	25,000,000,000
2	28/10/2008	Citigroup Inc.	New York	NY	25,000,000,000
3	28/10/2008	JP Morgan Chase & Co.	New York	NY	25,000,000,000
4	28/10/2008	Wells Fargo & Company	San Francisco	CA	25,000,000,000
5	28/10/2008	Morgan Stanley	New York	NY	10,000,000,000
6	28/10/2008	The Goldman Sachs Group Inc.	New York	NY	10,000,000,000
7	31/12/2008	The PNC Financial Services Group Inc.	Pittsburgh	PA	7,579,200,000
8	14/11/2008	U.S. Bancorp	Minneapolis	MN	6,599,000,000
9	14/11/2008	SunTrust Banks Inc.	Atlanta	GA	4,850,000,000
10	14/11/2008	Capital One Financial Corporation	McLean	VA	3,555,199,000
11	14/11/2008	Regions Financial Corporation	Birmingham	AL	3,500,000,000
12	31/12/2008	Fifth Third Bancorp	Cincinnati	OH	3,408,000,000
13	01/01/2009	American Express Company	New York	NY	3,388,890,000
14	14/11/2008	BB&T Corp.	Winston-Salem	NC	3,133,640,000
15	28/10/2008	The Bank of New York Mellon Corp.	New York	NY	3,000,000,000
16	14/11/2008	KeyCorp	Cleveland	OH	2,500,000,000
17	31/12/2008	CIT Group Inc.	New York	NY	2,330,000,000
18	14/11/2008	Comerica Inc.	Dallax	TX	2,250,000,000
19	28/10/2008	State Stree Corporation	Boston	MA	2,000,000,000
20	14/11/2008	Marshall & Ilsley Corporation	Milwakee	WI	1,715,000,000
21	14/11/2008	Northern Trust Corporation	Chicago	IL	1,576,000,000
22	14/11/2008	Zions Bancorporation	Salt Lake City	UT	1,400,000,000
23	14/11/2008	Huntington Bancshares	Columbus	OH	1,398,071,000
24	19/12/2008	Synovus Financial Corp.	Columbus	GA	967,870,000
25	05/12/2008	Popular, Inc.	San Juan	PR	935,000,000

Figure 7.6 Funds Disbursed before January 20, 2009

Chrysler, two of the nation's largest automakers, were teetering on the edge of bankruptcy as consumer demand collapsed. Federal intervention was deemed essential to prevent further economic dislocation, and funds were allocated to support these companies (see Figure 7.7) (Anginer and Warburton, 2010; Canis and Yacobucci, 2010; Helper and Henderson, 2014).

Defending his decision, Bush later stated: "I didn't want there to be 21 percent unemployment. [. . .] I did not want to look back and say, 'Bush could have done something but chose not to do it'" (Glass, 2018). His successor, President Obama, later affirmed the necessity of these measures, calling them

Society	City, State	Date	Investment ($)
GMAC	Detroit, MI	29/12/2008	5,000,000,000.00
General Motors	Detroit, MI	29/12/2008	884,024,131
		31/12/2008	13,400,000,000
Chrysler FinCo	Farmington Hills, MI	16/01/2009	1,500,000,000
Chrysler	Auburn Hills, MI	02/01/2009	4,000,000,000

Figure 7.7 Automotive Industry Financing Program 2009

"a necessary step to avoid collapse in our auto industry that would have devastating consequences for our economy and our workers" (Reuters, 2008).

The crisis response, while controversial, was instrumental in stabilizing the financial system and preventing a deeper economic catastrophe. The measures initiated under the Bush administration laid the groundwork for continued intervention under the Obama administration, which oversaw further economic recovery efforts in the years that followed.

7.6 Final Remarks

Bush's industrial policy actions were driven by international and domestic factors. The ascension of China to the WTO, and the subsequent integration into the global economy and global supply chains put pressure on the US's success in manufacturing. The cheap imports available from China led to a growing trade deficit and required intervention in the economy to save US jobs and industries. Additionally, 9/11 placed national security at the top of the agenda for Americans and the Bush administration. The terrorist attacks created the need to increase domestic production of defense tools and ratchet up US military strength. The instability in the Middle East after 9/11 also drove industrial policy actions in energy. Bush focused on preserving American energy independence to prevent undue reliance on the region.

Domestically, Bush responded to concerns raised by the public in regard to the economic downturn as well as pressure from industries affected by the "China shock." First, Bush responded quickly to the economic collapse through the Housing and Economic Recovery Act to aid the American public. He also instituted broad bailouts through TARP to preserve the American banking industry. In addition to the domestic pressure throughout the economic crisis, Bush responded to US industry concerns due to the "China shock." In particular, the steel industry was effective at lobbying Bush to institute temporary tariffs which were instituted in 2002.

All these actions were colored by Bush's ideology. His free-market stance resulted in industrial policy being provided in the form of tax cuts and incentives for investment, rather than direct support in the form of grants toward certain industries. His administration also maintained a skepticism toward climate change—and overall opposition to intervening in the service of the environment—that resulted in significant support to fossil fuel industries and limited subsidies for renewable energies.

Bush's support was targeted toward specific sectors and regions. The Energy Policy Act of 2005 was particularly focused on fossil fuel companies that were concentrated in the Gulf of Mexico, Alaska, and shale fields.

These tax incentives were beneficial to companies like ExxonMobil, Chevron, and Halliburton. Bush also increased defense contracts in the aftermath of 9/11 with specific benefits for defense and aerospace companies. The military engagements in the Middle East required more fighting power than was provided by Boeing, Lockheed Martin, and Northrop. Bush also instituted tariffs that were requested by the domestic industry in the aftermath of the China shock, with temporary steel tariffs as an important example.

Bush used tax credits, trade protection, and deregulation to institute his industrial policy. In line with his free-market viewpoints, Bush hoped to stimulate private investment and growth by reducing the tax burden for firms. The Energy Policy Act, the Economic Growth and Tax Relief Reconciliation Act, and the Jobs and Growth Tax Relief Reconciliation Act used tax reductions extensively to benefit companies. Furthermore, Bush responded to the "China shock" by placing trade protections and tariffs on certain industries to avoid widespread industry exposure to the influx of cheap imports. Finally, Bush sought to create favorable business conditions and induce growth by rolling back environmental and financial regulations.

There were distinct political coalitions for and against Bush's industrial policy programs. The industrial policy programs instituted by the Bush administration were very favorable to the US Chamber of Commerce and industry lobbies. In particular, his policies were extremely beneficial to oil and gas, defense and aerospace, and financial institutions which subsequently supported him. In addition, voters in states that heavily relied on these industries benefited and supported these policies. Bush instituted his policy with the guiding ideology of creating permissive business conditions under free-market principles which were appealing to the Republican base as well as libertarian think tanks. While Bush did aim to raise corporate accountability and reporting standards through the Sarbanes-Oxley Act in 2002, the Securities and Exchange Commission (SEC) ultimately lacked strong regulation of the mortgage market and credit default swaps (Wood, 2009). The loosening of such regulations allowed major investment banks to reduce their capital reserves, increasing their risk exposure, and emboldened commercial lenders to engage in trading products like collateralized debt obligations and mortgage-backed securities, which culminated in the collapse of the subprime housing bubble and the subsequent 2007–2008 financial crisis.

However, these industrial policy programs were opposed extensively by environmental groups, labor unions, and Democratic lawmakers. The extensive support to the oil and gas industry resulted in minimal investment and significant disadvantages for renewable companies. In addition, the focus on fossil fuels was opposed by groups like the Sierra Club, the Natural Resources Defense Council, and Greenpeace. Unions expressed concern that the Bush administration was not doing enough to prioritize the interests of workers and was instead offering tax cuts to big businesses. At the same time, the manufacturing industry was witnessing the continual loss of jobs to outsourcing, especially in the wake of the China shock. Therefore, there was harsh criticism of Bush's inability to preserve manufacturing jobs in the United States and prioritize union labor. These concerns for workers' rights and the environment were echoed by Democratic lawmakers.

Bush's industrial policy was successful at stimulating the economy, strengthening the defense industry, and cementing energy independence. Consumer spending and business investment increased in the wake of the Bush tax cuts and tax credit programs in the early 2000s. These policies also had long-term consequences of cementing pro-business tax policies in future US administrations. Next, the investments in the defense industry resulted in expansive government contracts and military resources in the wake of 9/11. As a result, these industries were successful in developing high-tech manufacturing and research in cybersecurity, missile defense, and drone technology. Finally, the expansion of fossil fuel industries did increase domestic fuel production and secured energy independence from the Middle East.

The industrial policy programs under the Bush administration had serious negative effects on income inequality, environmental progress, and regulatory oversight. By prioritizing a permissive business environment and low corporate taxes, tax policy in the United States became increasingly regressive, placing more of the burden on citizens rather than big businesses. These changes occurred at the same time as middle-class manufacturing jobs were declining, creating massive structural setbacks in inequality. Furthermore, the prioritization of fossil fuels also limited the success of renewable energy and set back the United States from achieving and cooperating on international environmental goals. Finally, the deregulation of the financial industry—continued from previous Republican administrations in the 1980s and 1990s—led to the collapse of the housing bubble and financial markets in the 2008 financial crisis. Therefore, while these interventions were successful to some extent, they had long-term negative consequences.

8

Obama

Crisis, the Bailout, and Promoting National Industry

8.1 Introduction

The election of President Obama should have coincided with a diversion from the past. This was the central message that then-Senator Obama had used to initiate and win the election. "Time for change" is the most effective slogan that summarized Obama's position, which carried him from his first election to the end of his long campaign (Coe and Reitzes, 2010; Ivie and Giner, 2009). "In six days, we can choose hope over fear, unity over division, the promise of change over the power of the status quo. [. . .] America's time for change has come" (Obama, 2008). This was a change that should have dispelled fears of the war on terrorism and the Great Financial Crisis, as well as rebuilt the image of the United States internationally.

Senator Obama, since the announcement of his first presidential candidacy, had proposed that he was the man who embodied the necessary change in US politics. Obama positioned himself as someone who could guarantee a strong discontinuity with the Bush administration and opposition to Republican projects. After the Financial Crisis broke out, Obama was able to push the events in his favor by presenting himself as a representative of alternative economic interests. Obama focused on working- and middle-class Americans, who did not benefit from a bailout during the Great Recession. Obama attempted to position himself in direct opposition to the economic interests of the political establishment, which Obama equated with his challenger, McCain, and Republicans who had governed over the last eight years:

> We are in the middle of the worst economic crisis since the Great Depression. 760,000 workers have lost their jobs this year. Businesses and families can't get credit. Home values are falling. Pensions are disappearing. Wages are lower than they've been in a decade, at a time when the cost of healthcare and college have never been higher. It's getting harder and harder to make the mortgage, or fill up your gas tank, or even keep the electricity on at the end of the month. [. . .] For eight years, we've seen Washington take care of the extremely well-off and well-connected, and now my opponent is making the same old arguments to

Governing Growth. Marco R. Di Tommaso and Vinod K. Aggarwal, Oxford University Press.
© Oxford University Press (2026). DOI: 10.1093/oso/9780197821787.003.0008

justify the same old policies that have been a complete failure for the middle class. He wants to give more to billionaires, more to corporations that ship jobs overseas, more to the same people whose greed and irresponsibility got us into this crisis. We're here because we know they shouldn't get away with it any more (Obama, 2008).

In the last months of an intense election cycle, the economic crisis, as well as its effects on Americans, became the central theme of debate between the candidates. Uncertainty about the future became a common sentiment as possible panic scared markets, industries, and the whole American society. In this context, Obama characterized himself as someone who would have had no hesitation in the moment of emergency: a Commander-in-Chief who would be able to intervene promptly and lead the country out of the crisis. With a careful rhetoric that didn't excessively target the average American's susceptibility, Obama spoke about a government that acts decisively to counter the crisis:

> I don't believe that the government can or should try to solve all our problems. I know you don't either. But I do believe that the government should do that which we cannot do for ourselves – protect us from harm and provide a decent education for our children; invest in new roads and new science and technology. It should reward drive and innovation and growth in the free market, but it should also make sure businesses live up to their responsibility to create American jobs, and look out for American workers, and play by the rules of the road (Obama, 2008).

Under these circumstances, Obama won the elections during a bleak November for the American economy, immediately clarifying the objectives that his new administration would pursue: relaunching the economy, reducing unemployment, promoting the competitiveness of American industry at an international level, and doing it all with due attention to social equity and environmental protection.

However, on January 21, 2009, the effective beginning of Obama's first term, the situation appeared even more critical than in November. The administration believed that there was no longer enough time to keep up with complex structural reforms that could fix the medium- and long-term problems with the economy. Obama's economic policy began at a very delicate moment, in which it was still necessary to mitigate the panic over the possible collapse of the national economy. In other words, the escalation of the crisis was the first factor that prevented the immediate change of course that was promised during the election campaign. Many of the initiatives promoted at the end of the Bush era were promptly given continuity. It was difficult to propose policies that could encourage long-term structural changes, which is what the public, national industry, banks, and trade unions had asked for.

In any case, the difficulties of promoting change had another origin, which was considered more structural and did not depend on the exceptional nature of the moment. Even in the Obama era, the industries that had always asked for and obtained special relations with the government would continue to do so: the banking system, industrial-military complex, and automotive industry. Adding to this traditional demand were the emerging interests of ICT, green energy, and health industries that had supported the election of the new president. In other words, old and new interests both shared the need to revive growth by combating the crisis. Not only did they seek to recover from the crisis, but they also sought to be protected from international competitors and expand the extension of their external markets.

8.2 The Actions to Combat the Crisis

Despite Obama's promise to address the economic concerns of the people, his administration continued with the strategy that Bush implemented in the last months of his term. First, a rescue intervention for banks—the Financial Stability Plan (FSP)—was approved by Congress in February 2009. Via the FSP, the government, among various initiatives, bought $2 trillion worth of loans from banks to encourage increased liquidity in the system and establish a climate of trust. However, this grand intervention was not particularly impactful: indeed, banks continued to refuse granting new loans due to negative expectations on the general economic trend (Di Tommaso and Schweitzer, 2013). Second, the TARP initiatives continued. After the large amount of funds allocated by the Bush administration, Obama resumed loans to banks and credit institutions after he took office. This was the so-called TARP II: more than 11 billion dollars were allocated under the only Capital Purchase Program (CCP), an intervention that involved over 400 American banks. Figure 8.1 shows the list of the 25 banking groups that received the largest amount of TARP II funds, after January 20, 2009, for a total of about 7.5 billion dollars.[1]

However, Obama went beyond the FSP and the simple continuity of TARP II. The American Recovery and Reinvestment Act (ARRA) was the first major intervention that stayed true to Obama's campaign promise of differentiating himself

---

[1] Please refer to the same Figure 7.6 presented in the previous chapter, which shows the main companies that received funds from the Bush administration within the CCP.

N.	Date	Istitute name	City	State	Investment ($)
1	26/06/2009	The Hartford Financial Services Group, Inc.	Hartford	CT	3,400,000
2	13/03/2009	Discover Financial Services	Riverwood	Il	1,224,558
3	10/07/2009	Lincoln National Cot.	Radnor	PA	950,000
4	30/01/2009	Flagstat Bancorp, Inc.	Troy	MI	266,657
5	30/01/2009	Privatebancorp, Inc.	Chicago	IL	243,815
6	20/02/2009	First Merchants Corporation	Muncie	IN	116,000
7	23/01/2009	1st Source Corporation	South Bend	IN	111,000
8	30/01/2009	Anchor Bancorp Wisconsin, Inc.	Madison	WI	110,000
9	30/01/2009	W.T.B. Financial Corporation	Spokane	WA	110,000
10	06/03/2009	First Busey Corporation	Urbana	IL	110,000
11	13/02/2009	Westamerica Bancorporation	San Rafael	CA	83,726
12	27/02/2009	Integra Bank Corporation	Evansville	IN	83,586
13	13/03/2009	First Place Financial Corp.	Warren	OH	72,927
14	26/06/2009	Metropolitan Bank Group, Inc.	Chicago	IL	71,526
15	27/03/2009	Apline Banks Of Colorado	Glenwood Springs	CO	70,000
16	24/04/2009	Standard Bancshares, Inc.	Hickory Hills	IL	60,000
17	06/02/2009	Lakeland Bancorp, Inc.	Oak Ridge	NJ	59,000
18	23/01/2009	Liberty Bancshares, Inc (Ar)	Jonesboro	AR	57,500
19	27/02/2009	Lakeland Financial Corporation	Warsaw	IN	56,044
20	23/01/2009	Wsts Financial Corporation	Wilmington	DE	52,625
21	11/09/2009	Community Bancshares Of Mississippi, Inc. / Community Bancshares Of Mississippi	Brandon	MS	52,000
22	13/02/2009	Communityone Bancorp / Fnb United Corp.	Asheboro	NC	51,500
23	07/08/2009	U.S. Century Bank	Miami	FL	50,236
24	24/07/2009	First American Bank Corporation	Elk Groove Village	IL	50,000
25	17/07/2009	First South Bancorp, Inc.	Lexington	TN	50,000

Figure 8.1 Funds Disbursed after January 20, 2009

from the Bush administration. The framework of the ARRA was still focused on rescue, but it also supported employment for the weakest sections of the population affected by the crisis and stimulated the revival of the entire economy. The newly elected president intended to use the ARRA to immediately validate his credibility by giving a clear signal to the nation and international markets that the Obama administration would prioritize domestic employment. More than 260,000 subsidized jobs were created in order to jumpstart the economy (Shah, 2017). It was an impressive package to be promoted so early—less than a month after the start of his presidential term. As the ERP (2010) notes, the "President signed the Recovery Act in Denver on February 17, just 28 days after taking office. At an estimated cost of $787 billion, the Act is the largest countercyclical fiscal action in American history" (pp. 51–52).

The ARRA was an extraordinary intervention, which was primarily intended to address the economic emergency. About a third of the law's budget was made available to support families and businesses. Among the most important interventions, the Making Work Pay lowered taxes for an "average" family by about $800 per year in 2010 and 2011. The ARRA then allocated approximately $14 billion for support to the elderly, veterans, and people with disability (ERP, 2010).[2] The program also allocated some $90 billion to support those directly affected by the crisis: subsidies and insurance for the unemployed and funds for the most serious cases under the Supplemental Nutrition Assistance Program. Finally, an important part of the funds made available by ARRA was used in the form of tax reductions to individual States to prevent them from unduly reducing the level of public spending or considerably increasing the tax burden.[3]

Additionally, within the ARRA, selective industrial policy interventions were proposed, which were intended to impact specific sectors of the economy and the wider national industry. These interventions were promoted with the idea of combining economic objectives with more complex social objectives. Indeed, the 2010 ERP states:

The Administration has also focused special attention on certain areas where particular national needs are urgent. These include investments in building a «smart grid» to enhance the reliability, flexibility, and efficiency of the electricity transmission grid; research on renewable energy technologies like wind, solar, and biofuels; and support for research into advanced vehicle technologies. These investments are motivated not only by the perception that technological breakthroughs are possible and would be highly valuable, but also by the enormous potential benefits that such breakthroughs could have in terms of enhancing national security, mitigating pollution, and stemming climate change. These are also investments that have a direct impact on creating high-paying, durable jobs—something that is particularly valuable at a time of high unemployment (ERP, 2010, p. 272).

[2] Other initiatives were subsequently aimed at reducing those social inequalities that had been in many cases exacerbated by the long crisis. The main proposals put forward by the administration in this area concerned the raising of the minimum wage and the expansion of the Earned Income Tax Credit for workers without children.

[3] In subsequent years, challenges associated with the expansion of public debt became increasingly pronounced, particularly at the federal level. Beginning with the second term of the Obama administration, significant attention was directed toward addressing fiscal challenges, notably the implications of the fiscal cliff in early 2013, as well as the development of long-term debt reduction strategies. Within this framework, there was a heightened emphasis on the implementation of impact assessment methodologies for public programs, with the objective of enhancing administrative efficiency and reducing expenditures (ERP, 2014).

CAPITAL	Estimated cost (2009–2019) billions of dollars
Transport infrastructure	30
Environment conservation	28
Building construction	23.9
Public Security and Defense	8.9
Economic Development	14.6
Subsidies for companies	11.7
LABOR	
University scholarships	17.3
Special training	12.2
Aid for Children with disadvantages	13
Other	10.3
TECHNOLOGY	
Scientific Research	18.3
Clean Energy	78.5
Health	32
Broadband	6.9
Other	6.7
TOTAL PUBLIC INVESTMENT	**300.6**

Figure 8.2 ARRA: Investments for long-run growth, by category

Source: Council of Economic Advisors, The Economic Impact of ARRA Five Years Later: Final Report to the Congress, 2014.

In this context, about a third of the total resources made available by ARRA were immediately allocated to the promotion of specific economic sectors considered strategic for the well-being of the country, including the energy sector, green industries, broadband sector, nanotechnology, automotive, and healthcare (ERP, 2010, pp. 53–54). Figure 8.2 shows the allocation of ARRA resources as part of the expenditure planned from 2009 to 2019 in public investments (amounting to approximately $300 billion). The resources are divided into capital investments (including transportation, environmental conservation, and construction) as well as workforce investments and new technologies (including environmental, healthcare technologies, and broadband connections).

In line with this strategic perspective and willingness to intervene selectively, the Obama administration introduced a strategy specifically aimed at the manufacturing sector (Executive Office of the President, 2009). In August 2010, the US Manufacturing Enhancement Act was promoted (Jones, 2012) as the law that would relaunch American manufacturing, while in June 2011, the Advanced Manufacturing Partnership (AMP) Plan was developed (Obama White House, 2011).

The basic idea behind these initiatives was to recreate the conditions for national (and international) manufacturing to take root, grow, and innovate in the United States.[4] The administration promoted detailed back-shoring policies with the explicit objective of encouraging the return of American manufacturing firms from abroad (ERP, 2014). Back-to-manufacturing is theorized and encouraged by highlighting the role that manufacturing can play in driving economic growth, innovation, and employment processes (Tregenna, 2009, 2014; Andreoni and Scazzieri, 2014). Within this framework, great care is taken for the ability to attract (and select) foreign productive investments.

A particular legislative innovation in this field is the Select USA Initiative, initially discussed in 2009, before being launched in 2011 and strengthened in 2013 (ERP, 2014).[5] The program envisioned the establishment of teams led by American ambassadors (of the 32 countries considered most strategic for the US economy) to encourage foreign investment in the United States (Chung and Jackson, 2013). The Make It In America Initiative was an Obama-era manufacturing agenda emphasizing regional economic development, workforce skills, and supply-chain strengthening. The National Manufacturing Strategy further elaborated on this policy framework (Executive Office of the President, 2012, 2014). The Obama administration's strategy sought to strengthen public-private partnerships and enhance interagency coordination to expedite and expand investment in advanced manufacturing technologies. Particular emphasis was placed on facilitating access to these innovations for small and medium-sized enterprises, thereby promoting broader industrial competitiveness and economic growth.

While the Obama administration created a framework that directed attention to supporting the manufacturing sector, the Obama administration sought to develop a structural intervention plan for improving the banking and financial sectors. The continuity in the TARP policy, as mentioned above, responded to the insistent requests for help from the banking sector and the need to avoid immediate bankruptcy. However, it was also necessary to modify existing principles and norms in these sectors, which would not be achieved through bailing out failing institutions. At the end of the electoral campaign, Obama had called himself the defender of Main Street ("the ordinary citizens") as opposed to the interests of Wall Street ("the palaces of finance"). In this way, he intended to make credit institutions liable and increase the transparency

---

[4] See White House, Office of the Press Secretary, February 13, 2013, White House, Office of the Press Secretary (2013) *Fact sheet: The President's plan to make America a magnet for jobs by investing in manufacturing*, 13 February. Washington, DC: The White House. Available at: https://obamawhitehouse.archives.gov/the-press-office/2013/02/13/fact-sheet-president-s-plan-make-america-magnet-jobs-investing-manufacturing (Accessed: March 2016).

[5] See in particular the website dedicated to the initiative: U.S. Department of Commerce, SelectUSA (2016) *SelectUSA initiative*. Available at: https://www.selectusa.gov (Accessed: August 2016).

of the financial system. Thus, the Consumer Financial Protection Agency was established with the aim of protecting consumers from the abuse of the financial system:

> The Consumer Financial Protection Agency will have the power to ensure that consumers get information that is clear and concise, and to prevent the worst kinds of abuses. Consumers shouldn't have to worry about loan contracts designed to be unintelligible, hidden fees attached to their mortgages, and financial penalties whether through a credit card or debit card that appear without warning on their statements. [...] By setting ground rules, we'll increase the kind of competition that actually provides people better and greater choices, as companies compete to offer the best product, not the one that's most complex or confusing (Obama White House, 2009b).

The enactment of the 2010 Dodd-Frank Wall Street Reform and Consumer Protection Act coincided with the establishment of this agency. This legislation created the Financial Stability Oversight Council, an entity tasked with overseeing the stability of the financial system as a whole. Additionally, the Act introduced regulatory measures aimed at enhancing the transparency and security of financial products, bolstering investor protection, and expanding the authority of supervisory bodies in financial fraud investigations. It can be argued that the profound impact of the global Financial Crisis rendered the regulation of the banking and financial sector more politically and rhetorically palatable:

> There are those who would suggest that we must choose between markets unfettered by even the most modest of regulations and markets weighed down by onerous regulations that suppress the spirit of enterprise and innovation. But if there is one lesson we can learn from the last year, it is that this is a false choice. Common sense rules of the road do not hinder the markets but make them stronger. Indeed, they are essential to ensuring that our markets function, and function fairly and freely (Obama White House, 2009b).

However, the debate on the concrete effects of these statements remains open. Despite the above-mentioned measures introducing greater constraints to the financial system, many believe that the Obama administration was not able to impose a truly radical reform of the sector (Coffee, 2011; Appelbaum and Batt, 2014; Di Tommaso and Schweitzer, 2013).

Alongside his attention to the manufacturing and financial sectors, Obama negotiated trade deals and initiatives meant to promote American goods abroad while reducing tariffs that domestic manufacturers had to pay. In 2010, Obama released his first executive order to create the National Export Exchange Initiative. Here, Obama outlines his reasoning for focusing on international trade:

> A critical component of stimulating economic growth in the United States is ensuring that U.S. businesses can actively participate in international markets by increasing their exports of goods, services, and agricultural products. Improved export performance will, in turn, create good high-paying jobs" (Executive Order 13534, National Export Initiative 2010).

Obama especially sought to target small businesses by helping remove trade barriers and create new export markets through the financing of federal export assistance and trade missions. While this was a short executive order, and relatively early in the Obama administration, it set up the Obama Administration as a fierce supporter of the expansion of US export power as a means of overcoming the Financial Crisis. Furthermore, it also set the stage for larger trade deals that would come later in his administration.

The most important of the Obama trade deals was the Trans-Pacific Partnership (TPP). The TPP originated from the Trans-Pacific Strategic Economic Partnership (TPSEP or P4 Agreement), signed in 2005 by Brunei, Chile, New Zealand, and Singapore to promote trade liberalization (Aggarwal and Evenett, 2013; Aggarwal, 2016). The United States joined the negotiations in 2008, expanding the agreement into a broader regional pact. Over time, other nations, including Japan, Canada, Australia, and Vietnam, joined, making it a 12-member trade agreement. It aimed to reduce tariffs, promote investment, set labor and environmental standards, and enhance digital trade. The TPP was finalized in 2016 under US leadership, aiming to set high trade standards. It encompassed around 40% of the world's economy and was a pivotal step in Obama's "pivot to Asia" plan (Donnan and Sevastopulo, 2015). The overall goal of the TPP was to liberalize world trade while creating jobs within the United States to strengthen American industries, but this goal was never realized as President Trump withdrew from the accord two years later.

8.3 Policies for "Special" Sectors

8.3.1 An Ongoing Story: The Automobile Industry

As highlighted in multiple sections of this book, the American automotive industry has long played a pivotal role in shaping US industrial policy, frequently drawing the attention and support of the federal government. Since its inception, it has been regarded as a strategically important sector, essential to economic growth, national security, and employment. This was evident in the early twentieth century when the nascent automobile industry benefited from protective tariffs and government subsidies to foster domestic development (Hounshell, 1984).

Government support intensified during both World Wars, as the industry became a critical supplier of military vehicles and equipment, significantly expanding its capacity to meet wartime demand (Milward, 1979). The postwar boom reinforced the industry's importance, cementing its position as a key driver of American economic prosperity. However, this close relationship was particularly evident during times of crisis. In the 1970s and 1980s, amid economic stagnation, oil price shocks, and rising foreign competition, the federal government directly intervened to stabilize the sector. The Carter and Reagan administrations took active measures to protect American automakers, most notably with the 1980 Chrysler bailout, where the US government provided $1.5 billion in loan guarantees to rescue the struggling company from collapse. This intervention underscored the industry's "too big to fail" status and reinforced its privileged position within US economic policymaking (Ben-Ishai and Lubben, 2011).

The 2008 crisis made the automotive sector the object of special government attention. Chrysler and General Motors (GM) found themselves on the verge of bankruptcy, and both the Bush administration and the Obama administration chose to intervene. The failure of both firms could not be accepted: the large number of employees and the heavy weight these two companies alone had on the US economy once again made them special interlocutors and "too big to fail." Indeed, the domino effect would have dragged down the entire sector, the national manufacturing industry, and soon, the entire American economy (Krippner, 2011). The effects on employment, as well as the local economies where the two companies were concentrated, would have been devastating. The government's bailout intervention, while defying the dogmas of the economic theories that Republican rhetoric often cited, was, for Bush, de facto obligated. Then, as happened at the time of Carter and Reagan, the government's concerns for the automotive industry proved to be bipartisan. However, even in this field, there was little room for real change. The Bush administration decided to take action to save the two companies and the bailout, regulated by the Chrysler and GM Loan and Security Agreements,[6] was subsequently carried out by the Obama administration without hesitation.

We cannot, and must not, and we will not let our auto industry simply vanish. This industry is like no other—it's an emblem of the American spirit; a once

---

[6] See Congressional Oversight Panel (2009).

and future symbol of America's success. It's what helped build the middle class and sustained it throughout the 20th century. It's a source of deep pride for the generations of American workers whose hard work and imagination led to some of the finest cars the world has ever known. It's a pillar of our economy that has held up the dreams of millions of our people (Obama, 2009c).

The government's intervention in rescuing General Motors (GM) and Chrysler during the 2008–2009 Financial Crisis followed different approaches, but in both cases, its role was central. These interventions were facilitated through the Troubled Asset Relief Program (TARP), established under the Emergency Economic Stabilization Act of 2008, which allocated $17.4 billion to support the struggling US auto industry (Di Tommaso and Schweitzer, 2013). Of this amount, $13.4 billion was directed toward GM, while the remaining funds were used to stabilize Chrysler.

In response to the 2008 Financial Crisis, the US government intervened to prevent the collapse of General Motors (GM) by acquiring a 60% ownership stake in exchange for $30.1 billion in financial assistance (U.S. Department of the Treasury, 2009). However, the intervention extended beyond financial aid, encompassing comprehensive restructuring measures aimed at improving GM's management, general operations, and long-term competitiveness (White House, 2009.

Recognizing poor leadership and operational inefficiencies as key factors in GM's decline, the Obama administration mandated the resignation of CEO Rick Wagoner in March 2009 as part of a broader effort to reform corporate governance and enhance accountability (Obama White House, 2009a). Following this, the administration implemented strategic downsizing measures, including the elimination of underperforming brands such as Pontiac, Saturn, and Hummer, along with the closure of numerous production facilities and dealerships to reduce costs and streamline operations (U.S. Department of the Treasury, 2009).

The intervention culminated in GM filing for Chapter 11 bankruptcy protection on June 1, 2009, allowing the company to restructure its operations, reduce debt, and emerge as a more viable entity (U.S. Department of the Treasury, 2009). The government's intervention, which combined large-scale TARP financial assistance with a bankruptcy-based restructuring, played a central role in GM's return to profitability and renewed competitiveness, and the U.S. Treasury completed the sale of its remaining GM shares in December 2013 (U.S. Department of the Treasury, 2013; Canis and Webel, 2013).

The Chrysler case followed a different path. Rather than acquiring ownership, the US government played a direct role in negotiating the company's sale to Fiat (see details below). This approach allowed Chrysler to avoid outright nationalization, while still securing much-needed financial and structural support.

The administration facilitated the transition by ensuring that Fiat gained a controlling interest, integrating Chrysler into its global operations while maintaining production in the United States (Ben-Ishai and Lubben, 2011).

Ultimately, both interventions reflected the government's broader strategy: not just to rescue failing companies, but to enforce structural adjustments that would enhance long-term industry sustainability.

> This is a company that has a particular claim on our American identity. It's a company founded in the early years of the American automobile industry; a company that helped make the 20th century an American Century. [. . .] Chrysler has not only been an icon of America's auto industry and a source of pride for generations of American workers; it's been responsible for helping build our middle class, giving countless Americans the chance to provide for their families, sending their kids to college, saving for a secure retirement. It's what hundreds of thousands of auto workers and suppliers and dealers and their families rely on to pay their bills in communities across our industrial Midwest and across our country (Obama, 2009c).

This intervention was in evident continuity with the previous administration. As already mentioned, in an attempt to help stabilize the company, in December 2008, the Bush administration had already allocated $4 billion. The purpose of the loan was to allow the company to continue operating, covering the mere operating costs during the first quarter of 2009, while the details of the plan were defined to maintain its long-term viability. As a condition for obtaining loan agreements, Chrysler undertook a restructuring plan in February 2009, describing the actions necessary to achieve and maintain long-term financial stability.

On February 17, 2009, Chrysler presented its plan requesting $5 billion from the US government for financial assistance to meet counter-expected lower revenues, driven by an economy that continued to be stagnant (Ferrado and Morris, 2014; Ben-Ishai and Lubben, 2011). In order to evaluate the company's restructuring plans and make decisions about future public support actions, President Obama set up a presidential task force on February 20, 2009. In this context, the Treasury Secretary took over the responsibility for deciding all issues relating to the company, including future decisions regarding the granting of additional financial assistance. On March 30, 2009, the president announced that the restructuring plan presented by Chrysler had not been able to define a credible path for the future stability of the company, meaning that no new federal investments were justified. At the same time, the chairman pointed to a series of actions that Chrysler would have to undertake to receive further assistance, stipulating that Treasury officials would work closely with Chrysler to adopt such measures.

In fact, the Obama administration was directly acquiring the company's management in exchange for the opportunity to receive government support (Ben-Ishai and Lubben, 2011).

The Presidential Task Force had identified several weaknesses for Chrysler: a limited presence in international markets, which made the company more vulnerable to economic fluctuations on the domestic market and unable to exploit economies of scale, a poor quality of production compared to competitors, a mix of products that did not cover the segment of small cars, and the lack of productive investments essential for competitiveness. According to the task force, Chrysler was not able to operate independently in the markets and had to find a partner to be able to consolidate its long-term profitability.[7] It was following these conclusions that President Obama personally encouraged and participated in the negotiations between Chrysler and Fiat. An initial agreement was reached in April 2009, and the US government supported the operation with a commitment of over $6 billion. The agreement provided for the transfer of all Chrysler's assets to Fiat, while Fiat committed itself to transfer its technological equipment and management services, as well as allow the exploitation of its commercial network for Chrysler (Pfleeger and Caputo, 2012; Ben-Ishai and Lubben, 2011). In the following years, the negotiations continued and ended in 2014 with the acquisition of all of Chrysler's shares by Fiat.

Finally, it should be remembered that despite the Obama administration's direct intervention focused on GM and Chrysler, Ford also benefited from significant government support. Ford did not receive TARP or ARRA funds but benefited in 2009 from $5.9 billion in federal loans made available under the Advanced Technology Vehicles Manufacturing Program. This initiative was promoted by the Energy Department to encourage industrial reconversion and investment in the development of electric motors and low-energy consumption. This industrial policy intervention created different objectives that were directly supported by President Obama:

> We have a historic opportunity to help ensure that the next generation of fuel-efficient cars and trucks are made in America. [. . .] These loans – and the additional support we will provide through the Section 136 program – will create good jobs and help the auto industry to meet and even exceed the tough fuel economy standards we've set, while helping us to regain our competitive edge in the world market (Quality News, 2009).

---

[7] See the US Government Accountability Office, *Report to Congressional Committees, Auto Industry, Summary of Government Efforts and Automakers' Restructuring to Date*, GAO-09-553, April 2009.

Ford continued to receive special government support: $250 million in 2010 from the Export-Import Bank of the United States to finance the purchase of 200,000 vehicles (produced at facilities in Illinois, Michigan, Missouri, Kentucky, and Ohio) destined for foreign markets, in particular Canada and Mexico. This industrial policy intervention was aimed at supporting exports which would, in turn, have a positive effect on employment and help boost national growth:

> My administration is announcing a new $250 million Export-Import Bank loan guarantee for Ford. [. . .] We're tired of just buying from everybody else – we want to start selling to other people, because we know we can compete. That's how we're going to grow our economy. That's how we're going to support millions of good jobs for American workers to do what they've always done: build great products and sell them around the world (Obama, 2010b).

Through TARP and other measures, $426.35 billion was given to banks and auto companies, while the sale of the stock and interest payments generated $441.7 billion. As such, the program overall made the government $15.3 billion (Weisman, 2014). Furthermore, the program is widely credited with stabilizing employment across the U.S. auto industry (Congressional Oversight Panel, 2010). These workers provided a valuable asset to the economy by keeping the American auto industry alive, especially for Ford, GM, and Chrysler. The program increased the productivity and sales of US automobiles both domestically and internationally. However, there was an overall loss from the auto industry bailouts of $9.5 billion, mostly from General Motors (Weisman, 2014). President Obama still considered the bailouts a victory due to the net profit gained, as well as the recovery of American auto companies from one of the worst economic crises in American history.

8.3.2 The Case of ICT Industries

Since the Clinton administration, information and communication technology (ICT) industries have held a unique and privileged status in US industrial policy. Unlike traditional sectors, ICT rapidly gained central importance in the national political and economic landscape, leading successive governments to implement targeted reforms and interventions. The sector's rapid expansion in the 1990s prompted the Telecommunications Act of 1996, a landmark reform that dismantled the longstanding AT&T monopoly and introduced a competitive telecommunications market. This deregulation facilitated new market entrants in the telephone and cellular industries while also introducing measures to directly support technological advancement (ERP, 2000). The overarching goal was to enhance competition, thus driving innovation and strengthening the US position in the global technology race (ERP, 2000).

In the early 2000s, the Bush administration pursued policies aimed at further liberalizing the information and communication technology (ICT) sector, emphasizing competition and private investment in ICT infrastructure. However, the 2008 Financial Crisis prompted a shift in federal policy under the Obama administration, leading to direct public intervention in the industry. Recognizing ICT as the backbone of modern economic infrastructure, the administration adopted a proactive industrial policy to expand broadband coverage and enhance digital connectivity nationwide (FCC, 2010).

The National Broadband Plan of 2010 became the centerpiece of this strategy. Released by the FCC on March 17, 2010, the plan outlined a roadmap for initiatives to stimulate economic growth, spur job creation, and improve America's capabilities in education, healthcare, homeland security, and public safety. It emphasized government investment in broadband as a driver of economic growth and social inclusion, recognizing broadband as fundamental to economic expansion, employment, and global competitiveness (FCC, 2010).

The plan introduced policy reforms and federal investments to increase broadband accessibility, particularly in rural and underserved communities. It also proposed innovative partnerships between federal, state, and local governments and private sector entities to ensure a nationwide broadband infrastructure (Pew Charitable Trusts, 2010). Additionally, the American Recovery and Reinvestment Act (ARRA) of 2009 allocated approximately $7.2 billion to fund broadband expansion projects, reinforcing the administration's commitment to investing in technological infrastructure as a pillar of economic recovery (FCC, 2010).

By positioning broadband expansion as a central component of economic development, the National Broadband Plan aimed to bridge the digital divide and ensure that all Americans had access to the benefits of a connected society. The policy marked a shift toward recognizing digital connectivity as a form of critical infrastructure, akin to transportation and energy networks, requiring sustained federal oversight and investment (FCC, 2010).

President Obama framed broadband expansion as a historical infrastructure challenge, drawing parallels with past national projects like the Transcontinental Railroad and the Interstate Highway System. In a statement on March 16, 2010, he underscored broadband's role in unleashing innovation, creating jobs, enhancing security, and promoting democratic engagement, declaring:

> America today is on the verge of a broadband-driven Internet era that will unleash innovation, create new jobs and industries, provide consumers with new powerful sources of information, enhance American safety and security,

and connect communities in ways that strengthen our democracy. Just as past generations of Americans met the great infrastructure challenges of the day, such as building the Transcontinental Railroad and the Interstate highways, so too must we harness the potential of the Internet (Obama White House, 2010).[8]

To implement this vision, the American Recovery and Reinvestment Act (ARRA) of 2009 allocated $7.2 billion for broadband expansion through two major programs: 1) Broadband Technology Opportunities Program (BTOP)—managed by the US Department of Commerce, focusing on network infrastructure, public computing centers, and broadband adoption projects; and 2) Broadband Initiatives Program (BIP)—administered by the US Department of Agriculture, targeting rural broadband expansion to address geographic disparities in connectivity.

The Obama administration prioritized bridging the digital divide by addressing the vast inequalities in Internet access across different socioeconomic and geographic groups. This intervention recognized that broadband expansion was not merely a sector-specific economic initiative but a transformative policy with far-reaching implications for the American economy and society (ERP, 2016).

The push for universal high-speed connectivity was based on its critical role in enhancing American businesses' competitiveness, particularly in driving productivity, innovation, new organizational models, and improved market access. At the same time, the federal investment in ICT infrastructure was designed to increase workforce inclusion, along with supporting education and skills development, and ultimately reducing social inequalities. By expanding digital access, the policy aimed to ensure that all citizens could fully participate in economic, civic, and political life, reinforcing broadband technology as a key enabler of equal opportunity in the twenty-first century (ERP, 2016).[9]

8.3.3 Energy Sector and Green Industries

The energy sector and "green" industries had been among the key focuses of the Obama administration since the 2008 election campaign. Besides the many political objectives, essential economic and social issues were also invoked in the rhetoric and practice of President Obama's government. Among those

---

[8] Statement from the President on the National Broadband Plan, The White House Office of the Press Secretary, March 16, 2010.

[9] In 2013, the ConnectEd program was also promoted with the specific objective of alleviating social inequalities, aiming at promoting a greater diffusion of high-speed Internet connections among American families (ERP, 2016). Within this initiative, in particular, the Federal Communications Commission (FCC) has invested 2 billion dollars in two years, along with further investments by private partners.

goals were reducing dependence on foreign oil and energy costs, improving industrial efficiency, creating skilled jobs, reducing pollution, and broadly promoting a higher quality of life (Di Tommaso and Schweitzer, 2013). To this end, ARRA was immediately used as a tool of selective industrial policy aimed at strategically encouraging the development of American green industries for the national interest. This intervention was not only a response to the crisis, but it also aimed to promote structural change in American industry, economy, and society:

> From China to India, from Japan to Germany, nations everywhere are racing to develop new ways to producing and use energy. The nation that wins this competition will be the nation that leads the global economy. [. . .] That's why the Recovery Act that we passed back in January makes the largest investment in clean energy in history, not just to help end this recession, but to lay a new foundation for lasting prosperity. The Recovery Act includes $80 billion to put tens of thousands of Americans to work developing new battery technologies for hybrid vehicles; modernizing the electric grid; making our homes and businesses more energy efficient; doubling our capacity to generate renewable electricity. These are creating private-sector jobs weatherizing homes; manufacturing cars and trucks; upgrading to smart electric meters; installing solar panels; assembling wind turbines; building new facilities and factories and laboratories all across America. And, by the way, helping to finance extraordinary research (Obama, 2009b).

In 2009, approximately $90 billion was allocated to this sector, including roughly $60 billion in direct spending and incentives for productive activities and about $30 billion in tax credits (Council of Economic Advisers, 2010). Among the eight major categories of the American Recovery and Reinvestment Act (ARRA) clean energy investments, renewable energy generation received the largest portion, estimated at $26.6 billion (Council of Economic Advisers, 2010). Beyond direct investments, renewable energy technologies such as wind turbines and solar panels were incentivized through extended federal tax credits and new loan guarantees (Council of Economic Advisers, 2010). A key mechanism for supporting renewable energy under the American Recovery and Reinvestment Act of 2009 (ARRA) was the extension and modification of federal tax incentives for renewable electricity production and investment. ARRA extended the renewable electricity Production Tax Credit (PTC) for electricity generated from qualified renewable resources such as wind, biomass, geothermal, hydropower, and landfill gas, while also allowing taxpayers eligible for the PTC to elect instead to claim a 30 per cent Investment Tax Credit (ITC) for certain facilities; the legislation also eliminated the previous $4,000 cap on the small wind ITC and removed restrictions on subsidised energy financing (Internal Revenue Service, 2009a). ARRA further created the Section 48C Qualifying Advanced Energy Project Credit, establishing a competitive 30 per cent investment tax credit for certified advanced energy manufacturing projects (Internal Revenue Service, 2009b; United States Congress, 2009). In its initial allocation, the programme awarded approximately $2.3 billion in credits to 183 US clean-energy manufacturing facilities, supporting domestic advanced energy manufacturing capacity (U.S. Department of Energy, 2013; Obama White House, 2010).

In 2013, the administration announced a second competitive allocation of $150 million in previously unawarded Section 48C credits, administered jointly by the Department of Energy and the Internal Revenue Service, extending the program's impact on clean energy manufacturing (U.S. Department of Energy, 2013).

In 2009, more than $80 billion was allocated to this sector, including $60 billion in direct incentives for productive activities and $30 billion as tax credits (ERP, 2010). Among the eight major categories of the ARRA's clean energy investments, renewable energy generation made up the largest share of the legislation's appropriations, estimated at $26.6 billion (ERP, 2010). In addition to direct investments, the installation of renewable energy technologies like wind turbines and solar panels was promoted through incentives like renewed federal tax credits and new loan guarantees (ERP, 2010). One such incentive was the Production Tax Credit (PTC) for renewable electricity generation, which the American Recovery and Reinvestment Act of 2009 extended for facilities using qualified renewable resources such as wind, biomass, geothermal, hydropower, and landfill gas, while also allowing developers eligible for the PTC to instead elect a 30 per cent Investment Tax Credit (ITC) for certain facilities; the Act further removed the previous $4,000 cap on small wind ITC claims and eased restrictions on subsidised energy financing (Internal Revenue Service, 2009a). ARRA also created the Section 48C Qualifying Advanced Energy Project Credit, establishing a competitive 30 per cent investment tax credit to support domestic advanced energy manufacturing; in its first allocation round, the programme awarded approximately USD 2.3 billion in tax credits to 183 clean-energy manufacturing facilities in the United States (Internal Revenue Service, 2009b; U.S. Department of Energy, 2013; Obama White House, 2010).

Years after the end of the Financial Crisis, an additional $150 million in previously unawarded Section 48C tax credits were competitively allocated through a joint Department of Energy–Internal Revenue Service process, indicating that the ARRA had continuing effects on domestic manufacturing several years after its enactment (U.S. Department of Energy, 2013).

Another tool provided by the federal government to support clean energy development was the Department of Energy's loan guarantee authority. Through the Loan Programs Office, the Department operated the Clean Energy Financing Program under Title XVII of the Energy Policy Act of 2005, providing direct loans and partial guarantees of commercial debt to clean energy enterprises—particularly those deploying innovative technologies that are technically proven but not yet widely commercialized. The scope of the Title XVII program expanded substantially following amendments enacted through the Infrastructure Investment and Jobs Act and the Inflation Reduction Act (U.S. Department of Energy, 2024).

The ARRA included substantial support for transportation infrastructure, providing approximately $48.1 billion for Department of Transportation programmes, of which around $8 billion was allocated specifically to intercity passenger rail and high-speed rail capital projects (United States Congress, 2009; Congressional Research Service, 2020). ARRA also amended the Internal Revenue Code to modify and expand incentives for plug-in electric vehicles, revising Section 30D of the Code to allow a tax credit consisting of a base amount of $2,500 plus additional amounts tied to battery capacity, up to a maximum of $7,500 for qualifying plug-in electric drive motor vehicles; additional provisions applied to low-speed vehicles and conversions (United States Congress, 2009; Internal Revenue Service, 2009c). The Internal Revenue Service subsequently issued administrative guidance on these provisions through Notice 2009-58 (Internal Revenue Service, 2009c). In addition to these transportation and vehicle incentives, ARRA funded broader clean-energy and efficiency programs through separate appropriations managed primarily by the Department of Energy. In addition, $300 million was invested through the General Services Administration into the purchase of energy-efficient vehicles produced in America (Di Tommaso and Schweitzer, 2013). To reduce electricity consumption, the government invested $4 billion in the construction of a more modern electrical "smart" grid. ARRA then provided tax credits for the renovation of private homes in accordance with energy efficiency standards (Di Tommaso and Schweitzer, 2013). Section 1121 of the American Recovery and Reinvestment Act of 2009 increased the residential energy property credit for energy efficiency improvements to 30 per cent of qualified expenditures, with an aggregate cap of $1,500 for 2009 and 2010 (Internal Revenue Service, 2009a; United States Congress, 2009). Section 1122 implemented a similar change for certain alternative energy equipment. This supported construction companies and encouraged innovation in the construction sector.

Among the most important investments planned within ARRA was a massive allocation of 400 million dollars for the establishment of the Advanced

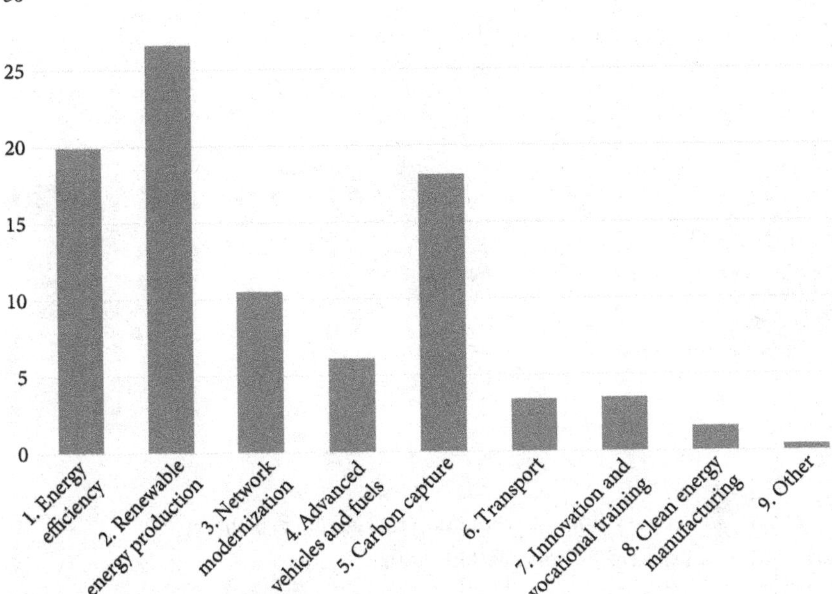

Figure 8.3 Recovery Act, Clean Energy Allocations by Category (in billions of dollars)

Source: Economic Report of the President (ERP, 2010)

Research Projects Agency-Energy (ARPA-E), an agency created to encourage investment in research projects for advanced energy technologies (ERP, 2010). Figure 8.3 provides a summary of some of ARRA's main expenditure items aimed at promoting the improvement of the energy sector and the green industries.[10]

Within this incentive framework for green industries, and in particular, for encouraging renewable energy (which in 2011 accounted for 12% of national energy production, see Figure 8.4), the Obama administration's energy policy

---

[10] Along with the interventions presented here, in the field of environmental policies, the administration had also provided for the Cap and Trade program, included in the 2009 American Clean Energy and Security Act (ERP, 2010). However, this program has never been implemented due to the loss of the majority in the Chamber during the mid-term elections in 2010 (Di Tommaso and Scheweitzer, 2013). The Cap and Trade system would have substantially set a total annual limit on greenhouse gas emissions and divided this amount into "allowances" (corresponding to the right for an enterprise to emit one ton of polluting gas into the atmosphere). These allowances would have then been allocated to companies through an auction and the companies would have been free to market them among themselves, thus creating a "compensation" market. The system, in addition to ensuring that no uncertain level of pollution is exceeded, could have encouraged companies to find the most cost-effective technologies on the market, in order to reduce carbon emissions, with a consequent boost to innovation in this sector (ERP, 2010).

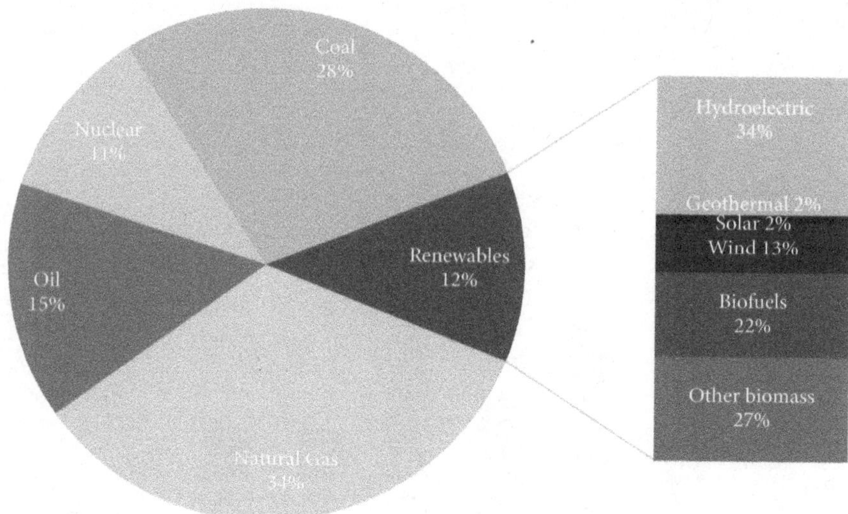

Figure 8.4 US Primary Energy Production by Category: 2011
Source: Economic Report of the President (ERP, 2010)

paid particular attention to the substitution of overseas oil imports with national production:

> The Pentagon has declared our dependence on fossil fuels a security threat. Veterans from Iraq and Afghanistan are traveling the country as part of Operation Free, campaigning to end our dependence on oil. The young people of this country—that I've met all across America—they understand that this is the challenge of their generation (Obama, 2009b).[11]

As shown in Figure 8.5, since the beginning of the 1980s (i.e., at the end of the oil crisis in 1979), oil imports from abroad had progressively grown with the growth in domestic consumption, with domestic production simultaneously experiencing a gradual reduction. In the years of the recent Great Financial Crisis, this trend was reversed: in 2007, oil imports began to fall sharply, partly due to a reduction in domestic demand caused by the recession, but also thanks to a significant increase in domestic production. However, this was also a result of recent technological developments in the extractive sector, partly the result of research funded by the government, which made it possible in the United States

---

[11] *Remarks by the President Challenging Americans to Lead the Global Economy in Clean Energy*, The White House Office of the Press Secretary, October 23, 2009.

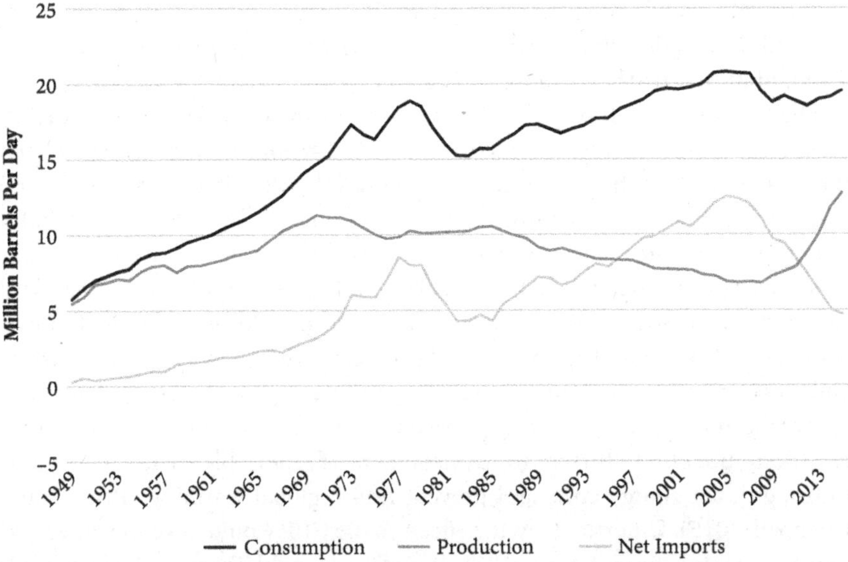

Figure 8.5 US Net Oil Consumption, Production, and Imports: 1983–2015 (in thousands of barrels per day)
Source: Data from the US Energy Information Agency

to extract shale oil and shale gas at significantly reduced costs (thanks to the controversial technique of fracking, the hydraulic crushing of the rock in the subsoil through the injection at high pressures of liquids and solvents) (ERP, 2013).

The Obama administration was centrally concerned with reducing its dependence on foreign oil. This led not only to the development of green energy sources, but also the growth of internal oil production. It is worth recalling that in 2013 (for the first time since 1995) domestic oil production exceeded the level of net imports.

In addition to promoting the extraction of fossil fuels at home, the Obama administration married its goals of reducing consumption of foreign oil and promoting environmental improvements through stricter automobile fuel efficiency standards. The Corporate Average Fuel Economy (CAFE) standards were initially passed in 1975 in the wake of the OPEC oil embargo (Feigenbaum and Morris, 2017). CAFE standards—initially for passenger cars and light trucks but later extended to medium-duty and heavy-duty vehicles—"regulate how far our vehicles must travel on a gallon of fuel" (National Highway Traffic Safety Administration, 2024). The standards have changed over time. The Energy Independence and Security Act of 2007 required a 35-mpg fuel economy by 2020 (Feigenbaum and Morris, 2017). In 2009, an Obama administration directive established a fuel economy standard of 27.3 mpg—slightly lower than the Bush administration that preceded it—and scheduled annual increases in the standard until it reached 35 mpg in 2020 (Feigenbaum and Morris, 2017).

The estimated effects of the CAFE standards are mixed. On the one hand, they seem to have induced automakers to improve technology in cars, saving fuel, but they may have contributed to vehicular fatalities (by affecting the weight of cars) and harmed automakers' competitiveness (National Research Council, 2002).

Furthermore, the Obama Administration pledged an overall decrease in carbon emissions through the controversial Clean Power Plan which set a standard for a 32% decrease in carbon dioxide emissions from 2005 levels by 2030 (Environmental Protection Agency, 2015). Specifically, this plan targets the carbon emissions from power plants, such as coal and natural gas burning plants. The goal of this policy is not only to improve the health of Americans from dangerous emissions, but also to further the development of renewable energy in an effort to bring down energy costs and prevent future global warming (Perkins and Chappell, 2015). Unfortunately, the effects of the CPP would never be fully measured as just two years later in 2017, President Donald Trump rolled back this initiative in an attempt to strengthen the coal industry (Davenport and Rubin, 2017).

8.3.4 Obamacare and Health Industries

A field of intervention that had great visibility in American and international public opinion was the reform of the health system, the so-called "Obamacare." This was a policy area that the president had wanted to invest an important share of his political capital in from the beginning of his first term: "We did not come here just to clean up crises. We came here to build a future. So tonight, I return to speak to all of you about an issue that is central to that future and that is the issue of health care" (Obama, 2009d).[12]

This reform was based on two main laws: the Patient Protection and Affordable Care Act (PPACA) and the Health Care and Education Reconciliation Act, both approved by Congress in 2010. These interventions established a priority of extending healthcare coverage to millions of American citizens who had, for years, remained excluded from any insurance program. More generally, the reform also sought to reduce the cost of managing the entire national health service. The aim was to innovate the system of diffusion and information sharing concerning patients, therapies, and medical treatments. This improvement in

---

[12] *Remarks by the President to a Joint Session of Congress on Health Care*, White House, Office of the Press Secretary, September 9, 2009.

the management of information could contribute not only to an improvement in the quality and effectiveness of the services but also create a general reduction in the costs of the national health system.[13]

Obamacare was also guided by an intention to promote greater social equity. It aimed to encourage pathways of change that would lead toward the universality of health coverage and an improvement in the costs and quality of the national healthcare system. In this regard, trying to include over 40 million citizens in medical assistance schemes has been a long and complex operation, encountering many obstacles and resistance. It was an intervention with a strong political appeal that polarized the attention of the public and the media for months. Indeed, this was a step that many progressive politicians before Obama had failed to achieve.

Moreover, this was a difficult reform that may have altered the balance between established interests and, in some way, the relationships between companies, workers, and the government. This may have also created a long-lasting impact on labor costs, workers' rights and protections, and worker productivity. The reform would have increased the number of medical insurances included in labor contracts and purchased by companies for their employees, leading to a reduction of costs and greater risk sharing.

The reform also promised to improve the health of Americans by reducing the impact of health on public accounts: it would reduce chronic situations, promote prevention, as well as improve the effectiveness and efficiency of the national health system by positively impacting the public budget. Not only did Obama's healthcare reform reduce adverse selection in insurance markets through expanded risk pooling, it also sought to restrain healthcare costs by increasing bargaining power and competition among insurers and providers (Gruber, 2011; Blumenthal, Abrams and Nuzum, 2015).

It is worth noting that Obamacare also promised an important stimulating effect on the national health industries that produce goods and services to meet the health demand.[14] In this sense, we are dealing with a strategic and selective intervention aimed at particular industries, which can play an important role within policies to combat the Financial Crisis and revitalize the national economy: First, the reform sought to lead to a significant increase in the demand for health insurance, with an extension of the national insurance market of about 40 million new policies. This increase would undoubtedly stimulate the development of the insurance sector, but, simultaneously, it is reasonable to argue that it could boost the demand for a long list of other sectors in the American

---

[13] For a more detailed discussion of healthcare reform see Di Tommaso and Schweitzer (2013).

[14] For a more detailed discussion of the concept of Health Industry, see Di Tommaso and Schweitzer (2005, 2010).

economy, e.g., pharmaceutical, biomedical, or biotechnology, along with, more generally, the supply chains linked to the provision of healthcare services, from research to ICT, communication and specialized manufacturing (Di Tommaso and Schweitzer, 2005, 2013).

8.3.5 Special Measures for Small Businesses

From the outset of his presidency, Barack Obama placed significant emphasis on supporting small and medium-sized enterprises (SMEs). This focus was not only a continuation of his campaign rhetoric but also a direct response to the Financial Crisis that had disproportionately affected small businesses. Unlike large financial institutions that benefited from substantial government bailouts, small businesses lacked the same level of institutional resilience and access to credit. As Obama stated:

> Small businesses are the heart of the American economy. They're responsible for half of all private sector jobs and they created roughly 70 percent of all new jobs in the past decade. So small businesses are not only job generators, they're also at the heart of the American Dream (Obama White House, 2009a).

Recognizing the vulnerability of small businesses in the wake of the Great Recession, the Obama administration introduced a series of policies aimed at providing financial relief, fostering growth, and promoting innovation in the SME sector. One of the first major initiatives was the allocation of more than $700 million to the Small Business Administration (SBA) under the American Recovery and Reinvestment Act of 2009. These funds were used primarily to subsidize loan fees, increase government guarantees, and expand access to credit for small businesses (U.S. Small Business Administration, 2009). The goal was to alleviate financial constraints on SMEs and prevent closures due to restricted credit availability.

In addition, the Obama administration launched the Small Business Jobs Act of 2010, which provided $2 billion in new tax incentives aimed at encouraging entrepreneurship and start-up formation. The act also established the State Small Business Credit Initiative and the Small Business Lending Fund, managed by the Department of the Treasury, to increase lending to small businesses (ERP, 2012; Di Tommaso and Schweitzer, 2013). Furthermore, in 2014, Congress approved the Consolidated Appropriations Act, which raised the budget for the Small Business Investment Company's Venture Capital Program from $3 billion to $4 billion, ensuring that more capital was available to high-potential small firms (Dilger, 2014).

Recognizing the need for US SMEs to compete in global markets, the SBA introduced specialized initiatives such as the Export Market Entry Training Program and the Export Trade Assistance Program, designed to enhance SME export capabilities (Di Tommaso and Schweitzer, 2013). These programs provided technical assistance, export financing, and market entry strategies to small firms looking to expand internationally.

The Manufacturing Extension Partnership (MEP), a public–private initiative housed within the National Institute of Standards and Technology, received increased funding during the Obama administration. In fiscal year 2010, the administration requested and secured $124.7 million for MEP—an increase of roughly 13% over the previous year. Although this fell short of doubling the program's funding, it nonetheless represented a significant boost aimed at enhancing support for small and medium-sized manufacturers (National Institute of Standards and Technology, 2010). MEP operates through a national network of centers in all fifty states and Puerto Rico, delivering comprehensive solutions to help small and medium-sized manufacturers improve productivity, access new markets, and develop innovative products. These centers provide services such as process improvements, workforce training, supply chain development, and technology acceleration. The program has been particularly valuable for SMEs facing challenges exacerbated by the Financial Crisis, including limited human capital, outdated infrastructure, and restricted access to financing. By offering tailored advisory services, MEP centers assist SMEs in overcoming these structural weaknesses, thereby enhancing their competitiveness and capacity for innovation.

In addition to direct financial assistance, the Obama administration introduced initiatives to support economic development at the regional and community levels. The Economic Development Administration, under the 2010 federal budget, received $50 million for Regional Planning and Matching Grants to assist less-developed areas in fostering economic growth. These grants focused on improving infrastructure, enhancing workforce development, and attracting new businesses to economically distressed regions (U.S. Department of Commerce, 2010).

Moreover, during the peak years of the recession, the administration implemented the National Emergency Plan for Communities and Regions, a Department of Labor program initiated in 2010. This program provided funding for vocational training in regions with high unemployment rates, helping displaced workers acquire new skills and transition into sustainable employment (Di Tommaso and Schweitzer, 2013).

8.4 Expenditures and Investments for Defense and National Security

Along with the economic crisis, the Obama administration inherited from the Bush administration the management of the wars in Iraq and Afghanistan, as well as the wider fight against terrorism. In terms of rhetoric, Obama took a radical distance from the approach adopted by his predecessor in his first election campaign.

The promise to end the armed conflicts that had begun in the early 2000s, together with a broader shift in U.S. foreign and military policy, gave the new Obama administration unusually high international visibility (Ikenberry, 2011). The promises of change in this critical area also generated strong expectations from the first days in the White House and the historic speech given in Cairo in June 2009 (Obama, 2009e).[15] These expectations and programmatic speeches in 2009, even before the facts, resulted in the awarding of the Nobel Peace Prize to President Obama.

It is hard to argue that the Obama administration during its eight years achieved effective results that fundamentally altered the United States' involvement in armed conflicts (Kreps, 2011; Glennon, 2016). During the two Obama terms, the American military intervention, in its various forms, continued in a long list of countries: Afghanistan, Iraq, Pakistan, Libya, Syria, Yemen, Chad, Nigeria, Mali, Cameroon, Somalia, and Uganda. The foreign policy solutions proposed and hoped for at the beginning of the first term of office struggled to take off. The Arab Spring was left alone and soon lost its driving force. Bin Laden and Gaddafi were killed, while Assad was tolerated. The threat of al-Qaeda did not become less dangerous as ISIS grew ever more violent.

In other words, the war on terrorism required and justified a strong commitment from the United States that remained permanently involved in global military operations. In parallel, the fear of threats and internal attacks on American soil motivated massive government investment in the national security system. This was a situation in which Americans, like in the Cold War, got used to living with a constant threat, which required the government to invest heavily in security and defense. As in Eisenhower's time, the military-industrial complex continued to demand attention from the government.

Certainly, the Great Financial Crisis and subsequent fiscal constraints might have suggested a sustained containment of U.S. military spending. While some restraint did occur, it was driven less by strategic political choice than by technical budgetary mechanisms. In 2011, amid a confrontation over the federal

[15] See Obama, B. (2009e) *Remarks by the President on a new beginning,* Cairo University, 4 June. Washington, DC: The White House. Available at: https://obamawhitehouse.archives.gov/the-press-office/remarks-president-cairo-university-6-04-09

debt ceiling, the Obama administration and Congress enacted the Budget Control Act, which raised the debt limit while imposing caps on discretionary spending (U.S. Congress, 2011). When the bipartisan Joint Select Committee on Deficit Reduction failed to agree on further deficit reduction, the Act triggered automatic sequestration, leading to modest but across-the-board reductions in defense spending beginning in fiscal year 2013 rather than a deliberate reassessment of U.S. military commitments (Congressional Budget Office, 2011; Congressional Budget Office, 2013).

While the Budget Control Act of 2011 authorized a cumulative increase in the federal debt ceiling of up to $2.1 trillion, it did not include any corresponding tax increases to address long-term debt dynamics. Instead, the Act established the Joint Select Committee on Deficit Reduction, charging it with identifying at least $1.2 trillion in deficit reduction over ten years, failing which automatic sequestration would be triggered (U.S. Congress, 2011; Congressional Research Service, 2011). To avoid a government shutdown, Republicans and Democrats agreed to the Budget Control Act, each walking away with something they wanted. Democrats wanted to increase spending, and Republicans wanted to prevent tax hikes for the upper class and corporations. As a result, the tax ceiling was raised with no plausible method for reducing the deficit and a committee was created to somehow address this critical issue. However, the law also established transversal, automatic, and indiscriminate cuts to government expenditure (i.e., a sequestration in technical terms) in cases where an agreement on the type of expenditure to be reduced had not been reached in Congress. This was exactly what happened since March 2013, also influencing military spending (ERP, 2014).[16]

It can be argued that Obama tried to change not so much the degree of military involvement, but rather its nature. This was also part of Obama's decision to promote a gradual withdrawal of US troops from Iraq and Afghanistan (Sherman and Jacobson, 2015) and a general reluctance of the United States to use "large-scale" military force in Libya and Syria, which had characterized the interventions in Iraq and Afghanistan (Warren and Bode, 2015) (Figure 8.6).

Moreover, the massive investment in the "Drone Program" tells a story about military intervention that changes and impacts public opinion, but probably not

---

[16] Together with the cuts in public spending provided for by the 2011 Budget Control Act, some important tax exemptions introduced by the Bush administration in 2001 within the Alternative Minimum Tax (AMT) were due to expire at the beginning of 2013, as well as a series of measures to support the economy introduced by Obama for face the emergency of the crisis, leading to a substantial increase in the tax burden. The concomitance of the reduction in public spending and a general tax increase was leading the American economy to the so-called fiscal cliff, a severe recession caused by the simultaneous reduction of public spending and the increase in taxes, as indicated by the provisions of the Congressional Budget Office (2012). This uncertainty was partly resolved by the American Taxpayer Relief Act, approved by the Congress on January 1, 2013, which avoided the implementation of excessively recessive policies (ERP, 2013, p. 51).

	2008	2009	2010	2011	2012	2013	2014	2015
Military Personnel	138,940	147,348	155,690	161,608	152,266	150,825	148,923	145,206
Operation and maintenance	244,836	259,312	275,988	291,038	282,297	259,662	244,481	247,239
Military Procurement	117,398	129,128	133,603	128,003	124,712	114,912	107,485	101,342
Research & Development, Test and evaluation	75,120	79,030	76,990	74,871	70,396	66,892	64,928	64,124
Military Constructions	11,563	17,614	21,169	19,917	14,553	12,318	9,823	8,114
Housing	3,590	2,721	2,173	3,432	2,331	1,829	1,354	1,198
Other	3,185	1,499	90	−805	4,296	1,357	903	−4,724
SUB-TOTAL DOD	594,632	636,742	666,703	678,064	650,851	607,795	577,897	562,499
Atomic Energy	17,122	17,546	19,308	20,410	19,246	17,634	17,416	18,692
Defense Other activities	4,312	6,724	7,474	7,080	7,755	8,017	8,144	8,373
TOTAL DOD	616,066	661,012	693,485	705,554	677,852	633,446	603,457	589,564

Figure 8.6 National Defense Expenditures (in millions of dollars)

Source: https://www.whitehouse.gov/omb/information-resources/budget/historical-tables/

in substance and extent of involvement in military action (Warren and Bode, 2015). Through the special "drones" program, the administration maintained a high military commitment at the international level without risking a deterioration in the internal consensus of military action (Jacobson and Sherman, 2015).

Focusing on our interest in industrial policy, the Obama administration's commitment to the military continued to play an important industrial role. Quite simply, the global war on terrorism had the same impact on growth and innovation as the Cold War itself. In this context, two cases seem to merit particular attention: robotics and nanotechnologies.

The demand for drones used for military purposes was the main push for the implementation of specific federal programs for technological development in the field of robotics (Weiss, 2014). The Obama administration launched the National Robotics Initiativein 2011 as part of the Advanced Manufacturing Partnership Plan (Obama White House, 2011). Initially, the National Science Foundation, the National Aeronautics and Space Administration, the National Institutes of Health, and the Agriculture Department made a total of about $70 million available to support research in the field of next-generation robots (which can be used in the manufacturing sector, health, agriculture, and military) (Obama White House, 2011). Along with investing in research and development, an important role for the growth of new industries in robotics was once again played by public procurement. For example, from 2000 to 2011, the Pentagon's equipment for unmanned aerial vehicles (drones) had grown from less than 50 to over 7,000. In spite of the reduction in military spending invoked by many, the US Air Force continued to increase its investments in new drones, allocating about $5 billion in the 2012 budget for development programs in this field.[17]

---

[17] For more information see Weiss (2014).

A similar case concerns public support for the development of nanotechnologies. This is a research field focused on assembling materials and components at the atomic or molecular level to create structures with new properties. Developments in this field are potentially applicable to a wide range of sectors, such as electronics, energy, environmental products, materials, medical, pharmaceutical, manufacturing, and defense (Weiss, 2014). Military interest, particularly in reducing electronic equipment volume and lightening soldiers' loads, has led several federal agencies, especially the US Army, to invest in nanotechnology—making the sector a national priority (Weiss, 2014).

The National Nanotechnology Initiative (NNI)—the first national program in the field of nanotechnology—was launched in 2000 by the Clinton administration, but it experienced an important boost under Obama. The agencies and departments originally involved in the program (the Department of Defense, the National Science Foundation, the Energy Department, NASA, the National Institute of Standards and Technology, and the National Institute of Health) have grown from six to twenty-five, coordinating research and development efforts among themselves. In this regard, funds for the NNI have progressively grown. The Obama administration had allocated $1.8 billion in the 2011 budget (Di Tommaso and Schweitzer, 2013) and a further $2.1 billion in the 2012 budget (Weiss, 2014).

The initiative also mobilized private industry, which invested additional resources through partnerships with federal agencies, setting up industrial consortia and specialized engineering centers to accelerate the commercialization of the achieved results. In this regard, for example, the Institute for Soldier Nanotechnologies and the Nanoelectronics Research Initiative were set up (Weiss, 2014).

8.5 Investments in Knowledge

As part of its broader agenda to strengthen education, basic research, and scientific and technological advancement, ARRA allocated approximately $100 billion toward these sectors (ERP, 2010). This substantial investment expanded the budgets of key federal research agencies, including the National Institutes of Health (NIH), the National Science Foundation (NSF), the Department of Energy's Office of Science, and the National Institute of Standards and Technology (NIST) under the Department of Commerce. Additionally, funding was allocated to support innovation through basic research conducted by the Department of Defense (ERP, 2010).

Recognizing the importance of intellectual property in fostering innovation, the Obama administration pursued significant reforms in patent policies. The

America Invents Act of 2011 streamlined patent application processes, reducing bureaucratic delays and improving the efficiency of the US Patent and Trademark Office (ERP, 2012). President Obama emphasized this approach in a 2011 speech:

> We have to do everything we can to encourage the entrepreneurial spirit, wherever we find it. We should be helping American companies compete and sell their products all over the world. We should be making it easier and faster to turn new ideas into new jobs and new businesses. And we should knock down any barriers that stand in the way. Because if we're going to create jobs now and in the future, we're going to have to out-build and out-educate and out-innovate every other country on Earth (Obama, 2011).

The Obama administration placed significant emphasis on enhancing the education and professional training system to better align workforce skills with labor market demands. Recognizing the importance of a highly skilled workforce in driving economic growth and global competitiveness, the administration launched several key initiatives aimed at strengthening education at multiple levels.

One of the earliest efforts was the American Graduation Initiative (AGI), introduced in 2009, which sought to bolster community colleges and other local education programs, particularly in fields experiencing skill shortages (White House, 2009). The initiative aimed to increase the number of college graduates, improve institutional resources, and provide targeted training for in-demand industries. Similarly, the Early Learning Challenge Fund, established in 2010 and administered jointly by the Department of Education and the Department of Health and Human Services, focused on fostering innovative educational models and teacher training programs to improve early childhood education outcomes (Executive Office of the President, 2011).

To support advanced education in science and technology, the administration also significantly expanded funding for the National Science Foundation's Graduate Research Fellowships. Funding for these fellowships was substantially increased, leading to a marked rise in financial support for doctoral students in science, technology, engineering, and mathematics (STEM) fields, reinforcing the administration's commitment to research and innovation (National Science Foundation, 2012).

A major budgetary initiative in President Obama's Fiscal Year 2015 Budget was the Opportunity, Growth, and Security Initiative, which allocated an additional $56 billion for investments in education, research, infrastructure, and national security (Executive Office of the President, 2014). This initiative aimed to balance investments between civilian and military sectors, supporting a wide range of projects, including early childhood education and vocational training to enhance workforce readiness and basic and applied research in health, energy efficiency, and renewable energy technologies. It also created the National Network for Manufacturing Innovation, with plans to establish forty-five advanced research institutes nationwide. Finally, it sought to modernize critical infrastructure, including the national electricity grid and aviation system and enhance public administration efficiency, streamlining government operations to improve service delivery.

The Workforce Innovation and Opportunity Act of 2014 revised the Workforce Investment Act of 1998, creating a state board of workforce development to oversee investments in career-building programs for low-skilled and undereducated workers. A key component of this initiative was the American Jobs Center, a "one-stop service delivery system" designed to improve coordination between agencies and provide job seekers with access to education, career services, and training. Additionally, the Border Security, Economic Opportunity, and Immigration Modernization Act of 2013 sought to attract high-skilled talent from abroad, further strengthening the US workforce and enhancing economic growth.

Finally, the Obama administration placed a strong emphasis on policies that advanced scientific progress and innovation. Federal contributions to Research and Development (R&D) were consistently increased, with targeted investments in specific research areas. Notable initiatives included the development of green technologies, climate change research, and expanded funding for disease research, including efforts to combat cancer and neurodegenerative diseases such as Alzheimer's.

8.6 Final Remarks

Obama's approach to industrial policy during his presidency was driven by international and domestic factors that were largely a result of the 2008 Financial Crisis. Internationally, the United States was expected to play an important role in stabilizing the global economy after the worldwide economic downturn and the global Financial Crisis. At the same time, China's growing economic competitiveness was threatening US supremacy over emerging technology and manufacturing.

Domestically, Americans were dealing with serious levels of unemployment as a result of the 2008 Financial Crisis and economic downturn. Obama faced pressure, especially from those bearing the brunt of the crisis, to alleviate these conditions through industrial policy programs. Along with individuals that were harmed, affected industries and sectors—particularly the automotive industry—pushed the Obama administration to assist them in recovery. However, the financial stimulus packages that Obama considered were frustrated by political polarization in Congress. Partisan disputes limited the scope of what the Obama administration could implement to address these issues. The lack of structural reform and the deviation from Keynesian fiscal policy by Congress left the United States in a precarious state for the future, despite the immediate economic relief. Throughout his two terms, the United States budget deficit increased by $6.781 trillion, a 58% increase from Bush's last budget (Amadeo, 2021). Bush had cut taxes during the 2001 crisis but failed to raise them again subsequently. Congress during the Obama administration continued this trend by deficit spending during the 2008 crisis, but failed to raise taxes once the crisis was alleviated, causing the deficit to balloon.

The conflicting policies within Congress and pressure surrounding international trade led Obama to target specific sectors to alleviate the strain of the Financial Crisis and economic downturn. His industrial policy programs focused on revitalizing manufacturing, the automotive industry, renewable energy firms, and the technology sector. These programs reflected the Obama administration's ideological approach toward Keynesian economics, US competitiveness, and climate change. Obama's administration was open to providing large-scale stimulus packages, given their belief in spurring growth through these targeted government interventions. In addition, Obama's investment in high technology sectors, start-ups, and R&D reflects his belief in and prioritization of American competitiveness. There was significant investment in Silicon Valley in technology firms and start-ups, reflecting these beliefs. Finally, while building up the bread and butter of American manufacturing industries during this period, Obama also leveraged the opportunity for large-scale stimulus packages to prioritize green energy and tackle the threat of climate change.

Obama's industrial policy was operationalized through direct financial support for firms and infrastructure, increased regulation, public–private partnerships, workforce training programs, and adjustments to trade agreements. First, the Obama administration instituted large-scale bailout programmes and financial support for distressed sectors of the economy—most notably the automotive industry, which received roughly $80 billion in federal assistance under the Troubled Asset Relief Program (Canis and Webel, 2013; U.S. Department of the Treasury, 2013). In addition to these broad financial packages, Obama also instituted industrial policy through more targeted measures. First, the administration rolled out a range of tax credits for the renewable energy sector and for renewed research and development. In addition, the administration aimed to make investment in emerging technologies less risky by providing loans to renewable energy and high technology. Next, by placing increased regulations on industries receiving this financial support, Obama raised the standards in line with environmental goals. For example, the administration introduced higher fuel efficiency standards and carbon emissions regulations while providing support for the auto industry. The Obama administration also prioritized public-private partnerships to foster investment and innovation—namely, the National Network for Manufacturing Innovation and the Advanced Research Projects Agency-Energy. To bolster the workforce's capacity and skills, the Obama administration introduced workforce training measures, particularly in the areas of STEM and through initiatives like the Workforce Innovation and Opportunity Act. Finally, the Obama administration attempted to promote exports and trade through the formation of the Trans-Pacific Partnership and the National Export Initiative.

These measures were instituted through both presidential and legislative means. Obama issued a series of executive orders, particularly to develop the clean energy priorities of his administration. He also issued presidential memoranda to guide administrative agencies on these issues. After receiving this guidance, regulatory agencies then produced regulations and standards in line with the administration's stated goals. The primary stimulus packages to support the domestic public were passed in the legislature. For example, the American Recovery and Reinvestment Act, the Affordable Care Act, and the Workforce Innovation and Opportunity Act were negotiated and voted on by Congress.

There were distinct domestic coalitions supporting and opposing Obama's industrial policy. Given the administration's focus on promoting the environment and clean energy, these policies were particularly well received by progressive and environmental advocacy groups, as well as the companies receiving the direct financial support in the technology and clean energy industry. Additionally, the revival of manufacturing and workforce training was supported by groups that had been struggling during the beginning of the Financial Crisis. For example, the United Auto Workers and AFL-CIO received many of the benefits of the bailout of the automotive sector and were therefore extremely supportive of these measures.

On the other hand, the focus of the industrial policy programs also faced opposition. Namely, Republican lawmakers were opposed to extensive government intervention in the economy and its impact on the national debt. Their viewpoints were substantiated by the advocacy and research from conservative think tanks that prioritized the free market. The extensive support for clean energy also raised concerns from oil, gas, and coal companies as well as voters in states where their activity was concentrated. Even the industries that had benefited from extensive bailouts—like automakers—were concerned about the Obama administration's simultaneous increased regulation of emissions and fuel efficiency.

Obama's policies were successful in alleviating the effects of the Financial Crisis and stabilizing the U.S. economy. In particular, the American Recovery and Reinvestment Act played an important role in reducing unemployment and supporting economic recovery in the aftermath of the 2008 crisis (Congressional Budget Office, 2014). The bailouts to the U.S. auto industry, while extensive, helped avert a collapse of the sector and facilitated its restructuring amid intense international competition (Congressional Oversight Panel, 2011; U.S. Department of the Treasury, 2013). The Obama administration's focus on the clean energy sector was also successful, with nearly a thirty-fold increase in solar capacity between 2009 and 2016 (Obama White House, 2016).

However, there were also serious failures during Obama's presidency on industrial policy. The Clean Power Plan, while boosting the clean energy industry, was difficult to implement and faced serious legal opposition. Despite the benefits of the ARRA in job creation, many of the jobs created were concentrated in the construction industry and were only temporary. In addition, the program was unable to address the fundamental structural issues associated with growing automation and technology in manufacturing. Thus, the long-term benefits of the program were limited. The limited reform to the financial sector created more faith in government bailouts of banks, potentially allowing for more risky investment strategies in the future. While unconventional, the Obama administration's conditional aid to the automotive sector simultaneously saved the car manufacturing in the short term and created structural change that was necessary for future success.

9

The Trump Eruption

9.1 Introduction

Donald Trump's 2016 presidential campaign and subsequent tenure in the Oval Office marked a distinct shift in ideology and policy from the previous administration and within the Republican Party. Within the domestic sphere, Trump utilized traditional neoliberal principles by simplifying the US tax code, reducing income and business taxes, while also decreasing welfare spending and overall government expenditure, in the hopes of stimulating investment and business development. However, one place Trump increased spending was within defense, especially when it came to research and development. On the other hand, in terms of international policy, President Trump's goal to bring back American industry was marked with protectionist policy, trade wars, and intimidating rhetoric toward American companies looking to move operations abroad. By and large, the main beneficiaries of these policies have been wealthier individuals and companies that have taken advantage of the decrease in regulation and taxes.

9.2 The First Campaign: A New Coalition

In 2016, the evolution of the global political and economic order was changing rapidly. The Syrian Civil War did not appear close to an agreed resolution among the parties involved, with ISIS not showing signs of retreat while consolidating its presence in other war fronts such as in Libya. At the same time, several Islamist terrorist attacks destabilized a series of European nations, fueling an increasing consensus toward right-wing movements.

In June 2016, British citizens voted in the Brexit referendum to leave the European Union, changing the political equilibrium of the US strategic partnership with the continent and undermining the market's confidence in a global investment climate upswing. Meanwhile, Putin's Russia proved to be increasingly proactive and effective in pursuing its interests in the Middle East, while simultaneously using cyber-spying and clandestine funding of anti-system movements to interfere in the internal affairs of many Western countries. Finally, China consolidated its commercial supremacy in different international markets, while

Governing Growth. Marco R. Di Tommaso and Vinod K. Aggarwal, Oxford University Press.
© Oxford University Press (2026). DOI: 10.1093/oso/9780197821787.003.0009

becoming more aggressive with respect to the territorial disputes concerning the control of the South China Sea (Schwab, 2016).

In this context, the US presidential campaign was radically disrupted during the Republican Party's primaries by Donald J. Trump. Trump, a total outsider who was diametrically opposed to the Obama administration, promoted an unconventional and populist rhetoric. He sought to delegitimize the past political establishment, both Democratic and Republican, who he argued were obsessive globalists. In his view, such policies were harmful to the national interest, and he criticized both Democrats and the traditional Republican Party. During the campaign, he launched severe attacks against the moderate candidate Marco Rubio, the neocon competitor Ted Cruz, and scathing attacks on George Bush in the context of the Iraq War. At the end of the primaries, in July 2016, the Republican convention anointed Trump as the official party candidate challenging the Democrat Hillary Clinton for the White House (Economist Intelligence Unit, 2024).

During the 2016 presidential campaign, Donald Trump adapted his political discourse by integrating elements of the traditional Republican platform, including the Tea Party's free-market principles and policies favoring major conservative economic interests such as the tobacco, carbon, oil, and financial industries (Williamson et al., 2011). However, his most significant rhetorical innovation was his direct appeal to white working-class voters, leveraging anti-globalization and protectionist themes. He framed the offshoring of American industrial jobs as a failure of the Democratic establishment, embodied by Hillary Clinton, echoing long-standing populist critiques of elite economic policies (Judis, 2016).

Trump's campaign was notable for its unprecedented use of social media, particularly Twitter, which facilitated a process of political disintermediation. This direct communication strategy enabled the centralization of decision-making within a small circle of advisers and helped polarize public opinion around key economic and social issues—such as employment, taxation, migration, and national security—by offering immediate, often scapegoat-driven explanations (Kreis, 2017; Ott, 2017). This approach marked a distinct departure from traditional political messaging, further reshaping American electoral dynamics. Research suggests that Trump's use of Twitter enabled him to set the tone of political discourse through norm-breaking, highly personalized communication that bypassed traditional media filters. Rather than operating primarily through conventional agenda-setting mechanisms, this strategy contributed to heightened polarization and the coarsening of public debate by privileging immediacy, provocation, and affect over sustained policy discussion (Ott, 2017).

In addition, it is important to point out the intersection of economic pressures that go beyond the traditional Republican laissez-faire precepts. In particular, Trump's electoral economic agenda seemed to have captured the political pressures arising from immigration and trade. He pointed to international agreements—like NAFTA and TPP—as destructive for the interests of the working class. In this perspective, the two main slogans adopted by Trump—"America First" and "Make America Great Again (MAGA)"—should be interpreted as a rather successful attempt to match the rising demand for economic closure by the losers of globalization (Di Tommaso et al., 2017).

Trumponomics—as was often termed Trump's economic strategy—included a mix of laissez-faire proposals for the business sector, large-scale investment in physical infrastructure, and protectionist trade policies (Di Tommaso et al., 2019). Trump's economic message blended traditional Republican supply-side tax cuts with a populist-nationalist critique of globalization.

One of Trump's central promises was corporate tax reduction, which he argued would incentivize multinationals to repatriate jobs and investment. He proposed lowering the corporate tax rate from 35% to 15%, increasing the standard deduction, and eliminating the deductibility of interest expenses on new investments (Nunns et al., 2015, 2016). His broader individual tax plan included consolidating the number of income tax brackets from seven to three (12%, 25%, 33%), repealing the 3.8% net investment income tax, and expanding standard deductions (Gale et al., 2018). To offset revenue losses, Trump pledged a spending review with Obamacare as a primary target, framing it as a costly regulatory burden on businesses (Blahous, 2012).

With regard to infrastructure, Trump sought to surpass Hillary Clinton's $300 billion proposal, arguing that America's declining infrastructure—ranked 12th globally in 2016 by the World Economic Forum—needed urgent investment (Schwab, 2016). His plan aimed to unlock up to $1 trillion in projects by offering tax credits to private companies willing to finance and invest in infrastructure (Ross and Navarro, 2016). His economic advisors projected that every $200 billion in infrastructure spending could generate $88 billion in wages and boost GDP growth by over 1%. However, critics warned that heavy reliance on private financing could lead to excessive toll-based infrastructure rather than addressing broad public needs (Edwards, 2017).

Trump's slogans *"Make Trade Fair Again"* and *"Bring Manufacturing Jobs Back to America"* exemplified his trade and industrial policy. He blamed China and Mexico for protectionist and interventionist policies that disadvantaged American industry. Key proposals included withdrawing from the TPP, renegotiating or exiting NAFTA, and shifting toward bilateral agreements rather than multilateral trade pacts (Irwin, 2017). He also advocated using the US Trade Representative to identify trade violations, impose tariffs on currency manipulators—primarily targeting China—and file WTO cases against unfair trade practices (Bown, 2019). Additionally, Trump proposed aggressive tariffs against countries engaged in illegal trade activities, a stance that signaled his later tariff wars as president. By merging pro-business tax policies with populist economic nationalism, Trump's economic platform marked a break from the free-trade orthodoxy of previous Republican administrations while continuing to uphold traditional conservative priorities.

The core objective of Trump's economic agenda was to revitalize domestic manufacturing employment by prioritizing reshoring industrial jobs and reversing what he saw as the negative consequences of globalization. From his perspective, economic openness and international trade were fundamentally unfair to US traditional industries, a viewpoint rooted in economic nationalism and protectionist rhetoric (Irwin, 2017). He framed past trade agreements, such as NAFTA and TPP, as threats to American workers, arguing that free trade disproportionately benefited foreign competitors, particularly China and Mexico (Bown, 2019). His industrial policy proposals thus sought to reduce trade deficits, repatriate supply chains, and impose punitive tariffs on nations engaged in what he described as unfair trade practices (Di Tommaso et al., 2019).

Trump's appeal to the working-class electorate played a crucial role in securing his unexpected win in the 2016 electoral battle. While Republican candidates traditionally drew support from business owners, wealthier voters, and suburban conservatives, Trump successfully expanded the party's voter base to include disaffected blue-collar workers, particularly in states with declining manufacturing employment (Gest, 2016; Cramer, 2016). This was especially evident in the industrial Midwest, where Trump won Ohio, Michigan, Pennsylvania, and Wisconsin—all states that had previously backed Barack Obama. Michigan, for example, had not voted Republican since 1988, yet it flipped to Trump by a narrow margin of just 10,704 votes (McQuarrie, 2017). In Florida—a pivotal swing state—Trump's economic populism and his focus on immigration and trade policies strengthened Republican backing, particularly among White working-class voters (Mason, 2018).

Trump's strongest support came from the lower middle class, White Protestant voters, and less-educated workers employed in manufacturing, mining, and industrial sectors (Kochhar and Cilluffo, 2018). Exit polls showed that 67% of White voters without a college degree voted for Trump. This demographic increasingly felt left behind by globalization and automation (Tyson and Maniam, 2016). Meanwhile, his campaign's populist economic rhetoric resonated in rural and deindustrialized areas, where job losses contributed to economic stagnation and disillusionment with the political establishment (Hochschild, 2016).

9.3 Governing: 2017–2020: The General Economic Approach

The first two years of the Trump administration were marked by a combination of controversial declarations and substantive policy actions, many of which were consistent with his electoral campaign promises. While constrained initially by various institutional interests—such as Wall Street, congressional Republicans, and corporate lobbying groups—which sought continuity in economic policy, Trump frequently challenged the status quo (Di Tommaso et al., 2019). His "Trumponomics" agenda emphasized tax cuts, deregulation, protectionist trade policies, military spending, and fiscal conservatism.

The first major economic policy document of the Trump administration was the Budget of the US Government for Fiscal Year 2018, titled "A New Foundation for American Greatness," followed by the 2019 budget, "Efficient, Effective, Accountable: An American Budget." These documents outlined the administration's economic philosophy, attributing economic stagnation to bad trade deals, excessive regulation, and high corporate taxes. The 2018 report explicitly criticized globalization and international trade agreements for allegedly hollowing out American industries and communities, stating, "Horrible trade deals that have exported American jobs have led to cities and towns devastated by unfair trade policies" (OMB, 2018, p. 6).

In addition, the budget aggressively targeted federal regulations, particularly environmental regulations. The administration blamed regulatory policies, such as Light Duty Fuel Economy Standards and Power Plant Emissions Regulations, for imposing an estimated compliance cost of $10 billion per year on businesses (Di Tommaso et al., 2019, p. 7). Furthermore, the budget criticized permitting processes for infrastructure projects and claimed that high corporate tax rates were suppressing business investment, particularly in manufacturing and energy sectors.

The 2018 budget proposal sought to reduce federal spending by $3.6 trillion over ten years, with the stated goal of limiting the national debt-to-GDP ratio to 60%. The key measures proposed included repealing Obamacare and restructuring Medicaid by realigning financial incentives between federal and state governments and reforming the welfare system, blaming it for fostering dependency on public subsidies rather than incentivizing employment.

In addition, the budget proposal aimed to reduce Social Security Disability Insurance and retirement benefits, arguing that these programs imposed an unsustainable fiscal burden (OMB, 2018, pp. 9–12). Further goals included simplifying the tax code and reducing both personal and corporate income taxes, which were positioned as essential for boosting investment and job creation (OMB, 2018, p. 13).

In parallel, the budget proposed a 2% systematic decrease in federal discretionary spending per year, with one key exception: military and defense spending was expanded significantly. The increase in military expenditures was offset by sharp cuts in non-defense programs, reflecting a reallocation of federal resources toward national security.

The spending reductions proposed by the Trump administration disproportionately affected lower-income and middle-income Americans. According to the Center on Budget and Policy Priorities, the administration's 2021 budget proposed cutting $1.6 trillion over ten years from programs such as Medicaid, the Supplemental Nutrition Assistance Program, and other assistance programs for low- and middle-income individuals. Additionally, the Tax Policy Center's analysis of the Tax Cuts and Jobs Act of 2017 indicates that higher-income households and corporations received substantial tax reductions, with the largest cuts as a share of income going to taxpayers in the 95th to 99th percentiles of the income distribution (Kogan et al., 2020; Tax Policy Center, 2017).

The administration's economic strategy revealed a clear alignment with traditional corporate interests, reinforcing a trickle-down growth philosophy (Di Tommaso et al., 2017). Despite Trump's electoral rhetoric about prioritizing blue-collar workers and revitalizing industrial employment, his actual fiscal policies favored capital-intensive industries and high-income groups. The sharp reductions in social welfare programs and Medicaid—while maintaining tax incentives for large businesses—demonstrated continuity with traditional Republican economic orthodoxy rather than the economic nationalism and worker-centric policies that Trump had promised on the campaign trail.

Although Trump frequently criticized free trade and globalization for harming American workers, his administration's fiscal measures prioritized corporate tax cuts and military expansion over direct industrial investment. While his campaign promised a reconfiguration of domestic production to benefit the "losers of globalization," his actual policies largely reflected corporate interests and traditional conservative economic principles.

This contradiction was particularly evident in the treatment of federal spending. While Trump's budget emphasized cutting non-defense spending and limiting the federal deficit, the expansion of military spending and corporate tax cuts effectively offset any potential deficit reduction. As a result, the federal budget deficit increased significantly during his first two years in office, despite his administration's commitment to fiscal conservatism.,

Under the Trump administration, defense investment became the top federal budget priority, reflecting his broader "America First" security strategy. The administration increased the discretionary budget of the Department of Defense (DoD) by $52 billion in 2017, raising the total defense budget to $639 billion. This surge in spending positioned military funding as the single largest component of discretionary federal expenditures. .Almost half of this funding was allocated to military research and development (R&D). The DoD received 45.4% of total federal R&D funding, with most of it channeled through the Pentagon's Research, Development, Test, and Evaluation program (GAO, 2020). Significant investments in next-generation weaponry, artificial intelligence (AI), cyber warfare capabilities, and hypersonic missile technology continued the historical trend of prioritizing military technological superiority (CBO, 2018).

In August 2018, President Trump signed the John S. McCain National Defense Authorization Act (NDAA) for Fiscal Year 2019, authorizing a record-high $717 billion defense budget (NDAA, 2018). Trump described it as: "the most significant investment in our military and our warfighters in modern history" (Trump, Twitter, 2018a).

The budget included $616.9 billion for the Pentagon's base budget, covering personnel, operations, procurement, and modernization of military equipment; $69 billion for Overseas Contingency Operations (OCO) funding, mainly supporting ongoing military operations in the Middle East and counterterrorism efforts; and $21.9 billion for nuclear weapons programs—managed by the Department of Energy—with a focus on modernizing the US nuclear arsenal (NDAA, 2018).

The increase in defense spending was justified by the administration as necessary to rebuild the US military, which Trump frequently claimed had been weakened under previous administrations. His rhetoric emphasized military strength as essential for national security, economic growth, and global power projection: "Our military is building and is rapidly becoming stronger than ever before. Frankly, we have no choice!" (Trump, Twitter, 2017c). He went on to note, "I just signed Bill. Our Military will now be stronger than ever before. We love and need our Military and give them everything—and more. First time this has happened in a long time. Also means JOBS, JOBS, JOBS!" (Trump, Twitter, 2018e).

By linking military expansion to economic and industrial revitalization, Trump framed defense investment as a job creation tool, reinforcing his protectionist economic strategy. This linkage was reflected in expanding procurement contracts for major defense companies such as Lockheed Martin, Boeing, Northrop Grumman, and Raytheon, which benefited from increased spending on fighter jets, naval ships, and missile defense systems (SIPRI, 2019). It also granted investments in the defense industrial base, ensuring continued political and economic support from defense-sector workers and contractors (Kurc and Bitzinger, 2021).

The Trump administration extensively employed rhetoric-driven economic policymaking to influence corporate decisions and public perception regarding manufacturing job creation. This approach, which combined public pressure, expectation management, and legislative action, was particularly evident in efforts to repatriate manufacturing jobs and revitalize American industry (Di Tommaso et al., 2019).

Trump's strategy to encourage domestic industrial investment can be categorized into three key mechanisms. First, he focused on blaming companies that outsourced jobs. His strategy can be seen in his 2016 campaign when he frequently criticized free-trade agreements and accused corporations of betraying American workers. For instance, in August 2016, he tweeted: "Vast numbers of manufacturing jobs in Pennsylvania have moved to Mexico and other countries. That will end when I win!" (Trump, Twitter, 2016).

Once in office, Trump escalated this rhetoric, singling out major automakers such as Toyota and General Motors (GM), threatening punitive tariffs on companies that outsourced production. Two notable examples include his attack on Toyota and GM: "Toyota Motor said it will build a new plant in Baja, Mexico, to build Corolla cars for U.S. NO WAY! Build a plant in the U.S. or pay big border tax" (Trump, Twitter, 2017b). And on GM: "General Motors is sending Mexican-made models of Chevy Cruze to U.S. car dealers—tax-free across borders. Make in the U.S.A. or pay big border tax!" (Trump, Twitter, 2017a).

Trump's administration employed public pressure campaigns to deter companies from offshoring jobs, aiming to influence their investment decisions. For instance, in 2016, Carrier Corporation announced plans to relocate its Indianapolis manufacturing operations to Mexico, which would have resulted in significant job losses in the United States. Following public and political pressure, including direct engagement from President-elect Trump, Carrier agreed to retain some jobs in Indiana in exchange for state incentives (Reuters, 2021). However, despite such interventions, the broader trend of offshoring persisted. Data indicates that from 2016 to 2020, the US Department of Labor certified over 200,000 workers as having lost their jobs due to offshoring, a figure comparable to previous administrations (Reuters, 2021).

While these public pressure efforts led some companies to adjust their short-term strategies, long-term structural factors continued to drive manufacturing decisions. Global supply chains, labor costs, and automation remained significant determinants. Rising labor costs in traditionally low-cost countries, along with increased expenses related to transportation and quality control, prompted businesses to reevaluate their offshoring strategies (Boston Consulting Group, 2018). Additionally, advancements in automation and artificial intelligence have transformed supply chains, enabling companies to enhance efficiency and reduce costs, further influencing decisions on manufacturing locations (Global Trade Magazine, 2023).

Second, beyond direct corporate pressure, Trump cultivated business confidence among domestic manufacturers by repeatedly declaring the revival of US industry. His strategy relied on constant public statements and announcements designed to reinforce the perception of industrial resurgence, even when concrete policy actions were lacking. For example, at the National Association of Manufacturers annual conference in 2017, Trump declared:

> For decades, the policy of Washington, DC, on the subject of manufacturing was a policy best summarized in one word: surrender. They surrendered. Under my administration, the era of economic surrender is over, and the rebirth of American industry is beginning (Trump, 2017a)

Similarly, he celebrated supposed job creation successes through Twitter, as seen in August 2018:

> Almost 500,000 Manufacturing Jobs created since I won the Election. Remember when my opponents were saying that we couldn't create this type of job anymore. Wrong, in fact these are among our best and most important jobs! (Trump, Twitter, 2018b).

While these claims reinforced confidence in the manufacturing sector, their substance was debated. Economic analysts noted that many of the manufacturing jobs created during Trump's tenure were a continuation of pre-existing trends rather than a direct result of his policies (Scott, 2020).

In August 2017, President Trump's Manufacturing Jobs Initiative was disbanded after several business leaders resigned in protest of his remarks concerning the Charlottesville rally. Notably, Merck CEO Kenneth Frazier, Under Armour CEO Kevin Plank, and Intel CEO Brian Krzanich were among those who stepped down, leading to the dissolution of the council. This series of resignations significantly undermined the administration's credibility in fostering industry-government collaboration (Egan, 2017).

Third, the most substantive policy action supporting Trump's industrial agenda was the drastic reduction of corporate income taxes through the Tax Cuts and Jobs Act (TCJA) of 2017. While his campaign initially proposed a corporate tax rate cut from 35% to 15%, the final legislation lowered it to 21%—a significant reduction, nonetheless. Trump framed the tax cuts as a pivotal factor in reversing offshoring and boosting domestic investment:

> The corporate tax rate, as you know, will be lowered from 35 to 21 percent. That means that more products will be made in the USA. A lot of things are going to be happening in the USA. We're going to bring back our companies. They've already started coming back. I think they had certain confidence in me and they figured we were going to get this done. But they have already started. (Trump, 2017c).

The TCJA also introduced full expensing (100% bonus depreciation) for capital investments in short-lived assets, a provision particularly beneficial for manufacturers investing in new equipment and facilities (Muresianu and York, 2024). However, while the tax cuts boosted corporate profits and stock buybacks, the impact on domestic manufacturing job creation was mixed. As Zwick and Mahon (2017) note, investment did increase, but primarily in automation and capital assets, not in labor-intensive job creation. Moreover, manufacturing job growth under Trump was comparable to pre-2016 trends, suggesting limited additional impact from tax cuts alone (Chodorow-Reich et al., 2024). And many companies used tax windfalls for stock buybacks rather than wage increases or domestic expansion (Bivens, 2018).

9.4 An Aggressive Trade Policy

Despite campaign promises of broad tariffs on Chinese imports, Trump's trade policy began with targeted, sector-specific measures.[1] One of the first significant actions was the initiation of a Section 201 investigation under the Trade Act of 1974, which aligns with Article XIX of the GATT. This provision permits the implementation of safeguards when a surge in imports causes serious injury to domestic industries. Following the International Trade Commission's determination of such injury, the administration imposed tariffs in January 2018 on washing machines and solar panels. These tariffs were structured as tariff-rate quotas, scheduled to decrease over three to four years, with few exceptions. Countries like China, South Korea, and Japan announced their intent to retaliate, with their tariffs expected to take effect in 2021, adhering to WTO procedures.

Subsequently, the administration invoked Section 232 of the Trade Expansion Act of 1962, a measure that allows for trade restrictions on the grounds of national security, as outlined in GATT Article XXI. Historically, this provision has been sparingly used. In March 2018, following a Commerce Department assessment, the administration imposed tariffs of 10% on aluminum and 25% on steel imports. As Trump noted:

> We're going to use American steel, we're going to use American labor, we are going to come first in all deals." (Tweeted in April 2017); "Steel is a big problem, I mean, they're dumping steel. Not only China, but others. We're like a dumping ground, okay? They're dumping steel and destroying our steel industry. They've been doing it for decades, and I'm stopping it. It'll stop. (The New York Times, 2017).

---

[1] This section on trade draws heavily on Aggarwal and Reddie (2021).

Certain countries, including Australia, Argentina, Brazil, and South Korea, secured exemptions by agreeing to limit their exports. In response, many affected nations promptly retaliated and notified the WTO of their actions.

Trade disputes with China clearly deserve special attention. In particular, despite several declarations on the complementarity of the two economies and the need for mutually beneficial cooperation, a quick spiral of protectionist actions and reactions between the United States and China ensued between January and November 2018, leading to a trade war concerning both agricultural and manufacturing products, as well as technology and intellectual property.

Under Section 301 of the Trade Act of 1974, the US Trade Representative was directed to investigate China's alleged violations of US intellectual property rights (CRS, 1974). This statute permits the United States to withdraw trade concessions or impose tariffs if a foreign country's actions are deemed unjustifiable and detrimental to US commerce. Although utilized during the Reagan administration, its application diminished following the establishment of the WTO's Dispute Settlement Body, as the United States preferred seeking WTO approval for such measures.

In March 2018, after determining an adverse impact on the United States, the administration enacted a series of tariff measures, prompting Chinese retaliation. These actions included a 25% US tariff on $50 billion worth of Chinese goods in July 2018, with China responding with equivalent tariffs on US imports. In September 2018, the United States imposed a 10% tariff on an additional $200 billion of Chinese imports, scheduled to increase to 25% on January 1, 2019. China countered with 5–10% tariffs on an additional $60 billion of US goods (Congressional Research Service, 2019).

In total, the China-specific Section 301 tariffs affected approximately $364 billion of imports in 2018, which imposed tens of billions of dollars of costs on US firms (Lee and Varas, 2022). The tariffs disrupted supply chains in multiple sectors. This was the case, especially given the fact that many of the tariffs were levied on intermediate goods, which in turn raised input prices for domestic producers and hampered their competitiveness (Amiti, et al., 2019). The 2018 China tariff shock disrupted firm-to-firm relations and made US firms expend resources on renegotiations with suppliers or search costs to find replacement suppliers (Grossman et al., 2024). Among the industries that were affected by the Section 301 tariffs were consumer goods companies that imported goods from China, leading to their opposition to the tariffs (Jackson and Harden, 2023). Technology companies that sourced from China also opposed the tariffs because they faced increased costs without bringing back jobs and production from China (Analysis of Section 301 Tariff Impacts, 2022; Johnson and Wong, 2024).

The trade war was then officially placed on hold for ninety days from early December 2018 to allow negotiations toward a trade deal, after the meeting that

Donald Trump and Xi Jinping had during the G-20 Summit in Buenos Aires: "My meeting in Argentina with President Xi of China was an extraordinary one. Relations with China have taken a BIG leap forward! Very good things will happen. We are dealing from great strength, but China likewise has much to gain if and when a deal is completed. Level the field!" (Trump, Twitter, 2018c).

The negotiations were focused on technology transfer issues, protection and enforcement of intellectual property rights, tariff and non-tariff barriers, cyber-theft, and market-distorting forces (for instance, subsidies and state-owned enterprises according to the US side), as well as other structural issues, such as trade deficit and the role of currencies in the US-China trading relationship.

A mix of optimism and continuing threats characterized Trump's rhetoric in these 90-day deadline negotiations (by March 1, 2019), as illustrated by the following Twitter post in December 2018:

> President Xi and I want this deal to happen, and it probably will. But if not remember I am a Tariff Man. When people or countries come in to raid the great wealth of our Nation, I want them to pay for the privilege of doing so. It will always be the best way to max out our economic power. We are right now taking in $billions in Tariffs. MAKE AMERICA RICH AGAIN (Trump, Twitter, 2018d)

The escalation continued into 2019, with further tariff increases and threats of additional measures. A partial agreement between the United States and China was reached on January 15, 2020, temporarily easing tensions.

9.5 Trump's Investment Regulations

In 2018, the United States intensified its efforts to safeguard national security by enacting the Foreign Investment Risk Review Modernization Act (FIRRMA). This legislation significantly broadened the scope of the Committee on Foreign Investment in the United States (CFIUS), an interagency body responsible for evaluating foreign investments for potential security threats (Jackson, 2019). FIRRMA expanded CFIUS's jurisdiction beyond its previous mandate under the Foreign Investment and National Security Act of 2007, enabling the committee to scrutinize a wider array of transactions (Jackson, 2019).

Notably, FIRRMA extended CFIUS's authority to include non-controlling investments in US businesses involved in critical technologies, critical infrastructure, or those collecting sensitive personal data of US citizens (Jackson, 2019). Additionally, the legislation emphasized rigorous examination of real estate transactions near military installations or other sensitive national security sites (Jackson, 2019).

Aggarwal and Reddie (2020) contextualize FIRRMA within the broader framework of U.S. economic statecraft, identifying it as a strategic effort to expand regulatory oversight of foreign direct investment. They argue that this shift reflects a growing recognition of the economic dimensions of national security and the need for more comprehensive policy instruments to address emerging vulnerabilities.

Considering the long-run strategic economic and political importance attributed to the automotive industry by the US government (Tassinari, 2019), it is critical to discuss the key elements characterizing Trump's rhetorical practices. First, Trump explicitly recognized its strategic relevance for the US economy—especially through meetings with prominent entities—such as: "We have, at this table, the biggest car manufacturers in the world..... We're working on how to build more cars in the United States" (Trump, 2017b).

Second, since the electoral campaign, Trump has implicitly incentivized automakers to reshore manufacturing in the United States through rhetoric. On the one hand, he chastised car manufacturers who have moved—or were planning to move—production abroad, such as in the GM case:

> Very disappointed with General Motors and their CEO, Mary Barra, for closing plants in Ohio, Michigan and Maryland. Nothing being closed in Mexico & China. The U.S. saved General Motors, and this is the THANKS we get! We are now looking at cutting all @GM subsidies, including for electric cars [...] I am here to protect America's Workers!" (Trump, Twitter, 2018f).

On the other hand, he openly praised companies (e.g., Ford, Fiat-Chrysler, GM, Toyota, Mazda) that announced investment plans in US plants, such as:

> Ford said last week that it will expand in Michigan and U.S. instead of building a BILLION dollar plant in Mexico. Thank you Ford & Fiat C!" (Trump, Twitter, 2017d).

Such rhetoric-based strategy clearly created an implicit system of threats, incentives, and rewards for companies to reshore—and even to change previous offshoring plans, as in the case of GM and Toyota—without the use of any traditional policy tools: "It will only get higher. Car companies and others, if they want to do business in our country, have to start making things here again. WIN!" (Trump, Twitter, 2017e).

Third, Trump and his advisors continuously raised expectations for protectionism. The strong rhetoric via Twitter between March and April 2018 blamed what his administration conceives as "big trade imbalances" and "stupid trade" with the European Union and China. This was followed in May 2018 by the official investigation under Section 232 of the Trade Expansion Act of 1962, as in the case of steel, justified by concerns that vehicle and parts imports threatened the industry's health and its ability to research and develop advanced technologies. It is hard to believe that no concrete action would follow, having created high expectations for protectionism.

9.6 Regulatory Changes

With respect to regulations, a political give-and-take was advanced by proposing to roll back efficiency rules. The administration sought to eliminate the Corporate Average Fuel Economy—seen by automakers as a regulatory burden on greenhouse gas emissions and fuel economy standards for automobiles—in exchange for more car production and hiring in the United States.

Trump continued to pursue an approach directed to attribute a new centrality to the manufacturing sector; on the other hand, different from Obama's interest in the upgrading of the advanced manufacturing industries. The concerns of the Trump administration reveal a concern with prioritizing a return to traditional manufacturing sectors that required more workers and fewer skills, such as coal mining, steel, textiles, and cars.

From this perspective, the development of the green industry has been clearly downgraded by Trump as compared to the robust efforts of the Obama administration (Gross, 2020). Indeed, several declarations and actions contributed to dismantling the system of incentives provided by Obama for reducing carbon emissions and promoting renewable energy: leaving the Paris Agreement on global warming in June 2017; repealing the 2015 Clean Water Role regulation concerning water resource management; the review of the Obama's Clean Power Plan concerning the restriction of greenhouse gas emissions and the identification of emissions' social costs; reversing the temporary ban on mining coal and steam protection; the launch of the America First Energy Plan, along with ending Obama's Climate Action Plan, prescribing a reduction in the regulations on domestic fossil fuel extraction, and the introduction of incentives to revitalize the creation of jobs in oil, gas, and coal production (Vakhshouri, 2017; Di Tommaso et al., 2019).

Trump planned to reverse Obama's rejection of the construction of the Keystone XL (KXL) extension pipeline to transport oil from Canadian tar sands to the United States. The pipeline was controversial for several reasons, including its path through Native American territory, its environmental impacts, and potential safety issues for those in the surrounding areas. Since the pipeline was never built, the exact economic impacts are uncertain. The number of jobs it would have created ranges from around 21,000 to 59,000 for the first two years depending on different estimates. However, it has been mostly agreed that after being built, it would take roughly fifty employees to maintain the pipeline. The possible revenue and effect on prices have only been inconclusive (Department of Energy, 2022). However, President Trump and many supporters say that the failure of the KXL pipeline has led to high gas prices and cost tens of thousands of jobs. Thus, the KXL pipeline has become a hot topic in recent years and shows Trump's support for the oil and gas industry that surpasses other environmental and safety concerns.

Similarly, another domestic industry that had taken a hit despite Trump's "protectionism" was agriculture and livestock. The Trump administration gutted several regulations for the meat-packing industry including dissolving the Grain Inspection, Packers and Stockyards Administration (GIPSA). GIPSA prevented agribusiness from retaliating against growers who organized unions, negotiated in bad faith, and imposed unequal pay to farmers. The dissolution of GIPSA left a hole in agribusiness oversight that led to increases in farmers' input prices combined with decreased farmgate prices, significantly lowering profits. Trump's trade war has also decreased agricultural exports significantly. For the state of Iowa, the corn, soybean, and hog markets lost $1.6 billion. The effects were mostly felt by small and medium farmers who lost significantly from decreased exports as well as decreased regulations (Willingham, 2020). President Trump's policies toward the agricultural sector are representative of his policies in general: protect big business, ignore the small, and instill protectionist policies.

To conclude this period, Trump's State of the Union addresses in 2018 and 2019 explicitly mentioned all the above-mentioned priorities, promises, and actions, making full use of his capacity to raise expectations, shape behaviors, and create incentives or disincentives for economic agents. This rhetoric can be seen as aimed at simultaneously fulfilling both the requests for radical anti-globalization and protectionist change by his political base, as well as the requests for continuity by the strongest interests of American capitalism:

> Americans fill the world with art and music. They push the bounds of science and discovery. And they forever remind us of what we should never forget: The people dreamed this country. The people built this country. And it is the people who are making America great again" (Trump, 2018).

> The agenda I will lay out this evening is not a Republican agenda or a Democrat agenda. It's the agenda of the American people. [...] We must keep America first in our hearts. We must keep freedom alive in our souls (Trump, 2019).

Despite his rhetoric, Trump's protectionist policy actions did not meaningfully boost overall employment. Trump's expansive use of tariffs, by raising prices of intermediate inputs and by inviting retaliation, hurt domestic manufacturing.

Flaaen and Pierce (2019) found that businesses more exposed to the tariffs were worse off, as the effects of retaliatory tariffs more than offset the protective effects of reduced import penetration. According to data from the Bureau of Labor Statistics, the total number of persons employed in manufacturing slightly increased from 12.366 million in January 2017, when Trump took office, to 12.780 million in February 2020, the last full month before COVID shutdowns (Federal Reserve Economic Data, 2025). But these numbers are far below peaks in the second half of the twentieth century and actually do not represent an increase at all in manufacturing employment as a share of total nonfarm employment, which slightly decreased from approximately 8.5% in January 2017 to approximately 8.4% in February 2020 (Federal Reserve Economic Data, 2025). US manufacturing employment in the twenty-first century seems to be driven more by secular trends than by policymakers. On its own terms of averting offshoring and bringing manufacturing back to US shores, the Trump administration has not succeeded (Scott, 2020). By contrast to his trade and industrial policies, Trump's tax reforms did meaningfully stimulate growth, boost employment, increase investment, and bolster manufacturing (Chodorow-Reich et al., 2024).

9.7 Final Remarks

Trump's approach to industrial policy was driven by both domestic and international factors. Trump entered office when US-China tensions and trade deficits were continuing to grow. Therefore, concerns about China's technological advancement and broad subsidies to domestic industry motivated industrial policy programs focused on stricter trade and investment measures. Trump's domestic coalitions were animated by these international factors, calling for the revitalization of US manufacturing and the protection of domestic production after witnessing the outcomes of the "China shock." After facing decades of deindustrialization and witnessing the precarity of global supply chains, voters wanted Trump to prioritize these industrial policy programs.

Trump's administration focused its industrial policy on specific sectors, companies, and regions to address these concerns. First, Trump instituted extensive tariffs in his first administration—and has done so aggressively in his second term—on steel, aluminum, and automobiles. Section 232 of the Trade Expansion Act was used to impose 25% tariffs on steel and 10% on aluminum imports. Trump also used Section 301 tariffs to combat the influx of Chinese goods into the United States using the justification that China was using unfair trade practices because of the theft of intellectual property and vast subsidies for domestic industries. These measures aimed to revitalize American manufacturing and provide protection for domestic suppliers. Additionally, Trump was very concerned about Chinese companies gaining access to US intellectual property, which led to a focus on the technology and telecommunications sector. In particular, Trump placed restrictions on some Chinese companies to prevent them from building 5G infrastructure in the United States—including Huawei and ZTE. At the same time, Trump bolstered CFIUS by passing FIRRMA. This act required additional review of investment in critical technologies in foreign countries and had a significant impact on technology companies. Finally, Trump's industrial policy focused on expanding domestic energy production and supporting fossil fuel companies by removing regulations that had been developed under the Obama administration. A similar plan is in place for Trump's second administration, with executive orders already passed that benefit the fossil fuel industry.

The effects of these industrial policy programs were beneficial to manufacturing regions, particularly in the Midwest. By creating manufacturing jobs in Ohio, Michigan, and Pennsylvania, Trump was able to appeal to his domestic base and fulfill his campaign promises of promoting "Buy American" initiatives. In addition, the deregulation of the fossil fuel industry was lucrative for states that had many energy companies like Texas, West Virginia, and North Dakota. For example, the Keystone XL and Dakota Access pipelines would increase economic growth in these states and were developed after deregulation took place. There were extensive domestic coalitions in support of these industrial policy programs. The industries that benefited from tariffs and trade restrictions, specifically the steel, aluminum, and automotive industries, were vocal about their support for the programs. Additionally, unions that saw increased jobs and expansion of wages under these policies—like the United Steelworkers—were supportive of these tariffs. Similarly, the fossil fuel industry benefited from the deregulation of environmental standards and the increase in domestic energy production. These policies also appealed to Trump's voter base, which favored populist and protectionist approaches to the economy.

However, there was also opposition to his industrial policy proposals amongst those harmed by the changes to tariffs and export controls. In particular, tech companies that had extensive supply chains and networks in China saw increased costs and disrupted operations as a result of the changes. In addition, consumer goods companies that imported goods from China also opposed tariffs, as they raised prices for companies and disrupted their inventory. Another group that was harmed by Trump's industrial policy was the agriculture sector—in particular, corn, soybean, and pork farmers. The changes to tariffs extensively impacted their ability to export their products in an economically efficient manner. States that were heavily dependent on agriculture for their economy—like Iowa, Kansas, and Nebraska—also expressed their concerns about how the tariffs were impacting their state's industry.

The effects of Trump's industrial policy programs were mixed. Domestic industries that were targeted by Trump's industrial policy programs—like steel and fossil fuels—saw an increase in production and international market share. Trump's policy also began the process of reshoring critical infrastructure and industries to secure the domestic supply chain, an issue of heightened concern during this time due to the COVID-19 Pandemic. In particular, Trump's policy focused on the reshoring of pharmaceuticals, PPE, and semiconductors.

The impact of the programs on the manufacturing sector and subsequent job creation was fairly limited. The majority of jobs created were short-term contracts, and so the program did not reach the high expectations of reshoring US domestic production. In addition, the increased tariffs on Chinese imports resulted in disruptions to the supply chain and higher prices on consumer goods. Trump's proposals for his second administration, with more comprehensive tariffs across industries, would likely magnify these impacts. These measures heightened international tension between the United States and China, as well as the United States and its international allies, given the abandonment of the international regime for free trade.

10
The Joe Biden Years

10.1 Introduction

Joe Biden's campaign was promoted as an antithesis to Donald Trump's, in which Trump had "failed" in progress and handling COVID-19. Biden promoted his own policies as filling in the gaps where Trump had faltered. Similar to Trump, Biden's policies reflected a desire among the American people for a stronger and more resilient domestic economy in the wake of mass globalization. However, while Trump addressed the issue through tax cuts, welfare reductions, and military spending, Biden's policies, such as the Build Back Better Act and the Inflation Reduction Act (IRA), worked to stimulate the economy through investment. The government's focus turned to towards job creation, clean energy, infrastructure development, and other anti-cyclical policies meant to help the post-COVID economy. Biden further utilized more progressive principles of raising money to fund these policies such as promising to increase taxes on the rich.

His main goal was to ease the average American's mind that had been plagued with the job loss and economic uncertainty of the pandemic by promising a return to normalcy, both by pre-pandemic standards, but also from a tumultuous Trump presidency. His plans have been successful in improving infrastructure, clean energy, and job growth, but as the Biden presidency ends, there are still many issues being faced in enacting these policies. Without him running for a second term, much of this would have been carried on by his Vice-President and Democratic nominee Kamala Harris.

10.2 Biden's Election in Tumultuous External Conditions

Biden entered office facing two international crises: the COVID-19 pandemic and US–China tensions. The industrial policy pursued by Biden was largely informed by and reactive to these events. First, Biden's campaign responded to the intense job loss and economic slowdown caused by the COVID-19 pandemic by advocating for public infrastructure works. Reminiscent of The New Deal, Biden's proposed policies included repairing and building bridges, roads, and highways, as well as addressing the degradation of utility infrastructure across the country (Parilla et al., 2024).

Governing Growth. Marco R. Di Tommaso and Vinod K. Aggarwal, Oxford University Press.
© Oxford University Press (2026). DOI: 10.1093/oso/9780197821787.003.0010

Where would the funding come from for this massive expenditure? Like any politician trying to appeal to working-class voters, Biden promised to pay for the new infrastructure and public jobs by raising taxes on the rich. By spending money, Biden aimed to stimulate the economy after the COVID-19 recession and enhance the US response to climate change by investing in more green energy methods. Biden used his own policies to attack Trump's lack of progress made during his own presidency, pointing out how the incumbent president had made similar promises to restore America's infrastructure but had fallen short during the pivotal COVID years. On the other hand, Trump's campaign promises focused on continuing accomplishments during his term, such as limiting the DACA program, approving the Keystone Pipeline, removing clean energy regulations, and implementing tariffs on China. These policies were criticized by Biden's campaign for being counter-productive, and he promised to repeal many of them while still asserting America's dominance over China and growing America's domestic manufacturing, especially in the auto industry (Beattie, 2024).

The key point here is that Biden's election promises needed to be strong in order to inspire Americans still suffering from the socioeconomic issues created during the COVID-19 pandemic, especially in key swing states that had decided Trump's victory in 2020. Unemployment peaked in April 2020 at over 15%, just two months after it was 3% in February. By the time the November election rolled around, unemployment was still almost 7% (Unemployment Rates During the COVID-19 Pandemic: In Brief, 2021).

Most of these job losses were in the lowest-paying sectors, which heightened economic inequality among already marginalized groups. For instance, black and Latino Americans experienced slower job recovery than white workers. Furthermore, official unemployment statistics only account for those searching for work, but some 1.3 million Americans gave up searching for work during the pandemic. Other workers retained their jobs but didn't receive pay due to business closures. These conditions are why reducing unemployment and closing the inequality gap were focuses of Biden's plans for infrastructure, such as in the IRA.

Furthermore, the pandemic demonstrated that the global supply chain was fragile since restrictions on trade made it much harder to receive key parts for manufacturing, increasing the cost of goods. During the pandemic, stimulus checks and boredom led to an increase in online shopping, which further put stress on global supply chains. In no situation was the stress and fragility more obvious than in the 2021 Suez Canal Obstruction, where one container ship, the *Ever Given*, blocked trade in the Suez Canal causing hundreds of ships with billions of dollars of trade to be held up for days. To Biden, in order to prevent more disasters a resilient domestic supply chain needed to be built (White House, 2021a).

Abroad, US–China trade tensions and protectionism have been increasing since the late 2010s, causing high-value-added and technological industries (e.g., semiconductors, digital assets) to be important to national interest. Thus, Biden campaigned on the idea of reestablishing America's manufacturing sector, which would eventually become part of his Chips Act once in office, with one of the prides of Biden being the semiconductor plant being built in Arizona.

When Biden entered the presidency in 2021, he was faced with a post-pandemic global economy that was fragile and still recovering. The pandemic reshaped the world as we know it, and exposed many glaring holes in our current institutions that made us ill-equipped for such a sudden emergency. Thus, the Biden Presidency would have to reckon with these many issues.

10.3 Biden's Approach to Industrial Policy

After his election, Biden's industrial policy can be grouped into two broad types. First, at the beginning of his administration Biden prioritized public infrastructure works to bolster job creation in the wake of COVID-19. Second, Biden focused on strengthening key US industries' supply chains and increasing domestic production in industries critical to national security and public health.

In January 2021, Biden began his term with an industrial policy that focused on harnessing the federal government's reach and purchasing power to support US domestic industries. Guidelines for federal financial assistance and procurement were introduced to maximize the use of US-made goods and services, streamline procurement bureaucracy, and promote enforcement. A Made in America Office was established in the Office of Management and Budget to centralize the review and approval of agencies' requests for exceptions to Made in America Laws. This review process included evaluating whether the cost advantage of a foreign-sourced product results from the use of dumped or injuriously subsidized steel, iron, or manufactured goods. Additionally, proposed and granted exception waivers were to be made public to provide transparent market intelligence to interested parties (Chu et al., 2024; White House, 2021e).

The Code of Federal Regulations was also amended to measure domestic content by the value added to the product through US-based production or US job-supporting economic activity rather than cost. It increased the numerical threshold for domestic content from 55% to 75% as well as price preferences for domestic end products and construction materials (Federal Register, 2022). Specific attention was paid to information technology that were commercial items, where existing laws constraining the application of Made in America Laws would be reviewed.

In February 2021, the Biden administration began working on strengthening key domestic industries through introducing reviews and assessments to improve supply chain resilience for industries including semiconductors, rare earth elements, and pharmaceuticals. The influence of COVID-19 can be seen, as efforts in the pharmaceutical industry are specifically designed to complement ongoing work to secure supply chains of critical COVID-19 items such as personal protection equipment. Key industries here are generally relevant to national security (e.g., defense), high value-added and technological products (e.g., high-capacity batteries) and public health (e.g., agriculture and food production). 100-day supply chain reviews were required for the following specific industries: semiconductors, advanced packaging, high-capacity batteries (including electric vehicle batteries), critical and strategic minerals (including rare earth elements), as well as pharmaceuticals and active pharmaceutical ingredients. One-year sectoral supply chain assessments were required for the following industrial bases as well: defense including areas where civilian supply chains are dependent upon "competitor nations," public health and biological preparedness, critical sectors and subsectors of ICT technology, transportation, agriculture and food production, as well as digital networks, services, assets and data (White House, 2021a).

Media coverage at the time was cautiously optimistic since the media generally praised the Biden administration for acknowledging American supply chain issues which had been exposed by the COVID-19 pandemic and looked forward to future legislation that would boost US manufacturing in key industries, but questioned how the government would compel companies to improve resilience. The 100-day supply chain reviews revealed significant structural weaknesses due to factors such as unfair trade practices by competitor states, just-in-time production, private and public prioritization of low-cost labor and private sector focus on short-term returns rather than long-term investment. It also recommended improving supply chain resiliency via collaborating across entire industries, beyond individual companies' actions (White House, 2021a).

The American Rescue Plan Act was enacted in March 2021 (U.S. Department of Transportation, 2021). This program focused specifically on issues caused by COVID-19 to provide additional relief for the economy, public health, state and local governments, individuals, as well as businesses. From March through the end of 2021, the Biden administration implemented a series of major investments into public infrastructure works on a scale not seen since the New Deal of the 1930s. This investment is wide-ranging, covering sectors such as transportation, water, power, housing and other buildings. It also encompassed job creation via federal hiring to engage in these public infrastructure improvements. The American Jobs Plan was first proposed, and then the priorities from this plan were signed into law as the Bipartisan Infrastructure Law and Build Back Better Act.

The March 2021 American Jobs Plan began with major investments in public infrastructure, emphasizing resilience against climate change. This plan invests 1% of the US's GDP over eight years, totaling $2 trillion over the course of the 2020s. $621 billion was invested into transportation infrastructure. The plan included the improvement of roadways, with the modernization of 20,000 miles of highways, roads, and main streets, as well as repairing the ten most significant bridges in the United States and the worst 10,000 smaller bridges. In addition, the plan impacted public transit via the replacement of buses and rail cars, repair of stations, renewal of airports, as well as expansion of transit and rail into new communities. In terms of utilities, all lead pipes and service lines would be eliminated from drinking water systems, electric transmission lines would be installed, orphan oil and gas wells, and abandoned mines would be capped, and high-speed broadband would be extended to populations including rural communities. Buildings such as housing, commercial buildings, schools, childcare facilities, federal facilities-especially veteran-serving facilities-would be constructed, rehabilitated, and retrofitted (White House, 2021b).

In November 2021, the Bipartisan Infrastructure Law, also known as the Investment Infrastructure and Jobs Act, was enacted, incorporating most of the American Jobs Plan's infrastructure goals. This deal increased the amount of federal investment in public works. $55 billion was invested in expanding water infrastructure and the elimination of lead service pipes. $65 billion was invested into broadband internet infrastructure deployment. For roads and bridges, surface transportation programs were reauthorized for five years, and $110 billion was additionally invested into road and bridge repair. $89.9 billion would be invested into public transit over the next five years, including $39 billion into modernizing transit. For airports and ports, repair and maintenance backlogs would be addressed, congestion and emissions would be reduced, and electrification and low-carbon technologies would be expanded. $17 billion was invested in port infrastructure and waterways and $25 billion was invested into airports. For passenger rail, $66 billion was invested to clear Amtrak's maintenance backlog, modernize the Northeast Corridor and expand rail beyond the Northeast and mid-Atlantic. $7.5 billion was invested into a national electric vehicle charger network, including the deployment of chargers along highway corridors and within communities. Over $65 billion was invested into power infrastructure, including building new transmission lines and setting up new programs to support the development, demonstration, and deployment of clean energy technologies (Chu et al., 2024; White House, 2021c).

Outside of improving public infrastructure, over $50 billion was invested in infrastructure protection against droughts, heat, floods, wildfire weatherization, as well as cyber-attacks. Finally, $21 billion was invested in cleaning up legacy pollution including Superfund and brownfield sites, reclamation of abandoned mine land, and capping of orphaned oil and gas wells. The White House hailed the successes of the Bipartisan Infrastructure Law, and the policy is generally viewed positively by the public as a rejuvenation of aging infrastructure.

Implementation since 2021 has been smooth, though constrained by cost: For instance, more than 23 million low-income households have gained access to free or discounted high-speed internet through the Affordable Connectivity Program, but benefits ended in April 2024 due to a lack of additional Congress funding (U.S. Congress, 2025). Awards have been split evenly between states without significant political bias, even for competitive grants. Demand for skilled labor is projected to increase, thereby increasing workers' bargaining power. At the same time, there is also a far higher federal funds-driven demand for these infrastructure jobs than workers willing to fill them, in sectors such as welding and construction. For instance, prison inmates are being trained for broadband installation and maintenance jobs at community colleges in Ohio, with companies that historically have rejected ex-convicts eager to hire them once they finish their sentences.

These industries already have long-term skilled labor shortages, caused mostly by older workers retiring without new workers entering the trades. The sudden inflow of federal infrastructure funding is only exacerbating the worker shortage, leading to increased costs for projects due to the higher wages that workers are demanding. Alongside increases in material costs after the COVID-19 pandemic, the cost of implementing projects is increasing and can potentially limit the total number of projects able to be funded by the Bipartisan Infrastructure Law. Yet, the Biden administration has been responding to the worker shortage by collaborating with local governments and companies on training and apprenticeship programs, focusing on training historically excluded groups such as ex-convicts to potentially take advantage of the situation as a "feature, not a bug" (Parilla et al., 2024).

The Build Back Better Act of November 2021 incorporated other aspects of the American Jobs Plan. In terms of industrial policy, it provided additional funding for job placement, career services, safe drinking water projects, energy efficiency projects, electric vehicles, zero-emission heavy-duty vehicles, public health infrastructure, and supply chain resiliency, cybersecurity, small business assistance and development, as well as transit services and clean energy projects in low-income communities. As a collective, these policies form the bulk of the Biden administration's industrial policy as it relates to public infrastructure (White House, 2021d).

In terms of implementation, Biden's public infrastructure industrial policies have been shown to benefit economically distressed communities (Parilla et al., 2024). The private sector has invested $82 billion in counties with high unemployment and relatively low median income since 2021, within industries targeted by the abovementioned bills. This constitutes twice these counties' share of national GDP and twice their share of all private investment received from 2010 to 2020, which represents a change of policies that have traditionally funneled investment and employment into a few metropolitan areas. Structurally, this redistribution is a direct result of the bills' provisions, which include bonus funding to companies investing in low-income communities.

After setting a strong policy base of supporting US domestic industries and public infrastructure investment, the Biden administration concentrated on specific industries over the course of 2022. A January 2022 executive order (No. 14067) aimed to balance US competitiveness and leadership in financial innovation with mitigation of misuse and risk. The executive order specifically acted with respect to digital assets. With the understanding that digital finance was increasing in popularity, Biden wanted to outline a commitment to providing safety for these assets to both consumers and businesses, but also to protect the national security of the United States by preventing financial crimes. Furthermore, the government has been ill-equipped to respond to new online banking and investing apps that introduce more complex systems and middlemen that can pose security risks.

The August 2022 CHIPS and Science Act specifically focused on the semiconductor manufacturing sector, with financial incentives and assistance to encourage domestic production as well as significant scientific and technological R&D investment across multiple federal agencies. Semiconductors have been an integral part of development and innovation since their invention, but US semiconductor manufacturing capacity has dropped from nearly 40% of global supply in 1990 to 12% today. Notably, the United States heavily relies on East Asia in semiconductor manufacturing, as the region controls 75% of global production. The United States had fallen behind in production of them to countries like Taiwan and South Korea. For the United States, this meant an increasing reliance on global supply chains and countries, such as China, that the United States has contentious relations with (President's Council of Advisors on Science and Technology, 2022).

Thus, the CHIPS and Science Act provided subsidies for building chip manufacturing plants as well as tax subsidies and funding for innovation in chip manufacturing. As a result, this bill intensifies the US–Chinese decoupling process. The Act prohibits funding recipients from expanding semiconductor manufacturing in China and countries defined by US law as posing a national security threat to the United States. These restrictions would apply to any new facility unless the facility produces legacy semiconductors predominately for that country's market.

The bill also aims to boost the nation's science and technology research and address China's anti-competitive trade practices. Since Biden's first year in office, the Biden-Harris Administration has implemented an industrial strategy to revitalize US manufacturing, create more domestic jobs, and strengthen American supply chains. The Act aligns with this strategy.

The bill has been met with both positive and negative reactions. Many were hopeful that the billions of dollars put into building chip plants would eventually be able to reclaim semiconductor supremacy; however, two years later, the proposed semiconductor fabrication plant in Arizona still has not been finalized despite all the monetary allocations. Furthermore, implementing restrictions on doing business with China is a contentious move. It may garner support from American industry and more protectionist politicians, but at the same time, China is still a massive business partner with the United States, and prohibiting company expansion in China could dissuade firms from taking the money in the United States.

The Chairman of the China Semiconductor Industry Association opposed the Act firmly, claiming that the US legislation contains elements that violate fair market principles and that it is intended to give China's rivals a helping hand. "It contains essentially discriminatory clauses in market competition and creates an unfair playing field, which goes against the World Semiconductor Council principles," the Chinese association is quoted as saying (Time, 2022). Furthermore, other Chinese agencies say that this bill will disrupt normal business for chip manufacturing companies worldwide.

The IRA was passed in the same month and focused on climate change mitigation. The IRA invests $369 billion in an unprecedented move for US policy on climate change and clean energy. The IRA continues the Biden administration's pattern of large-scale industrial policy and public investment, in which the government enables private industry to drive development. The Act builds on some climate-related actions within the Bipartisan Infrastructure Law, such as electricity grid modernization, infrastructure for electric vehicles, passenger rail and public transit, improving resilience to extreme weather, and cleaning up legacy pollution.

Several of the IRA's energy provisions also synergize with Made in America Laws by offering bonus credits to projects that meet domestic content requirements for steel, iron, or other manufactured projects. Tax credits were extended for carbon sequestration, as well as wind, biomass, geothermal, solar, landfill gas, trash, qualified hydropower, marine, and hydrokinetic energy. Notably, a new tax credit was also created for zero-emission nuclear electric power. Clean fuels, namely biodiesel, renewable diesel, sustainable aviation fuel, and clean hydrogen, were given tax credits (White House, 2022).

Other tax incentives were also extended to the expansion of clean energy and efficiency, including personal and commercial electric vehicles, charging and refueling property, and the production of clean electricity. Other issues such as drought response and preparedness, offshore wind, as well as greenhouse gas and other air pollution emissions reduction also received funding. For instance, in terms of grants and loans, $27 billion was provided to the Environmental Protection Agency for awarding competitive grants for clean energy and climate projects that reduce greenhouse gas emissions. The Department of Energy Loan Programs Office was also provided with $40 billion in loan authority, supported by $3.6 billion in credit subsidy, for loan guarantees for innovative clean energy projects, including renewable energy systems, carbon capture, nuclear energy, as well as critical minerals processing, manufacturing, and recycling (White House, 2022).

The IRA represented a political compromise short of the original Build Back Better plan's tax and industrial policy package as proposed by Biden's administration. Democrats and Republicans split along party lines, with Republicans united in opposition to the bill in a 50–50 Senate. The bill therefore required the support of every Democratic Senator, which gave conservative Democratic Senator Joe Manchin of West Virginia "de facto veto power" over the legislation. Manchin has ties to the fossil fuel industry, particularly coal, which is an important economic sector in West Virginia. In order to secure his vote, many aspects of the original Build Back Better proposal were scaled back, including its industrial policy aspects. Throughout the Biden administration, Manchin's stance has shifted dramatically and repeatedly, causing delays in passing legislation (Kapur and Sarlin, 2022).

The IRA finally passed as a result of a surprise deal between Manchin and Senator Chuck Schumer, the Democrat majority leader, which represented a compromise between the Build Back Better plan and Manchin's own claim two weeks prior to the deal's announcement that he would not support climate or tax proposals in the short term. Where Build Back Better had initially promised more than $3.5 trillion of spending, the IRA took into account Manchin's strong concerns regarding inflation and federal spending, reducing spending to $369 billion. Yet, controversy over potential legislative loopholes and the details of implementation still remained through 2023 and 2024, even as Manchin himself congratulated Biden for record-breaking oil, natural gas and renewable energy production due to the IRA and Bipartisan Infrastructure Law (Snell, 2022).

Beyond the political process of passing the policy, public reception of the IRA has generally been positive, with the international community as well as US climate activists considering it a key piece of climate legislation that will shape the global economy in the next few decades.

In terms of implementation, the IRA's decisive public investment in clean energy has encouraged the private sector to increase its own investment, with many businesses taking advantage of the law's uncapped tax incentives. For instance, $28 billion in new manufacturing investment was announced immediately after the Act was passed, concentrated on the manufacturing of electric vehicles and their batteries, as well as solar panels. Yet, local contexts such as city governments' capacity to handle the application process for programs, as well as the lack of public knowledge about programs available to households, have impeded implementation (Einstein et al., 2023). The survey also found that local permitting processes have created a fragmented environment and building regulatory structure that clean energy companies struggle to navigate. In sum, the private sector has responded healthily to the IRA, but individual households still lack awareness and require communication on a local level to fully take advantage of the Act's programs.

A September 2022 executive order (No. 14081) focused on biotechnology and biomanufacturing, seeking to grow the emerging industry toward innovative solutions in health, climate change, energy, food security, agriculture, supply chain resilience, and national and economic security. It aimed specifically to develop genetic engineering technologies and techniques, scale up production and commercialization, reduce biological risks including promotion of biosafety and biosecurity as well as safeguarding the US bioeconomy against foreign adversaries and competitors. Policy actions domestically include coordination of federal investment in key R&D areas, fostering a biological data ecosystem, improving and expanding domestic biomanufacturing production capacity and processes, increasing piloting and prototyping efforts, boosting sustainable biomass production and creating climate-smart incentives for agricultural producers and forest landowners, expanding market opportunities for bioenergy and biobased products and services, as well as training and support for the relevant workforce (Gallo and Kuiken, 2022; President's Council of Advisors on Science and Technology, 2022).

In terms of institutional support for the growing industry, the policy clarifies and streamlines regulations, promotes standards, establishes metrics, and develops systems for assessment and policymaking. To mitigate biological risk, it prioritizes biological risk management by providing for research and investment in applied biosafety and biosecurity innovation, as well as proactively assessing threats, risks, and potential vulnerabilities, including digital intrusion, manipulation, and exfiltration by foreign adversaries. Outside the United States, the policy will engage with the international community to enhance biotechnology R&D.

Finally, a July 2023 executive order (No. 14104) further ensured federal investment into domestic industries' R&D would benefit domestic industries, by mandating that new technologies and products developed with US governmental support must be manufactured in the United States.

10.4 The Rise of Kamala Harris

Biden was set to run a re-election campaign in 2024, continuing many of the "Bidenonmics" policies described above. However, a disastrous presidential debate against President Trump heightened concerns among Democratic elites and voters that Biden was not prepared for another four years as president due to his age. After reassurances that he would continue to run, Biden eventually stepped aside in July 2024 and endorsed Kamala Harris to pursue the Democratic presidential nomination (Bade, 2024). While her policy positions were relatively underdeveloped and unknown on industrial policy given the brevity of her campaign, we've provided a broad sketch of our expectations if Harris had been elected in terms of industrial policy. Kamala Harris served as Biden's vice president and thus played an instrumental role in both the passage of the CHIPS Act and the IRA. Her administration was expected to continue many of the "Bidenomics" policies in place, while also forming her own economic policy agenda through a focus on improving conditions for the middle class and promoting responsible business.

Harris' trade and industrial policy would have largely maintained continuity with the Biden administration. The measures that Biden has taken regarding these issue areas are still widely popular, and "the pressures of public opinion and Congress will largely be the same" if Kamala is elected in November (Beattie, 2024). Harris would likely have continued the focus on investing strategically in the manufacturing sector, infrastructure, and green energy (Politi and Smith, 2024). Kamala's policies also would have remained more precisely focused and sector specific, relative to Trump's universal and broad-based tariff policy ideas (Beattie, 2024).

In addition, Harris campaigned on improving domestic production and manufacturing jobs in key battleground states like Michigan, Pennsylvania, and Wisconsin. The Biden administration's focus on this issue has resulted in the creation of twenty new auto and battery plants in the United States, creating over 250,000 jobs—a sharp divergence from the loss of 90,000 manufacturing jobs during the Trump administration. During the "Economic Opportunity Tour," Harris herself announced $100 million in support for small auto manufacturers and suppliers (Bade, 2024; Politi and Smith, 2024). The major investments in auto manufacturing have focused on building capacity for electrical vehicle manufacturing. The Biden-Harris administration earmarked up to $15.5 billion in grant and loan funding for retooling and converting auto factories transitioning to EVs, prioritizing facilities at risk of closing or recently closed (White House, 2024). Their investments have also recognized the advanced training of workers is important for these investments in the industry to be effective and shore up domestic capacity.

The Biden-Harris administration has invested $24 million in advanced manufacturing workforce training (Fact Sheet, 2024). Harris was expected to continue these investments in improving manufacturing industries in battleground states and investing in the green energy transition. The previous work and continued campaign promises in this space generated support for Harris, with an endorsement from the United Auto Workers. Not only did these groups support Harris' economic policies, but they also worried about the potential effects of Trump's trade policies (Rogers and Williams, 2024). Despite these positive developments, Harris faced implementation challenges of IRA and CHIPS Act investment incentives. 40% of these projects are delayed due to increased costs and waning confidence in the market (Chu et al., 2024). Therefore, the conditions on the ground might not match the lofty goals of the industrial policy programs.

One area of divergence from the Biden administration was Harris' approach to the cryptocurrency industry. Given Trump's growing support in Silicon Valley circles—in part because of his openness to cryptocurrency—Kamala's advisors approached leading crypto companies, including Coinbase, Circle, and Ripple Labs, to improve relations. In general, Harris acted as a pro-business candidate for the Democratic Party in the 2020 primary, and this move can be seen as a continuation of that role that developed during her time in the Senate. Harris' campaign sought to change the perception that Democrats are anti-business, promoting the message of being "pro-business, responsible business" (Politi and Smith, 2024).

Furthermore, Harris' campaign has shifted from Biden's economic policy by focusing on using economic tools to benefit the middle class. Harris discussed increasing tax credits for small businesses and re-upping the Child Tax Credit (Luhby and Lobosco, 2024). In addition, she touted her role in the Biden administration in capping insulin costs and capping rental increases. Affordable housing was also a priority that would have carried over into her administration, continuing the rental increase caps and increasing the supply of affordable housing for US voters.

10.5 Final Remarks

Biden entered office facing many of the same international challenges as existed during the Trump administration. US–China tensions and the supply chain vulnerabilities exposed by the pandemic motivated much of his industrial policy. At the same time, Biden was focused on reviving investment and attention to green technology and policy after the Trump administration. There was pressure on Biden from the international community to revive these programs in the aftermath of Trump's secession from the Paris Agreement and deregulation of the fossil fuel industry. Domestically, the United States was in the process of recovering from the COVID-19 pandemic and required support from the federal government to promote new jobs and combat unemployment. Furthermore, there was bipartisan support—in response to the impacts of COVID-19—to improve infrastructure and domestic manufacturing in order to combat the vulnerability of supply chains.

The Biden administration focused its industrial policy on (1) promoting public infrastructure and (2) developing domestic supply chains and manufacturing. The Biden administration initially addressed the COVID-19 emergency and its subsequent downstream effects on the economy and unemployment through investments in public infrastructure. These policies were enacted through job training programs and federal infrastructure funding. This funding focused on improving the electrical grid, clean water, transportation, and access to broadband internet. The upgrades to public infrastructure were beneficial to companies that were considering expansion into previously disadvantaged communities, as well as the people who lived in locations with limited infrastructure and investment.

Next, the CHIPS Act and IRA focused on building out domestic supply chains and manufacturing capability. These programs were enacted through extensive tax incentives and subsidies for new investment—both in high technology industries and green industries. These programs targeted subsidies toward Rust Belt states—like Michigan, Indiana, Ohio, and Pennsylvania—that are also battleground states in national elections. In addition, subsidies have flowed to Sun Belt states specifically for green energy and semiconductor manufacturing.

Biden's industrial policy was well received by labor unions in the United States, environmental groups and companies, high technology industries, and local governments that received subsidies. First, the creation of new, high-quality manufacturing jobs by the Biden administration was supported by the recipients of said jobs, largely union laborers in the construction, energy, and automotive industries. In addition, the subsidies and tax incentives offered through the IRA and CHIPS Act were targeted at companies in the green energy and high-tech sectors; recipients of these incentives were highly supportive of the program, as it aided their ability to expand their business. Finally, the local governments that received either infrastructure or investment through Biden's industrial programs also largely supported the initiative as the program built up the local community, created new jobs, and expanded the infrastructure base.

At the same time, Biden's industrial policy, particularly the CHIPS Act, received international pushback. For example, China's semiconductor industry association, criticized the extensive subsidies that were being provided to companies that relocated or built additional manufacturing facilities in the United States. While their reaction was less strong, US allies also raised concerns about the massive subsidy packages being offered in the United States that made it more difficult for the EU, South Korea, or other trading partners to attract high-tech investment and build out their domestic capacity. Furthermore, these policies were increasingly contested by the Republican party especially as Biden ran for re-election. In particular, Republican lawmakers raised concerns about the costs of the IRA and CHIPS Act, the transfer of funds to foreign firms to build US manufacturing plants, and the effect on the national debt.

11
Trump's Return

11.1 Introduction

Since his inauguration in January 2025, President Trump has embarked on an aggressive expansion of US industrial and trade policy-melding traditional Republican deregulation with a more muscular form of economic nationalism. Building on his "America First" rhetoric from the 2024 campaign, the administration has simultaneously: (a) rolled back environmental and clean-energy programs; (b) doubled down on domestic manufacturing incentives; (c) unleashed a new wave of tariffs, export controls, and investment restrictions aimed squarely at strategic rivals, especially China; and (d) launched a campaign against government size and costs associated with its intervention.

This chapter first sketches the key themes of his 2024 platform, then details how, in the first six months of his new mandate, those campaign promises have translated into sweeping executive actions reshaping supply chains, technology controls, and global trade relationships.

11.2 Trump's Second Campaign in 2024

During the 2024 election, Trump distilled his America-First agenda into a three-pronged industrial blueprint: reverse Biden's clean-energy push, supercharge domestic manufacturing, and weaponize tariffs against strategic rivals.

Candidate Trump vowed to "cap or terminate" the Inflation Reduction Act's clean-energy tax credits—especially those for electric vehicles and renewables—arguing they unfairly subsidized political opponents' strongholds (Subran et al., 2024, p. 22). Some observers predicted he would cap rather than fully repeal IRA credits, focusing dismantling efforts on clean-energy and EV incentives (Subran et al., 2024, p. 22).

Simultaneously, he unveiled a Strategic National Manufacturing Initiative pledging $55 billion per year in new subsidies for raw materials, chemicals, steel, autos, and critical minerals—explicitly financed by higher customs duties—and backed by stringent "domestic content" requirements (Subran et al., 2024, p. 3, 22). He railed against foreign CHIPS Act recipients—singling out TSMC's

Governing Growth. Marco R. Di Tommaso and Vinod K. Aggarwal, Oxford University Press.
© Oxford University Press (2026). DOI: 10.1093/oso/9780197821787.003.0011

Arizona plant—and promised to redirect every dollar toward US-owned firms (Subran et al., 2024, p. 22). To hedge against future reversals, some manufacturers shifted planned investments into reliably Republican states—"just in case, you probably want to be in a red state so that someone from the same party is going to fight for you and your rights" (Chu et al., 2024).

Trump also courted emerging-tech constituencies. With JD Vance as his running mate, he pledged to "end the 'persecution' of the crypto industry" and replace SEC Chair Gary Gensler with Paul Atkins, whose approach is deemed more crypto-friendly (Asgari, 2024; Rogers, 2024). Silicon Valley responded: CEOs of major tech firms were invited to the inauguration, and Apple alone committed $500 billion and 20,000 jobs to expand US chip and server manufacturing (Allen and Berkowitz, 2025).

On trade, he proposed a universal tariff of 10–20% on all imports—and up to 60% on Chinese goods—to be imposed "day one," targeting transport machinery, metals, and chemicals. He amplified doubts about Taiwan's role in US semiconductor leadership, suggesting Taipei should pay for its defense (Simpson, 2024) and lamenting that Taiwan had "hollowed out" America's chip industry (Culpan, 2024). He also signaled that added tariff revenue would help offset large corporate and individual income-tax cuts (Tax Foundation, 2024).

Finally, the Trump campaign was characterized by another big project that was able to polarize and collect a great consensus. His anti-government positions and promises to drastically reduce the cost of government, represented as a self-seeking, inefficient, and mismanaged bureaucracy. Here, the continuity with the past and the President Reagan and Bush narratives is evident. The traditional government failure argument has been all used since the very beginning of the campaign, and the launch of the new Department of Government Efficiency—the soon-to-be very popular DOGE—resulted in a very effective and remunerative rhetorical investment. During the campaign, it was presented not just as an administrative reform plan, but as one of the central symbols of Trump's intent to challenge established bureaucratic power. The DOGE project was supported by a simple rhetoric, blending cost-cutting, anti-regulation, and general anti-elite messaging:

> In 2022, fraud and improper payments alone cost Americans an estimated hundreds of billions of dollars, but with our action plan, we will fully eliminate fraud and improper payments within six months ... This will save trillions of dollars. It's massive. For the same service you have right now" (Trump, 2024).

The President, on Inauguration Day, delivered on many of these pledges. On January 20, Trump froze $300 billion in IRA grants and loans—though tax credits remained intact—signed orders dismantling Biden-era environmental subsidies, declared a national energy emergency, and expedited oil and gas expansion. January 20 also marked the beginning of a new phase that was destined to revolutionize the national and equilibria the international order: a season of tariff announcements, actions, counter-announcements, and counter-measures. It was also the launch day for the DOGE plan, led by one of Trump's most influential campaign supporters, Elon Musk.

Having sketched these campaign commitments and inauguration moves, we now turn to Section 11.3 to the specific executive orders, investigations, and tariff actions that between February and May 2025 have reshaped US industrial and trade policy.

11.3 Policy Implementation and Escalation (February–May 2025)

After retaking office in January 2025, President Trump swiftly began to implement his America First agenda through a flurry of executive actions, trade directives, and regulatory reversals. These moves centered on his effort to restore domestic manufacturing, reshoring critical industries, and intensifying economic confrontation with strategic rivals, especially China.

The following months witnessed a sweeping transformation in US economic, industrial, and trade policy, marked by announcements and actions for "the domestication" of the global value chain, the support of select industries, the control of exports, the restriction of some typologies of imports and foreign investments, reshoring, and the aggressive use of tariffs. All these intentions and actions have been justified in the name of "the American national interest," which, according to President Trump's view, demands to be promoted and defended from abroad. He found no need to refer to the traditional economic literature and modeling, market failures, comparative or competitive advantage principles, or to other similar theoretical arguments and empirical evidence. Economic policy in general, industrial policy and trade policy in particular, were designed, announced, and implemented in reference to the national interest in a "Make American Great Again" and "American first" perspective:

> From this day forward, our country will flourish and be respected again all over the world. We will be the envy of every nation, and we will not allow ourselves to be taken advantage of any longer. During every single day of the Trump administration, I will, very simply, put America first. … Our sovereignty will be reclaimed. Our safety will be restored (Trump, 2025c).

Selective policies and protectionist actions targeting specific sectors are justified in order to defend the US's national interest and the American people. In terms of industrial policy goals, the Hamiltonian "preference for manufacturing" is one of the main assumptions of President Trump's strategy for growth, prosperity, and security. Therefore, rebuilding an autonomous domestic manufacturing is declared a national priority. Traditional industries like oil, steel, automobile, and shipping are declared different from others, deserving immediate government support and protection:

> America will be a manufacturing nation once again, and we have something that no other manufacturing nation will ever have—the largest amount of oil and gas of any country on earth—and we are going to use it. We'll use it. We will bring prices down, fill our strategic reserves up again right to the top, and export American energy all over the world. We will be a rich nation again, and it is that liquid gold under our feet that will help to do it. With my actions today, we will end the Green New Deal, and we will revoke the electric vehicle mandate, saving our auto industry and keeping my sacred pledge to our great American autoworkers. In other words, you'll be able to buy the car of your choice. We will build automobiles in America again at a rate that nobody could have dreamt possible just a few years ago. And thank you to the autoworkers of our nation for your inspiring vote of confidence. We did tremendously with their vote. I will immediately begin the overhaul of our trade system to protect American workers and families. Instead of taxing our citizens to enrich other countries, we will tariff and tax foreign countries to enrich our citizens (Trump, 2025c).

In terms of industrial policy tools, President Trump has continued to prioritize tariffs. His policy approach, at this point, should be defined as McKinleyian—at least according to his own reinterpretation of McKinley's economic policy practices and goals. President Trump's model presents tariffs as one of his central policy instruments, capable of achieving broader industrial and economic objectives. In this respect, tariffs are promoted as tools for re-shaping the global value chain and thus relaunching the national industry. However, Neo-Mckinleyians have more ambitious goals: revolutionizing the international economic and political order, consolidating the relationships with the dominant Big-Business, funding tax cuts, and thus feeding domestic political consensus.

Thus, given the aims of this plan, it should not surprise that during the inauguration day speech, President Trump clearly paid homage to President McKinley who "... made our country very rich through tariffs. . ." And a few hours later, he signed an executive order renaming America's tallest peak in honor of him and his tariffs-based industrial policy approach:

Renaming of Mount McKinley. (a) President William McKinley, the 25th President of the United States, heroically led our Nation to victory in the Spanish-American War. Under his leadership, the United States enjoyed rapid economic growth and prosperity, including an expansion of territorial gains for the Nation. President McKinley championed tariffs to protect U.S. manufacturing, boost domestic production, and drive U.S. industrialization and global reach to new heights" (Trump, 2025d).

11.3.1 Supply Chain Security and Strategic Materials

In his second term, President Trump has prioritized the reconfiguration of US supply chains as a matter of both economic policy and national security. Early moves by the administration emphasized insulating American production from geopolitical risks and foreign dependencies—especially those involving China. On February 6, 2025, USTR nominee Jamieson Greer testified before the Senate Finance Committee, emphasizing the administration's commitment to strengthening domestic production and supply chain resilience. He proclaimed that "America should be a country of producers" and advocated for restructuring the international trading system to better align with US economic and national security interests (U.S. Senate Committee on Finance, 2025).

A major component of this effort has been reducing reliance on foreign sources of critical minerals. In April 2025, Trump signed an executive order directing the Commerce Department to initiate a Section 232 investigation into whether US imports of key minerals—including rare earth elements, lithium, cobalt, and other high-tech inputs—pose a threat to national security (White House, 2025a). The investigation aims to assess whether dependency on overseas suppliers, many of them located in or tied to China, leaves the United States vulnerable to supply disruptions. Notably, the order states that if Commerce finds that imports threaten national security and the President imposes tariffs under Section 232, those new tariffs will supersede the general 10% reciprocal tariff for the covered materials. In other words, a special higher duty might be applied to critical mineral imports to encourage local sourcing.

This focus on industrial inputs has extended into broader reviews of the defense industrial base. The administration ordered sweeping evaluations of whether additional imports—beyond those already targeted by steel, aluminum, and auto tariffs—should be subject to Section 232 remedies (White House, 2025b, Section 4). In fact, President Trump has already directed investigations into imports of copper, timber, and lumber products to determine if foreign dominance in those markets harms US economic stability and security (White House, 2025a). These inquiries, like the critical minerals effort, could lead to trade restrictions designed to nurture domestic supply chains in construction materials, electronics, and other defense-related sectors.

The administration has also reinforced existing trade barriers aimed at revitalizing domestic production. Trump's renewed commitment to the 25% tariff on autos is intended to pressure automakers to shift production back to the United States (Executive Office of the President, 2025a). Similarly, the steel and aluminum tariffs were reinforced in 2025 to close loopholes that allowed global overcapacity—much of it driven by foreign government subsidies—to weaken US metals supply chains (White House, 2025c). Together, these measures reflect a broader push to harden US supply chains and assert control over the production of critical goods in an increasingly adversarial global environment.

11.3.2 Technology Controls and Investment Restrictions

Parallel to supply chain security efforts, the Trump administration dramatically escalated controls on technology transfers and foreign investment. The America First Trade Policy memorandum ordered rigorous reviews of US export control regimes, directing the State and Commerce Departments to assess whether existing controls adequately protected America's "technological edge" and limited strategic technology transfers to foreign rivals (White House, 2025b, Section 4c). The scope encompassed semiconductors, artificial intelligence, aerospace technology, and emerging categories such as "connected" products—including "connected" vehicles—that could pose security risks. The memo urges the Secretary of Commerce to consider broader security measures on information and communication technology (White House, 2025b, Section 4d). By tightening export controls, the United States aims to secure its supply chain of critical technologies, ensuring cutting-edge chips and components remain available to US industry and military, and not diverted to empower rivals.

China has been the primary target of these technological restrictions. In February 2025, Trump signed a national security memorandum directing the Committee on Foreign Investment in the United States (CFIUS) to tighten scrutiny on Chinese investment in strategic sectors, surpassing the level of oversight implemented by the previous administration. The "America First Investment Policy" explicitly stated that China was "exploiting United States capital to develop and modernize its military, intelligence, and other security apparatuses," establishing a new standard allowing "only those investments that serve American interests" (White House, 2025d). In practice, this means CFIUS will aggressively block or unwind Chinese acquisitions in sectors like technology, critical minerals, energy, and infrastructure (White House, 2025d, Section 2f).

Trump's order also raised the prospect of new restrictions on outbound US investment into China, signaling that American companies may soon be barred from investing in sensitive Chinese tech fields such as semiconductors, AI, quantum computing, biotechnology, and aerospace. (White House, 2025d, Section 2j). Consistent with Trump's campaign pledges, officials indicated that the administration may prohibit Chinese firms from owning US real estate or infrastructure in critical sectors like energy and telecom (White House, 2025d, Section 2k). This was reinforced by public messaging: the State Department's China policy page was pointedly updated to decry China's "restrictive" market and unfair trade practices.

11.3.3 Reshoring and Domestic Production Revival

A central objective of Trump's second-term industrial strategy is the revival of domestic manufacturing through reshoring—bringing back production of critical goods to the United States. Consistent with his first-term rhetoric and campaign promises, Trump has explicitly linked this effort to national security, arguing that the United States must "reduce dependence on other countries" for vital goods (White House, 2025b) and ensure the capacity to make essential products domestically, especially in times of crisis or conflict (White House, 2025e).

To achieve these goals, the administration has pursued a suite of policies aimed at expanding federal procurement preferences, reducing regulatory barriers, and incentivizing domestic investment. Simultaneously, the administration has reduced regulatory barriers that impede domestic manufacturing facility expansion. A notable action is Trump's Executive Order on domestic pharmaceutical production, signed in May 2025. According to a White House fact sheet, this order is designed to "facilitate the restoration of a robust domestic manufacturing base for prescription drugs," including the active ingredients and raw materials needed for medicines (White House, 2025e). Simultaneously, the FDA is instructed to increase inspections and fees for foreign drug producers to ensure they meet US standards, implicitly raising the cost of offshoring production.

Trump's approach also includes sector-specific initiatives to catalyze investment in priority industries. In March 2025, the administration launched the Investment Accelerator, a revamped program under the CHIPS Program Office tasked with renegotiating existing subsidy agreements to deliver what officials described as a "better deal for the American taxpayer" (White House, 2025f). This includes stricter requirements for job creation, domestic sourcing, and long-term capital commitments in semiconductor and advanced manufacturing projects.

The administration has also expanded its industrial ambitions to emerging technologies. In late January, Trump signed an executive order aimed at "sustaining and enhancing America's global AI dominance," mandating a full review of Biden-era artificial intelligence directives and empowering the White House Office of Science and Technology Policy to produce an action plan for advancing US leadership in AI (Executive Office of the President, 2025b).

Moreover, Trump has signaled support for significant tax relief to further incentivize reshoring (Leddy and Shaw, 2025). Proposals under consideration include lowering the corporate tax rate for domestic manufacturers and offering targeted credits for investments in strategic sectors. The combined effect is a two-pronged policy strategy: removing structural barriers that pushed firms offshore, while creating powerful new incentives to bring production back home.

11.3.4 Tariffs

After Trump's inauguration for his second term, his administration quickly announced sweeping industrial and trade policy changes, emphasizing the need to reduce dependence on other countries, benefit domestic workers and industries, stop illicit drugs from entering the country, and remedy trade deficits, with the overarching goal of strengthening national security (White House, 2025b).

Trump's administration repealed the *de minimis* import exceptions—which previously exempted imports under $800 from taxes—and instituted an *ad valorem* tax on these low-cost shipments instead (U.S. Customs and Border Protection and Department of the Treasury, 2025). This act, along with an additional 10% tariff on all imports from the PRC (White House, 2025g), were among the first actions taken in Trump's second administration, establishing the PRC as the primary target for tariffs.

The main action was then promoted in what President Trump called "Liberation Day," the moment of public announcement of the long list of reciprocal tariffs to be applied to foreign countries (see Figure 11.1):

For decades, our country has been looted, pillaged, and plundered by nations near and far, both friend and foe alike. American steelworkers, auto workers, farmers, and skilled craftsmen – we have a lot of them here with us today – they really suffered gravely. They watched in anguish as foreign leaders have stolen our jobs, foreign cheaters have ransacked our factories, and foreign scavengers have torn apart our once beautiful American dream. Our country and its taxpayers have been ripped off for more than fifty years, but it is not going to happen anymore. It's not going to happen. In a few moments, I will sign a historic executive order instituting reciprocal tariffs on countries throughout the world. Reciprocal. That means they do it to us and we do it to them (Trump, 2025a).

The policy rationales of this policy action are clearly listed below. In President Trump's words, presented in the "Regulating Imports with a Reciprocal Tariff to Rectify Trade Practices that Contribute to Large and Persistent Annual United States Goods Trade Deficits" (see Figure 11.1):

Large and persistent annual U.S. goods trade deficits have led to the hollowing out of our manufacturing base; inhibited our ability to scale advanced domestic manufacturing capacity; undermined critical supply chains; and rendered our defense-industrial base dependent on foreign adversaries. Large and persistent annual U.S. goods trade deficits are caused in substantial part by a lack of reciprocity in our bilateral trade relationships. This situation is evidenced by disparate tariff rates and non-tariff barriers that make it harder for U.S. manufacturers to sell their products in foreign markets. It is also evidenced by the economic policies of key U.S. trading partners insofar as they suppress domestic wages and consumption, and thereby demand for U.S. exports, while artificially increasing the competitiveness of their goods in global markets. These conditions have given rise to the national emergency that this order is intended to abate and resolve (Trump, 2025b).

In the same White House's official document, President Trump supported his "Liberation Day," recalling the last century's history of trade agreements with the rest of the world:

For decades starting in 1934, U.S. trade policy has been organized around the principle of reciprocity. Congress directed the President to secure reduced reciprocal tariff rates from key trading partners first through bilateral trade agreements and later under the auspices of the global trading system. Between 1934 and 1945, the executive branch negotiated and signed 32 bilateral reciprocal trade agreements designed to lower tariff rates on a reciprocal basis. After 1947 through 1994, participating countries engaged in eight rounds of negotiation, which resulted in the General Agreements on Tariffs and Trade (GATT) and seven subsequent tariff reduction rounds. However, despite a commitment to the principle of reciprocity, the trading relationship between the United States and its trading partners has become highly unbalanced, particularly in recent years. The post-war international economic system was based upon three incorrect assumptions: first, that if the United States led the world in liberalizing tariff and non-tariff barriers the rest of the world would follow; second, that such liberalization would ultimately result in more economic convergence and increased domestic consumption among U.S. trading partners converging towards the share in the United States; and third, that as a result, the United States would not accrue large and persistent goods trade deficits.

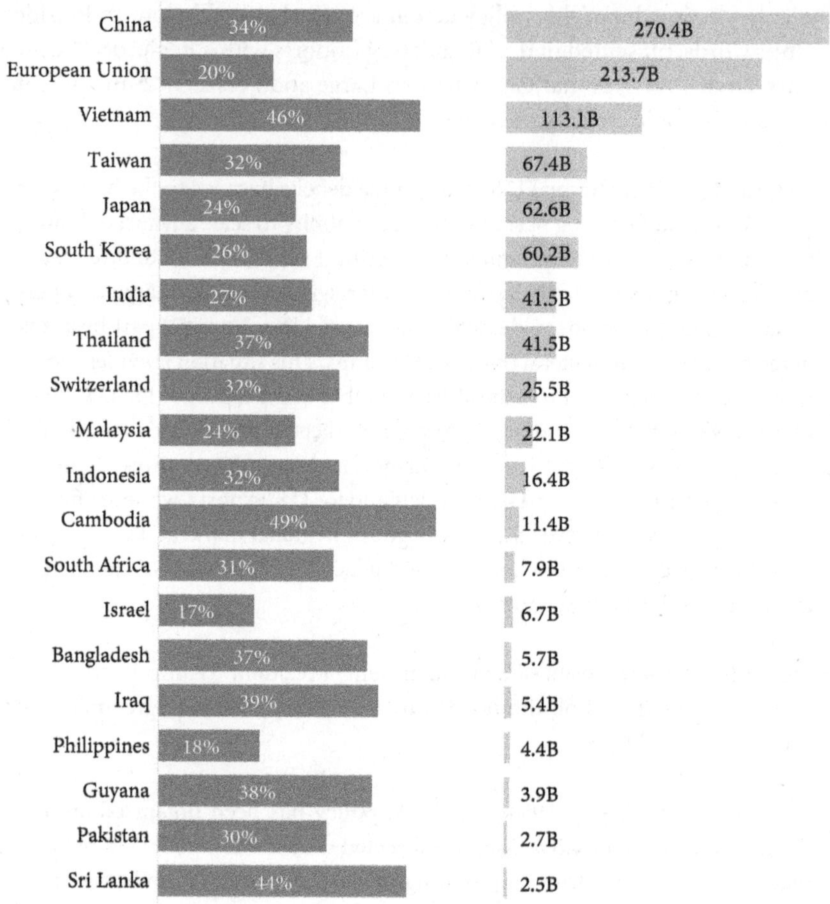

Figure 11.1 US Reciprocal Tariff and Trade Deficit

Source: CSIS Economics Program and Scholl Chair in International Business • White House, Annex I: Tariff Rates, April 2025; US Bureau of Economic Analysis, Trade Deficit Report, February 2025, aggregated at US Trade Deficit by Country. Countries with 2024 deficits under $1 billion are excluded from this table. The reciprocal tariff is adjusted; the US trade deficit in 2024 does not include December. https://www.csis.org/analysis/liberation-day-tariffs-explained

When Trump's global "reciprocal tariff" order took effect in early April, China retaliated swiftly, announcing steep counter-tariffs on US exports (White House, 2025h). The United States responded by piling on further tariffs targeting China on April 8 and 9, on top of the existing duties. Beyond reducing trade deficits, Trump also wielded tariffs in an effort to coerce changes in China's behavior (White House, 2025i). For instance, he invoked national emergency powers to punish China over the fentanyl opioid crisis in February 2025, in which an executive order targeted China's "synthetic opioid supply chain," resulting in an additional 20% tariff on Chinese imports as leverage to compel Beijing to curb illicit fentanyl exports (White House, 2025a). By mid-April, with tit-for-tat measures spiraling, Chinese goods were facing extraordinary tariff rates—in some cases effectively up to 125% under the reciprocal trade deficit tariff, plus 20% for the fentanyl sanctions, plus the pre-existing Section 301 tariffs (ranging from 7.5% to 25% on various products) (White House, 2025a). These compounded penalties drove total duties on certain Chinese imports into the triple digits.

Amid this escalation, diplomatic negotiations resumed in late April, culminating in a breakthrough US–China trade agreement announced on May 12, 2025. The White House hailed the deal as a "historic trade win" for the United States (White House, 2025i). Under the accord, both sides agreed to ease tensions and scale back their latest round of tariff increases and ease tensions. China consented to remove the retaliatory tariffs it had imposed since early April and suspend other punitive measures (White House, 2025i). Crucially, Trump did *not* remove the pre-existing tariffs—all Section 301 tariffs on Chinese goods, the national security (Section 232) tariffs, and the fentanyl-related tariffs remained in force.

US allies and neighbors have not been spared from Trump's hardball trade tactics, although his approach mixes pressure with select deal-making. Trump shocked Canada and Mexico by tying trade to immigration and drug policy: he threatened a 25% blanket tariff on all Mexican and Canadian exports unless those countries halted the flow of fentanyl and illegal migrants across the US border (White House, 2025i).

Trump's relations with the European Union have been similarly confrontational as he seeks to reduce trade deficits with Europe. He has repeatedly criticized Europe's trade policies—calling the European Union "nastier than China" on trade—and accused the bloc of outright scheming against the United States (Gijs et al., 2025). In early 2025, Trump targeted Europe, implementing a 10% across-the-board tariff for EU producers, as well as the reinstated 25% steel and aluminum tariffs and the new 25% auto import tariff (Laudani and Rabiega, 2025). As of early May, the European Union's $1.6 trillion trade relationship with the United States remains strained by these tariffs, with European officials bracing for potential further escalation (Gijs and Gavin, 2025).

Not all allies have fared poorly—Trump has shown selective flexibility for those willing to strike new arrangements. In May, he reached a limited trade pact with the United Kingdom, whose prime minister, Keir Starmer, had courted Washington for an agreement (Gijs et al., 2025). The US–UK deal modestly expands agricultural market access and lifts some US tariffs on British auto and steel exports, though it leaves in place the 10% baseline tariff on UK goods (Gijs et al., 2025). This marked the first tariff rollback Trump granted to any ally since his April tariff barrage. The symbolic accord with Britain—and the parallel tariff truce with China—illustrate Trump's transactional approach: countries that negotiate "in good faith" or meet US demands may earn tariff reductions, whereas those who resist face sustained pressure (Gijs et al., 2025).

11.4 Final Remarks

Trump's second term marks not a rupture but a striking continuation of the long-standing role the US federal government has played in steering industrial development. As this volume has argued, the supposed American aversion to intervention masks a deep and recurring pattern: across historical periods and partisan lines, US administrations have leveraged the tools of industrial policy to manage crises, restructure domestic industry, and assert national interests in global markets.

What distinguishes Trump's 2025 industrial policy agenda is not its novelty, but its coercive and overtly strategic form. Combining tariffs, investment restrictions, import and export controls, and reshoring incentives, Trump's second term retools industrial policy to directly confront geopolitical rivals, particularly China and to reshape the terms of global economic interdependence. These interventions reflect a convergence of goals long explored in this book: national security, strategic autonomy, technological sovereignty, preference for manufacturing, and the revival of domestic production. From critical minerals to semiconductors or pharmaceuticals to AI, the administration has tied industrial development to state power, using economic tools as instruments of diplomacy, deterrence, and domestic revival.

Trump's return to power does not simply represent the resurgence of protectionism or the retrenchment of globalization. It represents a new phase in the evolving relationship between the American state and its industrial base—one marked by a renewed willingness to wield industrial policy as a central tool of economic and geopolitical governance.

12

Governing Growth in the United States

Ten Points

This book tells the story of an American government that has consistently played an integral role in the country's industrial growth, structural changes, and development processes. We show that contrary to much of the conventional wisdom and rhetoric on the United States, successive administrations from Hamilton to Trump have engaged not only in the pursuit of classical macroeconomic interventions, but also in pursuing both horizontal and vertical industrial policies. Such policies have taken place even during administrations that were theoretically committed to the free-market models and principles.

To understand the evolution of American government policy in this field, we examined different periods in history with a common theoretical template. To this end, each chapter follows a similar logic. We begin by identifying the international, domestic, and ideational concerns that drove policy in each administration. Then we turn to what different administrations hoped to achieve in terms of goals, targets, tools, and implementation. To understand the political economy of these choices, we focus on the coalitional dynamics underlying the choices that administrations have made and then conclude by evaluating how industrial policies have worked or failed. Although our focus is on the United States, we believe that this political economy analysis can be extended beyond America to understand the pursuit of industrial policy around the world.

We summarize the results of our analysis in ten points.

12.1. What Has the Government Done?

The American government has acted with surprising long-term continuity on a plurality of fronts. Initially, the United States sought economic independence by forcefully and lucidly encouraging the birth of a national manufacturing industry. Over time, the government has consistently promoted the growth and development of its industries, particularly with defense industries. During critical historical moments, the government intervened to contain the excesses of capitalism, aiming to ensure the social sustainability of the processes of industrial

Governing Growth. Marco R. Di Tommaso and Vinod K. Aggarwal, Oxford University Press.
© Oxford University Press (2026). DOI: 10.1093/oso/9780197821787.003.0012

development and structural change. In particular, during challenging periods for the economy and society it acted by saving businesses, sectors, and regions to counteract shocks, crises, and recessions. In many cases, the government has fought unemployment, as well as social and territorial imbalances. It has developed special relationships with sectors of industry to guarantee a defense system that would allow the achievement, and then maintenance, of global military leadership.

Successive administrations have opposed, but also tolerated and encouraged, large concentrations of economic and industrial power. They have always supported the national industry by engaging in actions that ensured a progressive expansion of markets. In many sectors and for long periods, the United States has aggressively protected its industries from foreign competition. Moreover, across different eras, presidents supported American companies' efforts to penetrate foreign markets, both through trade and investment, with the negotiation of bilateral and multilateral international agreements. Different administrations have often promoted selective policies by choosing and supporting strategic industries and sought to drive the national innovation system through regulations and investment in public research, science, and technologies.

12.2 Permanent Growth and the Expanding Frontier

American administrations have always been dedicated to promoting the growth of national industry by consistently implementing industrial policies, even if they rarely called them that. The primary objective of the American government was to promote "a state of permanent growth" tied to the vision of "an ever-expanding frontier." This enabled the industry to access new markets, enhance efficiency, and foster innovation. Over extended periods, it also contributed to the mitigation of social tensions by generating employment, expanding workers' consumption capacity, and producing profits for businesses.

To manage this process, the government has responded to the demands of national industry—businesses, unions, and regions—through a variety of tools: protection, subsidies, investments, bailouts, public procurement, and support for entry into international markets. In return, the national industry has guaranteed continued political support for successive administrations. For decades, thanks to permanent accelerated growth, the majority of the population has been able to increase their expectations and consumption possibilities, generally improve their living conditions, and hope to join the middle class.

This was the case of the post-WWII era of prosperity, as well as in recent decades of globalization, which have once again brought the US years of accelerated growth. Focusing on the latter, the collapse of the Soviet bloc and the rise of Asia presented unique opportunities for American business and certain segments of its society. In other words, it marked another extraordinary expansion of the economic frontier. The entry into new large markets (i.e., China, Russia, Poland, etc.) and the establishment of a North-South division of labor that made possible the delocalization abroad (i.e., in Mexico, China, Vietnam, etc.) of low-value-added manufacturing. It was a model of accelerated globalization, with bipartisan support by administrations that reshaped the domestic economy—its specialization and its geography. All presidents from Clinton to the Bushes and Obama—de facto worked to support a project of deindustrialization and servitization of the American economy and society. They pursued domestic agendas through macroeconomic reforms and industrial policies, while proving highly effective in the international arena by promoting the global acceptance of free-market principles, approaches, and practices—such as privatization, liberalization, the free movement of goods, services, and capital, and the signing of bilateral and multilateral agreements. These efforts were strongly supported by US-led international institutions, including the IMF, World Bank, and WTO, as well as by influential American universities and economic schools, such as the University of Chicago.

More recently, however, the economic and social sustainability of this model has been challenged. New borders and frontiers are expected to be drawn, therefore Granting permanent growth to Americans thanks to US leadership in globalized "quasi-free markets" is not working anymore. First of all, the external conditions have radically changed because of the rise of economic and political power of China and many other emerging nations. Second, we have entered a new era of instability and shocks that makes the American strategic control of the global value chain not possible in the same way as in the past. Then, internally, new economic and social tensions made the previous model of domestic specialization and international globalization weak as well as socially and politically no longer sustainable.

The previous model of globalization has produced many winners in America, but also many losers. Growing disparities between territories, social classes, genders, ethnic groups, and generations are outcomes of the previous model and make the American economic and social equilibria not sustainable. Without a new robust welfare system, active regional strategies for the declining areas, and effective labor market policies, those whose activities and jobs have been displaced by foreign supply chains have led to politics of resentment.

Some of the first signals of weakness were not intercepted by Obama, and later, they continued to remain unaddressed by the Biden administration. By contrast, Trump, since his first campaign, found in the new domestic and international conditions elements ability to feed his rhetoric and policy proposals. He has been able to transform the Republican party through appealing to this disjuncture by building a coalition with business leaders and workers, the latter being the traditional focus of the Democratic party. A key part of his industrial and political strategy has been to appeal to both businesses and workers by calling for the "domestication of the global supply chain."

To make America great again, the promises of growth demand a redefinition of the new frontiers for American Business. First, the huge domestic demand should be protected from hostile foreign competitors and left, when possible, to the American Big Business. Second, all foreign markets that are in the new evolving geopolitical order—thanks to aggressive trade policy practices and announcements, bilateral economic and political negotiations, risk of war, and real military conflicts—will remain part of the new emerging American bloc. Last but not least, the very far frontiers that the new technologies are opening: American Big Business is ready for Mars and President Trump's support is ready to be offered.

12.3 Theory and Practices

From our reading of the American experience, we see that the actions of governments very often diverge from established economic theory. Most of the interventions mentioned in our re-reading of the American history of policy intervention—strategic actions, selective policies, protection of infant industries, consolidation of national champions, and rescues of companies and sectors—cannot be justified by mainstream economic theory that accepts industrial policy intervention only to correct market failures—and this further reduces its domain because of government failure arguments. There is a gap between economic theory and the majority of the policy practices we discussed in this book. A distance that in our times is even more impressive, given all the efforts that both the Biden and Trump administrations have made in promoting and governing growth through horizontal and vertical industrial policies.

This divergence from theory opens up margins of discretion to policymakers that can be hazardous. Consider rescue policies or selective policies: What justifies the rescue and selection actions of the strategic sectors? In an ideal world, these are actions that depend on the vision of enlightened and benevolent politicians who are truly interested in promoting the general interest. In nonideal worlds, these are choices that can degenerate into inefficiency, cronyism, and widespread corruption. Moreover, bailouts link the interests of a suffering industry to governments hungry for short-term consensus, creating a bond that is not conducive to structural change of the economy and society. Even selective policies that invest in strategic sectors for the future of a country, in the absence of innovative corrective measures, risk responding to the demand of existing and already organized interests and neglect the entry of innovators who might drive new businesses, technologies, and sectors.

Yet at the same time, the poverty of neoliberal economic theory is evident here: without any attention to business and worker structural adjustment policies that would allow for a smoother transition for these actors in the global economy, it is hardly surprising that we have seen a backlash against globalization. The neglect of theories that analyze how to efficiently pursue industrial policy in the name of open markets has ironically led to the very outcome that neoliberal economists have sought to avoid: the rise of protectionism, with Trump pursuing tariffs as the only tool of industrial policy and rejecting measures to help increase American competitiveness. A tariff-only policy—and the many swinging announcements in this field—produces domestic and global uncertainty that is expected to have very negative effects on growth, inflation, and employment. These policies are currently on the path to exacerbate social unsustainability and might continue to lead to economic stagnation, growing disparities, and political discontent.

12.4 Rhetoric and Reality

Another characteristic that emerges from our long-term analysis is the persistent gap between political rhetoric and the actual actions taken by governments. Political rhetoric often creates a division between those who claim to always favor the free market and oppose government intervention, and those who advocate for public intervention at every turn. This simplistic representation is frequently proposed as a solution to otherwise complex problems, effectively polarizing the electorate and generating consensus.

The Reagan years tell a lot about this strategy. Yet the situation did not change in the following decades, as seen in the Clinton-Trump 2016 and even in the last Biden-Trump presidential campaigns. The result, quite simply, is that governments do often intervene to bolster their industries but tend not to openly acknowledge it. Politicians champion the free market in the media, but do not hesitate to save banks and businesses on the verge of bankruptcy, or to be inactive with domestic big business, monopolies, oligopolies, and cartels.

This disconnect between the rhetoric of political discourse and actual intervention is a problem for our societies, hindering the reporting and evaluation of government action. Among these disconnects are claims by the current administration to help workers—but only a limited number. With the disruption of many industries such as autos and apparel, which have developed both global and regional supply chains as a result of NAFTA and USMCA, workers on the whole stand to lose despite the rhetoric of American job creation. Most striking is a lack of attention towards technological advancements in robotics and AI that will lead to significant job losses but increase profits for businesses.

12.5 Success and Failures

The experience of the United States showcases how the government has intervened to pursue a variety of industrial, economic, and social goals. However, simply acknowledging this continued and active presence may not be enough. Many argue that the mere presence of government intervention is not the main issue. The important questions are: Were American successes possible thanks to government intervention, or despite it? And even if we were willing to agree that the government's intervention had a positive impact on growth and development, what were the costs and benefits of its actions?

However, this is an old line of reasoning, which does not take us far. Long-term counterfactuals are not possible to calculate and are ultimately unhelpful, as they would remain exercises with no practical applications. Similarly, when conducting a long-term analysis that asks ambitious questions about the role of government in the processes of development and change of the economy and society, the calculation of net benefits is out of place. Throughout history, there has been continued action by American governments which has produced both costs and benefits. In summary, it is impossible and probably useless to determine what would have happened in the absence of the government and to establish the net costs or benefits of its action in the long run.

12.6 Technological Innovator

Throughout history, American administrations have demonstrated their ability to solve complex technological problems and to promote crucial paths of innovation. Notably, they have proven that they know how to drive national scientific and technological progress. Half a century ago, the government sent a man to the Moon and may soon send men and women to live on Mars. For over a century, American governments have guided and managed the most advanced national defense apparatus, consistently equipping the Navy, Air Force, and Army with cutting-edge military machines. In this context, the government literally invented the internet, the revolutionary global platform shaping our present and our future.

At the core of this organizational and innovative capacity lies the special relationship with the national military-industrial complex. Governments have allocated enormous quantities of public resources in this inherently protected sector, crucial for supporting large-scale innovations that demand patience, clarity, and the madness that investments in great innovations need. From some perspectives, this alliance can be considered successful since for over a century, American governments have guaranteed global military supremacy and international technological leadership. However, other issues bring this balance into question.

This gives rise to a number of questions: What were the opportunity costs of innovation driven by the military-industrial complex? Is it possible to demonstrate that—even from the point of view of the "innovating State," interested primarily in innovation but distracted by other issues—there were no alternative paths? Moreover, it is crucial to consider the implications of the public procurement system, which is a very delicate mechanism that often prioritizes secure income over profit, based on risk, competitiveness, and investment. We are faced with a potentially closed system protected from foreign competition and characterized by the presence of a few players who are usually large and too accustomed to dealing with governments. This has often created a dynamic in which the government-industry relationship can easily degenerate, favoring vote-buying, clientelism, and corruption. Finally, we cannot ignore the possibility that the military-industrial complex thrives on "threats" and "permanent wars." From this perspective, the history of the twentieth and twenty-first centuries holds many lessons, and our present demands careful and profound reflection.

12.7 Social Innovator

American administrations have demonstrated a remarkable ability to address complex issues that go beyond the dynamics of technological and economic innovation. By participating in two and a half centuries of continuous structural change in industry, the economy, and society governments have managed to ensure the stability of the system and, therefore, the sustainability of a process of permanent transformation. From this perspective, American governments have proven to be extraordinary social innovators, guiding and facilitating the transformation of their society by defending the continuity of the economic and political system. In this sense, the government had a central role because it encouraged the adoption of the "new" by fostering change and inhibiting regressive conservation. Little has changed in the core objectives of governments so that everything can change in society.

The succession of administrations rooted in antagonistic political traditions has, in fact, maintained consistent lines of intervention, facilitating the uninterrupted transformation of economic and social structures. Of course, we are witnesses to a change that has occurred within certain limits, and which has left many on the sidelines. However, it has also driven a process of social change and innovation that has managed to involve hundreds of millions of people over more than two centuries. This book helps explain why administrations as theoretically antagonistic as those of Reagan and Obama, or Biden and Trump, exhibit many common features during periods of accelerated transformations and socioeconomic crisis. The demand for continuity inherent in the capitalist system has historically acted as a stabilizing force.

12.8 Good Government

The American experience also sheds light on the responsibilities that governments have assumed in both ordinary management and exceptional situations. Questioning the need for government intervention is a false problem. In America, as elsewhere, capitalism involves markets, businesses, commerce, and government. The question that deserves reflection is not whether the government must intervene but how it can intervene effectively.

There is much to be explored in this regard. It is not enough to simply advocate for intervention, after decades in which we have stubbornly gone in the opposite direction, we must start investing in the construction of "good governance" again. Building an effective, efficient, benevolent, and ambitious government stands as a central challenge of contemporary capitalism. Good governance does not "grow on trees": it is the result of a conscious and collective investment that requires time, consensus, skills, and resources. Markets fail, governments fail, and the societies we live in don't seem like the best of all possible worlds. Our goal is to seek remedies for these failures. Ultimately, what we all want are better markets and better governments. And why do we want them? Because we would like to live in better societies.

12.9 The Politics of Industrial Policy

The analysis of the American case compels us to reflect on the objectives of government intervention. It is clear that industrial policy—like economic policy in general—is not just a technical tool to achieve given objectives. Rather, it is a political intervention that can contribute significantly to (re)designing the societies of our future, beginning with discussions on the ultimate goals of government action. We are faced with an instrument that can determine the balance among the various interests that animate a society such as territories, sectors, classes, generations, and the like. These balances, which in dynamic contexts characterized by growth and structural change of the economy and society, are constantly called into question. Governments may choose to listen to the most powerful and organized interests, thereby securing the consensus needed to maintain the status quo. Or governments can opt to anticipate and promote societal demands for change by referring to new and emerging interests. From this perspective, industrial policy is a powerful tool wielded by the government that contributes to defining, from a dynamic perspective, the collective interests and future of a country.

12.10 Learning from the Past, Looking to the Future: Continuity and Change

In this book, we have emphasized the continuity of policy attitude over nearly two and a half centuries. In the United States, governments have consistently promoted policies targeting specific industries, with the goal of steering economic growth and the resulting structural transformation of both the economy and society. Such an approach has contributed to enhancing efficiency, fostering innovation, and generating broad-based prosperity, thereby reinforcing democratic institutions by extending material benefits across wide segments of the population.

However, we also believe that we may be at a turning point with the second mandate of President Trump because of international and domestic factors. Whereas some themes continue with the talk of American expansion, the current global context is radically different than nineteenth-century expansionism, the post-WWII era, or the more recent globalization golden age. The new evolving international economic, political, and military order, as well as the coexistence of a plurality of economic and political powers, demands a redefinition of the US position in the global context. A crucial question is how the United States can maintain its long-lasting leadership in technology and thus in the production of goods and services. In this new setting, the reshaping of the global value chains is demanded in different US business strategies and industrial policies. Managing the ongoing decoupling with China (and with other players, including the European Union) is limited by a plurality of interdependencies and suggests a trajectory of transformation of the international economic order that goes in the direction of a globalization by blocks. And no doubt that the adaptation to this transformative path demands very effective and visionary industrial policies.

Having said this, the domestic scenario is also challenging the previous model of growth and development policy. In many periods of American history, industrial policy interventions were designed and implemented to ensure social sustainability. Today, this last aspect seems to remain at the margin of industrial policy's concrete actions. Megatrends of digitalization and robotization, the most recent development in the AI industry, the process of servitization and delocalization abroad that have characterized the last decades of globalization, and the aggressive competition of the new industrial powers have tended to create a jobless society where disparities and inequalities are the norm and not the exception. This is a field that today should demand a rethinking of the role of industrial policy that, as it happened in American history, might also be a tool for granting social sustainability and fostering democracy.

Finally, a few final words on tariffs, the most visible and debated industrial policy tools promoted by the President Trump administration. As we have noted, they are very controversial instruments to deal with the rapid technological, economic, and political transformations we are currently facing at the domestic and international level. Ignoring the full range of measures, targets, and goals that—as we have shown in this book—have historically guided governments in bolstering the American economy, society, and security should be considered a dangerous path toward economic decline and social disorder.

References

Abend, G., 2014. *The Moral Background: An Inquiry into the History of Business Ethics*. Princeton, NJ: Princeton University Press.

Acharya, V.V., Richardson, M., van Nieuwerburgh, S. and White, L.J., 2011. *Guaranteed to Fail: Fannie Mae, Freddie Mac, and the Debacle of Mortgage Finance*. Princeton, NJ: Princeton University Press.

Adams, M.C.C., 1994. *The Best War Ever: America and World War II*. Baltimore, MD: Johns Hopkins University Press.

Adams, W. and Brock, J.W., 1986. *The Bigness Complex: Industry, Labor, and Government in the American Economy*. New York: Pantheon.

Aggarwal, V. and Aggarwal, S.N., 2023. "Rethinking the Political Economy of Industrial Policy," *L'Industria*, 4, pp. 583–626.

Aggarwal, V.K. and Evenett, S.J., 2010. "Financial Crisis, 'New' Industrial Policy, and the Bite of Multilateral Trade Rules," *Asian Economic Policy Review*, 5(2), pp. 221–244.

Aggarwal, V.K. and Evenett, S.J., 2012. "Industrial Policy Choice During the Crisis Era," *Oxford Review of Economic Policy*, 28(2), pp. 261–283.

Aggarwal, V.K. and Evenett, S.J., 2013. "A Fragmenting Global Economy: A Weakened WTO, Mega FTAs, and Murky Protectionism," *Swiss Political Science Review*, 19(4), pp. 550–557.

Aggarwal, V.K. and Reddie, A., 2021. "Economic Statecraft in the 21st Century: Implications for the Future of the Global Trade Regime," *World Trade Review*, 20(2), pp. 137–151.

Aggarwal, V.K. and Reddie, A.W., 2020. "New Economic Statecraft: Industrial Policy in an Era of Strategic Competition," *Issues & Studies*, 56(4), pp. 2040004.

Aggarwal, V.K., 1985. *Liberal Protectionism: The International Politics of Organized Textile Trade* (Studies in International Political Economy). Berkeley: University of California Press.

Aggarwal, V.K., 1987. *International Debt Threat: Bargaining Among Creditors and Debtors in the 1980s*. Berkeley, CA: Institute of International Studies, University of California.

Aggarwal, V.K., 1996. *Debt Games: Strategic Interaction in International Debt Rescheduling*. New York: Cambridge University Press.

Aggarwal, V.K., 1998. *Institutional Designs for a Complex World: Bargaining, Linkages, and Nesting*. Ithaca, NY: Cornell University Press.

Aggarwal, V.K., 1992. "The Political Economy of Service Sector Negotiations in the Uruguay Round," *The Fletcher Forum of World Affairs*, 16(1), pp. 35–54.

Aggarwal, V.K., 1993. "Building International Institutions in Asia-Pacific," *Asian Survey*, 33(11), pp. 1029–1042.

Aggarwal, V.K., 1994. "Comparing Regional Cooperation Efforts in the Asia-Pacific and North America," in A. Mack and J. Ravenhill, eds., *Pacific Cooperation: Building Economic and Security Regimes in the Asia Pacific Region*, New York: Routledge, pp. 40–65.

Aggarwal, V.K., 2000. "Withering APEC? The Search for an Institutional Role," in J. Dosch and M. Mols, eds., *International Relations in The Asia-Pacific: New Patterns of Power, Interest and Cooperation*, New York: St. Martin's Press, pp. 67–86.

Aggarwal, V.K., 2001. *Winning in Asia, European Style: Market and Nonmarket Strategies for Success*. New York: Palgrave Macmillan.

Aggarwal, V.K., 2009a. "Reluctance to Lead: U.S. Trade Policy in Flux," *Business and Politics*, 11(3), pp. 1–21. doi:10.2202/1469-3569.1257.

Aggarwal, V.K., 2009b. "The Dynamics of Trade Liberalization," in H. Milner and A. Moravcsik, eds., *Power, Interdependence, and Nonstate Actors in World Politics*, Princeton, NJ: Princeton University Press, pp. 164–184.

Aggarwal, V.K., 2016. "Mega-FTAs and the Trade-Security Nexus: The Trans-Pacific Partnership (TPP) and Regional Comprehensive Economic Partnership (RCEP)," *Asia-Pacific Issues*, No.123. Honolulu, HI: East West Center.

Aggarwal, V.K., Keohane, R.O. and Yoffie, D.B., 1987 "The Dynamics of Negotiated Protectionism," *American Political Science Review*, 81(2), pp. 345–366.

Aggarwal, V.K. and Ravenhill, J., 2001. *Undermining the WTO: The Case Against "Open Sectoralism". Asia Pacific Issues*, No. 50. Honolulu, HI: East-West Center.

Aghion, P., Boulanger, J. and Cohen, E., 2011. "Rethinking Industrial Policy," *Bruegel Policy Brief*.

Akyüz, Y., 2014. "Crisis Mismanagement in the United States and Europe: Impact on Developing Countries and Longer-Term Consequences," *South Centre Research Paper*, No. 50.

Allen, M. and Berkowitz, B., 2025. "Trump Manufacturing Win: Apple to Spend $500 Billion in U.S., Hire 20,000," *Axios*. https://www.axios.com/2025/02/24/apple-investment-trump-tim-cook.

Amadeo, K., 2024. "U.S. Inflation Rate by Year". *The Balance*. Available at: https://www.thebalancemoney.com/u-s-inflation-rate-history-by-year-and-forecast-3306093.

Amadeo, K., 2021. "U.S. Budget Deficit by President," *The Balance*. Available at: https://www.thebalancemoney.com/deficit-by-president-what-budget-deficits-hide-3306151.

Amiti, M., Redding, S.J. and Weinstein, D.E., 2019. "The Impact of the 2018 Trade War on U.S. Prices and Welfare," *Journal of Economic Perspectives*, 33(4), pp. 187–210.

Andreoni, A. and Scazzieri, R., 2014. "Triggers of Change: Structural Trajectories and Industrial Policy in Italy," *Cambridge Journal of Economics*, 38(6), pp. 1391–1420.

Anginer, D. and Warburton, A.J., 2010. "The Chrysler Effect: The Impact of the Chrysler Bailout on Borrowing Costs," *Policy Research Working Papers* No. 5460, October. Washington, DC: World Bank (Accessed 15 December, 2024).

Appelbaum, E. and Batt, R., 2014. *Private Equity at Work: When Wall Street Manages Main Street*. New York: Russell Sage Foundation.

ARPA-E, 2023. *ARPA-E History: Origins and Mission*. U.S. Department of Energy.

Asgari, N., 2024. "A Major Ad-Vance for Crypto," *Financial Times*. Available at: https://www.ft.com/content/c17891f6-0cbb-40d4-92cc-62e148eedfeb (Accessed: November 10, 2024).

Atkinson, R.D. and Mayo, M., 2010. "*Refueling the U.S. Innovation Economy: Fresh Approaches to Science, Technology, Engineering, and Mathematics (STEM) Education,*" Information Technology and Innovation Foundation.

Attali, J., 2009. *A Brief History of the Future: A Brace and Controversial Look at the Twenty-first Century*. New York: Arcade Publishing.

Attali, J., ed., 2010. *After the Crisis: How Did It Happen?* Paris: ESKA Publishing.

Audretsch, D.B., 2003. "Standing on the Shoulders of Midgets: The U.S. Small Business Innovation Research Program (SBIR)," *Small Business Economics*, 20(2), pp. 129–135. https://doi.org/10.1023/A:1022259931084.

Ayres, L.P., 1919. *The War with Germany: A Statistical Summary*, 2nd edition. Washington: Government Printing Office.

Bade, G., 2024. "Harris' Next Challenge: How to Talk About the Economy," *POLITICO*. https://www.politico.com/newsletters/politico-nightly/2024/07/26/harriss-next-challenge-how-to-talk-about-the-economy-00171280 (Accessed: November 11, 2024).

Baker, D., 2024. "The Biden-Harris Misery Index in Historical Context," *Center for Economic and Policy Research*, September 13. https://cepr.net/the-biden-harris-misery-index-in-historical-context (Accessed: December 3, 2024).

Bailey, T. and Merritt, D., 1997. "School-To-Work For The College Bound," *Education Resources Information Center*. https://eric.ed.gov/?id=ED405476.

Baldwin, R.E. and Richardson, J.D., 1987. "Recent U.S. Trade Policy and Its Global Implications," in: C.I. Bradford Jr. and W.H. Branson, eds., *Trade and Structural Change in Pacific Asia*, Chicago, IL: University of Chicago Press, pp. 121–156. https://www.nber.org/

books-and-chapters/trade-and-structural-change-pacific-asia/recent-us-trade-policy-and-its-global-implications (Accessed: November 9, 2024).

Baquie, S., Huang, Y., Jaumotte, F., Kim, J., Machado Parente, R., Pienknagura, S., 2025. "Industrial Policies: Handle with Care," *IMF Staff Discussion Note*, SDN/2025/002., Washington, DC: International Monetary Fund.

Barbieri, E., Di Tommaso, M.R. and Zhang, M., 2015. "Industrial Development in China: Local Institutional Trajectories and Global Competition". *China Economic Review*, 34, pp. 52–65.

Barnett-Hart, A.K., 2009. T*he Story of the CDO Market Meltdown: An Empirical Analysis*. Harvard Kennedy School.

Baron, D.P., 2000. *Business and Its Environment*. London: Pearson.

Bernstein, B.J., 1967. "The Debate on Industrial Reconversion: The Protection of Oligopoly and Military Control of the Economy," *The American Journal of Economics and Sociology* 26(2), pp. 159–172. doi: 10.1111/j.1536-7150.1967.tb00998.x.

Baumol, W.J., Panzar, J.C. and Willig, R.D., 1983 "Contestable Markets: An Uprising in the Theory of Industry Structure: Reply," *The American Economic Review*, 73(3), pp. 491–496.

Beattie, A., 2024. "How Bidenomics will survive Biden's departure." *FinancialTimes*. Available at: https://www.ft.com/content/f22ff7bc-c279-4d16-949c-d18a16a7178b (Accessed: November 11, 2024).

Ben-Ishai, S. and Lubben, S.J., 2011. "A Comparative Study of Bankruptcy as Bailout." *SSRN*. https://papers.ssrn.com/sol3/papers.cfm?abstract_id=1780550.

Bernanke, B., 2005. "The Global Saving Glut and the U.S. Current Account Deficit." *Federal Reserve Bank Speech*.

Bernanke, B.S., 2015. *The Courage to Act: A Memoir of a Crisis and Its Aftermath*. W.W. Norton & Company.

Bianchi, J. and Mendoza, E.G., 2010. "Overborrowing, Financial Crises and 'Macro-prudential' Taxes". *NBER Working Paper* No. 16091, National Bureau of Economic Research.

Bianchi, P.,1988. *Antitrust e gruppi industriali*. Bologna: Il Mulino.

Bideleux, R. and Jeffries, I., 1998. *A History of Eastern Europe: Crisis and Change*. London: Routledge.

Bingham, R., 1998. *Industrial Policy American-style: From Hamilton to HDTV*. Milton Park: Routledge.

Birdsall, N. and Fukuyama, F., 2011. "The Post-Washington Consensus: Development After the Crisis," *Foreign Affairs*, 90(2), pp. 45–53.

Biven, W.C., 2002. *Jimmy Carter's Economy: Policy in an Age of Limits*. Chapel Hill: University of North Carolina Press (The Luther H. Hodges Jr. and Luther H. Hodges Sr. Series on Business, Entrepreneurship, and Public Policy). https://uncpress.org/book/9781469614557/jimmy-carters-economy/ (Accessed: November 9, 2024.

Bivens, J., 2007. *Globalization and American Wages: Today and Tomorrow*. Washington, DC: Economic Policy Institute.

Bivens, J., 2018. *The Tax Cuts and Jobs Act: Corporate Stock Buybacks Surge as Worker Gains Lag*. Washington, DC: Economic Policy Institute.

Blahous, C., 2012. *The Fiscal Consequences of the Affordable Care Act*. Mercatus Center, George Mason University. https://www.mercatus.org/publications/government-spending/fiscal-consequences-affordable-care-act.

Blanchard, O., 2012. "Monetary Policy in the Wake of the Crisis," in O. Blanchard, D. Romer, M. Spence, and J.E. Stiglitz eds., *The Wake of the Crisis: Leading Economists Reassess Economic Policy*. Cambridge, MA: MIT Press, pp. 1–21.

Blanchard, O., Dell'Ariccia, G. and Mauro, P., 2012. "Rethinking Macroeconomic Policy." *IMF Staff Discussion Note*. Washington, DC: International Monetary Fund.

Blinder, A., 2013. *After the Music Stopped: The Financial Crisis, the Response, and the Work Ahead*. Penguin Press.

Block, F., 2008. "Swimming Against the Current: The Rise of a Hidden Developmental State in the United States," *Politics & Society*, 36(2), pp. 169–206. Available at: https://doi.org/10. 1177/0032329208318731.

Block, F. and Keller, M.R., 2011. *State of Innovation: The U.S. Government's Role in Technology Development*. Paradigm Publishers.

Blumenthal, D., Abrams, M. and Nuzum, R., 2015. "The Affordable Care Act at Five Years," *New England Journal of Medicine*, 372(25), pp. 2451–2458.

Bonvillian, W.B., 2004. "Meeting the New Challenge to U.S. Economic Competitiveness." *Issues in Science and Technology*, 19(4), pp. 75–82.

Boston Consulting Group, 2018. "How Shifting Costs are Altering the Math of Global Manufacturing." *Boston Consulting Group*. https://web-assets.bcg.com/img-src/BCG-How-Shifting-Costs-Are-Altering-the-Math-of-Global-Manufacturing-Dec-2018_tcm9-208907. pdf.

Botero, G., 1588. The Cause of the Greatnesse of Cities. Three Bookes, With Certaine Observations concerning the Sea. Translated from *Delle cause della grandezza delle città* by Sir Thomas Hawkins. London: Printed by E.P. for Henry Seile, 1635, pp. 85–86.

Bourne, E.G., 1894. "Alexander Hamilton and Adam Smith." *The Quarterly Journal of Economics*, 8(3), pp. 328–344.

Bown, C.P., 2019. "The 2018 US-China Trade Conflict: A Retrospective." *Peterson Institute for International Economics.*

Breslin, S., 2013. *China and the Global Political Economy*. Basingstoke: Palgrave Macmillan.

Broadberry, S. and Harrison, M. eds., 2005. *The Economics of World War I*. Cambridge: Cambridge University Press.

Buchanan, J.M., 1983. "Rent Seeking, Noncompensated Transfers, and Laws of Succession," *The Journal of Law and Economics*, 26(1), pp. 71–85.

Buigues, P. and Sekkat, K., 2009. *Industrial Policy in Europe, Japan and the USA: Amounts, Mechanisms and Effectiveness*. Palgrave Macmillan.

Bureau of Labor Statistics, n.d. "CPI Inflation Calculator," Available at: http://data.bls.gov/cgi-bin/cpicalc.pl.

Bush, G.H.W., 1992. "Remarks at Texas A&M University in College Station, Texas, The American Presidency Project." https://www.presidency.ucsb.edu/documents/remarks-texas-am-university-college-station-texas (Accessed: November 10, 2024).

Bush, G.W., 1999. *A Charge to Keep*. New York: William Morrow.

Bush, G.W., 2000. "American Rhetoric: President Elect George W. Bush - 2000 Victory Speech," December 13. *American Rhetoric: Online Speech Bank*. https://www.americanrhetoric.com/speeches/gwbush2000victoryspeech.htm (Accessed: February 15, 2026).

Bush, G.W., 2008a. "Address to the Nation on the National Economy | The American Presidency Project." September 24. https://www.presidency.ucsb.edu/documents/address-the-nation-the-national-economy.

Bush, G.W., 2008b. "President Bush Discusses Financial Markets and World Economy," November 13. *The White House*. https://georgewbush-whitehouse.archives.gov/news/releases/2008/11/20081113-4.html (Accessed: December 15, 2024).

Canis, B. and Webel, B., 2013. "The Role of TARP Assistance in the Restructuring of General Motors, CRS Report R41978, 9 May 2013." *Congressional Research Service*. Available at: https://business.cch.com/BANKD/CRS-Report-R41978.pdf.

Canis, B. and Yacobucci, B.D., 2010. "The U.S. Motor Vehicle Industry: Confronting a New Dynamic in the Global Economy." *Congressional Research Service.*

Cárcamo-Huechante, L.E., 2006. "Milton Friedman: Knowledge, Public Culture, and Market Economy in the Chile of Pinochet," *Public Culture*, 18(2), pp. 413–435. https://doi.org/10. 1215/08992363-2006-010.

Carter, G., 1968. "State in, State Out: A Pattern of Development Policy." *Journal of Economic Issues*, 2(4), pp. 365–383.

Chang, H.J., 1994. *The Political Economy of Industrial Policy*. New York, NY: St. Martin's Press.

Chang, H.J., 2007. *Bad Samaritans: The Myth of Free Trade and the Secret History of Capitalism.* New York: Random House Business Book.

Chang, H.J., 2003. "Kicking Away the Ladder: Infant Industry Promotion in Historical Perspective," *Oxford Development Studies*, 31(1), pp. 21–32.

Chang, H.J. and Andreoni, A., 2020. "Industrial Policy in the 21st Century," *Development and Change*, 51(2), pp. 324–351.

Chantrill, C., n.d. *Defense Spending in Twentieth Century.* US Government Spending. Available at: https://www.usgovernmentspending.com/.

Cherif, R. and Hasanov, F., 2021. "Industrial Policy Against Pandemics," *Industrial and Corporate Change*, 34(5), pp. 1029–1043. https://doi.org/10.1093/icc/dtab042.

Chodorow-Reich, G., Ohrn, E., Zwick, E. and Zidar, O., 2024. "The Effects of the Tax Cuts and Jobs Act on Investment, Employment, and wages," *Quarterly Journal of Economics*, 139(1), pp. 65–131.

Chu, A., Roeder, O., Basarkar, R. and White, A. 2024. "Delays Hit 40% of Biden's Major IRA Manufacturing Projects," *Financial Times.* https://www.ft.com/content/afb729b9-9641-42b2-97ca-93974c461c4c (Accessed: November 10, 2024).

Chung, J.H. and Jackson, J.K., 2013. *SelectUSA: Foreign Investment Promotion.* Washington, DC: Congressional Research Service.

Clarke, L., 1985. "The Origins of Nuclear Power: A Case of Institutional Conflict." *Social Problems* 32(5), pp. 474–487. doi: 10.2307/800776.

Clinton, W.J., 1993. Remarks to the Seattle APEC Host Committee, The American Presidency Project. Available at: https://www.presidency.ucsb.edu/documents/remarks-the-seattle-apec-host-committee (Accessed: November 9, 2024).

Clinton, W.J., 1994. Remarks on Goals of the Summit of the Americas in Miami, The American Presidency Project. Available at: https://www.presidency.ucsb.edu/documents/remarks-goals-the-summit-the-americas-miami (Accessed: November 10, 2024).

Clinton, W.J., 2000. "Full Text of Clinton's Speech on China Trade Bill," *The New York Times* Web Archive. Available at: https://archive.nytimes.com/www.nytimes.com/library/world/asia/030900clinton-china-text.html (Accessed: November 11, 2024).

CNN, 2008. "Bush Says U.S. Working to Reduce Impact of Financial Turmoil," *CNN*, 18 September. Available at: https://georgewbush-whitehouse.archives.gov/news/releases/2008/09/20080915-2.html (Accessed: November 11, 2024).

Cochran, T.C., 1950. "North American Railroads: Land Grants and Railroad Entrepreneurship," *The Journal of Economic History*, 10(1), pp. 53–67.

Coe, K. and Reitzes, M., 2010. "Obama on the Stump: Features and Determinants of a Rhetorical Approach." *Presidential Studies Quarterly*, 40(3), pp. 391–413.

Coffee, J.C. Jr., 2011. Systemic Risk after Dodd-Frank: Contingent Capital and the Need for Regulatory Strategies beyond Oversight. New York: Columbia Law School, Center for Law and Economic Studies, Working Paper No. 423.

Collins, F.S., Green, E.D., Guttmacher, A.E. and Guyer, M.S., 2003. "A vision for the future of genomics research," *Nature*, 422(6934), pp. 835–847.

Congressional Budget Office, 2011. *Estimated impact of the Budget Control Act of 2011 on Discretionary Spending.* Washington, DC: CBO.

Congressional Budget Office, 2012. *Economic Effects of Reducing the Fiscal Restraint that is Scheduled to Occur in 2013.* Washington, DC: CBO.

Congressional Budget Office, 2013. *The Budget and Economic Outlook: Fiscal Years 2013 to 2023.* Washington, DC: CBO.

Congressional Budget Office, 2014. *Estimated Impact of the American Recovery and Reinvestment Act on Employment and Economic Output in 2014.* Washington, DC: CBO.

Congressional Budget Office, 2014. The Macroeconomic and Budgetary Effects of the American Recovery and Reinvestment Act of 2009: April 2014 Report. Available at: https://www.cbo.gov/publication/45291.

Congressional Budget Office (CBO). 2018. Long-Term Implications of the 2019 Future Years Defense Program.

Congressional Budget Office (CBO), 2024. "Final Report on the Troubled Asset Relief Program." May 31. https://www.cbo.gov/publication/60220.

Congressional Oversight Panel, 2009. *The Use of TARP Funds in the Support and Reorganization of the Domestic Automotive Industry*, September Oversight Report, 9 September. Washington, DC: Congressional Oversight Panel. Available at: https://www.govinfo.gov/content/pkg/CHRG-111shrg52863/pdf/CHRG-111shrg52863.pdf.

Congressional Oversight Panel, 2010. *The Continuing Role of TARP in the U.S. Economy*. Washington, DC. https://www.govinfo.gov/content/pkg/CPRT-111JPRT57397/pdf/CPRT-111JPRT57397.pdf.

Congressional Oversight Panel, 2011. *March Oversight Report: The Final Report of the Congressional Oversight Panel*, 16 March 2011. Available at: https://www.congress.gov/112/cprt/JPRT64832/CPRT-112JPRT64832.pdf.

Congressional Research Service (CRS), 1974. Section 301 of the Trade Act of 1974. https://www.congress.gov/crs-product/IF11346.

Congressional Research Service (CRS), 1988. H.R.4848 - 100th Congress (1987–1988): Omnibus Trade and Competitiveness Act of 1988. August 23. https://www.congress.gov/bill/100th-congress/house-bill/4848.

Congressional Research Service, 2011. *The Budget Control Act of 2011*. Washington, DC: CRS.

Congressional Research Service (CRS), 2019. *China's Retaliatory Tariffs on U.S. Goods*. Washington, DC: CRS.

Congressional Research Service, 2020. *Transportation Infrastructure Investment as Economic Stimulus: Lessons from the American Recovery and Reinvestment Act of 2009*, CRS Report R46343, 5 May 2020. Available at: https://www.congress.gov/crs-product/R46343.

Congressional Research Service (CRS), 2021. Safeguards: Section 201 of the Trade Act of 1974. [online] Available at: https://crsreports.congress.gov/product/pdf/IF/IF10786 (Accessed: November 30, 2024).

Congressional Research Service (CRS), 2021. Unemployment Rates During the Covid-19 Pandemic: In Brief. https://crsreports.congress.gov/product/pdf/R/R46554/9# (Accessed: November 11, 2024).

Consumer Technology Association, 2022. *Analysis of Section 301 Tariff Impacts on Imports of Consumer Technology Products*. Arlington, VA: Available at: https://www.wita.org/wp-content/uploads/2022/08/CTA_Section-301-Tariff-Whitepaper.pdf (Accessed: December 9, 2024).

Council of Economic Advisers, 1982. *Economic Report of the President, 1982*. Washington, DC: U.S. Government Printing Office.

Council of Economic Advisers, 1984. *Economic Report of the President, 1984*. Washington, DC: U.S. Government Printing Office.

Council of Economic Advisers, 2010. *Economic Impact of the American Recovery and Reinvestment Act of 2009: Second Quarterly Report*. Washington, DC: Executive Office of the President. Available at: https://obamawhitehouse.archives.gov/the-press-office/economic-impact-american-recovery-and-reinvestment-act-2009-second-quarterly-report.

Crandall, R.W., 2005. *Competition and Chaos: U.S. Telecommunications since the 1996 Telecom Act*. Washington, DC: Brookings Institution Press.

Cramer, K.J., 2016. *The Politics of Resentment: Rural Consciousness in Wisconsin and the Rise of Scott Walker*. University of Chicago Press.

Crockett, D.A., 2002. *The Opposition Presidency: Leadership and the Constraints of History*. College Station: Texas A&M University Press.

Culpan, T., 2024. "Trump Is Wrong About Taiwan's Chip Industry," *Bloomberg*.com. https://www.bloomberg.com/opinion/articles/2024-07-18/trump-is-wrong-about-taiwan-s-chip-industry (Accessed: November 10, 2024).

Cummings, B., 1984. "The Origins and Development of the Northeast Asian Political Economy: Industrial Sectors, Product Cycles, and Political Consequences," *International Organization*, 38(1), pp. 1–40.

Davenport, C. and Rubin, A.J., 2017. "Trump Signs Executive Order Unwinding Obama Climate Policies," *New York Times*, 28 March. https://www.nytimes.com/2017/03/28/climate/trump-executive-order-climate-change.html.

Davis, W., 2014. "Eisenhower's Atomic Power for Peace III: CAP and Power Demonstration Reactors." *American Nuclear Society*, March 20. https://www.ans.org/news/article-1537/eisenhowers-atomic-power-for-peace-iii-cap-and-power-demonstration-reactors/.

De Laffemas, B., 1597. "Reiglement général pour dresser les manufactures en ce royaume." Monstroeil. Paris. France. (in English: The General regulation for the establishment of manufactures).

Department of Energy, 2022. Keystone XL Extension Permit Revocation: Energy Costs and Job Impacts. https://www.daines.senate.gov/wp-content/uploads/2023/01/12.23.22-KXL-Pipeline-Job-Loss-and-Impacts-on-Consumer-Energy-Costs-001245.pdf (Accessed: December 8, 2024).

Department of Labor, 2013. ETA News Release: Obama Administration Awards $20.5 Million for Make it in America Challenge Grants to Spur Business Investment and Job Creation. https://www.dol.gov/newsroom/releases/eta/eta20131022.

Destler, I.M., 1995. *American Trade Politics*. 3rd edn. Washington, DC: Institute for International Economics.

Deyo, F., 1987. *The Political Economy of the New Asian Industrialism*. Ithaca: Cornell University Press.

Di Tommaso, M.R., Prodi, E., Di Matteo, D. and Barbieri, E. 2025. "Structural Change and its Discontents," *Structural Change and Economic Dynamics*, 72, pp. 438–455.

Di Tommaso, M.R., Rubini, L. and Barbieri, E. 2013. *Industrial Development in Developing and Emerging Countries: The Role of Governments, Market and Institutions*. Edward Elgar Publishing.

Di Tommaso, M.R., Tassinari, M., Bonnini, S. and Marozzi, M. 2017. "Industrial Policy and Manufacturing Targeting in the US: New Methodological Tools for Strategic Policymaking," *International Review of Applied Economics*, 5(31), pp. 1–23.

Di Tommaso, M.R. and Giovannelli, S. 2006 Nazioni Unite e sviluppo industriale. Per un intervento di politica industriale nell"interesse della comunità delle nazioni. Milan: Franco Angeli.

Di Tommaso, M.R. and Schweitzer, S.O., 2005. *Health Policy and High-Tech Industrial Development*. Edward Elgar Publishing.

Di Tommaso, M.R. and Schweitzer, S.O., 2010. "Production and Transfer of Academic Knowledge: Policy Targets and Implications for the Health Industry." *International Journal of Healthcare Technology and Management*, 11(4), p. 227. doi:https://doi.org/10.1504/IJHTM.2010.036009.

Di Tommaso, M.R. and Schweitzer, S.O., 2013. *Industrial Policy in America: Breaking the Taboo*. Cheltenham, UK and Northampton, MA, USA: Edward Elgar.

Di Tommaso, M.R., 2020. "Una strategia di resilienza intelligente per il dopo coronavirus. Sulla centralità della domanda e offerta di politica industrial," *L'industria*, 41(1), pp. 3–20.

Di Tommaso, M.R. and Tassinari, M., 2014. "Government and Industry in the United States, Past Practices and the Debate on the Present Policies," *L'industria*. 3, pp. 369–408.

Di Tommaso, M.R. and Tassinari, M., 2017. *Industria governo e mercato. Lezioni americane*. Bologna: Il Mulino.

Di Tommaso, M.R., Pollio, C., Rubini, L. and Barbieri, E. 2024. *Industry Organization and Industrial Policy: Production and Innovation, Development and Public Interest*. Bologna: Il Mulino. ISBN: 978-88-15-3883-84.

Di Tommaso, M.R., Prodi, E., Matteo, D. and Mariotti, I., 2022. "Local Public Spending, Electoral Consensus, and Sustainable Structural Change," *Structural Change and Economic Dynamics*, 63(10), pp. 435–453.

Di Tommaso, M.R., Rubini, L. and Barbieri, E. 2013a. *Southern China: Industry, Development and Industrial Policy.* Abington: Routledge. Available at: https://www.routledge.com/Southern-China-Industry-Development-and-Industrial-Policy/DiTommaso-Rubini-Barbieri/p/book/9781138115767 (Accessed: November 11, 2024).

Di Tommaso, M.R., Rubini, L. and Barbieri, E., 2013b. *Industrial Development in Developing and Emerging Countries: The Role of Governments, Market and Institutions.* Edward Elgar Publishing.

Di Tommaso, M.R., Tassinari, M. and Ferrannini, A. 2019. "Industry and Government In the Long-Run: The True Story of the American Model," in P. Bianchi, C. Ruiz Duran, and S. Labory, eds., *Transforming Industrial Policy for the Digital Age: Production, Territories, and Structural Change.* Cheltenham: Edward Elgar, pp. 83–111.

Dicken, P., 2011. *Global Shift: Mapping the Changing Contours of the World Economy.* Sage.

Dilger, R.J., 2014. "SBA Small Business Investment Company Program." *Congressional Research Service.* CRS Report No. R41456. https://www.congress.gov/crs-product/R41456 (Accessed: December 10, 2024).

DiLorenzo, T.J., 1984 "The Political Economy of National Industrial Policy," *Cato Journal,* 4(2), pp. 587–607.

Dobbin, F., 1994. *Forging Industrial Policy: The United States, Britain, and France in the Railway Age.* Cambridge: Cambridge University Press.

Donnan, S. and Sevastopulo, D., 2015. "US, Japan and 10 countries strike Pacific trade deal," *Financial Times,* 5 October.

Dorn, J.A., 1984 "Introduction: Planning America, Government or the Market?," *Cato Journal,* 4(2), pp. 365–380.

Duffy, R. 1997. *Nuclear Politics in America: A History and Theory of Government Regulation.* Lawrence: University Press of Kansas.

Dunlop, J.B., 1993. *The Rise of Russia and the Fall of the Soviet Empire.* Princeton, NJ: Princeton University Press. https://press.princeton.edu/books/paperback/9780691001739/the-rise-of-russia-and-the-fall-of-the-soviet-empire (Accessed: November 10, 2024).

Economic Report of the President (ERP) 2013. "Annual Report of the Council of Economic Advisers." U.S. Government Printing Office.

Economic Report of the President (ERP) 2014. "Annual Report of the Council of Economic Advisers." U.S. Government Printing Office.

Economic Report of the President (ERP) 2016. "Annual Report of the Council of Economic Advisers." U.S. Government Printing Office.

Economic Report of the President (ERP), 2000. "Annual Report of the Council of Economic Advisers." U.S. Government Printing Office.

Economic Report of the President (ERP), 2009. "Economic Report of the President Transmitted to the Congress." U.S. Government Printing Office.

Economic Report of the President (ERP), 2010. "Annual Report of the Council of Economic Advisers." U.S. Government Printing Office.

Economic Report of the President (ERP), 2012. "Annual Report of the Council of Economic Advisers." U.S. Government Printing Office.

Economic Report of the President (ERP), 1981. Washington, DC: United States Government Printing Office. https://www.presidency.ucsb.edu/sites/default/files/books/presidential-documents-archive-guidebook/the-economic-report-of-the-president-truman-1947-obama-2017/1981.pdf.

Economic Report of the President, 1982. Washington, DC: U.S. Government Printing Office.

Economic Report of the President (ERP), 1984. Washington, DC: United States Government Printing Office. https://www.presidency.ucsb.edu/sites/default/files/books/presidential-documents-archive-guidebook/the-economic-report-of-the-president-truman-1947-obama-2017/1984.pdf (Accessed: 9 November 2024).

Economic Report of the President (ERP), 1986. Washington, DC: United States Government Printing Office. https://www.presidency.ucsb.edu/sites/default/files/books/presidential-documents-archive-guidebook/the-economic-report-of-the-president-truman-1947-obama-2017/1986.pdf.

Economic Report of the President (ERP), 1988. Washington, DC: United States Government Printing Office. https://www.presidency.ucsb.edu/sites/default/files/books/presidential-documents-archive-guidebook/the-economic-report-of-the-president-truman-1947-obama-2017/1988.pdf.

Economic Report of the President (ERP), 1989. Washington, DC: United States Government Printing Office. https://www.presidency.ucsb.edu/sites/default/files/books/presidential-documents-archive-guidebook/the-economic-report-of-the-president-truman-1947-obama-2017/1989.pdf.

Economic Report of the President (ERP), 1990. Washington, DC: United States Government Printing Office. https://fraser.stlouisfed.org/files/docs/publications/ERP/1990/ERP_1990.pdf.

Economic Report of the President (ERP), 1991. Washington, DC: United States Government Printing Office. https://www.presidency.ucsb.edu/sites/default/files/books/presidential-documents-archive-guidebook/the-economic-report-of-the-president-truman-1947-obama-2017/1991.pdf.

Economic Report of the President (ERP), 1992. Washington, DC: United States Government Printing Office. https://www.presidency.ucsb.edu/sites/default/files/books/presidential-documents-archive-guidebook/the-economic-report-of-the-president-truman-1947-obama-2017/1992.pdf.

Economic Report of the President (ERP), 1993. Washington, DC: United States Government Printing Office. https://www.presidency.ucsb.edu/sites/default/files/books/presidential-documents-archive-guidebook/the-economic-report-of-the-president-truman-1947-obama-2017/1993.pdf.

Economic Report of the President (ERP), 1994. Washington, DC: United States Government Printing Office. https://www.presidency.ucsb.edu/sites/default/files/books/presidential-documents-archive-guidebook/the-economic-report-of-the-president-truman-1947-obama-2017/1994.pdf.

Economic Report of the President (ERP), 1995. Washington, DC: United States Government Printing Office. https://fraser.stlouisfed.org/title/economic-report-president-45/1995-8094 (Accessed: November 9, 2024).

Economic Report of the President (ERP), 1996. Washington, DC: United States Government Printing Office. https://www.presidency.ucsb.edu/sites/default/files/books/presidential-documents-archive-guidebook/the-economic-report-of-the-president-truman-1947-obama-2017/1996.pdf (Accessed: November 9, 2024).

Economic Report of the President (ERP), 1997. Washington, DC: United States Government Printing Office. https://www.presidency.ucsb.edu/sites/default/files/books/presidential-documents-archive-guidebook/the-economic-report-of-the-president-truman-1947-obama-2017/1997.pdf (Accessed: November 10, 2024).

Economic Report of the President (ERP), 1998. Washington, DC: United States Government Printing Office. https://www.govinfo.gov/content/pkg/ERP-1998/pdf/ERP-1998.pdf (Accessed: November 11, 2024).

Economic Report of the President (ERP), 1999. Washington, DC: United States Government Printing Office. https://www.presidency.ucsb.edu/sites/default/files/books/presidential-documents-archive-guidebook/the-economic-report-of-the-president-truman-1947-obama-2017/1999.pdf (Accessed: November 11, 2024).

Economic Report of the President (ERP), 2000. Washington, DC: United States Government Printing Office. https://fraser.stlouisfed.org/title/economic-report-president-45/2000-8099 (Accessed: November 11, 2024).

Economic Report of the President (ERP), 2001. Washington, DC: United States Government Printing Office. https://www.presidency.ucsb.edu/sites/default/files/books/presidential-documents-archive-guidebook/the-economic-report-of-the-president-truman-1947-obama-2017/2001.pdf.

Economic Report of the President (ERP), 1965. Washington, DC: United States Government Printing Office. https://www.presidency.ucsb.edu/sites/default/files/books/presidential-documents-archive-guidebook/the-economic-report-of-the-president-truman-1947-obama-2017/1965.pdf.

Economic Report of the President (ERP), 1966. Washington, DC: United States Government Printing Office. https://www.presidency.ucsb.edu/sites/default/files/books/presidential-documents-archive-guidebook/the-economic-report-of-the-president-truman-1947-obama-2017/1966.pdf.

Economic Report of the President (ERP), 1974. Washington, DC: United States Government Printing Office.

Economist Intelligence Unit, 2024. US election: its impact on industrial policy. https://www.eiu.com/n/us-election-its-impact-on-industrial-policy/ (Accessed: February 15, 2025).

Edey, M., 2009. "The Global Financial Crisis and its Effects," *Economic Papers: A Journal of Applied Economics and Policy*, 28(3), pp. 186–195.

Edwards, C., 2017. *Infrastructure Investment: A Federal Perspective*. Cato Institute.

Efficient, Effective, Accountable. An American Budget for Fiscal Year 2019. 2018. Archives.gov. Office of Management and Budget. https://trumpwhitehouse.archives.gov/wp-content/uploads/2018/02/budget-fy2019.pdf (Accessed: November 10, 2024).

Egan, M., 2017. "White House business panels collapse as CEOs flee Trump," *CNN Money*. August 16.

Einstein, K.L., Glick, D.M., Palmer, M., Fox, S. and LeBlanc, E. 2023. "2023 Menino Survey of Mayors," *Boston University*. Available at: https://www.surveyofmayors.com/files/2024/03/2023-Menino-Survey-IRA-Report-Final.pdf (Accessed: November 11, 2024).

Eisenhower, Dwight D., 1961. President Dwight D. Eisenhower's Farewell Address 1961 National Archives. https://www.archives.gov/milestone-documents/president-dwight-d-eisenhowers-farewell-address. [Original source: Box 38, Speech Series, Papers of Dwight D. Eisenhower as President, 1953-61, Eisenhower Library; National Archives and Records Administration.]

Eisinger, P., 1990. "Do the American States Do Industrial Policy?," *British Journal of Political Science*, 20(4), pp. 509–535. Available at: https://doi.org/10.1017/S0007123400005962.

Engelhardt, T., 1995. *The End of Victory Culture: Cold War America and the Disillusioning of a Generation*. New York: Basic Book.

Environmental Protection Agency, OAR, 2015. "FACT SHEET: Overview of the Clean Power Plan." https://archive.epa.gov/epa/cleanpowerplan/fact-sheet-overview-clean-power-plan.html.

Etzioni, A., 1983. "The MITIzation of America?," *Public Interest*, 72(44), pp. 44–51.

European Bank for Reconstruction and Development, 1996. *Annual Report 1996*. London: EBRD.

Evenett, S., Jakubik, A., Martín, F., and Ruta, M., 2024. "The Return of Industrial Policy in Data," in *IMF Working Papers*, Volume 2024: Issue 001 - DOI: https://doi.org/10.5089/9798400260964.001.

Executive Office of the President, 2009. "A Framework for Revitalizing American Manufacturing." *govinfo.gov*. https://www.govinfo.gov/app/details/GOVPUB-PREX-PURL-LPS121438.

Executive Office of the President, 2011. *Fact sheet: President Obama"s Early Learning Agenda*. Washington, DC: The White House.

Executive Office of the President, 2012. *A National Strategic Plan for Advanced Manufacturing*. Washington, DC: National Science and Technology Council. Available at: https://www.manufacturing.gov/sites/default/files/2018-01/nstc_feb2012.pdf.

Executive Office of the President, 2014. *The President's Budget for Fiscal Year 2015*. Washington, DC: Office of Management and Budget.

Executive Office of the President, 2025a. "Adjusting Imports of Automobiles and Automobile Parts Into the United States." *Presidential Document. Federal Register*, April 3. https://www.federalregister.gov/documents/2025/04/03/2025-05930/adjusting-imports-of-automobiles-and-automobile-parts-into-the-united-states.

Executive Office of the President, 2025b. "Removing Barriers to American Leadership in Artificial Intelligence. Executive Order 14179." *Federal Register*, January 31, 90 FR 8741–8742. https://www.federalregister.gov/documents/2025/01/31/2025-02172/removing-barriers-to-american-leadership-in-artificial-intelligence.

Executive Order No. 13534, 2010. "National Export Initiative", *Federal Register*, 75(50), pp. 12433–12435.

Falk, G., Nicchitta, I.A, Nyhof, E.C., and Romero, P.D., 2021. "Unemployment rates during the COVID-19 pandemic (CRS Report No. R46554)". Congressional Research Service. https://crsreports.congress.gov/product/pdf/R/R46554/9.

Farber, H.S. and Western, B., 2001. "Ronald Reagan and the Politics of Declining Union Organization." Working Paper No. 460, Industrial Relations Section, Princeton University. Available at: https://collaborate.princeton.edu/en/publications/ronald-reagan-and-the-politics-of-declining-union-organization/.

Federal Communications Commission (FCC), 2010. *Connecting America: The National Broadband Plan*. Washington, DC: Federal Communications Commission. Available at: https://www.fcc.gov/general/national-broadband-plan.

Federal Energy Regulatory Commission, 2020. *Energy Policy Act of 2005*. Washington, DC: Federal Energy Regulatory Commission. Available at: https://www.ferc.gov/enforcement-legal/legal/federal-statutes/energy-policy-act-epact-2005.

Federal Register, 2022. "Federal Acquisition Regulation: Amendments to the FAR Buy American Act Requirements." 7 March. Available at: https://www.federalregister.gov/documents/2022/03/07/2022-04173/federal-acquisition-regulation-amendments-to-the-far-buy-american-act-requirements (Accessed: December 10, 2024).

Federal Reserve Economic Data. Manufacturing Employment (MANEMP), 2025. Federal Reserve Bank of St. Louis. https://fred.stlouisfed.org/series/MANEMP (Accessed: February 14, 2025).

Feigenbaum, B. and Morris, J., 2017. "CAFE Standards in Plain English." *Reason*. https://reason.org/wp-content/uploads/2017/01/pb137_cafe_standards.pdf.

Ferrado, M. and Morris, J., 2014. "Fiat conquista il 100% di Chrysler. Marchionne: "Saremo costruttori globali'." Il Sole 24 ORE.

Ferrannini, A., Barbieri, E., Biggeri, M. and Di Tommaso, M.R., 2021. "Industrial Policy for Sustainable Human Development in the Post-COVID19 Era," *World Development*, 137, 105215.

Fewsmith, J., 2001. *China since Tiananmen: From Deng Xiaoping to Jiang Zemin*. Cambridge: Cambridge University Press.

First Summit of the Americas: Declaration of Principles 1994 Organization of American States, 1994. https://www.oas.org/juridico/english/DeclaI.html (Accessed: November 10, 2024).

Flaaen, A. and Pierce, J., 2019. "Disentangling the Effects of the 2018–2019 Tariffs on a Globally Connected U.S. Manufacturing Sector," *Board of Governors of the Federal Reserve System*, 2019.0(86).

Foot, R., 1995. *The Practice of Power: U.S. Relations with China Since 1949*. Oxford: Clarendon Press.

Frame, W.S., et al., 2015. "The Rescue of Fannie Mae and Freddie Mac." *Journal of Economic Perspectives*, 29(2), pp. 25–52.

Frank, D., 1999. *Buy American: The Untold Story of Economic Nationalism*. Boston: Beacon Press.

Frankel, J., 2015. "The Plaza Accord, 30 Years Later," *National Bureau of Economic Research*. http://www.nber.org/papers/w21813.

Franz, D.R. and Zajtchuk, R., 2002. "Biological terrorism: Understanding the threat, preparation, and medical response." *Disease-a-Month* 48(8), pp. 493–564.

Freyer, T., 1992. *Regulating Big Business: Antitrust in Great Britain and America 1880–1990*. Cambridge: Cambridge University Press.

Friedman, M., 1951. "Neoliberalism and Its Prospects," *Collected Works of Milton Friedman Project records. Hoover Institution Library & Archives, Stanford, CA.* https://digitalcollections.hoover.org/objects/57816/neoliberalism-and-its-prospects.

Friedman, M., 1975. *An Economist's Protest*. Thomas Horton and Daughters.

Fukuyama, F., 1992 *The End of History and the Last Man*. New York, NY: Free Press.

Gale, W.G., Krupkin, A. and Rueben, K., 2018. *Effects of the Tax Cuts and Jobs Act: A Preliminary Analysis*. Washington, DC: Urban-Brookings Tax Policy Center.

Gallo, M.E. and Kuiken, T., 2022. *White House Initiative to Advance the Bioeconomy, E.O. 14081: In Brief. CRS Product R47274*. Congressional Research Service. Available at: https://www.congress.gov/crs-product/R47274.

Gans, H.J., 1967. *The Levittowners: Ways of Life and Politics in a New Suburban Community*. New York: Pantheon Books.

Gansler, J.S., 2011. *Democracy's Arsenal: Creating a Twenty-First-Century Defense Industry*. MIT Press.

Gest, J., 2016. *The New Minority: White Working Class Politics in an Age of Immigration and Inequality*. Oxford University Press.

Gijs, C. and Gavin, G., 2025. "US gets back to EU on trade war — hinting at Trump's willingness to find a deal." *Politico*, May 14. https://www.politico.eu/article/us-gets-back-to-eu-on-trade-war-%E2%80%95-hinting-at-trumps-willingness-to-find-a-deal/ (Accessed: May 26, 2025).

Gijs, C., Desrochers, D. and Hawkins, A., 2025. "Trump's tariff deals send Europe to the back of the line." *Politico*, May 12. https://www.politico.eu/article/donald-trump-tariff-deal-send-europe-back-line/ (Accessed: May 26, 2025).

GIS Geography, 2023. 10 Uses and Applications of GPS Technology. Available at: https://gisgeography.com/gps-uses/ (Accessed: February 15, 2026).

Glaser, L.K., 1986. "Provisions of the Food Security Act of 1985." *Economic Research Service*. https://ers.usda.gov/sites/default/files/_laserfiche/publications/41995/15127_aib498a_1_.pdf.

Glass, A., 2018. "Bush Signs Auto Industry Bailout." *Politico*, December 19.

Glennon, M.J., 2016. " National Security and Double Government". New York: Oxford University Press.

Global Trade Magazine, 2023. The Impact of Automation and AI on Supply Chain Efficiency: Transforming Logistics for the Future. https://www.globaltrademag.com/the-impact-of-automation-and-ai-on-supply-chain-efficiency-transforming-logistics-for-the-future/.

Glykou, I. and Pitelis, C.N., 2011. "On the Political Economy of the State, the Public-Private Nexus and Industrial Policy," *Policy Studies*, 32(4), pp. 461–478.

Goldberg, P.K. and Knetter, M.M., 1997. "Goods Prices and Exchange Rates: What Have We Learned?," *Journal of Economic Literature*, 35(3), pp. 1243–1272.

Gonyea, D., 2013. "What Has NAFTA Meant For Workers? That Debate's still Raging." *National Public Radio*. December 17. Available at: https://www.npr.org/2013/12/17/251945882/what-has-nafta-meant-for-workers-that-debates-still-raging

Government Accountability Office (GAO), 2020. Pentagon's RDT&E Spending and Emerging Technologies.

Grabbe, H., 2006. *The EU's Transformative Power: Europeanization Through Conditionality in Central and Eastern Europe*. Basingstoke: Palgrave Macmillan.

Graham Jr., O.L., 1992. *Losing Time: The Industrial Policy Debate*. Cambridge, MA: Harvard University Press. Available at: https://www.hup.harvard.edu/books/9780674539358 (Accessed: November 9, 2024).

Greenaway, D., 1992. "Trade Related Investment Measures and Development Strategy," *Kyklos*, 45(2), pp. 139–159. Available at: https://doi.org/10.1111/j.1467-6435.1992.tb02111.x.

Grillo, M. and Silva, F., 1989. *Impresa, concorrenza e organizzazione: Lezioni di economia e politica industriale*. Rome: La Nuova Italia Scientifica. Available at: https://www.carocci.it/prodotto/impresa-concorrenza-e-organizzazione (Accessed: February 20, 2026).

Gross, S., 2020. What is the Trump Administration's Track Record on the Environment? Available at: https://www.brookings.edu/articles/what-is-the-trump-administrations-track-record-on-the-environment/ (Accessed: February 15, 2025).

Grossman, G.M., Helpman, E. and Redding, S.J., 2024. "When Tariffs Disrupt Global Supply Chains," *American Economic Review*, 114(4), pp. 988–1029. Available at: https://doi.org/10.1257/aer.20211519.

Gruber, J., 2011. *Health Care Reform: What It Is, Why It's Necessary, How It Works*. New York: Hill and Wang.

Grubler, A. and Wilson, C., 2014. *Energy Technology Innovation: Learning from Historical Successes and Failures*. Cambridge University Press.

H.R.803 - Workforce Innovation and Opportunity Act, 2014.

Hacker, J.S. and Pierson, P., 2005. *Off center: The Republican Revolution and the Erosion of American Democracy*. New Haven, CT: Yale University Press.

Haggard, S. and Kaufman, R.R., 1995. *The Political Economy of Democratic Transitions*. Princeton, NJ: Princeton University Press.

Haggard, S., 1990. *Pathways from the Periphery: The Politics of Growth in the Newly Industrializing Countries*. Ithaca: Cornell University Press.

Haggard, S., 2004. "Institutions and Growth in East Asia," *Studies in Comparative International Development*, 38(4), pp. 53–81.

Hamilton, A., 1791. "Alexander Hamilton's Final Version of the Report on the Subject of Manufactures, December 5," *Founders Online, National Archives*, https://founders.archives.gov/documents/Hamilton/01-10-02-0001-0007. [Original source: The Papers of Alexander Hamilton, vol. 10, December 1791–January 1792, ed. Harold C. Syrett. New York: Columbia University Press, 1966, pp. 230–340.]

Hammes, D. and Wills, D.T., 2005. "Black Gold: The End of Bretton Woods and the Oil Price Shocks of the 1970s." *Independent Review* 9(4), pp. 501–511

Harrison, M., ed., 1998. *The Economics of World War II: Six Great Powers in International Comparison*. Cambridge: Cambridge University Press.

Hausmann, R. and Rodrik, D., 2003. "Economic Development as Self-Discovery," *Journal of Development Economics*, 72(2), pp. 603–633.

Hausmann, R., Rodrik, D. and Sabel, C., 2007. "Reconfiguring industrial policy: a framework with an application to South Africa." *CID Working Paper*, No. 168. Cambridge: Center for International Development at Harvard University.

Hawley, E.W., 1974. *The New Deal and the Problem of Monopoly: A Study in Economic Ambivalence*. Princeton, NJ: Princeton University Press.

Helper, S. and Henderson, R., 2014. "Management Practices, Relational Contracts, and the Decline of General Motors." *Journal of Economic Perspectives* 28(1), pp. 49–72.

Helper, S. and Henderson, R., 2014. "Management Practices, Relational Contracts, and the Decline of General Motors." *Journal of Economic Perspectives*, 28(1), pp. 49–72.

Higgs, Robert. 1992. "Wartime Prosperity? A Reassessment of the U.S. Economy in the 1940s." *Journal of Economic History* 52(1), pp. 41–60. doi: 10.1017/S0022050700010251.

Hill, G.F., 1951. "Government Engineering Aid to Railroad before the Civil War," *Journal of Economic History*, 11(3), pp. 235–246.

History.com Editors, 2023. Great Migration: Definition, Causes & Impact. *HISTORY*, December 15.

Hochschild, A.R., 2016. *Strangers in Their Own Land: Anger and Mourning on the American Right*. The New Press.

Hoekman, B.M. and Mavroidis, P.C., 1997. *Law and Policy in Public Purchasing: The WTO Agreement on Public Procurement*. Ann Arbor, MI: University of Michigan Press. Available at: https://scholarship.law.columbia.edu/books/145.

Hogan, M.J., 1987. *The Marshall Plan: America, Britain and the Reconstruction of Western Europe, 1947–1952*. Cambridge: Cambridge University Press.

Holzer, H.J., 2001. *What Employers Want: Job Prospects for Less-Educated Workers*. New York: Russell Sage Foundation.

Hopewell, K., 2016. *Breaking the WTO: How Emerging Powers Disrupted the Neoliberal Project*. Stanford University Press.

Horton, E., 2017. "The Legacy of the 2001 and 2003 'Bush' Tax Cuts | Center on Budget and Policy Priorities," Center on Budget and Policy Priorities, October 23. doi: https://www. cbpp.org/research/the-legacy-of-the-2001-and-2003-bush-tax-cuts.

Hounshell, D.A., 1984. *From the American system to mass production, 1800–1932: the development of manufacturing technology in the United States*. Baltimore Etc.: The Johns Hopkins University Press.

Huang, Y., 2008. *Capitalism with Chinese Characteristics: Entrepreneurship and the State*. Cambridge: Cambridge University Press.

Hufbauer, G.C. and Schott, J.J., 2005. *NAFTA Revisited: Achievements and Challenges*. Washington, DC: Institute for International Economics.

Hufbauer, G.C. and Schott, J.J., 2009. *Buy American: Bad for Jobs, Worse for Reputation*. Washington, DC: Peterson Institute for International Economics.

Ingrassia, P. and White, J.B., 1995. *Crash Course: The American Automobile Industry's Road from Glory to Disaster*. New York: Random House.

Internal Revenue Service, 2009a. *Energy Provisions of the American Recovery and Reinvestment Act of 2009 (ARRA)*, FS-2009-10, April 2009. Available at: https://www.irs.gov/pub/ irs-news/fs-09-10.pdf.

Internal Revenue Service, 2009b. *Notice 2009-72: Qualifying Advanced Energy Project Credit*. Available at: https://www.irs.gov/pub/irs-drop/n-09-72.pdf.

Internal Revenue Service, 2009c. *Notice 2009-58: Qualified Plug-In Electric Vehicle Credit under Section 30*, Internal Revenue Bulletin 2009-30, 27 July 2009. Available at: https://www.irs. gov/pub/irs-drop/n-09-58.pdf.

Ikenberry, G.J., 2011. *Liberal Leviathan: The Origins, Crisis, and Transformation of the American World Order*. Princeton, NJ: Princeton University Press.

Irwin, D.A., 2004. *The Aftermath of Hamilton's "Report on Manufactures," Journal of Economic History*, 64(3), pp. 800–821. https://doi.org/10.1017/S0022050704002979.

Irwin, D.A., 2017. *Clashing Over Commerce: A History of US Trade Policy*. University of Chicago Press.

Irwin, D.A., 1996. "The U.S. Japan Semiconductor Trade Conflict," in A.O. Krueger, ed., *The Political Economy of Trade Protection*. [online] University of Chicago Press, pp. 5–14. Available at: http://www.nber.org/chapters/c8717 (Accessed: November 30, 2024).

Isserman, A.M. and Rephann, T.J., 1995. "The Economic Effects of the Appalachian Regional Commission: An Empirical Assessment of 26 Years of Regional Development Planning," *Journal of the American Planning Association*, 61(3), pp. 345–364.

Ivie, R.L. and Giner, O., 2009. "American Exceptionalism in a Democratic Idiom: Transacting the Mythos of Change in the 2008 Presidential Campaign," *Communication Studies*, 60(4), pp. 359–375.

Jackson, E. and Harden, B., 2023. Inflation, Uncertainty, Lost Jobs: Sec 301 Tariffs in Review, Retail Industry Leaders Association. Available at: https://www.rila.org/blog/2023/ 09/inflation-uncertainty-lost-jobs-sec-301-tariffs-in (Accessed: December 9, 2024).

Jackson, J.K., 2019. The Committee on Foreign Investment in the United States (CFIUS). RL33388. Washington, DC: Congressional Research Service. Available at: https://crsreports.congress.gov/product/pdf/RL/RL33388/69.

Janeway, E., 1951. *The Struggle for Survival: A Chronicle of Economic Mobilization in World War II.* New Haven, CT: Yale University Press, 1951.

Johnson, C., 1982. *MITI and the Japanese Miracle: The Growth of Industrial Policy, 1925–1975.* Stanford: Stanford University Press.

Johnson, C., 1984 *The Industrial Policy Debate.* San Francisco, CA: Institute for Contemporary Studies.

Johnson, K. and Wong, M., 2024. The Trouble with Tariffs, Information Technology Industry Council. Available at: https://www.itic.org/news-events/techwonk-blog/the-trouble-with-tariffs (Accessed: December 9, 2024).

Johnson, L.B., 1964. *Remarks at the University of Michigan.* Gerhard Peters and John T. Woolley, The American Presidency Project.

Jones, D.S., 2014. *Masters of the Universe: Hayek, Friedman, and the Birth of Neoliberal Politics* - Updated Edition. Princeton University Press. https://doi.org/10.1515/978140085 1836.

Jones, R.W., 2012. "Manufacturing Renaissance? US Industrial Policy After the Crisis," *International Economics and Economic Policy*, 9(3–4), pp. 269–285.

Jorde, T.M. and Teece, D.J., 1992. "Antitrust, Innovation, and Competitiveness," *Oxford Review of Economic Policy*, 8(4), pp. 54–73.

Jorgenson, D.W., 2005. *Productivity, Volume 3: Information Technology and the American Growth Resurgence.* Cambridge, MA: MIT Press.

Judis, J.B., 2016. *The Populist Explosion: How the Great Recession Transformed American and European Politics.* New York: Columbia Global Reports.

Kamensky, J., 2001. "*A Brief History of Vice President Al Gore's National Partnership for Reinventing Government During the Administration of President Bill Clinton: 1993–2001,*" University of North Texas. https://govinfo.library.unt.edu/npr/whoweare/historyofnpr.html (Accessed: November 11, 2024).

Kapur, S. and Sarlin, B., 2022. "Manchin Says Build Back Better is 'Dead.' Here's What he Might Resurrect," *NBC News*, February 3. https://www.nbcnews.com/politics/congress/manchin-says-build-back-better-dead-here-s-what-he-n1288492.

Kennedy, J.F., 1961. Address to Joint Session of Congress May 25. John F. Kennedy Presidential Library and Museum.

Keohane, R., 1984. *After Hegemony.* Princeton: Princeton University Press.

Ketels, C.H.M., 2007. "Industrial Policy in the United States," *Journal of Industry, Competition and Trade*, 7(2), pp. 147–167.

Khan, M., Watkins, M., Aminuzzaman, S., Kahir, S. and Khan, M., 2022. "Win-Win: Designing Dual-Use in Climate Projects for Effective Anti-Corruption in Bangladesh." *Climate and Development*, 14(10), pp. 921–934.

Kiely, R., 2015. *The BRICs, US "Decline" and Global Transformations.* Basingstoke: Palgrave Macmillan.

Klein, A. and Meissner, C.M., 2024. "Did Tariffs Make American Manufacturing Great? New Evidence from the Gilded Age," *National Bureau of Economic Research*, Working Paper 33100. doi: 10.3386/w33100

Knowlton, B. and Br/International Herald Tribune, 2003. "Bush Rescinds Tariffs on Steel Imports, Averting Trade War." *The New York Times*, December 4.

Kochhar, R. and Cilluffo, A., 2018. *Income Inequality in the U.S. Is Rising Most Rapidly Among Asians.* Pew Research Center.

Kogan, R., Romig, K. and Beltran, J., 2020. "Trump's 2021 Budget Would Cut $1.6 Trillion From Low-Income Programs," *Center on Budget and Policy Priorities*, February 10.

Koujianou G. and Knetter, M.M., 1997. "Causes and Consequences of the Export Enhancement Program for Wheat," in: R.C. Feenstra, ed., *The Effects of U.S. Trade Protection and Promotion Policies*. University of Chicago Press, pp. 273–296. https://www.nber.org/system/files/chapters/c0316/c0316.pdf (Accessed: December 1, 2024).

Kreis, R., 2017. "The 'tweet politics' of Donald Trump," *Journal of Language and Politics*, 16(4), pp. 607–618.

Kreps, S.E., 2011. *Coalitions of Convenience: United States Military Interventions after the Cold War*. Oxford: Oxford University Press.

Krippner, G.R., 2011. *Capitalizing on Crisis*. Cambridge, MA: Harvard University Press.

Krueger, A.O., 1974. "The Political Economy of the Rent-Seeking Society," *American Economic Review*, 64(3), pp. 291–303.

Krueger, A.O., 1990. "Government Failures in Development," *Journal of Economic Perspectives*, 4(3), pp. 9–23. Available at: https://doi.org/10.1257/jep.4.3.9.

Krugman, P., 2009. *The Return of Depression Economics and the Crisis of 2008*. W.W. Norton & Company.

Krugman, P.R., 1997. "Growing World Trade: Causes and Consequences." *Brookings Papers on Economic Activity*, 1, pp. 327–343.

Kurc, Ç. and Bitzinger, R., 2018. "Defense Industries in the 21st Century: A Comparative Analysis—The Second e-Workshop," *Comparative Strategy*, 37(3), pp. 255–259. doi: 10.1080/01495933.2018.1497318.

Kurc, C. and Bitzinger, R.A., 2021. *Defense Industries in the 21st Century: A Comparative Analysis*. London: Routledge.

Kuznets, S., 1955. "Economic Growth and Income Inequality," *The American Economic Review*, 45(1), pp. 1–28.

Kwoka, J.E. and White, L.J., eds. 1999. *The Antitrust Revolution: Economics, Competition, and Policy*, 3rd edn. Oxford: Oxford University Press.

Lardy, N.R., 1998. *China's Unfinished Economic Revolution*. Washington, DC: Brookings Institution Press.

Laudani, P. and Rabiega, M., 2025. "How Trump's Chaotic Trade War has Evolved." *Reuters*, May 12. https://www.reuters.com/business/autos-transportation/how-trumps-chaotic-trade-war-has-evolved-2025-05-12/ (Accessed: May 26, 2025).

Lazonick, W. and Tulum, Ö., 2011 "US Biopharmaceutical Finance and the Sustainability of the Biotech Business Model," 40(11). https://doi.org/10.2139/ssrn.2257932.

Leddy, M. and Shaw, T., 2025. "Experts Delve into Business, Manufacturing Provisions in House Tax Reform Bill." https://tax.thomsonreuters.com/news/experts-delve-into-business-manufacturing-provisions-in-house-tax-reform-bill/ (Accessed: May 26, 2025).

Lee, T. and Varas, J., 2022. "The Total Cost of U.S. Tariffs," *American Action Forum*. https://www.americanactionforum.org/research/the-total-cost-of-tariffs/ (Accessed: December 9, 2024).

Le Grand, J., 1991. "The Theory of Government Failure," *British Journal of Political Science*, 21(4), pp. 423–442.

Leiner, Cerf, Clark, Kahn, Kleinrock, Lynch, Postel, Roberts, and Wolff, 1997. "A Brief History of the Internet." *Internet Society*.

Lens, S., 2003. *The Forging of the American Empire: From the Revolution to Vietnam: A History of U.S. Imperialism*. London: Pluto Press.

Lerner, J., 1999 "The Government as Venture Capitalist: The Long-Run Impact of the SBIR Program," *The Journal of Business*, 72(3), pp. 285–318. Available at: https://doi.org/10.1086/209616.

Lester, R.E. (1993) The Johnson Administration and Pacification in Vietnam: The Robert Komer–William Leonhart Files, 1966–1968. University Publications of America. Available at: https://huongduongtxd.com/pacificationvietnam.pdf

Levinson, M., 2019. *An Extraordinary Time: The End of the Postwar Boom and the Return of the Ordinary Economy*. New York: Basic Books.

Lin, J. and Chang, H.J., 2009. "Should Industrial Policy in Developing Countries Conform to Comparative Advantage or Defy It? A Debate Between Justin Lin and Ha-Joon

Chan." *Developmental Policy Review*, 27(5), pp. 483–502. https://doi.org/10.1111/j.1467-7679.2009.00456.x.

Lin, J.Y., 2012. "From Flying Geese to Leading Dragons: New Opportunities and Strategies for Structural Transformation in Developing Countries," *Global Policy*, 3(4), pp. 397–409.

Lincoln, E.J., 1990. *Japan's Unequal Trade*. Washington, DC: Brookings Institution.

List, F., 1885. *The National System of Political Economy, translated from the Original German edition published in 1841 by Sampson Lloyd*. London: Longmans, Green, and Company.

Living New Deal, n.d. *Programs: History of the New Deal*. https://livingnewdeal.org/history-of-the-new-deal/programs/ (Accessed: July 8, 2025).

Lloyd, J.M., 1982. *Railroads and Land Grant Policy: A Study in Government Intervention*. New York: Academic Press.

Louis J. and Williamson, S.H., 2026. "What Was the U.S. GDP Then?," *MeasuringWorth*. https://measuringworth.com/datasets/usgdp/.

Luckey, J.R., 2009. The Buy American Act: Requiring Government Procurements to Come from Domestic Sources. Congressional Research Service (CRS Report No. RL33536). Washington, DC: Library of Congress.

Luhby, T. and Lobosco, K., 2024. "Here's what Harris is Proposing for the Economy". *CNN*. https://www.cnn.com/2024/09/03/politics/harris-economic-proposals (Accessed December 5, 2024).

MacMartin, S.M., Silva, A.T., Vázquez, I.P. and Werner, R.L., Jr., 2025. *The History and Evolution of Homeland Security in the United States: From the Constitution Through 9/11 to the Present*. CRC Press.

Macro Trends, n.d. "S&P 500 Index - 90 Year Historical Chart." (Accessed: November 19, 2024).

Macrotrends, 2024. "S&P 500 Historical Returns". Available at: https://www.macrotrends.net/2324/sp-500-historical-chart-data.

Magness, P.W., 2023. "The Problem of the Tariff in American Economic History, 1787–1934," *Cato Institute*, September 26. https://www.cato.org/publications/problem-tariff-american-economic-history-1787-1934.

Mason, L., 2018. *Uncivil Agreement: How Politics Became Our Identity*. University of Chicago Press.

Maurer, M. ed., 1978. *The U.S. Air Service in World War I*. Washington, D.C.: The U.S. Government Printing Office, Stock Number 008-070-00.

Mazzucato, M., 2013. *The Entrepreneurial State: Debunking Public vs. Private Sector Myths*. London: Anthem Press.

McAndrews, L.J., 2006. *The Era of Education: The Presidents and the Schools, 1965–2001*. 1st edn. Urbana: University of Illinois Press. https://www.press.uillinois.edu/books/?id=p075797 (Accessed: 11 November 2024).

McKinley, W., 1897. " Message to Congress, 15 March," in: W. McKinley, Message to Congress. The American Presidency Project. Available at: https://www.presidency.ucsb.edu/documents/message-congress-40 (Accessed: December 10, 2024).

McQuarrie, M., 2017. "The Revolt of the Rust Belt: Place and Politics in the Age of Anger," *The British Journal of Sociology*, 68(S1), S120–S152.

Merry, R.W., 2017. *President McKinley: Architecture of the American Century*, New York: Simon and Schuster.

Milward, A.S., 1979. *War, Economy and Society, 1939–1945*. Berkeley: University of California Press.

Mishkin, F.S., 2012. *The Economics of Money, Banking, and Financial Markets*. 10th ed. Pearson.

Moessner, R. and Allen, W.A., 2011. "Banking Crises and the International Monetary System in the Great Depression and Now1," *Financial History Review*, 18(1), pp. 1–20.

Moran, T.H., Graham, E.M. and Blomström, M., 2005. *Does Foreign Direct Investment Promote Development?* Washington, DC: Peterson Institute for International Economics.

Moretti, E., 2012. *The New Geography of Jobs.* Houghton Mifflin Harcourt.

Mowery, D.C., Nelson, R.R., Sampat, B.N. and Ziedonis, A.A., 2001. "The Growth of Patenting and Licensing by U.S. Universities: An Assessment of the Effects of the Bayh–Dole Act of 1980," *Research Policy*, 30(1), pp. 99–119.

Mowery, D.C. and Sampat, B.N., 2005. "Universities in National Innovation Systems," in J. Fagerberg, D.C. Mowery, and R.R. Nelson eds., *The Oxford Handbook of Innovation.* Oxford: Oxford University Press, pp. 209–239.

Mun, T., 1630. *England's Treasure by Forraign Trade. Or, the Ballance of our Forraign Trade is the rule of our Treasure. Written by Thomas Mun, published by his son John Mun of Bearsted.* London: J[ohn] G[rismond] for Thomas Clark, 1664.

Muresianu, A. and York, E., 2024a. How Did the Tax Cuts and Jobs Act Change Cost Recovery?, Tax Foundation. https://taxfoundation.org/blog/tax-cuts-and-jobs-act-expensing/ (Accessed: December 9, 2024).

Muresianu, C. and York, E. 2024b. *The Long-Term Impact of the 2017 Tax Cuts and Jobs Act.* Tax Foundation.

National Bureau of Economic Research, 2021. *Long-Run Trends and the Natural Rate of Unemployment.* https://www.nber.org/reporter/2021number2/long-run-trends-and-natural-rate-unemployment?page=1&perPage=50.

National Defense Authorization Act (NDAA) for FY 2019, 2018. U.S. Government Publishing Office.

National Highway Traffic Safety Administration (NHTSA), 2024. *Corporate Average Fuel Economy (CAFE) Standards.* Washington, DC: U.S. Department of Transportation. Available at: https://www.nhtsa.gov/laws-regulations/corporate-average-fuel-economy.

National Institute of Standards and Technology, 2010. *Manufacturing Extension Partnership: FY2010 Budget Justification.* Washington, DC: U.S. Department of Commerce.

National Research Council, 2001. *The Advanced Technology Program: Assessing Outcomes.* Washington, DC: National Academy Press.

National Research Council, 2002. *Effectiveness and Impact of Corporate Average Fuel Economy (CAFE) Standards.* Washington, DC: National Academies Press.

National Science Foundation, 2012. *Merit Review Highlights: Graduate Research Fellowship Program.* Arlington, VA: NSF.

Naughton, B., 2007. *The Chinese Economy: Transitions and Growth.* Cambridge, MA: MIT Press.

Naval History and Heritage Command (NHHC), 1917. Vice Admiral William S. Sims, Commander, United States Naval Forces Operating in European Waters to United States Ambassador to Great Britain Walter Hines Page.

Naval History and Heritage Command (NHHC), 2018. H-023-1: The Contribution of the U.S. Navy During World War I.

Nester, W.R., 1997. *American Industrial Policy: Free or Managed Trade.* London: Macmillan.

New York Times, 1890. "UP GO THE PRICES NOW; HOW THE M"KINLEY TARIFF TAXES THE NECESSARIES OF LIFE. MERCHANTS ARE MARKING UP ALMOST EVERYTHING THAT MEN WEAR, EAT, OR KEEP HOUSE WITH." *New York Times*, October 21. https://www.nytimes.com/1890/10/21/archives/up-go-the-prices-now-how-the-mkinley-tariff-taxes-the-necessaries.html.

New York Times, 1989. "Excerpts from Brady Remarks on Debt," *New York Times*, 11 March. https://www.nytimes.com/1989/03/11/business/excerpts-from-brady-remarks-on-debt.html (Accessed: December 10, 2024).

Niskanen, W.A., 1988 "U.S. Trade Policy," The Cato Review of Business & Government. Available at: https://www.cato.org/regulation/fall-1988/us-trade-policy.

Nixon Goes to China, 1972. UPI. Available at: https://www.upi.com/Archives/Audio/Events-of-1972/Nixon-Goes-to-China/ (Accessed: 11 November 2024).

Nixon, R., 1973. "Address to the Nation on Project Independence," 7 November, in *Foreign Relations of the United States, 1969–1976, Volume XXXVI, Energy Crisis, 1969–1974, Document 237*, U.S. Department of State. Available at: https://history.state.gov/historicaldocuments/frus1969-76v36/d237.

Norton, R.D., 1986 "Industrial Policy and American Renewal," *Journal of Economic Literature*, 24(1), pp. 1–40.

Nunns, J., Burman, L., Rohaly, J. and Rosenberg, J., 2015. *An Analysis of Donald Trump's Tax Plan*. Tax Policy Center.

Nunns, J., Burman, L., Rohaly, J. and Rosenberg, J., 2016. *An Analysis of Donald Trump's Revised Tax Plan*. Tax Policy Center.

Obama White House, 2009a. "Fact Sheet on Obama Administration Auto Restructuring Initiative for General Motors".

Obama White House, 2009b. "Remarks by the President on Financial Rescue and Reform at Federal Hall." [online] *whitehouse*.gov. Available at: https://obamawhitehouse.archives.gov/the-press-office/remarks-president-financial-rescue-and-reform-federal-hall (Accessed: 16 Dec. 2024).

Obama White House, 2010. "Statement From the President on the National Broadband Plan." https://obamawhitehouse.archives.gov/the-press-office/statement-president-national-broadband-plan?utm_source=chatgpt.com (Accessed: 16 Dec. 2024).

Obama White House, 2010. *Fact Sheet: $2.3 Billion in New Clean Energy Manufacturing Tax Credits*, 8 January 2010. Available at: https://obamawhitehouse.archives.gov/the-press-office/fact-sheet-23-billion-new-clean-energy-manufacturing-tax-credits.

Obama White House, 2011. "President Obama Launches Advanced Manufacturing Partnership". https://obamawhitehouse.archives.gov/the-press-office/2011/06/24/president-obama-launches-advanced-manufacturing-partnership.

Obama White House, 2016. "Fact Sheet: The Recovery Act Made The Largest Single Investment in Clean Energy In History, Driving The Deployment Of Clean Energy, Promoting Energy Efficiency, And Supporting Manufacturing".

Obama, B., 2008. *Remarks in Canton, Ohio Presenting Presidential Campaign "Closing Argument"*. *The American Presidency Project*. https://www.presidency.ucsb.edu/documents/remarks-canton-ohio-presenting-presidential-campaign-closing-argument.

Obama, B., 2009a. "Obama's Remarks to Small Business Owners, Community Lenders and Members of Congress". *The New York Times*. https://www.nytimes.com/2009/03/16/us/politics/16obama-biz.html.

Obama, B., 2009b. "Remarks by the President Challenging Americans to Lead the Global Economy in Clean Energy". *whitehouse.gov*. https://obamawhitehouse.archives.gov/the-press-office/remarks-president-challenging-americans-lead-global-economy-clean-energy.

Obama, B., 2009c. "Remarks by the President on the Auto Industry," April 30. *whitehouse.gov*. https://obamawhitehouse.archives.gov/the-press-office/remarks-president-auto-industry.

Obama, B., 2009d. "Remarks by the President to a Joint Session of Congress on Health Care". *whitehouse.gov*. https://obamawhitehouse.archives.gov/the-press-office/remarks-president-a-joint-session-congress-health-care.

Obama, B., 2009e. *Remarks by the President on a New Beginning, Cairo University, 4 June*. Washington, DC: The White House. Available at: https://obamawhitehouse.archives.gov/the-press-office/remarks-president-cairo-university-6-04-09.

Obama, B., 2010a. *Remarks by the President on Wall Street Reform*, 22 April. New York: The White House. Available at: https://obamawhitehouse.archives.gov/the-press-office/remarks-president-wall-street-reform.

Obama, B., 2010b. *Remarks by the President on the American Auto Industry and the American Economy*, 26 May. Washington, DC: The White House. https://obamawhitehouse.archives.gov/the-press-office/2010/08/05/remarks-president-american-auto-industry-and-american-economy.

Obama, B., 2011. *Remarks by the President at Signing of the America Invents Act*, September 16. The White House, Office of the Press Secretary.

Office of Management and Budget (OMB), 2018. *A New Foundation for American Greatness: Budget of the U.S. Government for Fiscal Year 2018*. The White House.

Office of Science and Technology Policy (OSTP), 2006. *American Competitiveness Initiative: Leading the World in Innovation*. White House.

Office of Science and Technology Policy (OSTP), 2014. "Open Government Plan". https://obamawhitehouse.archives.gov/sites/default/files/microsites/ostp/ostp_2014_open_gov_plan.pdf.

Office of the Historian, n.d. "The Soviet Invasion of Afghanistan and the U.S. Response, 1978–1980," *State.gov*. Available at: https://history.state.gov/milestones/1977-1980/soviet-invasion-afghanistan. (Accessed: 11 November 2024).

Office of the Historian, 2019. "Milestones: 1969–1976 - Office of the Historian," *State.gov*. Available at: https://history.state.gov/milestones/1969-1976. (Accessed: 11 November 2024).

Office of Science and Technology Policy (OSTP), 2006. American Competitiveness Initiative: Research and Development Funding in the President's 2007 Budget [PDF]. *Executive Office of the President*. https://nsf-gov-resources.nsf.gov/attachments/108276/public/ACI.pd.

Ott, B.L., 2017. "The Age of Twitter: Donald J. Trump and the Politics of Debasement," *Critical Studies in Media Communication*, 34(1), pp. 59–68. doi: 10.1080/15295036.2016.1266686.

Owen, G., 2012. "Industrial Policy in Europe since the Second World War: What Has Been Learnt?" ECIPE Occasional Paper, No. 1/2012. Brussels: European Centre for International Political Economy.

Pack, H. and Saggi, K., 2006 "Is There a Case for Industrial Policy? A Critical Survey," *The World Bank Research Observer*, 21(2), pp. 267–297. Available at: https://doi.org/10.1093/wbro/lkl001.

Paget, L.R. ed., 1896. *McKinley Masterpieces. Selection from the public addresses in and out of the Congress*. Boston, MA: Joseph Knight Company Publishing.

Pang, J., 2013. "In Malaysia, a Historic Chance for Reform." *The New York Times*, May 4.

Parilla, J., Haskins, G., Bermel, L., Hansmann, L., Muro, M., Cummings, R. and Deese, B., 2024. "Strategic Sector Investments are Poised to Benefit Distressed US Counties," *MIT CEEPR*. https://ceepr.mit.edu/wp-content/uploads/2024/02/MIT-CEEPR-RC-2024-02.pdf (Accessed: November 11, 2024).

Paulson, H., 2010. *On the Brink: Inside the Race to Stop the Collapse of the Global Financial System*. Business Plus.

Perkins, L. and Chappell, B., 2015. "President Obama Unveils New Power Plant Rules In 'Clean Power Plan'". *National Public Radio*. https://www.npr.org/sections/thetwo-way/2015/08/03/429044707/president-obama-set-to-unveil-new-power-plant-rules-in-clean-power-plan.

Perrotta, C., 2014. "Thomas Mun's England's Treasure by Forraign Trade: the 17th-Century Manifesto for Economic Development," *History of Economics Review*, 59(1), pp. 94–106. doi: 10.1080/18386318.2014.11681258.

Pew Charitable Trusts, 2010. *Bringing America Up to Speed: States' Role in Expanding Broadband*. Washington, DC: Pew Charitable Trusts.

Pfleeger, S.L. and Caputo, D.D., 2012. "Leveraging Behavioral Science to Mitigate Cyber Security Risk," *Computers & Security*, 31(4), pp. 597–611. doi:https://doi.org/10.1016/j.cose.2011.12.010.

Pierce, J.R. and Schott, P.K., 2012. "The Surprisingly Swift Decline of U.S. Manufacturing Employment," *National Bureau of Economic Research*. https://www.nber.org/papers/w18655.

Piven, F.F. and Cloward, R.A. 2005. *Poor People's Movements: Why They Succeed, How They Fail*. New York: Vintage Books.

Politi, J. and Smith, C., 2024. "Kamalanomics: Harris's Economic Vision for America's Middle Class," *Financial Times*. https://www.ft.com/content/949ead2b-68e2-4064-9cfa-187ec629a84b (Accessed: November 11, 2024).

Porter, M.E., 1998. "Clusters and the New Economics of Competition," *Harvard Business Review*, 76(6), pp. 77–90.

Preliminary Details and Analysis of the Tax Cuts and Jobs Act, 2017. 241. Washington, DC: Tax Foundation. https://taxfoundation.org/research/all/federal/final-tax-cuts-and-jobs-act-details-analysis/ (Accessed: December 9, 2024).

President's Council of Advisors on Science and Technology, 2022. Revitalizing the U.S. Semiconductor Ecosystem. Executive Office of the President, September 20. https://bidenwhitehouse.archives.gov/wp-content/uploads/2022/09/PCAST_Semiconductors-Report_Sep2022.pdf.

Prestowitz, C.V., 1988. *Trading Places: How We Allowed Japan to Take the Lead*. New York: Basic Books.

Prodi, R. and De Giovanni, D., 1988. "Mutamenti concorrenziali e regole del gioco," in Bianchi, P., ed., *Antitrust e gruppi industriali*. Bologna: Il Mulino.

Quality News, 2009. *Obama Awards $8 Billion in Loans for Advanced Automotive Technologies*. [online] *Qualitymag*.com. Available at: https://www.qualitymag.com/articles/86346-obama-awards-8-billion-in-loans-for-advanced-automotive-technologies?   (Accessed: December 16, 2025).

Rabbeno, U., 1895. *The American Commercial Policy: Three Historical Essays*. London: Macmillan and Co.

Ravenhill, J., 2000. *APEC and the Construction of Pacific Rim Regionalism*. Cambridge: Cambridge University Press.

Reagan, R., 1981. "Inaugural Address." *Ronald Reagan Presidential Library and Museum*, January, 20. https://www.reaganlibrary.gov/archives/speech/inaugural-address-1981.

Reagan, R., 1985. "Foreword Written for a Report on the Strategic Defense Initiative," *Ronald Reagan Presidential Library & Museum*. https://www.reaganlibrary.gov/archives/speech/foreword-written-report-strategic-defense-initiative (Accessed: December 3, 2024).

Reich, R.B., 1982. "Why the U.S. Needs an Industrial Policy," *Harvard Business Review* 60(1), pp. 74–81.

Reich, R.B., 1984. *The Next American Frontier*. New York, NY: Penguin Books.

Reinert, E.S., Ghosh, J., Kattel, R., eds. 2016. *Handbook of Alternative Theories of Economic Development*. Cheltenham: Edward Elgar.

Reischauer, Robert D., 1986. "Fiscal Federalism in the 1980s: Dismantling or Rationalizing the Great Society." In *The Great Society and Its Legacy: Twenty Years of U.S. Social Policy, edited by Marvin Kaplan and Philip Cuciti*, pp. 179–197. Durham, NC: Duke University Press.

Remarks by President Clinton, President Bush, President Carter, President Ford, and Vice President Gore in Signing of NAFTA Side Agreements, 1993. Clinton Presidential Materials Project White House Virtual Library. Available at: https://clintonwhitehouse6.archives.gov/1993/09/1993-09-14-remarks-by-clinton-and-former-presidents-on-nafta.html (Accessed: November 9, 2024).

Reuters, 2008. Obama: Help to Automakers Was 'Necessary Step'. *Reuters*. [online] December, 19. Available at: https://www.reuters.com/article/markets/oil/obama-help-to-automakers-was-necessary-step-idUSN19392630/ (Accessed: February 15, 2025).

Reuters, 2021. "How Offshoring Rolled Along Under Trump, Who Vowed to Stop It," 19 January. https://www.reuters.com/business/how-offshoring-rolled-along-under-trump-who-vowed-stop-it-2021-01-19/ (Accessed: February 15, 2025).

Rice, C., 2000. "Promoting the National Interest," *Foreign Affairs*, 79(1), pp. 45–62.

Richardson, J.D., ed. 1920. *A Compilation of the Messages and Papers of the Presidents 1789–1897*, vol. 10, New York: Bureau of National Literature, pp. 393–397.

Richman, S.L., 1988. *The Reagan Record on Trade: Rhetoric vs. Reality.* Policy Analysis 107. Washington, DC: Cato Institute. https://www.cato.org/sites/cato.org/files/pubs/pdf/pa107.pdf.

Robbins, L., 1953. The Theory of Economic Policy in English Classical Political Economy. London: Macmillan & Co. Ltd.

Rodrik, D., 1996. "Understanding Economic Policy Reform." *Journal of Economic Literature,* 34(1), pp. 9–41.

Rodrik, D., 1998. "Globalisation, Social Conflict and Economic Growth." *The World Economy,* 21(2), pp. 143–158.

Rodrik, D., 2004. "Industrial Policy for the Twenty-First Century." *CEPR Discussion Papers, 4767.* London: Centre for Economic Policy Research.

Rodrik, D., 2013. *The Right Green Industrial Policies.* Project Syndicate, August 7. London: Palgrave Macmillan.

Roessner, P. ed., 2016. *Economic Growth and the Origins of Modern Political Economy: Economic Reasons of State, 1500–2000.* London/New York: Routledge.

Rogers, A., 2024. "Donald Trump vows to sack SEC boss and end 'persecution' of crypto industry." *Financial Times.* https://www.ft.com/content/03e8e1d2-4244-4eba-9248-9bbd8d1b0090 (Accessed: November 10, 2024).

Rogers, T.N. and Williams, A., 2024. "Kamala Harris gains endorsement of car workers as union support builds," *Financial Times.* Available at: https://www.ft.com/content/92d5a31e-145b-433f-9b81-6f5f5634c995 (Accessed: November 11, 2024).

Roosevelt, F.D., 1933. Statement on N.I.R.A. https://www.presidency.ucsb.edu/documents/statement-nira.

Roosevelt, F.D., 1937. Second Inaugural Address of Franklin D. Roosevelt. https://avalon.law.yale.edu/20th_century/froos2.asp.

Rosenberg, N. and Nelson, R.R., 1994. "American Universities and Technical Advance in Industry," *Research Policy,* 23(3), pp. 323–348.

Ross, W. and Navarro, P., 2016. Trump Versus Clinton On Infrastructure. https://www.novoco.com/public-media/documents/trump-v-clinton-infrastructure-2016.pdf (Accessed: February 15, 2025).

Ruttan, Vernon W., 2006. *Is War Necessary for Economic Growth? Military Procurement and Technology Development.* New York, NY: Oxford University Press.

Saad-Filho, A., 2005. "From Washington to Post-Washington Consensus: Neoliberal Agendas for Economic Development," in A. Saad-Filho and D. Johnston, eds., *Neoliberalism: A Critical Reader.* London: Pluto Press, pp. 113–119. https://doi.org/10.2307/j.ctt18fs4hp.16.

Saad-Filho, A., 2011. "Growth, Poverty and Inequality: Policies and Debates from the Post-Washington Consensus to Inclusive Growth," *Indian Journal of Human Development,* 5(2), 321–344.

Saad-Filho, A., 2021. "The Crisis This Time: Neoliberalism and the Pandemic." *L'Industria,* 42(4), pp. 621–648.

Sachs, J.D., 1989. "Conditionality, Debt Relief, and the Developing Country Debt Crisis," in J.D. Sachs ed., *Developing Country Debt and Economic Performance,* Vol. 1. Chicago: University of Chicago Press.

Sakwa, R., 2008. *Russian Politics and Society.* 4th edn. London: Routledge.

Sandel, M.J., 1996. *Democracy's Discontent: America in Search of a Public Philosophy.* Cambridge, MA: Belknap Press.

Satisfaction With the United States, 1979. Gallup. https://news.gallup.com/poll/1669/General-Mood-Country.aspx (Accessed: December 3, 2024).

Scheiber, H.N., 1987. "State Law and Industrial Policy in American Development, 1790–1987," *California Law Review,* 75(1), pp. 415–447.

Schoppa, L.J., 1997. *Bargaining with Japan: What American Pressure Can and Cannot Do.* New York: Columbia University Press.

Schott, J.J., 2004. "Free Trade Agreements: U.S. Strategies and Priorities," in J.J. Schott, ed. *Free Trade Agreements: U.S. Strategies and Priorities*. Washington, DC: Peterson Institute for International Economics.

Schrank, A. and Whitford, J., 2009 "Industrial Policy in the United States: A Neo-Polanyian Interpretation," *Politics & Society*, 37(4), pp. 521–553. Available at: https://doi.org/10.1177/0032329209351926.

Schultze, C.L., 1983. "Industrial Policy: A Solution in Search of a Problem." *California Management Review*, 25(4), pp. 5–15.

Schwab, K., 2016. The Global Competitiveness Report 2016-2017. *World Economic Forum*. https://www3.weforum.org/docs/GCR2016-2017/05FullReport/TheGlobalCompetitivenessReport2016-2017_FINAL.pdf (Accessed: December 9, 2024).

Schwartz, H., 2009a. *Subprime Nation: American Power, Global Capital, and the Housing Bubble*. Cornell University Press.

Schwartz, H., 2009b. "Origins and Consequences of the US Subprime Crisis," in H. Schwartz and L. Seabrooke, eds., *The Politics of Housing Booms and Bust*, Basingstoke: Palgrave, pp. 188–207.

Scott, R.E., 2020. *We Can Reshore Manufacturing Jobs, but Trump Hasn't Done It*. Washington, DC: Economic Policy Institute. Available at: https://www.epi.org/publication/reshoring-manufacturing-jobs/ (Accessed: December 9, 2024).

Serra, A., 1613. *A Short Treatise on the Wealth and Poverty of Nations*: ed. by Sophus Reinert, trans. by Jonathan Hun, London: Anthem Press.

Shah, R., 2017. "Jobs and Opportunity, America's Most Pressing Challenge." [online] *Rockefeller Foundation*. Available at: https://www.rockefellerfoundation.org/perspective/jobs-opportunity-americas-pressing-challenge/ (Accessed: February 26, 2025).

Shane, S., 2004. *Academic Entrepreneurship: University Spinoffs and Wealth Creation*. Cheltenham: Edward Elgar.

Shapira, P., 2001. "US Manufacturing Extension Partnerships: Technology Policy Reinvented?," *Research Policy*, 30(6), pp. 977–992. Available at: https://doi.org/10.1016/S0048-7333(00)00168-2.

Shenkin, T.S., 1994. "Trade-Related Investment Measures in Bilateral Investment Treaties and the GATT: Moving Toward a Multilateral Investment Treaty," *University of Pittsburgh Law Review*, 55(2), pp. 541–564.

Sherman, A. and Jacobson, L., 2015. "PolitiFact Sheet: Military spending under Obama and Congress". *Politifact*. https://www.politifact.com/article/2015/dec/14/politifact-sheet-our-guide-to-military-spending-/.

Sherman, J., 1890. Trusts: Speech of Hon. John Sherman, of Ohio, delivered in the Senate of the United States, Friday, March 21, 1890. Washington, DC: Government Printing Office. https://babel.hathitrust.org/cgi/pt?id=wu.89098552482&seq=1&q1=concentrated (Accessed: December 10, 2024).

Shirk, S.L., 2007. *China: Fragile Superpower*. Oxford: Oxford University Press.

Shonfield, A., 1965. *Modern Capitalism: The Changing Balance of Public and Private Power*. Oxford: Oxford University Press.

Simpson, J., 2024. "Chip stocks fall further after Trump's remarks on Taiwan defense. *The Guardian*," July 18. https://www.theguardian.com/business/article/2024/jul/18/chip-stocks-trump-taiwan-defence-semiconductor (Accessed: July 29, 2024).

Smith, A., 1776. *An Inquiry into the Nature and Causes of the Wealth of Nations*, vol. I. London: printed for W. Strahan and T. Cadell.

Smithsonian American Art Museum. "The Second Great Migration." *American Experience, Smithsonian Institution*. https://americanexperience.si.edu/wp-content/uploads/2015/02/The-Second-Great-Migration.pdf.

Snell, K., 2022. "After Spiking Earlier Talks, Manchin Agrees to a New Deal on Climate and Taxes," *NPR*, July 27. https://www.npr.org/2022/07/27/1114108340/manchin-deal-inflation-reduction-act.

Stabili, M.R., 1984. *America verso una società corporata: la AFL di Gompers*. Bari: Edizioni Dedalo.

Statista, 2023. "Annual Rate of Change of the Misery Index (Unemployment rate Plus Consumer Price Index) in the United States from January 1960 to September 2022" https://www.statista.com/statistics/1324607/us-misery-index/ (Accessed: 3 December 2024).

Statista, 2023. NASA's monetary obligations compared to Project Apollo's total costs from 1960 to 1973. https://www.statista.com/statistics/1342862/nasa-budget-project-apollo-costs/.

Stein, J., 1998 *Running Steel, Running America: Race, Economic Policy, and the Decline of Liberalism*. Chapel Hill: University of North Carolina Press.

Stiglitz, J., 2010. *Freefall: America, Free Markets, and the Sinking of the Global Economy*. W.W. Norton & Company.

Stiglitz, J. and Bilmes, L., 2008. *The Three Trillion Dollar War: The True Cost of the Iraq Conflict*. W.W. Norton & Company.

Stiglitz, J.E., 1989. "Markets, Market Failures, and Development," *The American Economic Review*, 79(2), pp. 197–203.

Stiglitz, J.E., 2002. *Globalization and Its Discontents*. New York, NY: W. W. Norton. https://wwnorton.com/books/9780393324396 (Accessed: 10 November 2024).

Stiglitz, J.E. and Lin, J.Y. eds., 2013. *The Industrial Policy Revolution I: The Role of Government Beyond Ideology*. London: Palgrave Macmillan UK. Available at: https://doi.org/10.1057/9781137335173.

Stockholm International Peace Research Institute (SIPRI), 2020. Trends in World Military Expenditure, 2019. SIPRI Fact Sheet, April. https://www.sipri.org/sites/default/files/2020-04/fs_2020_04_milex_0_0.pdf (Accessed: 10 November 2024).

Stone & Associates and Center for Regional and Economic Competitiveness, 2010. *Renewing the U.S. Commitment to a Strong Manufacturing Base: Expanding the Reach of the Manufacturing Extension Partnership*. Gaithersburg, MD: National Institute of Standards and Technology. https://www.nist.gov/system/files/documents/mep/MEP_Bus_Model_Report_Summary_July2010.pdf.

Strategic Defense Initiative (SDI), 1983. "U.S. Department of State," *Department Of State. The Office of Electronic Information, Bureau of Public Affairs*. Available at: https://2001-2009.state.gov/r/pa/ho/time/rd/104253.htm (Accessed: December 3, 2024).

Subran, L., et al., 2024. "Trumponomics: The Sequel." https://www.allianz.com/content/dam/onemarketing/azcom/Allianz_com/economic-research/publications/specials/en/2024/march/2024-03-13-Trump_Report-AZ.pdf (Accessed: February 15, 2025).

Sullivan, E.T., 1991. *The Political Economy of the Sherman Act. The First One Hundred Years*. Oxford: Oxford University Press.

Tassava, C.J., 2008. The American Economy during World War II. EH.Net Encyclopedia, edited by R. Whaples. https://eh.net/encyclopedia/the-american-economy-during-world-war-ii/.

Tassinari, M., 2014. "Industrial Policy in the United States. The Theoretical Debate, the Rhetoric, and the Practices in the Era of the Washington Consensus," *L'Industria. Rivista di Economia e Politica Industriale*, 35(1), pp. 69–100. Available at: https://doi.org/10.1430/77264.

Tassinari, M., 2019. *Capitalizing Economic Power in the US: Industrial Strategy in the Neoliberal Era*. Cham: Palgrave Macmillan. https://doi.org/10.1007/978-3-319-76648-5.

Taussig, F.W., 1910. *The Tariff History of the United States*. 5th edn, revised. New York: G.P. Putnam's Sons.

Taussig, F. W., 1930. *Inventors and Money-makers: Lectures on Some Relations Between Economics and Psychology Delivered at Brown University in Connection with the Celebration of the 150th Anniversary of the Foundation of the University*. New York: Macmillan.

Taussig, F. W., 1931. *Some Aspects of the Tariff Question: An Examination of the Development of American Industries Under Protection*, 3rd edn enl., *Harvard Economic Studies* 12. Cambridge, MA: Harvard University Press.

Tax Foundation, 2024. *Tracking the 2024 Presidential Tax Plans*. Tax Foundation. https://taxfoundation.org/research/federal-tax/2024-tax-plans/.

Tax Policy Center, 2017. Distributional Analysis of the Conference Agreement for the Tax Cuts and Jobs Act, December 18.

The New York Times, 2017. "Excerpts From Trump's Conversation With Journalists on Air Force One," *The New York Times*, July 13. https://www.nytimes.com/2017/07/13/us/politics/trump-air-force-one-excerpt-transcript.html (Accessed: February 15, 2025).

Thorelli, H.E., 1955. *The Federal Antitrust Policy: Origination of an American Tradition*. Baltimore, MD: The Johns Hopkins Press.

Time, 2022. "China Attacks U.S. Chip Handouts While Warning of a Market Slowdown." https://time.com/6206951/china-us-semiconductor-chips/ (Accessed: March 1, 2023).

Trade Enhancement Initiative for Central and Eastern Europe, 1991. *Foreign Policy Bulletin*. 2(1), pp. 92–92. doi:10.1017/S1052703600007590

Tregenna, F., 2009. "Characterising deindustrialisation: An analysis of changes in manufacturing employment and output internationally." *Cambridge Journal of Economics*, 33(3), pp. 433–466. doi: https://doi.org/10.1093/cje/ben032.

Tregenna, F., 2014. "A New Theoretical Analysis of Deindustrialization." *Cambridge Journal of Economics*, 38(6), pp. 1373–1390. doi: https://doi.org/10.1093/cje/bet029.

Trionfetti, F., 2000 "Discriminatory Public Procurement and International Trade," *The World Economy*, 23(1), pp. 57–76. Available at: https://doi.org/10.1111/1467-9701.00262.

Trump 2016 [Twitter] August 1. https://x.com/realDonaldTrump/status/760287440435187712.

Trump 2017a [Twitter] January 3. https://x.com/realDonaldTrump/status/816260343391514624.

Trump 2017b [Twitter] January 5. https://x.com/realdonaldtrump/status/817071792711942145

Trump 2017c [Twitter] April 16. https://x.com/realDonaldTrump/status/853604334944354305.

Trump 2017d [Twitter] January 9. https://x.com/realdonaldtrump/status/818461467766824961.

Trump 2017e [Twitter] January 15. https://x.com/realDonaldTrump/status/820632299037409280.

Trump 2018a [Twitter] August 13. https://x.com/realDonaldTrump/status/1029134567356149762?mx=2.

Trump 2018b [Twitter] August 3. https://x.com/realDonaldTrump/status/1025516607886577666?lang=en.

Trump 2018c [Twitter] December 3. https://x.com/realDonaldTrump/status/1069970500535902208?lang=en.

Trump 2018d [Twitter] December 4. https://x.com/realdonaldtrump/status/1069575605199482881.

Trump 2018e [Twitter] February 9. https://x.com/realDonaldTrump/status/961957671246159875.

Trump 2018f [Twitter] November 27. https://x.com/realDonaldTrump/status/1067494680416407552.

Trump, D.J., 2024. "Pres. Trump announces imposition of new tariffs in 'Liberation Day' remarks." Interview by Bloomberg Businessweek." Bloomberg. June 25. https://www.bloomberg.com/features/2024-trump-interview-transcript/.

Trump, D.J., 2017a. Remarks by President Trump to the National Association of Manufacturers. https://trumpwhitehouse.archives.gov/briefings-statements/remarks-president-trump-national-association-manufacturers/ (Accessed: February 15, 2025).

Trump, D.J., 2017b. Remarks by President Trump at a Roundtable with Automaker CEOs. *The White House*. https://trumpwhitehouse.archives.gov/briefings-statements/remarks-president-trump-roundtable-automaker-ceos/ (Accessed: December 10, 2024).

Trump, D.J., 2017c. Remarks by President Trump at the Signing of H.R. 1, the Tax Cuts and Jobs Act, 22 December. *The White House.* https://trumpwhitehouse.archives.gov/briefings-statements/remarks-president-trump-signing-h-r-1-tax-cuts-jobs-bill-act-h-r-1370/ (Accessed: December 10, 2024).

Trump, D.J., 2018. State of the Union Address. https://trumpwhitehouse.archives.gov/briefings-statements/president-donald-j-trumps-state-union-address/ (Accessed: November 10, 2024).

Trump, D.J., 2019. State of the Union Address. https://trumpwhitehouse.archives.gov/briefings-statements/president-donald-j-trumps-state-union-address-2/ (Accessed: November 10, 2024).

Trump, D.J., 2024. "Full Remarks: President Trump's Address to the New York Economic Club." Video. YouTube, April 5. Available at: https://www.youtube.com/watch?v=92Gx6NAZPsM (Accessed: 10 June 2025).

Trump, D.J., 2025a. "Announcement of Reciprocal Tariffs." *Speech, Rose Garden, White House,* Washington, D.C., April 2. https://www.youtube.com/watch?v=sGjnJlp1lfk (Accessed: June 10, 2025).

Trump, D.J., 2025b. "Regulating Imports with a Reciprocal Tariff to Rectify Trade Practices that Contribute to Large and Persistent Annual United States Goods Trade Deficits." *Executive Order, White House,* Washington, D.C., April 2. https://www.whitehouse.gov/presidential-actions/2025/04/regulating-imports-with-a-reciprocal-tariff-to-rectify-trade-practices-that-contribute-to-large-and-persistent-annual-united-states-goods-trade-deficits/ (Accessed: June 10, 2025).

Trump, D.J., 2025c. "The Inaugural Address." *White House, U.S. Capitol,* Washington, D.C., January 20. https://www.whitehouse.gov/remarks/2025/01/the-inaugural-address/ (Accessed: June 10, 2025).

Trump, D.J., 2025d. "Restoring Names That Honor American Greatness." *Executive Order, White House,* Washington, D.C., January 20. https://www.whitehouse.gov/presidential-actions/2025/01/restoring-names-that-honor-american-greatness/ (Accessed: June 10, 2025).

Tullock, G., 1967. "The Welfare Costs of Tariffs, Monopolies and Theft." *Western Economic Journal,* 5, pp. 224–232.

Turner, M.A., Angel, S., Leachman, M. and Wilson, M., 2002. *Promoting Economic Development in Distressed Communities: A Review of the Federal Empowerment Zone and Enterprise Community Program.* Washington, DC: Urban Institute.

Eisenhower, D.D., 1961. "Farewell Address to the Nation," 17 January. *The American Presidency Project.*

Tyson, A. and Maniam, S., 2016. *Behind Trump's Victory: Divisions by Race, Gender, Education.* Pew Research Center.

Tyson, L.D., 1992. *Who's Bashing Whom? Trade Conflict in High-Technology Industries.* Washington, DC: Institute for International Economics.

United States Agency for International Development, 2013. From Aid to Trade: USAID's Legacy in Europe and Eurasia. Washington, DC: USAID.

U.S. Army Center of Military History, n.d. U.S. Army in the World War I Era https://history.army.mil/portals/143/Images/Publications/catalog/77-2.pdf (Accessed: August 8, 2024).

U.S. Bureau of Labor Statistics, 2025. Unemployment Rate (UNRATE). Federal Reserve Bank of St. Louis (FRED). Available at: https://fred.stlouisfed.org/series/UNRATE.

U.S. Congress, 1938. *National Housing Act,* Public Law 75–424. Washington, DC: U.S. Government Printing Office.

U.S. Congress, 1970. *Emergency Home Finance Act,* Public Law 91–351. Washington, DC: U.S. Government Printing Office.

U.S. Congress, 1989. *Support for East European Democracy (SEED) Act of 1989,* Public Law 101-179. Washington, DC: U.S. Government Printing Office.

U.S. Congress, 2005. *Energy Policy Act of 2005*, Public Law 109–58. Washington, DC: U.S. Government Printing Office.

U.S. Congress, 2011. *Budget Control Act of 2011*, Pub. L. No. 112-25.

U.S. Congress, 2008. *Emergency Economic Stabilization Act of 2008*, Public Law 110–343. Washington, DC: U.S. Government Printing Office.

U.S. Congress, 2025. *The End of the Affordable Connectivity Program: Options for Consumers and Congress*. https://www.congress.gov/crs-product/IF12637.

U.S. Customs and Border Protection and Department of the Treasury, 2025. "Trade and National Security Actions and Low-Value Shipments." *Proposed Rule, Federal Register*, January 21, 90 FR 6852–6873. https://www.federalregister.gov/documents/2025/01/21/2025-01074/trade-and-national-security-actions-and-low-value-shipments.

U.S. Department of Commerce, 2010. "Annual Budget Report for the Economic Development Administration." *eda.gov*. https://www.eda.gov/sites/default/files/2022-02/EDA_FY_2010_Annual_Report.pdf.

U.S. Department of Energy, 2010. *Advanced Energy Manufacturing Tax Credit (Section 48C)*. Washington, DC: Department of Energy.

U.S. Department of Energy, 2013. *Energy Department Announces $150 Million in Tax Credits to Invest in U.S. Clean Energy Manufacturing*. Washington, DC: Department of Energy. https://www.energy.gov/eere/water/articles/energy-department-announces-150-million-tax-credits-invest-us-clean-energy.

U.S. Department of Energy, 2013. *48C Manufacturing Tax Credits: Fact Sheet*, April 2013. Available at: https://www.energy.gov/sites/prod/files/2013/04/f0/FACT%20SHEET%20--%2048C%20MANUFACTURING%20TAX%20CREDITS.pdf.

U.S. Department of Energy, 2024. *Energy Infrastructure Reinvestment (EIR) Financing Overview*. Washington, DC: U.S. Department of Energy. https://www.energy.gov/edf/title-17-energy-infrastructure-reinvestment-eir-financing.

U.S. Department of Justice and Federal Trade Commission, 1995. *Antitrust Guidelines for the Licensing of Intellectual Property*. Washington, DC: U.S. Department of Justice and Federal Trade Commission.

U.S. Department of Transportation, 2021. *American Rescue Plan Act of 2021*. https://www.transit.dot.gov/funding/american-rescue-plan-act-2021.

U.S. Department of the Treasury. About TARP. https://home.treasury.gov/data/troubled-assets-relief-program/about-tarp (Accessed: February 9, 2025).

U.S. Department of the Treasury, 2009. *Troubled Asset Relief Program: General Motors restructuring*. Washington, DC: U.S. Department of the Treasury. Available at: https://home.treasury.gov/data/troubled-assets-relief-program/automotive-programs/general-motors.

U.S. Department of the Treasury, 2013. *Treasury Sells Final Shares of GM Common Stock*, 9 December. Available at: https://home.treasury.gov/news/press-releases/jl2236.

U.S. Energy Information Administration, 2012. "CBECS 2012: Energy Usage Summary, Commercial Buildings Energy Consumption Survey." Available at: https://www.eia.gov/consumption/commercial/reports/2012/energyusage/.

U.S. Environmental Protection Agency, 2024. *Energy Policy Act of 2005*. Available at: https://www.epa.gov/laws-regulations/summary-energy-policy-act (Accessed: February 9, 2025).

U.S. Government Accountability Office (GAO), 2023. Troubled Asset Relief Program: Lifetime Cost. https://www.gao.gov/products/gao-24-107033.

U.S. Government Publishing Printing Office, 2004. Budget of the United States Government: Historical Tables Fiscal Year 2005. https://www.govinfo.gov/app/details/BUDGET-2005-TAB/.

U.S. Senate Committee on Finance, 2025. "Hearing to Consider the Nomination of Jamieson Greer, of Maryland, to be United States Trade Representative, with the Rank of Ambassador Extraordinary and Plenipotentiary." https://www.finance.senate.gov/hearings/hearing-to-consider-the-nomination-of-jamieson-greer-of-maryland-to-be-united-states-trade-representative-with-the-rank-of-ambassador-extraordinary-and-plenipotentiary.

U.S. Small Business Administration, 2009. *Recovery Act: Small Business Administration Implementation*. Washington, DC: U.S. Small Business Administration.

Unit, NPR Political, 2008. "Candidates Offer Joint Statement on Economic Crisis." *NPR*, September 25.

United States Census Bureau, 2012. "The Great Migration, 1910 to 1970." *United States Census Bureau*, September 13.

United States Code, 2023. Title 41 - Public Contracts, § 8302.

United States Congress, 1921. Federal Highway Act of 1921.

United States Congress, 2009. *American Recovery and Reinvestment Act of 2009*, Public Law 111-5, enacted 17 February 2009. Available at: https://www.congress.gov/bill/111th-congress/house-bill/1.

United States Congress, House of Representatives, 1790. Journal of the House of Representatives of the United States, 1790. *Congress.gov*. https://www.congress.gov/house-journal/140?q=%7B%22search%22%3A%22articleDates%3A1790-01-15%22%7D&s=2&r=1.

U.S. Department of Defense, 1986. *Very High Speed Integrated Circuits (VHSIC) Program: Technical Overview*. Defense Technical Information Center (DTIC) Report No. ADA168641.

US Department of Energy, Office of Environment, Health, Safety & Security, n.d. *Atomic Energy Act and Related Legislation*. U.S. Department of Energy.

U.S. General Accounting Office, 1985. *VHSIC: Progress and Problems in the Very High Speed Integrated Circuit Program*. Washington, DC: GAO. (GAO/NSIAD-85-146).

United States Government, 1974. *Annual Budget Message to the Congress: Fiscal Year 1975*, 4 February. Available at: https://www.presidency.ucsb.edu/documents/annual-budget-message-the-congress-fiscal-year-1975.

U.S. Small Business Administration, 2009. *Recovery Act: Small Business Administration Implementation*. Washington, DC: U.S. Small Business Administration.

EPA, 2013. OP. "Summary of the Energy Policy Act." *Overviews and Factsheets*, February 22.

United States: Executive Office of the President: Council of Economic Advisers, and United States George W. Bush, 2009. "Economic Report of the President 2009." *U.S. Government Printing Office*, January 1.

Vakhshouri, S., 2017. The America First Energy Plan: Renewing the Confidence of American Energy Producers. *Issue Brief, August, Atlantic Council*.

Verleger, Philip K., et al., 1979. "The U.S. Petroleum Crisis of 1979." *Brookings Papers on Economic Activity*, 1979(2), pp. 463–476. JSTOR. (Accessed: November 26, 2024).

Vlasic, B., 2011. *Once Upon a Car: The Fall and Resurrection of America's Big Three Auto Makers — GM, Ford, and Chrysler*. New York: William Morrow.

Vogel, D., 2012. *The Politics of Precaution: Regulating Health, Safety, and Environmental Risks in Europe and the United States*. Princeton, NJ: Princeton University Press.

Wade, R., 2003. *Governing the Market: Economic Theory and the Role of Government in East Asian Industrialization*. Princeton University Press.

Wade, R.H., 2012. "Return of Industrial Policy?," *International Review of Applied Economics*, 26(2), pp. 223–239. Available at: https://doi.org/10.1080/02692171.2011.640312.

Wade, R.H. and International Labour Office, 2014. *The Paradox of US Industrial Policy: The Developmental State in Disguise*. Geneva: ILO.

Wade, R.H., 2017. "The American Paradox: Ideology of Free Markets and the Hidden Practice of Directional Thrust." *Cambridge Journal of Economics*, 41(3), pp. 859–880.

War Production Board, 1945. *Wartime Production Achievements and the Reconversion Outlook: Report of the Chairman*. Washington, D.C.: War Production Board.

Warren, A. and Bode, I., 2015. "Altering the Playing Field: The U.S. Redefinition of the Use-of-force," *Contemporary Security Policy*, 36(2), pp. 174–199. doi: https://doi.org/10.1080/13523260.2015.1061768.

Washington, G., 1790. "First Annual Address to Congress," in G. Peters and J. T. Woolley, eds., *The American Presidency Project*. https://www.presidency.ucsb.edu/node/203158.

Washington, G., 1796. From George Washington to the U.S. Senate and House of Representatives, December 7. Founders Online, National Archives, https://founders.archives.gov/documents/Washington/05-21-02-0142. [Original source: The Papers of George Washington, Presidential Series, vol. 21, September 22, 1796–3 March 1797, ed. Adrina Garbooshian-Huggins. Charlottesville: University of Virginia Press, 2020, pp. 317–335.]

Webel, B. and Canis, B., 2015. "Government Assistance for GMAC/Ally Financial: Unwinding the Government Stake". *Congressional Research Service.* https://www.congress.gov/crs-product/R41846 (Accessed: December 8, 2024).

Weinstein, J., 1968. *The Corporate Ideal in the Liberal State: 1900–1918.* Boston, MA: Beacon Press.

Weinstein, O., 2012. *Firm, property and governance: From Berle and Means to the agency theory, and beyond. Accounting, Economics and Law: A Convivium,* 2(2). http://dx.doi.org/10.1515/2152-2820.1061.

Weisman, J., 2014. "U.S. Declares Bank and Auto Bailouts Over, and Profitable." *The New York Times.* https://www.nytimes.com/2014/12/20/business/us-signals-end-of-bailouts-of-automakers-and-wall-street.html.

Weiss, J., 2013. "Industrial Policy in the Twenty-First Century: Challenges for the Future," in Szirmai, A., Naudé, S. and Alcorta, I., eds., *Pathways to Industrialization in the Twenty-First Century: New Challenges and Emerging Paradigms. WIDER Studies in Development Economics.* Oxford: Oxford University Press, pp. 393–412.

Weiss, L., 2008. "Crossing the Divide: From the Military- Industrial to the Development-Procurement Complex," in *Berkeley Workshop on the "Hidden US Developmental State,"* pp. 20–21. San Francisco, CA.

Weiss, L., 2014. *America Inc.?: Innovation and Enterprise in the National Security State.* Ithaca, NY: Cornell University Press (Cornell Studies in Political Economy). https://www.cornellpress.cornell.edu/book/9780801479304/america-inc/ (Accessed: November 9, 2024).

Weiss, L. and Thurbon, E., 2006. "The Business of Buying American: Public Procurement as Trade Strategy in the USA," *Review of International Political Economy,* 13(5), pp. 701–724. https://doi.org/10.1080/09692290600950597.

White House, 1991. *Message to the Congress on United States assistance to Eastern Europe and the Soviet Union.* Washington, DC: The White House.

White House, 2009. *Fact sheet: President Obama"s American Graduation Initiative.* Washington, DC: The White House.

White House, 2021a. *Executive Order on America's Supply Chains.* White House. https://bidenwhitehouse.archives.gov/briefing-room/presidential-actions/2021/02/24/executive-order-on-americas-supply-chains/.

White House, 2021b. *Fact Sheet: The American Jobs Plan.* https://bidenwhitehouse.archives.gov/briefing-room/statements-releases/2021/03/31/fact-sheet-the-american-jobs-plan/.

White House, 2021c. *Fact Sheet: Bipartisan Infrastructure Deal.* https://bidenwhitehouse.archives.gov/briefing-room/statements-releases/2021/11/06/fact-sheet-the-bipartisan-infrastructure-deal/.

White House, 2021d. *Build Back Better Framework.* https://bidenwhitehouse.archives.gov/build-back-better/.

White House, 2021e. *Ensuring the Future is Made in all of America by all of America.* https://bidenwhitehouse.archives.gov/briefing-room/presidential-actions/2021/01/25/executive-order-on-ensuring-the-future-is-made-in-all-of-america-by-all-of-americas-workers/.

White House, 2022. *Fact Sheet: The Inflation Reduction Act Supports Workers and Families.* https://bidenwhitehouse.archives.gov/briefing-room/statements-releases/2022/08/19/fact-sheet-the-inflation-reduction-act-supports-workers-and-families/.

White House, 2024. *Fact Sheet: Vice President Harris Announces More Than $100 Million to Support American Auto Workers and Small Auto Suppliers.* https://bidenwhitehouse.archives.gov/briefing-room/statements-releases/2024/05/06/fact-sheet-vice-president-harris-announces-more-than-100-million-to-support-american-auto-workers-and-small-auto-suppliers/.

White House, 2025. *Fact Sheet: President Donald J. Trump Restores Section 232 Tariffs*. https://www.whitehouse.gov/fact-sheets/2025/02/fact-sheet-president-donald-j-trump-restores-section-232-tariffs/.

White House, 2025a. *Fact Sheet: President Donald J. Trump Ensures National Security and Economic Resilience Through Section 232 Actions on Processed Critical Minerals and Derivative Products*. https://www.whitehouse.gov/fact-sheets/2025/04/fact-sheet-president-donald-j-trump-ensures-national-security-and-economic-resilience-through-section-232-actions-on-processed-critical-minerals-and-derivative-products/.

White House, 2025b. *America First Trade Policy*. https://www.whitehouse.gov/presidential-actions/2025/01/america-first-trade-policy/.

White House, 2025c. *Fact Sheet: President Donald J. Trump Restores Section 232 Tariffs*. https://www.whitehouse.gov/fact-sheets/2025/02/fact-sheet-president-donald-j-trump-restores-section-232-tariffs/.

White House, 2025d. *America First Investment Policy. Presidential Memorandum*, February 21. https://www.whitehouse.gov/presidential-actions/2025/02/america-first-investment-policy/.

White House, 2025e. *Fact Sheet: President Donald J. Trump Announces Actions to Reduce Regulatory Barriers to Domestic Pharmaceutical Manufacturing*. https://www.whitehouse.gov/fact-sheets/2025/05/fact-sheet-president-donald-j-trump-announces-actions-to-reduce-regulatory-barriers-to-domestic-pharmaceutical-manufacturing/.

White House, 2025f. *Establishing the United States Investment Accelerator. Executive Order*, March 31. https://www.whitehouse.gov/presidential-actions/2025/03/establishing-the-united-states-investment-accelerator/.

White House, 2025g. *Imposing Duties to Address the Synthetic Opioid Supply Chain in the People's Republic of China. Executive Order*, February 1. https://www.whitehouse.gov/presidential-actions/2025/02/imposing-duties-to-address-the-synthetic-opioid-supply-chain-in-the-peoples-republic-of-china/.

White House, 2025h. *Fact Sheet: President Donald J. Trump Imposes Tariffs on Imports from Canada, Mexico, and China*. https://www.whitehouse.gov/fact-sheets/2025/02/fact-sheet-president-donald-j-trump-imposes-tariffs-on-imports-from-canada-mexico-and-china/.

White House, 2025i. *Fact Sheet: President Donald J. Trump Secures a Historic Trade Win for the United States*. https://www.whitehouse.gov/fact-sheets/2025/05/fact-sheet-president-donald-j-trump-secures-a-historic-trade-win-for-the-united-states/.

White, L.J., 2010. "Antitrust Policy and Industrial Policy: A View from the U.S.," in *Competition Law and Economics*, Cheltenham, UK: Edward Elgar. https://doi.org/10.4337/9781849807036.00033 (Accessed: November 9, 2024).

Williams, W.A., 1961. *The Contours of American History*. Cleveland, OH: World Publishing Company.

Williamson, J., 1990. "What Washington Means by Policy Reform," in J. Williamson ed., *Latin American Readjustment: How Much has Happened*. Washington: Institute for International Economics, pp. 7–20.

Williamson, S.D., 2012. "Liquidity, Monetary Policy, and the Financial Crisis: A New Monetarist Approach." *American Economic Review*, 102(6), pp. 2570–2605.

Williamson, V., Skocpol, T. and Coggin, J., 2011. "The Tea Party and the Remaking of Republican Conservatism." *Perspectives on Politics*, 9(1), pp. 25–43. https://scholar.harvard.edu/files/williamson/files/tea_party_pop_0.pdf (Accessed: February 15, 2025).

Willingham, C.Z., 2020. 10 Ways the Trump Administration Has Failed Rural America (and 10 Ways To Overcome It). *Center for American Progress*. https://www.americanprogress.org/article/10-ways-trump-administration-failed-rural-america-10-ways-overcome/ (Accessed: December 7, 2024).

Wilson, M.R., 2006. *The Business of Civil War: Military Mobilization and the State, 1861–1865.* Baltimore: JHU Press.

Williamson, J., 1994. *The Political Economy of Policy Reform.* Washington, DC: Institute for International Economics.

Wilson, W., 1917. *Address to the Nation,* 17 April. *The American Presidency Project.* Available at: https://www.presidency.ucsb.edu/documents/address-the-nation-0.

Wood, G., 2009. "Did Bush Cause the Financial Crisis?" *BBC News.* http://news.bbc.co.uk/2/hi/americas/7814704.stm (Accessed: December 3, 2024).

Woodward, D., 2014. *The American Army and the First World War.* Cambridge: Cambridge University Press.

World Bank, 2017. "Tapping the Potential of Drones for Development." https://www.worldbank.org/en/topic/transport/brief/drones-for-development. (Accessed: February 19, 2026).

World Trade Organization (WTO), 2016. *The History and Future of the World Trade Organization.* WTO Publications.

Yergin, D. and Stanislaw, J., 2002. *The Commanding Heights: The Battle for the World Economy.* New York: Simon & Schuster.

Zeleny, J., 2008. Obama and McCain Issue Joint Statement on the Economy, *The New York Times,* September 24. https://archive.nytimes.com/thecaucus.blogs.nytimes.com/2008/09/24/obama-debate-should-go-on/.

Zelizer, J.E., 2015. *The Fierce Urgency of Now: Lyndon Johnson, Congress, and the Battle for the Great Society.* New York: Penguin Press.

Zwick, E. and Mahon, J. 2017. "Tax Policy and Heterogeneous Investment Behavior." *American Economic Review,* 107(1), pp. 217–248.

Index

For the benefit of digital users, indexed terms that span two pages (e.g., 52–53) may, on occasion, appear on only one of those pages.

Figures in this index are indicated by *f* following the page numbers